Instructional Planning for Exceptional Children

Essays from Focus on Exceptional Children

Edward L. Meyen, *University of Kansas*
Glenn A. Vergason, *Georgia State University*
Richard J. Whelan, *University of Kansas Medical Center*

LOVE PUBLISHING COMPANY
Denver · London

All rights reserved. No part of this publication may be reproduced, stored in a retrieval system or transmitted, in any form or by any means, electronic, mechanical, recording or otherwise, without the prior written permission of the publisher.

Copyright © 1979 Love Publishing Company
Printed in the U.S.A.
ISBN 0-89108-079-1
Library of Congress Catalog Card Number 78-50503
10 9 8 7 6 5 4 3 2

CONTENTS

INTRODUCTION   1

PART 1 — ASSESSMENT
    Glenn A. Vergason, *Georgia State University*   3

Psychoeducational Assessment: An Integrated Viewpoint   5
    Margaret Walkenshaw, *Sequoyah Elementary School* (Kansas)
    Marvin Fine, *University of Kansas*

The Teacher's Role in Referral for Testing   19
    Mary Ross Moran, *University of Kansas*

Assessment and Programming in Mathematics
for the Handicapped   34
    H. A. Goodstein, *Hartford Insurance Group, Connecticut*

Informal Assessment for the Classroom   51
    Nancy K. Jobes and Linda White Hawthorne
    Georgia State University

Assessing Severely Handicapped Children   73
    Rebecca F. DuBose, Mary Beth Langley, and Vaughan Stagg
    George Peabody College

Nondiscriminatory Testing of Minority and Exceptional
Children   92
    Gordon Alley and Carol Foster, *University of Kansas*

Testing the Reading Achievement of Exceptional Learners   115
    Kathryn Blake, *University of Georgia*

PART 2 — INSTRUCTIONAL PLANNING
    Edward L. Meyen, *University of Kansas*   139

Implementation of IEPs: New Teacher Roles and
Requisite Support Systems   141
    Nancy D. Safer, Martin J. Kaufman, and Patricia A.
    Morrissey, *Bureau of Education for the Handicapped*
    Linda Lewis, *Nero & Associates*

Nine Steps to the Diagnostic Prescriptive Process
in the Classroom   177
    Mary Ross Moran, *University of Kansas*

Designing Instructional Games for Handicapped Learners   198
    Sivasailam Thiagarajan, *Indiana University*

General Principles and Guidelines in "Programming"
for Severely Handicapped Children and Young Adults   216
    Norris G. Haring, Alice H. Hayden, and Robin Beck
    University of Washington

Peer Use of Behavior Modification   236
    Harry E. Rosenberg, *Visalia Unified School District* (California)
    Paul Graubard, *Yeshiva University*

Language Programming for the Severely Handicapped   253
    Ken G. Jens, *University of North Carolina*
    Ken and Jane Belmore, *Madison Public Schools* (Wisconsin)

Mathematical Concepts and Skills: Diagnosis, Prescription,
and Correction of Deficiencies   279
    Lelon R. Capps and Mary M. Hatfield, *University of Kansas*

The Teacher's Role in Interpretation of Reports   294
    Mary Ross Moran, *University of Kansas*

The Helping Teacher/Crisis Teacher Concept   308
    William C. Morse, *University of Michigan*

The New Relationship Between Parents and Schools   325
    Peter Fanning, *Wichita Public Schools* (Kansas)

The Special Education Paraprofessional and the
Individual Educational Program Process   342
    Mary Goff and Phyllis Kelly, *Kansas State Department of Education*

PART 3 — EVALUATION
    Richard J. Whelan, *University of Kansas Medical Center*   349

Evaluating Full Service Special Education Programs   351
    Robert O. Brinkerhoff, *University of Virginia*

Evaluating Special Education Programs   374
    Clifford E. Howe and Marigail E. Fitzgerald, *University of Iowa*

Relating Educational Assessment to Instructional Planning   390
    Warren Heiss, *Montclair State College*

Special Education in the Mainstream: A Confrontation of Limitations?   406
    Barbara K. Keogh and Marc L. Levitt, *University of California-Los Angeles*

Program Evaluation: New Concepts, New Methods   424
    Gary D. Borich, *University of Texas*

Evaluation of Mainstreaming Programs   446
    Donald L. MacMillan, *University of California-Riverside*
    Melvin I. Semmel, *Indiana University*

AUTHOR INDEX   471

Introduction

Edward L. Meyen, *University of Kansas*
Glenn A. Vergason, *Georgia State University*
Richard J. Whelan, *University of Kansas Medical Center*

Instructional Planning for Exceptional Children is the third volume in a series that began with *Strategies for Teaching Exceptional Children* (1972) and was followed by *Alternatives for Teaching Exceptional Children* (1975). The first volume in the series dealt with general instructional models, practices, and evaluation. The second volume presented differential models and approaches, along with their rationale for educating exceptional children.

Each of the books, including the current one, has focused upon exceptional learners and the ways in which their education can be facilitated by appropriate program planning, delivery, and evaluation. The trend in content, however, has been from the general to the specific. This volume, *Instructional Planning for Exceptional Children*, centers primarily upon the classroom instructional environment; after all the delivery or administrative models have been analyzed and are selected for use, the challenges of teaching a child or group still remain. Models never taught a child. Only the child (through self teaching) or others actually teach.

Part 1 includes selections about formal and informal child assessment that describe the do's and don'ts of assessment that every teacher should know. Part 2 of the book deals with instructional planning and practices. Social and academic behaviors are included as part of the curriculum. Parents are brought in as partners with the professional educators to plan and deliver what is thought to be best for exceptional children. Part 3 is about program evaluation. It offers the teacher and administrator clear guidelines for evaluating the impact of instructional objectives and activities instituted to meet them. Use of the word "clear" does not imply *easy*. Evaluation, like teaching, is not easy. It requires many hours of diligent planning based upon precise assessments of children. The three main parts of this volume, then, represent areas important for helping children help themselves—assessment, teaching, and evaluation.

The winds of change have been influencing special education for many years. Conditions never have been static, although from a narrow time perspective, they may have appeared to be. Viewed from a broader perspective in which present time becomes constricted in relationship to the past and future, changes have been dramatic.

Sontag (Whelan & Sontag, 1974) has identified three sources of change: leverage, litigation, and legislation. Parent groups, often with the support of professionals, are vocal and powerful advocates for quality services. Their voices, when not heeded by duly elected legislative groups at local, state, and national levels, have been heard by the courts. Court decisions and parents stimulated reform legislation on behalf of the exceptional, a noteworthy example being the Education for All Handicapped Children Act (PL 94-142)—a culmination of these forces of change. This law marks the beginning of an era. Such a law—the hope and promise of the future—could not have been conceived without the cumulative changes of the past. The law is a carefully thought out, long-range plan for improving the lives of exceptional children. As a long-range plan, it has nothing to do with future decisions. Rather, it has to do with the impact of present decisions upon the future.

Many questions related to the future impact of this new legislative milestone remain. For example:

1. In view of the fact that the Individualized Education Program (IEP) requirement was thought necessary, what omissions and commissions in program planning still need to be corrected?
2. What will be the roles of the sending and receiving teachers in developing and implementing IEPs? If history repeats (and it usually does unless awareness of it is communicated), teachers will assume a passive role in team decisions. How do we ensure that teachers become leaders rather than followers?

Finding the answers and, more importantly, acting upon them will not be simple. Nevertheless, finding answers to these questions cannot be avoided, and now is the time to begin.

Serious advocates of quality programs for exceptional children hopefully can find a few answers in this book. We are at the beginning of a new beginning. This opportunity cannot be missed—and it won't be if all educators review their commitment to providing the best for children to whom they are responsible.

REFERENCE

Whelan, R. J., & Sontag, E. Prologue: Special education and the cities. In P. H. Mann (Ed.), *Mainstream special education.* Washington, DC: Council for Exceptional Children, 1974.

Part I
Assessment

Glenn A. Vergason, *Georgia State University*

Assessment is a process employing observation, task analysis, and testing to arrive at learning characteristics for educational, vocational, and social decision making about individuals. Such decisions are at the heart of all instruction, but especially special education. In earlier times one intelligence test might have been the only basis for decisions and placement, but during the last decade dramatic changes have taken place in what is considered to constitute assessment and in the roles of parents and professionals in this process. We have seen a move from testing to assessment, a move from classifying children to psychological and educational personnel working to describe the ways in which children learn best. We have seen a movement from the medical model (whereby we were diagnosing a disease or malfunction) to a more functional description of children's problems.

The early work of Alfred Binet appears to have been in the right direction for today's world. Binet sought to describe how children learn, and he had little interest in categorizing children. Professionals who followed in the years since 1905, however, employing revisions of his scale, led the field of special education into an overreliance on testing. This reliance seems to have been questioned rarely before the early 1970s. In looking back over the period of the 1950s and 1960s, when special classes were increasing rapidly in numbers, only a few voices of criticism were heard.

The first real test of the adequacy of assessment arose in *Diana v. State Board of Education* (1970), in which Mexican-American and Chinese-American children were claimed to be overrepresented in the population of special classes. The case was settled in favor of the plaintiff, resulting in the requirement to test children in their preferred language if bilinqual; reassessment of all children in special classes; and development of norms for children representing subpopulations. The same principles were present in

Larry P. v. *Riles* (1972), in which black children were identified as being overrepresented in special classes. Such cases laid the groundwork for what has been termed as nondiscriminatory testing—proper assessment should not lead to children from minority groups being placed in special classes when they really should not be there.

Until the 1970s children were tested and placed in special programs based largely on results from one test—usually the Stanford-Binet or the Wechsler Intelligence Scale for Children. This practice was contrary to the predominant definition of mental retardation and recommendations of the American Association on Mental Deficiency (1959). The definition of mental retardation emphasized the need to consider adaptive behavior in addition to measured intelligence. This multi-factor definition seems to have been widely ignored in practice until litigation and federal legislation resulted in its becoming a requirement in assessment.

The multi-factor assessment and reliance on more than one test carried over into current federal legislation, especially the Education for All Handicapped Children Act of 1975 (PL 94-142) and its regulations (*Federal Register,* August 23, 1977).

This law and regulations also have directed the field of special education away from one-person diagnosis or assessment toward placement committees in which a group of professional persons plus the parents study available assessment data from psychologists, teachers, physicians, and others to arrive at a group decision regarding diagnosis, placement, and educational programming. The requirement of an individualized education program (IEP) for each child receiving special education services makes great demands on the field of special education to develop reliable instruments and methods of assessing not only cognitive and academic abilities, but also areas such as physical education and affective skills.

The individuals who have written for this section have been quite sensitive to the changes in assessment, the role of teachers in this process, skills necessary for assessing academic subjects, and of understanding the use of informal approaches. These articles lead logically to the later sections on planning and evaluation, which derive from and depend upon the quality of assessment for success.

REFERENCES

Diana v. *State Board of Education,* Civil Action No. C 7307RFP (N.D., Cal., January 7, 1970, and June 18, 1973).

Heber, R. (Ed.). *A manual of classification of mental retardation.* Columbus, OH: American Association on Mental Deficiency, 1959.

Larry P. v. *Riles,* Civil Action N.C. 71-2270, 343F, Suppl. 1306 (N.D. Cal., 1972).

This work was especially commissioned by the editors to set the tone for this section of the book and has not previously appeared in print. The authors emphasize a positive approach to testing and assessment, including affective elements of assessment. In particular, they stress the contributions which the use of assessment measures can offer to teachers within the classroom. Tests are discussed under the headings of: classification, diagnostic testing, and task analysis, and include the potential contributions of each. Implications of PL 94-142 for assessment and the future also are addressed.

Psychoeducational Assessment: An Integrated Viewpoint

Margaret Walkenshaw, *Sequoyah (Kansas) Elementary School*
Marvin Fine, *University of Kansas*

The old adage of the blind men and the elephant has application to the psychoeducational assessment of children. In that tale, upon examining different parts of the elephant, each of the blind men argued with surety for his definition of the total elephant. Of course, each definition had been derived from a different perspective and produced entirely different definitions. In assessment, if an individual starts with a narrow frame of reference the resulting view of the problem will be restricted and considerably biased. Because we are talking here about assessing children with the goal of *helping* children, the emphasis should be on the child rather than on a grand scheme that pays homage to a theory and discounts the needs of the child.

The whole area of assessment has been under attack for many years, for a variety of reasons, from various groups. Major legal cases have pertained to assessment procedures. Some communities even have banned the use of certain kinds of tests. The consensus among professionals, however, seems to be that proper assessment procedures, adequately implemented in consideration of the specific child, can lead to valuable information which, in turn, can contribute to a helpful intervention with the child.

SOME HISTORICAL AND CONTEMPORARY ISSUES

American education has a history of being trend- and conflict-oriented, and the area of psychoeducational assessment has not been spared. With the emergence of the mental testing movement at the turn of the century, many persons were led to believe that we now had the answer for educating children—use mental tests to separate children into ability groupings and thus meet the needs of all children without unduly frustrating either the low or high ability students.

The closer we examined the concept of abilities, however, the more complicated the subject became, and the less realistic was the ability grouping ideology. Just as the child with a reading problem may be performing adequately in mathematics, so might the child superior in reading be performing in average fashion in another subject area. The attempts at ability grouping also reflected a serious myopic view within educational programming that precluded meeting the needs of children in other respects. For example, in one school district, after superior students had been culled from the general school population, those A students then were graded on a normal curve, resulting in over 75 percent of them dropping suddenly to B or lower. Needless to say, student and parent protests eventually deterred this practice.

The assessment procedures initially used to ability-place the children described above likely involved tests that gave standard scores based on norms. Such *norm-referenced* classification instruments, including intelligence and achievement tests, are still popular, and they represent one facet of an integrated assessment approach.

Another viewpoint on assessment was reflected in a letter sent to a teacher by a private clinic describing the progress of a child. The youngster had been doing poorly academically, and his parents had sought the help of this private clinic, which used a "neurological approach." The clinic's assumption was that neurological development could be inferred from peripheral motor behavior. Based on the developmental history and a current evaluation via certain procedures, they determined the child's "neurological age." They also assumed that learning was a function of appropriately developing neurological "structures." On these bases, they offered the child an intensive sensory-motor type of program. The report that followed the treatment program described how the child had made a two-year gain in neurological development, which of course pleased the parents. Unfortunately, however, the child's academic functioning had not improved.

The kind of service that the private clinic had offered was of a diagnostic nature and was *criterion-referenced*. Some diagnostic testing is also norm-referenced, as in the case of the Illinois Test of Psycholinguistic Abilities (Kirk, McCarthy, & Kirk, 1968). With this test, the child's psycholinguistic functioning is rated over 12 subtests, each one giving a score based on normative data.

An example of another approach to assessment—*task analysis*—was used by a kindergarten teacher we know. Concerned because a child was having great difficulty copying alphabet letters, she spent time observing him and then structured some specific tasks. The teacher learned that the child's inability to reproduce letters related to his more basic inability to consistently make vertical circles (as in the letter *b*) and to connect units of drawings. The teacher realized the fallacy in expecting this child to satisfactorily complete the assigned task given his level of perceptual-motor functioning. She then broke down the terminal task into its component parts and presented the child with some structured training experiences designed to build up his specific skills. In this instance, the child did succeed at the components and finally at completing some letters. Such informal diagnostic procedures of a task-analysis nature also are an important part of an integrated assessment approach.

DIMENSIONS OF ASSESSMENT

The foregoing discussion highlighted three dimensions in psychoeducational assessment of children:

(1) classification or categorization of the child and his/her problem,
(2) diagnosis of the problem area, and
(3) an analysis of the structure and content of learning.

Each dimension involved some kind of testing—which raises the question of how testing and assessment are related. In brief, testing is the systematic study of a sample of behavior, usually expressed in quantitative terms (for example, the measuring and reporting of an IQ score or a reading level would be a function of specific testing); assessment has a broader meaning and, for these authors, refers to the qualitative as well as quantitative study of the individual interacting with his/her environment. Assessment includes testing of various aspects of the individual, but goes beyond that. The coherent analysis of an individual as an active organism constitutes a true assessment.

Psychoeducational assessment is the study of an individual in an educational context, focusing on the quantitative and qualitative appraisal of his/her abilities, learning capacities, and emotionality as they relate to the child responding appropriately to the demands of the environment. The main purpose of psychoeducational assessment is to connect the outcomes of the assessment to educational planning for the child. Without this last component, the assessment process would be incomplete, as well as unnecessary.

Why involve a child in a psychoeducational assessment process in the first place? The answer, simply enough, is because of concern about the child. And a psychoeducational assessment process is considered to be a means of understanding the child and then preparing a special program to assist the youngster if one is necessary. The starting point typically is a teacher who is concerned, who already has had continuing contact with the child, and has discovered needs that are not being met. The teacher's approach likely has included a review of the child's cumulative record, possibly a conference with the parent, and then some decision about how to proceed. At some point, the teacher began to realize he or she did not know enough about certain things, or perhaps that the attempted program had not worked. Then, a referral likely was initiated to bring other persons, such as a school psychologist or learning disability consultant, into the picture.

The consultant entering the scene might retrace some of the territory already covered by the teacher, such as reviewing the child's cumulative record and past test information and, additionally, the teacher's experiences with and observations of the child. The consultant might spend some time observing the child in the classroom. Other valuable information likely will be obtained from the parents. Systematic testing of the child may seem advisable as a phase of this assessment process.

Although the total process of psychoeducational assessment is broader than a testing orientation, the data collection phase of assessment is in part test oriented. Three testing-based components of assessment can be considered.

Standardized Classification Testing

Testing as a way of learning something about the individual has great public appeal. Many women's magazines, for example, contain short questionnaires on everything from rating your sex appeal to how likely you are to become a child abuser. The score on the test is compared to a table that gives a rating from superior to deficient on the thing being measured. Usually, little explanation is offered as to the logic of the items, the basis on which the rating is determined, or how the test is able to predict in your daily life. If you've taken such tests, you probably are aware that, depending on how you felt that day or because of any number of other factors, your score might be considerably different on another day. These concerns about item selection, deviation of scores, predictability, and stability of performance speak to the psychometric properties of the test and are especially relevant to the historical use of classification instruments.

Classification systems tell you some things, but not others. Some of the difficulties school psychologists have encountered with teachers are a function of the psychologist having classified a child, for example, as educable mentally retarded while believing he or she gave the teacher (a) an understanding of the child, and (b) a direction for educating the child. Categorization of the child as educable mentally retarded initially may have satisfied a legal requirement. Second, it says that the child's learning efficiency historically has been low, as reflected in academic and intellectual scores. It does not, however, say anything about the youngster's specific academic problems, learning style, motivational characteristics, or other important factors such as cultural or family background as they relate to educational programming. Consequently, the broad use of such standardized instruments with atypical populations has led to charges of discrimination, and many states now have mandated that children be tested in "the language of their home" and that a variety of measures be used.

Stereotyping children and the subsequent developing of erroneous expectations is another problem related to classification or categorization. The labels *learning disabled, brain damaged, mentally retarded,* or *intellectually superior* conjure up many different images in teachers' minds which can lead to faulty expectations. Labels by themselves do not represent an understanding of the individual.

Classification instruments, typified by intelligence and achievement tests, often are standardized and are norm-referenced. The concept of standardization means that, to make sense out of the child's score, the test must be given in a prescribed manner. (Psychologists, because of their intensive training in testing, are particularly critical of anyone giving standardized tests who lacks sensitivity regarding how the way in which a test is administered can affect pupil behavior.) The raw scores obtained on such tests are converted into derived scores that say something about where the child falls in relation to other children. Examples of derived scores are standardized scores, grade equivalents, percentiles, and stanines.

Another important psychometric characteristic of standardized, norm-referenced instruments is the careful establishment of validity and reliability; this technical information is reported in test manuals and speaks to the key questions of, "What is the test measuring?" and "How stable is the measurement?" Ignoring these data may result in using an inappropriate test for a given child, or giving an incorrect interpretation to test scores.

Standardized classification testing can give useful information on current functioning levels and, in this way, can even serve as a baseline for subsequent retestings following remedial intervention. Instruments such as the Wechsler Intelligence Scales are important not only for establishing current levels of functioning, but also can serve as excellent determinants regarding the need for or emphasis on further diagnostic testing. The obtained scores may establish extent of the problem, or even whether a problem exists. Consider a child who functions poorly in class in terms of completing assignments. He or she may create the impression of not understanding the material, whereas achievement testing may disclose adequate knowledge and skill across academic areas, and would suggest that the student may not be applying himself or herself diligently in class.

The reader is referred to basic texts in the area of measurement and testing for complete presentations on standardized norm-referenced testing (Anastasi, 1968; Cronbach, 1960). Additionally, numerous excellent articles and books have dealt in detail with the cultural, discriminatory, and legal problems of formal testing (Bersoff, 1973; Phillips, 1973; Meyers, Sundstrom & Yoshida, 1973; Mercer, 1973; and Samuda, 1973).

Standardized Diagnostic Testing

Beyond the categorization of functioning level, the teacher will, of course, have questions regarding the nature of the child's difficulty. Numerous standardized diagnostic instruments have clearly defined administration, scoring, and interpretation. Many of those instruments—for example, The Marianne Frostig Test of Visual Perception (Frostig, Lefever, & Whittlesey, 1964) and the Illinois Test of Psycholinguistic Abilities (Kirk, McCarthy, & Kirk, 1968)—are norm-referenced; i.e., the scores obtained on these instruments can be understood in part by comparing the child's performance with that of a norm group.

In addition to norm-referenced tests, diagnostic tests also may be criterion-referenced. In these tests, someone has decided what the mastery area is (for example, the child being able to recognize beginning consonant sounds) and then decides what degree of correctness is considered satisfactory or problematic. An example of a criterion-referenced diagnostic test is the Basic Education Skills Inventory (SELECT-ED, Inc., 1972). The Durrell Analysis of Reading Difficulty (Durrell, 1955) is an example of a diagnostic test combining norm- and criterion-referenced subtests.

The arguments in favor of criterion-referenced testing revolve around the potential bias of norm-referenced testing as compared to the individual child-mastery orientation of criterion-referenced testing. But each has a worthwhile part in the total diagnostic battery calculated to fully understand the nature of a child's difficulties.

Another basis on which diagnostic tests differ from each other (aside from norm- versus criterion-referencing) is on a content versus process orientation. In content-oriented tests, the stimulus material presented to the child is essentially academic in nature. Examples would be a series of mathematics problems to complete, or consonant blends to identify. The test content has "curricular validity" in the way it correlates with actual classroom demands on the child. Process-oriented diagnostic tests, in contrast, make assumptions regarding psychophysical processes that underlie classroom learning. The Frostig Test (Frostig, Lefever, & Whittlesey, 1964) is an example of a process-oriented test with a focus on visual-motor functioning. The Illinois Test of Psycholinguistic Abilities (Kirk, McCarthy, & Kirk, 1968) is another example, with its focus on the intake, integration, and output of information using different sensory modalities. The Purdue Perceptual Motor Survey (Roach & Kephart, 1966) is another example of a diagnostic test that focuses on nonacademic areas with the implicit or explicit assumption that the psychophysical process being measured underlies adequate academic functioning. As one would expect, the prescribed remedial program varies depending on a person's orientation toward content or process.

One criticism of how some diagnostic tests have been used, in terms of problem identification and remediation, is that they are limited and ineffective attempts to train abilities (Smead, 1977; Eaves & McLaughlin, 1977; Ysseldyke & Salvia, 1974-75; Mann, 1971; and Hammill, Goodman, & Wiederhold, 1973-74). Standardized diagnostic tests, however, remain a potentially valuable source of information regarding a child's difficulties.

Analyzing the Structure of Learning (Task Analysis)

Recent years have witnessed a growing emphasis on informal assessment procedures of a task-analysis nature (Ysseldyke & Salvia, 1974-75; Siegel, 1972; Hammill, 1971; Junkala, 1973). The statement over 10 years ago by Schwartz (1967) calling for the training of diagnostician-educators has in fact received a response by many teacher training programs. Teachers, special and regular, are increasingly better trained in the classroom diagnosis of program planning for children with learning and behavior problems.

The task analysis approach clearly is behavioristic with its focus on small units of behavior and its rejection of inferential constructs. The approach basically is to identify a terminal task (for example, two-column addition that requires carrying) and to break it down into its component parts. Can the child visually recognize a written number? Add without carrying? Add a double column addition problem without carrying? Know how to carry? Put it all together to complete a two-column addition task requiring carrying? If not, where is the breakdown?

The approach also is experimental in nature in that sensitive diagnosticians may develop and administer the task steps as they work with the child. Furthermore, criteria for evaluating a child's performance on a task can vary according to the judgment of the teacher or diagnostician. For example, rate and accuracy might be identified as the crucial variables and, accordingly, the number of items successfully completed over a specified time period would be established as the criterion of success. Rate irrespective of accuracy might be the criterion in another situation, or vice versa.

A value of the task-analysis approach is that the knowledgeable teacher can work individually with children, task analyzing their behavior and then building in appropriate remedial steps. The task analysis of education objectives is properly the domain of the teacher, though he or she understandably may need to solicit backup consultation for some children. For a child presenting multiple problems, it makes good sense for other peer professionals to be involved.

The task-analysis approach is a variation of systems analysis. The skilled teacher is aware of how behaviors lock together sequentially, chaining toward some end point. Just as a systems analyst explores a malfunctioning system, so does the teacher conceptualize the units of production and analyze them systematically. The analysis can consider the input, association, and output of information, as well as the sensory modalities involved (Junkala, 1973).

From a norm-referenced test, one is able to generalize to other similar populations. This is an important value of the standardization and norming procedures associated with development and use of the test. Task analysis procedures, in contrast, are tailor-made for each individual child and, accordingly, what works with one child may not generalize to other children. A primary asset of task analysis is the individualization of diagnosis and subsequent remedial programming. Taken to an extreme, some proponents of task analysis have argued that normative measures, or even standardized diagnostic procedures, are unnecessary. This appears to these authors to be an overstatement of the case.

An Integrated Approach to Psychoeducational Assessment

As stated earlier, psychoeducational assessment is the study of the child in an educational context. The focus is on quantitative and qualitative appraisal of the child's abilities, learning capacities, emotionality, and how these three areas relate to the child's response to demands of the environment. Psychoeducational assessment must feed directly into curricular decisions and programming for the child; otherwise, it is an expendable luxury.

Although attempts have been made to polarize positions on assessment, in which one approach is touted as desirable and another approach viewed as incorrect, we believe that program decisions for children should be data based and, so as not to parallel the "blind men and the elephant" analogy, data from different sources of assessment are desirable. Data from any single source encourage biased or excessively narrow views of the child, the problem, and options for remediation. A number of persons have argued for such a comprehensive and integrated approach to assessment (e.g., Bateman, 1966-67; Adelman, 1971).

The Goal of Psychoeducational Assessment

Success experiences have been identified as an important cornerstone of a child's adequate personality development; also, a sense of success and the expectation of success are crucial motivators of productive intellectual and social pursuits by the child. This statement becomes dramatically clear to anyone who has spent time with children who have had prolonged exposure to personal failure. They have come to react to new ideas and new units of instruction more often than not with groans and negative anticipations. Therefore, the end goal of psychoeducational assessment should be to enable implementation of a program for the child that will lead to greater academic and social success and a greater sense of personal adequacy.

Assessment Procedures and Considerations

The three kinds of testing procedures described—classification, diagnostic, and task-analysis—each may have something to contribute toward understanding the child, but certainly not all these procedures have to be used with a given child. The "problem" most often is identified in the classroom by the teacher. The teacher's options for understanding the child and his or her difficulties include observing the child, talking with the child, reviewing past records, holding a parent conference, and, via task-analysis, experimenting with the child in the process of learning.

How children feel about themselves in the learning situation may have a greater impact on future learning than cognitive or sensory-motor factors. The emphasis in assessment procedures for children with learning problems has become decidedly cognitive over the most recent decades. One argument for discounting affective factors has been that helping a child with learning problems to feel better about himself/herself has led mainly to a well-adjusted learning disabled child. This is a shallow overstatement and supportive of a nonproductive polarization of theory and methodology. Most teachers are aware generally of how children feel about themselves within the classroom.

Formal classroom sociometrics can help to identify the isolated or rejected children, as will observation of friendship clusters. More specific to the learning situation, by observing how children approach tasks and by discussing their feelings and expectations, the teacher can appropriately learn about their affective nature.

Keeping in mind the interplay between cognitive and affective factors during daily, continued interaction with the child, if the teacher suspects that a child might have a problem that affects learning, a thorough assessment is in order. Current law requires that parental approval must be sought and received before proceeding and, aside from the legal aspects, it is wise and sound practice to involve parents in their children's learning experiences, placement, and special services, and to receive their input which can lead to a better understanding of the total child. Other professionals also can contribute to this understanding. Depending on the school district, the consultants might be school psychologists or remedial experts.

At this point, the scope of assessment broadens and probably will include some diagnostic and classification instruments to try to obtain a total view. Also, since the child's difficulties manifest themselves in the classroom as a behavior setting, some study of the child in interaction with that environment would be desirable. The assessment procedures should focus on cognitive, sensory-motor, and affective factors against the background of the settings within which the problems are occurring.

Psychoeducational assessment is, in part, a process of establishing and testing hypotheses. From a broad "what's happening" approach, the persons involved in the assessment begin to hypothesize as to specific problems. From a broad-based initial approach, the diagnostic processes narrow in focus as specific suspected problem areas are investigated. Diagnosticians who are restricted to a predetermined, set battery of tests or procedures turn the assessment function into a lock-step process and, while likely to discover some pertinent variable, also are likely to miss many.

Planning An Intervention

Presumably, what was attempted initially with the child has not worked—that is why the assessment occurred. The several persons potentially involved (teacher, school psychologist, social worker, learning disability consultant, parent) then should meet to plan the child's future program. Of course, the initial assessment and subsequent programming must comply with the fundamental due process issues, and the discussion here assumes parental consent to such intervention.

At the first team meeting, one of the members should be designated as team leader or coordinator. Each person should be asked to present pertinent information. This could involve background information as to the child's developmental history, prior school experience, home and community adjustment, and prior kinds of help offered the child. As a result, a picture of the current problem should begin to emerge. In what specific ways is the child having difficulty; also, in what ways is the child performing adequately?

A comprehensive, integrated psychoeducational assessment considers not only the child's weaknesses, but also the strengths, and the areas of satisfactory functioning. The history of psychological assessment has been deficiency-oriented. The suspicion of a teacher or principal that a child has a problem often has precipitated an evaluation procedure calculated to define the problem. In other words, the assumption that a problem exists has served as the basis and goal of the assessment. The fact is that most children are doing more things "right" than "wrong," as evidenced by their survival.

From a review of all these data, some hypotheses can be generated as to causal factors, correlative factors, and potentially successful curricular planning approaches. This phase of a conference broadens the perspective on the case and may frustrate those persons present who want a quick answer. As the discussion proceeds, the focus should narrow to several options that can intermesh to constitute the intervention program. The program needs to identify how the various personnel will be involved, what specific activities will be attempted and the overall goal to be achieved, how "success" will be gauged, and the projected time frame for this intervention. The persons involved in this planning activity should all have an opportunity to disagree, to brainstorm, and to feel a part of the helping process.

Often, aspects of the intervention program require input from the child, but sometimes the rhetoric, personal agendas, and biases cloud the fact that the child's welfare is the focus of the whole enterprise. The child has the greatest stake in the success or failure of the program, and to not include the child in relevant ways would be remiss. This inclusion means the child has the right to know what is being planned and has an opportunity to contribute ideas. His or her feelings and thoughts about various curricular placements (special class, resource room, working with an itinerant teacher, etc.) should be discussed. The child may have some valuable ideas on how to help himself or herself, or what curricular organization would be most comfortable and best able to generate motivation. For example, in remedial programming, the child could be placed in a small group, worked with individually, given programmed materials, or could work with a peer tutor. What are the child's feelings about these options?

Parental support for any in-school program is crucial. Certainly, it is possible to work successfully with children even if the parents are not fully supportive, but parental support and input provide a greater probability of success. The parent knows the child best, has "studied" the child longitudinally, and is aware of the youngster's likes, interests, and past successes and failures. Achieving parental support is a worthwhile endeavor, and parental support is most likely to occur if prior parental involvement has existed.

Continuous Evaluation

Historically, the format for evaluating an intervention program has been to make a judgment at the end of the academic year as to whether or not it worked. If the summative judgment was that the program was not effective, a great deal of time and energy had been wasted and, most importantly, the child was not helped. Either periodic evaluations of progress or a plan of continuous evaluations of a formative nature are preferable. Based on awareness of what progress is occurring, the intervention program can be modified, thereby continually increasing the probability of success.

Continuous evaluation is accomplished easily in a highly objectified, behavioral program. The day-to-day activities of the child can be charted and examined for changes. Variations in the treatment can be introduced and their impact made visibly apparent. In this way, content and structure of the program, as well as variations in reinforcement procedures, can be selectively varied and observed. At any point, evaluation statements can be made regarding the child's progress in the program.

Periodic evaluations also can occur to supplement the continuous evaluation. The diagnostic and classification instruments administered earlier can be readministered to complete the picture of progress. Unlike the adage of the blind men and the elephant, an integrated approach to psychoeducational assessment takes a *holistic* view of the child. Each aspect of assessment contributes toward the more complete picture of what is happening to the child and how the child is responding. Also, the persons involved, including parents and child, are concerned with a common objective—to assist the child, in the least restrictive way, to achieve academic and personal potentials within an educational setting.

Recently, litigation, legislation, and changes in professional attitudes have combined to significantly affect the lives of children with learning and developmental problems, particularly within the school system. Especially noteworthy is the Education for All Handicapped Children Act of 1975 (Public Law 94-142), which among other effects, has had a significant impact on assessment procedures.

IMPLICATIONS OF PUBLIC LAW 94-142 FOR ASSESSMENT

With the passage of Public Law 94-142, every exceptional child is assured an appropriate educational program that is carefully planned, well-documented, and regularly monitored and evaluated. To provide appropriate programs for all special children, school districts are responsible for developing systematic, nondiscriminatory identification and evaluation procedures. Screening methods to include all school age children serve as the first phase in identification of children who might be considered exceptional. Children who appear to be in need of special curricular adjustments are to be afforded a comprehensive evaluation which must be nondiscriminatory and multidisciplinary in nature, and is to include physical, psychological, educational, and environmental data. The purpose of such an evaluation is to provide the information necessary to develop an Individualized Education Program (IEP) designed to meet the specific needs of that child.

The IEP must be a written record developed in a meeting of educators, other professionals, parents, and, where appropriate, the child. The IEP is to be developed for every child needing special services, at the beginning of the school year, and is to be reviewed and revised, if necessary, at least annually. The content is to include statements as to the child's present levels of education performance, short-term instructional objectives which will move the child sequentially and measurably toward specified long-term goals, and the specific educational services and adjustments needed by the child. Beginning and projected termination dates for the delivery of special educational services must be stated, as well as a justification for the type of special programming decided upon and a statement as to the proposed extent of the child's participation in regular educational programs.

The implications of such rigorous specifications for the diagnostician or persons responsible for assessment are broad. To be of value in building an effective educational program for the student, the assessment must relate directly to the prescriptive program. Skills of the diagnostician have increased visibility and importance in translating findings into actual educational practice within the classroom. Assessment of each child must be broad enough to encompass academic as well as psychological and psychomotor functioning. The results obtained from such an integrated approach are consistent with psychoeducational assessment and its emphasis on a holistic view of the child, as described in this article. These methods and procedures, further, are exceedingly relevant and translatable to an appropriate individualized education program.

The recent flux of mandates to help exceptional children is testimony to our nation's concern, but it also is an indictment of education for its tardiness in meeting the needs of exceptional children. We endorse the comments made recently by Morse (1977) that:

> Our new-found conscience, expressed in the legal terms of *mandatory*, offers the greatest potential we have ever had for special education. Yet, one knows that great opportunities

Instructional Planning for Exceptional Children

also contain the potential for distortion . . . it is easy to subscribe to the illusion that administrative formats provide solutions when the significant issue is the quality of the psychoeducational experience actually provided each youngster (p. 60).

Psychoeducational assessment is the key to providing a quality psychoeducational experience. It will require special personnel to learn to work together in a cooperative planning approach. This, in turn, should lead to a broad, integrated approach to assessment with a clear focus on understanding and meeting the needs of the child.

REFERENCES

Adelman, H. S. Learning problems: A sequential and hierarchical approach to identification and correction. *Academic Therapy*, 1971, 6, (3).
Anastasi, A. *Psychological testing* (3rd ed.). New York: Macmillan, 1968.
Bateman, B. Three approaches to diagnosis and educational planning for children with learning disabilities. *Academic Therapy*, 1966-67, 2, 215-222.
Bersoff, D. N. Silk purses into sow's ears: The decline of psychological testing and a suggestion for its redemption. *American Psychologist*, 1973, 28, 892-899.
Cronbach, L. J. *Essentials of psychological testing* (2nd ed.). New York: Harper & Row, 1960.
Durrell, D. D. *Durrell analysis of reading difficulties*. New York: Harcourt, Brace, & World, 1955.
Eaves, R. C., & McLaughlin, P. A systems approach for the assessment of the child and his environment: Getting back to basics. *Journal of Special Education*, 1977, 11, 99-111.
Frostig, M., Lefever, D. W., & Whittlesey, J. R. *The Marianne Frostig developmental test of visual perception*. Palo Alto, CA: Consulting Psychologists Press, 1964.
Hammill, D. D. Evaluating children for instructional purposes. *Academic Therapy*, 1971, 6, 341-353.
Hammill, D., Goodman, L., & Wiederholt, J. L. Visual-motor processes: Can we train them? *Reading Teacher*, 1973-74, 27, 468-478.
Junkala, J. Task analysis: The processing dimension. *Academic Therapy*, 1973, 8, 401-409.
Kirk, S. A., McCarthy, J. J., & Kirk, W. O. *Illinois test of psycholinguistic abilities* (rev. ed.). Urbana: University of Illinois Press, 1968.
Mann, L. Psychometric phrenology and the new faculty psychology: The case against ability assessment and training. *Journal of Special Education*, 1971, 5, 3-14.
Mercer, J. The pluralistic assessment project: Sociocultural effects in clinical assessment. *School Psychology Digest*, 1973, 2, 10-18.
Meyers, C. E., Sundstrom, P. E., & Yoshida, R. K. The school psychologist and assessment in special education. *School Psychology Monograph*, 1973, 2, 3-57.
Morse, W. C. Acceptance speech upon receiving the Wallin Award. *Exceptional Children*, 1977, 44, 59-60.
Phillips, B. N. (Ed.). *Assessing minority group children* (a special issue of *Journal of School Psychology*). New York: Behavioral Publications, 1973.
Roach, E. G., & Kephart, N. C. *The Purdue perceptual-motor survey*. Columbus, OH: Merrill, 1966.
Samuda, R. J. Racial discrimination through mental testing: A social critic's point of view. *ERIC-ERCD Bulletin*, 1973, 42, 1-16.
Schwartz, L. Preparation of the clinical teacher for special education: 1866-1966. *Exceptional Children*, 1967, 34, 117-124.
SELECT-ED, Inc. *Basic education skills inventory*. Torrance, CA: B. I. Winch & Assoc., 1972.
Siegel, E. Task analysis and effective teaching. *Journal of Learning Disabilities*, 1972, 5.
Smead, V. S. Ability training and task analysis in diagnostic/prescriptive teaching. *Journal of Special Education*, 1977, 11, 113-125.
Ysseldyke, J. E., & Salvia, J. Diagnostic-prescriptive teaching: Two models. *Exceptional Children*, 1974-75, 41, 181-185.

This selection examines the teacher's role in assessment. Author Moran places considerable emphasis on the classroom teacher's importance in this regard, and indicates that all teachers must decide whether to rely on their own assessment of the student or to call upon other professional specialists. She offers practical suggestions on assessment of academic, psychomotor, cognitive, and affective functioning.

The Teacher's Role in Referral for Testing

Mary Ross Moran, *University of Kansas*

Over the past few years, the proliferation of diagnostic services made available to classroom teachers has increased the complexity of decisions they must make about assessment. They are asked to determine whether referral is indicated, and who should be asked to test a student. The following discussion represents an attempt to organize the teacher's task.

Bases for decision are discussed as follows: The Teacher's Role in Referral describes three levels of assessment, from academic performance through psychomotor, cognitive, and affective evaluation, offering suggestions for appropriate referral at each level, followed by guidelines for formulating useful referral questions and for preparing a student for referral. A brief concluding section explores the attitudes to be cultivated by the teacher who would benefit from the referral process.

Although some suggestions are incorporated for the testing to be conducted by the classroom teacher, the focus of this discussion is upon decisions about referral.

Instructional Planning for Exceptional Children

THE TEACHER'S ROLE IN REFERRAL

The basic question for any teacher is whether to rely upon her own assessment of a student's strengths and weaknesses or to refer the learner for evaluation by other professional specialists. The question is a serious one, and it requires a great deal of careful thought on the part of the teacher.

On the one hand, the teacher recognizes her responsibility to deal with academic problems herself, through modification of instruction; she knows that she is in the best position to judge a learner's academic skills because she works with him daily across subject areas. On the other hand, the teacher is aware that lowered academic performance can be a secondary symptom of underlying cognitive, perceptual, emotional, social, or medical problems which she is not trained to evaluate. How is she to decide which student can be adequately assessed in the classroom and which one requires the services of specialists?

This decision is never simple, but it can be aided by considering different levels of assessment. There are at least three *levels of assessment* which can be distinguished.

ACADEMIC FUNCTIONING LEVEL

On the surface level, the level which might be called Academic Functioning Level, a learner's academic strengths and weaknesses in each subject area can be identified and grade levels of achievement computed.

Sample Statements

This is the level at which it is reported that third-grader Joe has the following academic characteristics: "Independent reading level is Primer, instructional reading level is grade 2-1, listening capacity level is grade 3-1. Lowest scores on word recognition skills tests occurred on measures of sound blending, recognizing the visual forms of final consonants and blends, double vowels, and dipthongs. Overall grade level in math is 2-2, with lowered scores on place value, missing elements, and geometric forms. Spelling grade level is 2-0. Spelling is marked by omission of endings, b-d confusion, and inaccurate spacing of letters, with some correct letters in transposed order. Handwriting rate is scored at a grade level of 1-6. Manuscript letters are of uneven size with irregular spacing."

Typical Descriptors

Descriptors which might be used at this first level of assessment include grade level, grade equivalent, percentile, stanine, score, skill level, test profile, diagnostic test results, criterion level, mastery level, trial teaching.

Representative Tests

Of course, careful inspection of the child's daily written products and observation of his task behavior must be considered in addition to any special testing which is done at this level, because these factors carry strong implications for educational planning. At this level of assessment, some test instruments are appropriate, apart from the standardized group achievement tests which are always part of the classroom record. Individual testing may be conducted using an informal reading inventory constructed from the classroom series, the Classroom Reading Inventory (Silvaroli, 1973), a graded reading test such as the Standard Reading Inventory (McCracken, 1966), or the Diagnostic Reading Scales (Spache, 1963). If they have been trained in standardized procedures, teachers can and do use gross screening instruments such as the Peabody Individual Achievement Test (Dunn & Markwardt, 1970) or diagnostic instruments such as the Keymath (Connolly, Nachtman & Pritchett, 1971). Some teachers prefer the detailed skills information which can be obtained from measures such as the Basic Educational Skills Inventory (Adamson, Shrago & Van Etten, 1972). Others are developing their own criterion-referenced tests based upon classroom materials, or they are making systematic observations and records of a child's responses to trial teaching—two approaches which have proved particularly effective for individualized planning. All of the aforementioned approaches to obtaining a description of the child's academic performance are available to the regular classroom teacher, and she is in the best position to assess a child at this level. Even if it is determined that further evaluation is necessary, any child who is referred to a school psychologist or other ancillary personnel should first be assessed at this descriptive level by the classroom teacher. No one else can assess this level better than the teacher who has unlimited samples of the child's task behavior, written products, and the opportunity to carry out individual testing, observation, and trial teaching over time.

Considerations for Referral

There are a few situations in which a teacher might refer questions at this first level of assessment to other professionals. The special reading teacher, for example, might be asked to carry out some individual reading evaluations such as the Durrell Analysis of Reading Difficulty (Durrell, 1955) or the Gates-McKillop Reading Diagnostic Tests (Gates & McKillop, 1962) for youngsters whose reading problems have resisted the classroom teacher's efforts at diagnosis and remediation. An itinerant learning disabilities teacher or a resource room teacher might be asked to assist in diagnosis of skills deficits if the classroom teacher is not satisfied that she has enough description of a child's relative strengths and weaknesses to plan an individual program for a

Instructional Planning for Exceptional Children

specific student. The curriculum supervisor of reading or math might be consulted for recommendation of specific approaches to instruction to solve a specific problem.

But questions which can be resolved at the Academic Functioning Level are not appropriate for referral to a school psychologist, counselor, or clinical psychologist. Such personnel are not curriculum specialists, they are not specially trained in materials selection, and they are seldom in a position to make useful recommendations in regard to specific instructional practices. If the question concerns establishment of reading levels, skills levels in word recognition, comprehension, spelling, computation, numerical reasoning, writing, or other academic skills, the screening instruments widely used by psychologists, such as the Wide Range Achievement Test (Jastak & Jastak, 1965) or the Peabody Individual Achievement Test (Dunn & Markwardt, 1970), yield data too gross to be of diagnostic assistance to teachers in instructional planning; time lost in waiting for such test results will only delay the teacher's own assessment of these skills.

PSYCHOMOTOR OR PROCESS FUNCTIONING LEVEL

At the second level of assessment, which might be called the Level of Psychomotor or Process Functioning, sensory awareness is checked, modality preference or learning style can be established in terms of ability to work better with auditory or visual cues, and many of the perceptual and expressive subskills which are presumed to underlie academic skills can be inferred. It is beyond the scope of this article to discuss the advantages and disadvantages of testing psychomotor abilities or what research has said about the relevance of such testing to educational programming. Although testing of psychological process dimensions is discouraged by the research literature, one has only to observe school testing situations or inspect record folders to determine that such testing is being done and that educational decisions are being made on the basis of such test results. Indeed, some state mandates for special educational services have been written in such a way that testing of psychological correlates such as visual and auditory discrimination, memory, sequencing, and other subskill constructs must be reported for finding purposes. Decisions about whether or not such testing would be appropriate must be made according to local standards and philosophy. Because testing at this level is controversial, it will be discussed in greater detail than the first and third levels.

Sample Statements

This is the level of functioning which could be described by statements such as the following: "John's pattern of scores and test behavior indicated strengths in auditory discrimination, sequencing, closure, short-term auditory recall, and verbal skills. Performance items which required visual organization, with or without a model, revealed relative weaknesses in revisualization, spatial relationships, and directionality. These weaknesses account for John's difficulty in writing and spelling."

Typical Descriptors

Descriptors which might be used to identify characteristics at this level of functioning include visual acuity, form discrimination, figure-ground distinction, form constancy, visual closure, revisualization, visual sequential memory, eye-hand coordination, dexterity, laterality, directionality, discrimination of spatial relationships, body image, tactile or kinesthetic discrimination, auditory acuity, discrimination of sound, auditory figure-ground distinction, reauditorization, auditory sequential memory, auditory closure, speech articulation.

Representative Tests

Instruments used for second-level evaluation usually are those which isolate auditory, visual, and motor components of tasks, such as the Illinois Test of Psycholinguistic Abilities (Kirk, McCarthy & Kirk, 1968), Purdue Perceptual Survey Rating Scale (Roach & Kephart, 1966), Bender Visual-Motor Gestalt Test (Bender, 1938), Lincoln-Oseretsky Motor Development Scale (Sloan, 1954), Templin-Darley Tests of Articulation (Templin & Darley, 1960), Goodenough-Harris Drawing Test (Harris, 1963), and Southern California Perceptual-Motor Tests (Ayres, 1968).

The administration of such instruments of evaluation is usually considered to be the province of the trained psychologist, speech clinician, physical or occupational therapist, or a special educator with psychometric training. If such tests are determined to be needed, they should be used by one especially trained to administer and interpret them. Most tests at the second level of assessment would not be appropriate for administration by a regular classroom teacher. There may be exceptions, however. If a teacher decides that she wishes to do her own second-level assessment, some standardized tests are available to her.

As long as administration and scoring standards are rigidly followed, many people would agree that instruments such as the Developmental Test of Visual-Motor Integration (Beery & Buktenica, 1967), the Motor-Free Visual Perception Test (Colarusso & Hammill, 1972), or the Diagnostic Auditory Discrimination Test (Goldman, Fristoe & Woodcock, 1974) can be appropriately used by classroom teachers. Although considerable experience with these tests is required to establish a clinical basis for inferences to be drawn

Instructional Planning for Exceptional Children

from them, the scores can yield some useful information about how a given child performs these tasks under controlled classroom conditions. If most students in the classroom can successfully respond to the quiet subtest of the auditory discrimination test, for example, but Sally falls below the 10th percentile, this information is corroboration of classroom observation of this learner's difficulty with phonics instruction. This test result may be enough to encourage a teacher to engage in trial teaching of a more visual approach or a word-family approach to reading; the use of this test in a classroom can be justified for such a purpose.

The use of the test cannot be justified, however, if the teacher intends to make inferences from the test about Sally's "auditory discrimination" skills in general. No single test can be the basis for such an inference, and statements made about visual or auditory skills on the basis of any single instrument are certain to be misleading. This is why a school psychologist or clinician uses a battery of tests. As there is generally some degree of overlap of indicators in different tests, the presence of a single indicator provides the basis for a hypothesis which must be confirmed by additional indicators on other tests before a statement can be made about the auditory or visual skills of a given learner.

Although a classroom teacher may use some standardized tests for the purpose of confirming classroom observation, she is by no means limited to this method of obtaining further data at the Psychomotor or Process Level of assessment. By the use of informal test procedures, carefully designed and observed, a teacher can gain considerable information about a child's visual, motor and auditory subskills. Informal, teacher-made test procedures lack the precision of standardized tests, but they have the advantage of permitting the free substitution of stimulus and response modes which is impossible under standardized conditions. For example, if the student cannot write spelling words to dictation, the teacher can isolate the cause of such a problem by asking the student to spell the same words orally, then to select a correctly spelled word from a group of four minimally contrasted alternatives, and finally to copy the spelling words from printed cards. If all these procedures are followed, it should be possible to say with some certainty whether Johnny's problem with spelling is due to breakdown of auditory, visual, or motor components.

In addition to the advantage of alternative stimulus and response modes, informal teacher-made tests at the second level of assessment have the advantage of a firm relationship to terminal classroom behaviors. That is, a teacher who is assessing a child in a classroom to determine subskills is more likely to assess auditory functions by using curriculum materials such as a phonics worksheet, for example, than by asking a child to repeat digits. For this reason, results of such assessment are likely to be more directly interpretable into classroom practices. In contrast, many of the tasks of the ITPA (Illinois Test of Phycholinguistic Abilities) or the Ayres battery, for example, are so far removed from classroom tasks that it is difficult for most teachers to see any relevance of scores on those tasks to classroom work.

Considerations for Referral

Before one can talk of visual or auditory perception, it must be determined that the student has adequate sensory information to be processed. Therefore, any question of the student's visual or auditory sensory intactness should have high priority for referral. The school nurse usually performs only a Snellen chart screening and an audiometric sweep check; therefore, consultation might be sought with an orthoptic specialist, optometrist or ophthalmologist, the district hearing conservationist or a clinical audiologist.

Behavioral information which should lead a teacher to suspect a defect in vision might include covering one eye while reading or looking at the blackboard; moving a book or paper back and forth in the line of vision as if to bring it into focus; persistent rubbing of the eyes; closing eyes or resting forehead on arm frequently while reading; jerking or quick movement of the pupil of the eye; complaints of eye fatigue, double or blurred vision, chronic headaches.

Behavioral symptoms of possible hearing problems might include turning the head toward the direction of sound; lack of response to speech originating behind the learner; unusually close attention to the mouth of a speaker; requests for repetition of instructions when conditions are noisy or the pupil is farther from the teacher than usual; severe articulation problems, including omission of many consonant sounds, especially ending sounds such as /t/ and /s/; lack of response to phonics instruction, despite adequate instruction with a variety of methods over a period of time. Many of these symptoms are likely to be displayed by children with chronic and severe throat or upper respiratory infections, asthma, or allergies affecting the respiratory system.

If a child displays a cluster of these behaviors, or even one or two with frequency and consistency, a teacher should refer the child for sensory evaluation before considering other types of evaluation. If there are indications of such deficit, the results of academic or psychological testing cannot be adequately interpreted until sensory deficit has been ruled out.

At the second level of assessment, many professional persons might be consulted, other than the school psychologist or counselor. If there is a question of gross motor problems, a physical therapist might be asked to work with the physical education instructor to develop a modified program. If fine-motor skills are underdeveloped or uneven, an occupational therapist might be asked to offer suggestions for appropriate pencil-and-paper activities. If articulation is markedly delayed, the speech clinician should be

Instructional Planning for Exceptional Children

asked to evaluate the student. When second-level assessment is required, therefore, the teacher has a number of resources for assistance.

When a teacher refers a student for evaluation by a school psychologist or clinical psychologist, second-level assessment which takes place can frequently provide useful insights into a student's learning style. An experienced clinician can draw inferences about the student's strengths and weaknesses in terms of processes which cannot be directly observed, are difficult to isolate due to confounding or overlapping of task dimensions, and involve psychological constructs which are difficult to validate. The experience of the person drawing the inferences is critical—the same information can frequently be interpreted in more than one way, and a given battery of tests can result in conflicting information which must be reconciled in order to make meaningful statements about a student.

When should a referral be made for second-level assessment by a school or clinical psychologist? If the teacher has observational data to support a suspicion that Johnny demonstrates a specific severe perceptual or expressive deficit; if the teacher has attempted to gain further information herself by trial teaching and is not satisfied with what she has found; if Johnny is failing to profit from the instruction which the teacher has deemed suitable; and if the teacher is convinced that she cannot program effectively for the child without additional information on his subskills and most favorable learning style, or has reason to believe that he may require special services, then a referral for such testing is appropriate.

A referral for evaluation at this second level is not appropriate if the teacher is merely curious about whether the student may demonstrate some type of "learning disability." Such a determination is not enough to provide the basis for instructional programming. If testing of psychomotor processes establishes that Johnny is primarily a visual or auditory learner, or that a developmental lag in fine-motor skills explains his writing problems, these insights are worth having only if they lead the teacher to design an individual program for the student. Too frequently, a referral is made to determine "if there is a specific learning disability," and subsequent information is never incorporated into daily programming for the child.

Because many teachers lack confidence in their own ability to describe their students' learning characteristics, they make many referrals for process testing when they already have, or could obtain from classroom procedures, the information they need to do effective programming. If third-grader Johnny has not mastered manuscript printing, the teacher has a problem in instructional programming. If a psychologist's standardized tests establish that the problem is due to developmental lag in visual-motor integration skills, the teacher still has the same instructional programming problem. The psychologist's analysis of reversals and rotations on the Bender will not tell the teacher how to instruct the child any more than will her own observation of the student's attempts to write his name. In fact, the name-writing task, which is closer to the desired terminal behavior, is likely to yield more useful information. The teacher should be concerned about the child in the classroom because he cannot write, not because he cannot draw geometric figures. Referral for psychomotor or process testing should be considered, therefore, only if the teacher is prepared to translate such information into instructional practices. Instead of considering referral for second-level testing by a school psychologist, the teacher might consider requesting an inservice program on interpreting informal test results into methods and materials for instruction.

COGNITIVE AND AFFECTIVE FUNCTIONING LEVEL

The third level of assessment could be called the level of Cognitive and Affective Functioning. At this level, only a well-trained and experienced clinician is in a position to make statements about a student. The cognitive and affective characteristics of a given student can be discussed separately, of course, but they are combined here because they are considered to operate on the same level of abstractness and because they interact to some degree. A cognitive component might be described, for example, as the learner's ability to organize a plan of operation before beginning a motor task, but the affective component would be his willingness to delay movement and inhibit impulse in order to engage in preplanning. There is also some degree of overlap between the cognitive and phychomotor domains, but they have been separated for purposes of this discussion.

Sample Statements

At the third level of assessment, statements similar to the following might be made: "Johnny is currently functioning in the borderline range of intelligence. Test behavior as well as significantly lowered performance on tasks requiring concentration indicate that failure to achieve academically may be due to interference by emotional factors such as anxiety or intrusive thoughts. Verbal abilities such as categorization and association are at a low average level. Adaptive social behavior is age-appropriate and rules out the possibility that Johnny should be recommended for placement in an EMR classroom."

Typical Descriptors

Descriptors which may be used in the cognitive domain include analysis, synthesis, association, classification, deductive and inductive reasoning, problem-solving, prediction, and evaluation. Descriptors which may be used in the affective domain include attention, deliberation, compliance, effort, autonomy, inhibition, constriction.

Representative Tests

Tests which are appropriate to yield level three assessment are individual IQ measures such as the Wechsler Intelligence Scale for Children (Wechsler, 1974), the Stanford-Binet Intelligence Scale (Terman & Merrill, 1973), Leiter International Performance Scale (Arthur, 1952; Leiter, 1940), Nebraska Test of Learning Aptitude (Hiskey, 1966), and projective measures such as the Thematic Apperception Test (Murray, 1943) or the Rorschach Psychodiagnostic Plates (Rorschach, 1954). None of these is appropriate for use by the regular classroom teacher.

The reason for reserving assessment at the third level to experienced clinicians is that this is the level which most frequently is the basis for administrative decisions on delivery of special services or placement in special education classes. Because administrators are rightfully being made more accountable for such decisions, it is imperative that those providing data on which such decisions are made be carefully trained and experienced examiners.

Considerations for Referral

How does a teacher know when she should refer a student for cognitive or affective evaluation? If the student's social skills are those of a younger child and if he requires an unusual number of trials to master a task, it may be useful to request evaluation of level of intellectual functioning so that classroom expectations can be realistic or special instruction arranged. If a student's achievement is so far above that of others in the class that the teacher suspects he should be in a special accelerated program, testing may be needed to confirm such a placement. If a learner's day-to-day academic and social performance is so inconsistent that classroom observation and trial teaching do not answer questions about the child's academic and behavioral strengths and weaknesses, evaluation at the third level is indicated. If a student is typically withdrawn from peer and teacher contact or if acting-out behavior does not respond to classroom intervention over time; if a student engages in cruel or aggressive acts without remorse; if a learner consistently complains of vague physical illnesses and uses such complaints to avoid classroom tasks—in these situations referral for evaluation is indicated.

From a teacher's point of view, cognitive evaluation should not be necessary simply because the level of intellectual functioning is not known. If the teacher can program for the student so that he can respond to instruction, the IQ is probably irrelevant. Similarly, referral is not justified because there may be evidence of family conflict or situational emotional stress. Unless battering is suspected, the teacher's responsibility in such matters is to see to it that her own contacts with the child are always therapeutic. She cannot alter a parent's plan for divorce, for example, by confirming through testing that the child is not functioning academically because of emotional stress. However, a sharp change in academic or social behavior without evidence of any situational disturbance to account for it may be reason to consult with the counselor or school psychologist for evaluation of cognitive or affective functioning.

Guidelines for Referral Questions

Many teachers may react to these statements about appropriate levels of assessment with the question, "How can I control the type of evaluation which is conducted when I just refer a child to the psychologist, and I never know what kind of testing he will do?" The answer to that question is this: If a teacher writes an appropriate referral question, only the testing which answers that question should be conducted. School psychologists and other professionals would much prefer to focus their testing on specific questions rather than take a "shotgun" approach to evaluation. If irrelevant testing is reported while the teacher's questions about instructional planning remain unanswered, it may be because the teacher has not communicated effectively with the person to whom the student has been referred for testing.

What are the elements of an effective referral question? First, a good referral question is accompanied by all information already available to the teacher. It cannot be stressed too strongly that a teacher who refers a student must know everything that can be learned about him under classroom conditions before she should even consider referring the learner to someone else for testing.

It is totally inappropriate, for example, for a teacher to refer a student for evaluation of visual or auditory subskills involved in the reading process without simultaneously reporting to the potential examiner the student's instructional reading level, scores on skills tests in reading, and information about the student's level of vocabulary and grammar. If a teacher refers a child as a reading problem without providing the test information she already possesses, she cannot be surprised if the testing does not go beyond what she had already discovered. All relevant classroom test scores, behavioral observations, and reports of daily written products should be presented in summary form as part of the referral.

Second, the teacher should always report as part of a referral any intervention which she has already attempted with this student. For example, if she has conducted trial teaching of a VAKT (Visual-Auditory-Kinesthetic-Tactile) method of presenting sight words and has found it ineffective, she should report that information; otherwise, she is likely to find that the examiner will recommend just that procedure for the learner whose visual skills are relatively weak. Any special materials or methods which have been tried, and the length of time they have been applied, should be mentioned. Also, the textbooks and supplementary materials currently being used with the student should be listed. If the classroom operation includes a system of rewards or a token economy, that information should be provided so that any recommendation for intervention would be made within that framework. If these types of information are provided, the teacher should not find, as so many have reported, that the examiner has suggested interventions which had already been undertaken.

Third, the teacher must make a statement of what she has to know in order to instruct the student appropriately. That is, she has to be able to state what it is about the student that she cannot discover in the classroom. In the case of a reading problem, for example, she should be able to state that she would like to know whether Johnny demonstrates the subskills to profit from group reading instruction in the strongly phonics-oriented basal reader, or whether auditory skills are markedly below norms for his age. She may want to ask if Johnny's failure to complete written seatwork appears to be due to behavioral causes or deficient fine-motor skills. She may suspect that a student is unusually bright, and she wants to know how far she should push the child to achieve and how he can best be motivated since he is not now achieving. If the question is one of placement, it should be so stated: Does Johnny require individualized instruction in a small group situation such as a resource room or self-contained special class? Is Jim a candidate for placement in an EMR classroom on the basis of his difficulty in keeping up with the lowest groups in the class? Should Sally have reading instruction in the resource room but remain in the classroom for all other instruction?

Beyond the obvious benefits in terms of communication with the person to whom the student is referred, a teacher's close attention to these three components of a good referral question will clarify for the teacher her own goals and programs for a given student. If every teacher would discipline herself to compile this information—a list of academic achievement levels in each subject area; statements about word-recognition and comprehension reading skills, arithmetic computation skills, arithmetic reasoning skills, writing and spelling skills; comprehensive reports of all materials and methods which have been attempted with the student; precise questions about what the teacher needs to know about the child— she would probably find that she could answer many of her own instructional questions without referral. For those questions which she could not answer, she would be providing the basis for straightforward answers from a school psychologist or other ancillary personnel which would be more likely to solve her instructional programming difficulties.

GUIDELINES FOR PREPARING A STUDENT FOR REFERRAL

If the results of testing conducted by other professionals are to be of maximum usefulness to the teacher, testing should be conducted under optimal conditions. The teacher cannot control the selection of the testing room, the examiner's ability to establish rapport, or the noise from the playground. But she can, and should, attempt to motivate the student to cooperate with test procedures and develop a positive set for working at his best.

Motivation for testing is highly dependent upon the student's perception of the purpose of the evaluation, the assurance that he will learn the outcome of testing, and some understanding of the use to which test results will be put. Regardless of the child's age, he deserves a straightforward explanation of why the teacher is asking someone else to test him. The teacher might say, for example, "Jim, I can't figure out why you have so much trouble doing phonics worksheets with the class and I've asked someone else to try to help me find a way to make it easier for you." Or she might say, "I don't know how much work it is sensible to give you; I've asked someone else to help me find out how much you can handle."

The student deserves some assurance that he will receive feedback about the test results. It is astonishing how many teachers believe that the results of testing are the concern of administrators and parents, but never consider that such results should be the concern of the testee himself. Even a first grade child can understand test results at some level, and he should have a simple explanation of the findings. A teacher might say, for example, "After you have seen Mr. Jones, he will tell me what you did and then I will talk to you about it so you and I can decide which work is best for you." A child cannot be expected to care about his performance if he is never to know the outcome of the testing or how test results will be used to make decisions.

A student gains a positive work set largely from knowing that he is expected to work and from being told something about the tasks he will be asked to perform. This does not mean that test items are to be described in advance. Even if the teacher knows the exact tests to be administered, which she probably does not, it would invalidate any standardized test to describe tasks in detail. Instead, what is required is a set of statements which tell the child that he will probably be asked to answer some questions, use a pencil and paper, and put some things together with his hands. The teacher might add: "Some of the tasks will be like the ones you do in school, and some will be very different. Some will be too easy for you, perhaps, and others will be harder. What we expect you to do is just the very best you can."

It is a mistake to tell the student, as some teachers have done, that the session will consist of "playing games with Mr. Jones." If the student enjoys the tasks, that is to the advantage of all concerned; but he should not enter a testing situation with an expectation of games rather than work.

A young child who is unprepared for testing can find the experience bewildering or anxiety provoking. An older student may believe that something is terribly wrong with him if no one is willing to discuss the reasons for testing, and he may react with self-deprecation and hostility toward the adults who placed him in this position.

The teacher's responsibility to prepare a student for referral is part of her overall task of making the student a full partner in a cooperative undertaking—meeting educational objectives. If the teacher-learner relationship is to be cooperative rather than competitive, the student must view the process as a series of joint decisions toward mutual goals. He becomes a partner by being consulted about major steps in the process, by being offered reasons for actions to be taken, and by enlisting his support for the referral rather than imposing it upon him. A teacher who is willing to devote time and effort to preparing a student for referral will not only benefit from valid and useful test results, she will participate in humanizing the educational process.

REFERENCES

Adamson, G., Shrago, M., & Van Etten, G. *Basic educational skills inventory*. Olathe, KS: Select-Ed, 1972.

Arthur, G. The Arthur adaptation of the Leiter International Performance Scale. Washington, DC: Psychological Service Center Press, 1952.

Ayres, J. *Southern California perceptual-motor tests*. Los Angeles: Western Psychological Services, 1968.

Beery, K., & Buktenica, N. *Developmental test of visual-motor integration*. Chicago, IL: Follett, 1967.

Bender, L. *Bender visual-motor Gestalt test for children*. New York: American Orthopsychiatric Association, 1938.

Colarusso, R., & Hammill, D. *Motor-free visual perception test*. San Rafael, CA: Academic Therapy, 1972.

Connolly, A., Nachtman, W., & Pritchett, E. *Keymath diagnostic arithmetic test*. Circle Pines, MN: American Guidance Service, 1971.

Dunn, L., & Markwardt, F. *Peabody individual achievement test*. Circle Pines, MN: American Guidance Service, 1970.

Durrell, D. D. *Durrell analysis of reading difficulty*. New York: Harcourt, Brace & World, 1955.

Gates, A., & McKillop, A. *Reading diagnostic tests*. New York: Teachers College Press, 1962.

Goldman, R., Fristoe, M., & Woodcock, R. *Diagnostic auditory discrimination test*. Circle Pines, MN: American Guidance Service, 1974.

Harris, D. B. *Goodenough-Harris drawing test*. New York: Harcourt Brace Jovanovich, 1963.

Hiskey, M. S. *Nebraska test of learning aptitude*. Lincoln, NE: Marshall S. Hiskey, 1966.

Jastak, J. F., & Jastak, S.R. *Wide range achievement test*. Wilmington, DE: Guidance Associates, 1965.

Kirk, S., McCarthy, J., & Kirk, W. *Illinois test of psycholinguistic abilities*. Urbana, IL: University of Illinois Press, 1968.

Leiter, R. G. *Leiter international performance scale*. Santa Barbara, CA: Santa Barbara State College Press, 1940.

McCracken, R. A. *Standard reading inventory*. Klamath Falls, OR: Klamath Printing Company, 1966.

Moran, M. R. Nine steps to the diagnostic-prescriptive process in the classroom. *Focus on Exceptional Children*, 1975, 6, 1-14.
Murray, H. A. *Thematic apperception test.* Cambridge, MA: Harvard University Press, 1943.
Roach, E. G., & Kephart, N. C. *Purdue perceptual survey rating scale.* Columbus, OH: Charles E. Merrill, 1966.
Rorschach, L. G. *Rorschach psychodiagnostic plates.* New York: Grune & Stratton, 1954.
Silvaroli, N. *Classroom reading inventory.* Dubuque, IA: W. C. Brown Company, 1973.
Sloan, W. *Lincoln-Oseretsky motor development scale.* Chicago, IL: Stoelting, 1954.
Spache, G. *Diagnostic reading scales.* Monterey, CA: McGraw-Hill, 1963.
Templin, M., & Darley, F. *The Templin-Darley tests of articulation.* Iowa City, IA: Bureau of Educational Research and Service, State University of Iowa, 1960.
Terman, L. M., & Merrill, M. A. *Stanford-Binet intelligence scale.* Boston, MA: Houghton-Mifflin, 1973.
Wechsler, D. *Wechsler intelligence scale for children*—revised. New York: Psychological Corporation, 1974.

The author presents an analysis of assessment devices, both norm referenced and non-norm referenced. Mathematics learning is postulated to follow the highly structured form of math whether the person is handicapped or normal. The advantages and disadvantages of some of the present assessment instruments are reviewed for the reader, and the author concludes that current diagnostic tests and inventories in math leave much to be desired. Goodstein ends his article with a discussion of Project MATH and its emphasis on assessment and instruction.

Assessment and Programming in Mathematics for the Handicapped

H. A. Goodstein, *Hartford Insurance Group, Connecticut*

As a first step in the exploration of the topic of assessment and programming in mathematics for the handicapped, a set of philosophic assumptions (or biases) of the author should be shared. These are assumptions regarding the nature of mathematics, the handicapped learner, and their interaction vis-a-vis instruction. Mathematics is a body of concepts that is organized in a logical, sequential, hierarchical system. Notwithstanding differences in the formal descriptions that currently define this system, its inherent order or structure remains invariant. At the same time, however, the manifestation of the system, as operationalized through human performance, will remain imperfect since it reflects the effect of the environmental experiences and systematic instruction.

This assumption regarding the universal nature of mathematics prevents one from considering such possibilities as "mathematics for the normal child" as opposed to "mathematics for the handicapped child." That is, the system of mathematics that each learner must master to some degree remains invariate.

The logical structure of that system does not change for the gifted student or the student with developmental disabilities.

Handicapped children with learning difficulties in mathematics—whether described as mentally retarded, learning disabled, or emotionally disturbed—are characterized by a common problem. These children are not achieving the range of educational objectives in the manner or at an equivalent rate as the majority of their peers. Within all the psychomedical categories of handicap, substantial numbers of children present unique groupings of achievement and nonachievement. For these children, the most important educational decisions to be made are the determination of the range of educational objectives to be selected for instruction (strategy) and the specific instructional methods to be used to foster student achievement of those objectives (tactics).

When the characteristics of the learner are considered in conjunction with the structure of the content, certain implications become clear. The logical order of instruction in mathematics must remain relatively constant for handicapped children regardless of the nature of their specific disability. Changes in this order would only result in magnifying the achievement disabilities of handicapped children. Within the constraint, the educational task remains one of determining the range of topics (objectives) to be considered for instruction and the instructional methods selected to facilitate achievement.

The above set of assumptions allows the author to view issues in the assessment and instruction of mathematics for the handicapped as an extension, refinement, and specification of the issues that have impact on the education of all children. In other words, these assumptions allow for the normalization of or for mainstreaming the problems of mathematics instruction for handicapped children.

PROMINENCE OF INSTRUCTIONAL OBJECTIVES

A generalized revolution in instructional planning has taken place in the last decade. This revolution is marked by the prominence given to behaviorally stated instructional objectives in the process of educational planning. It is a generally accepted assumption that instructional objectives, in some form, should provide the basis for instruction and assessment. This assumption can be confirmed through examination of current educational literature, state educational plans, curriculum materials, and the syllabuses for teacher preparation programs. While its manifestation at the programming level of the classroom teacher is certainly incomplete, it is probably fair to state that the teacher who does not use instructional objectives in her classroom planning is considered outside the mainstream by the remainder of the educational establishment.

Some Problems

In view of the prominence given to instructional objectives in current approaches to instruction and assessment of all children, it is imperative that we examine some of the implications of their use for instructional planning with handicapped children. Goodstein (1974a) has proposed that conventionally formulated instructional objectives (e.g., Mager, 1962) have inherent limitations that can impede the teacher in the process of sequence or management of instruction. As instructional objectives become more precisely formulated, there exists a parallel need to formulate more alternative objectives. As listings of alternative objectives become more numerous, the ability of the teacher to use the listings of objectives to make sequencing decisions for curriculum planning becomes more limited.

Eisner (1967) has also pointed out that one of the biggest problem areas in the use of precisely formulated objectives is the sheer number of objectives that can be generated for any subject matter area. In special education, where the degree of specification sought may be well beyond that presumed necessary for the education of "average" children, the number of potential objectives generated can mushroom. This fact is attested to by the length of many current lists of instructional objectives in special education (e.g., Nofsinger, 1972).

Matrix Approach to the Specification of Instruction

As this author has previously proposed (Goodstein, 1974a), this problem, created by our need for specification in the process of generating instructional objectives, need not lead us to adopting the solution of reducing the level of specification. Rather, it should direct us toward construction of instructional systems that allow for the organization and management of all necessary specifications. This necessitates the creation of matrices for the display of those elements that impact the specificity level of instructional objectives (Goodstein, 1974a).

For example, in composing an instructional objective for mathematics instruction the following areas of specification might be considered: the stimulus situation created by the instructor (how the instructional task is presented), the manner in which the learner is required to respond, the learning requirement of the task (e.g., Gagne, 1965; Bruner, 1966), the mathematical topic (e.g., addition without renaming), and limits upon the range of examples to be used (e.g., three digit addends). While these areas of specification are not exhaustive of the existent possibilities, one could easily observe the multiplicative effect that differentiation within each of these areas could have upon the number of mathematics instructional objectives created.

The solution that this author and his colleagues at the University of

Connecticut have adopted in the development of instructional objectives for mathematics instruction with handicapped children (Cawley, Goodstein, Fitzmaurice, Lepore, Sedlak, & Althaus, 1975) has been to sequence instructional objectives primarily by mathematical topic and to arrange all further specification within organizing matrices. This allows the instructor to retain the degree of specificity necessary in order to individualize instruction to accommodate the instructional needs of handicapped children. It also provides for the instructor a logical structure for the sequencing and management of instruction. In essence, it assists in preventing the trees from obscuring the view of the forest. Further elaboration of this system for specifying instructional objectives will be made later in this paper.

CRITERION-REFERENCED ASSESSMENT

Concurrent with the growth of the behaviorally stated instructional objective as an instructional planning tool was the development of a new measurement tactic for the assessment of achievement. This measurement tactic has become known as criterion-referenced assessment (Glaser, 1963). Criterion-referenced instruments are collections of items that have been selected to assess the instructional outcomes of specific instructional objectives. Thus, it may be said that such items are referenced to particular instructional objectives. The use of the word criterion derives from the means of judging item performance. The use of absolute standards of performance (criteria) replaces standards derived from normative performance in the judgment of pupil (or item) adequacy. Readers who wish a more detailed discussion of the theoretical measurement framework underlying criterion-referenced instruments are referred to Popham and Husek (1969) and Glaser and Nitko (1971).

Briefly, criterion-referenced tests differ from norm-referenced tests, aside from their interpretation, in the manner by which items composing the tests are selected. Norm-referenced test items are ultimately selected on the basis of their statistical properties. Variance in performance among groups of learners is expected and sought. Additionally, items must adequately contribute to the discrimination of poor and able students. Criterion-referenced items are judged for adequacy only as to their content validity. A lack of variance in the performance of a group of learners can be expected when instruction is relatively effective or noneffective.

Problems with Norm-Referenced Instruments

As has been observed by Jones (1973), criterion-referenced instruments represent several improvements over norm-referenced instruments in the assessment of handicapped children. Exceptional children often perform at the lower extremes of the distribution of scores on norm-references achievement measures. Thus, the number of items that they can successfully master is limited. This can reduce the statistical reliability of scores of children scoring in this range. Also, the reduced number of accomplished items limits the diagnostic interpretation of the instrument for programming decisions that have to be made by the classroom teacher.

Since the selection of items for norm-referenced achievement measures is determined by their ability to distribute scores at any grade level over a wide distribution, exceptional children are expected not to be able to master a number of items. This negative selection factor mitigates against inclusion of a corresponding number of items that exceptional children could be expected to perform successfully. This is the case even when these items would be representative of the mathematics program for these children.

Perhaps the most important contribution of the development of criterion-referenced assessment strategies has been the intent to match assessment with instruction on a much closer basis than in the past. As has been alluded to earlier, handicapped children often require changes in strategy or tactics in mathematics instruction. This could include omission of certain nonessential topics or modifications of instructional procedures. Thus, norm-referenced instruments often may lack substantive content validity for handicapped populations. This should never be the case for true criterion-referenced instruments. The same objectives that are used for program planning and instruction should be used to generate assessment items.

The use of the word "true" in describing criterion-referenced tests suggests that the opposite condition "untrue" exists. several instruments have recently appeared that purport to be criterion-referenced, since they do not contain normative data and have been developed from a set of instructional objectives. However, it is this writer's opinion that, unless these same instructional objectives are used by the teacher in planning and instruction, these instruments are not very useful. In fact, many of these instruments become the basis very quickly for locally imposed normative expectations for performance. Scores generated from such instruments become benchmarks for judging the relative achievement of children. Consequently, in too many instances the original intent of such instruments to assess only those objectives for which instruction was planned or initiated has become obscured.

CURRENT DIAGNOSTIC TESTS

Present assessment instruments available for assisting the teacher in mathematics programming can be imperfectly classed as either achievement tests or diagnostic tests. The presumed distinction between the two classes of instruments resides in the intent of the diagnostic test to determine causality in the determination of nonachievement. It should be pointed out that simply because a test author determines to call his instrument a diagnostic test, this does not necessarily endow it with diagnostic properties (Cronbach, 1970). Within either class of instruments, the tests may be norm-referenced or non-norm-referenced. (This writer considers a test to be criterion-referenced only when its underlying objectives match those used by the classroom teacher for instruction.) Most current diagnostic tests in mathematics are non-norm-referenced. The one apparent exception to this trend is *Key Math* (Connolly, Nachtman & Pritchett, 1971). However, as will be pointed out later, the question as to whether *Key Math* functions as a diagnostic test is an open question.

Until recently the development of diagnostic instruments in determining the nature of arithmetical disabilities has been the province of mathematics educators. Mathematics educators have typically looked to the causality of disability as being determined to a large degree by the structure of the subject matter. This stands in marked contrast to the prevalent attitude of special education specialists to look toward the child as the first step in the determination of causality for disability (e.g., Johnson & Myklebust, 1967; Lerner, 1971; Frostig & Maslow, 1973).

The *Schonell Diagnostic Arithmetic Test* (Schnoell et al., 1957) reflects the position of its authors that a diagnostic test provides an analysis of skills, not an assessment. It covers only whole number combinations. The test tends to be lengthy for both the learner and the teacher. No actual modules for remediation exist once the child has been "diagnosed." This absence of a linkage between assessment and instruction for most diagnostic arithmetic tests, while prevalent, is regrettable.

Reisman (1972) has also developed a mathematics inventory for diagnosis. Reisman's basis for both diagnosis and instruction is task analysis. However, the computational sections of the inventory do not lend themselves to diagnostic use because subskills are not carefully controlled within the problems.

The *Buswell-John Diagnostic Chart for Individual Differences: Fundamental Process in Arithmetic* (Buswell & John, 1925) provides for an individual analysis of a pupil's difficulty in the four basic operations with whole numbers. The problems are arranged according to difficulty within each operation. The teacher has a checklist of errors which is used as the child orally explains his method of solving the problems. The test is not excessively long and is relatively easy to analyze for sequence of processes. This analysis, however, could be refined to help the teacher more accurately pinpoint where remediation is necessary. No systematic approach to the remediation process is given.

Key Math (Connolly et al., 1971) lends itself more to grade placement from a set of norms developed with a population of average children, rather than diagnosis. Failure on an item or set of items does not give the teacher a clear view of where diagnostic remediation should take place. Because of the normative nature of the test, substantial skill gaps exist between items arranged on any of its subtests. Additionally, failure to control the problems for the nature of the algorithm that the child might use to solve the problem creates difficulty in the interpretation of pupil performance for remediation. In fact, *Key Math* more closely resembles an individually administered achievement test than a diagnostic test.

Some additional problems regarding the use of *Key Math* with educable mentally retarded children were recently pointed out by this author (Goodstein, Kahn & Cawley, in press). The lack of items in the midrange of difficulty for the test causes many children to reach ceiling quite rapidly. This causes the test to lose its power to discriminate performance changes for many handicapped learners who make slow progress through those topics covered by midrange items. In fairness, this tends to be a characteristic of many standardized instruments that were norm-referenced by the performance of average children and subsequently used with handicapped achievers.

Of course, there also exist numerous standardized mathematics achievement tests or subtests of achievement batteries. These instruments tend to be less than useful in the assessment of handicapped children for instructional decision making. As was pointed out during our discussion of criterion-referenced assessment, norm referenced instruments largely lack content validity for the mathematics instruction for handicapped children and, perhaps more seriously, have structural inadequacies (e.g., limited range of appropriate items) that seriously limit their usefulness.

At this juncture, the author wishes to alert the reader that what may be perceived as an extremely critical comment regarding currently available assessment instruments in mathematics does not imply that their use is totally without merit. To the contrary, any information regarding the achievement of handicapped children in mathematics is desirable in contrast to absolute lack of such information which exists in many educational programs for handicapped children. What it does suggest, however, is that substantial room for improvement does exist, especially in the area of the development of diagnostic tests and inventories. Some suggestions for direction that such improvements could take will be offered later in this article.

PROJECT MATH

Little systematic attention to the improvement of mathematics instruction for handicapped children was given prior to this current decade. Recognizing this lack of attention, the Bureau for the Education of the Handicapped funded Dr. John Cawley and his associates at the University of Connecticut to begin a systematic inquiry into the nature of mathematics achievement among handicapped children and, subsequently, to develop a mathematics curriculum known as Project MATH (Cawley et al., 1975).

An understanding of the instructional system for Project MATH is necessary in order to clarify the assessment tactics that were adopted. It is hoped that these assessment tactics will provide a basis for the remainder of the discussion.

Project MATH has been described as a *multiple option curriculum* (Cawley, 1972). This label is derived from the multiple components that comprise the curriculum that are presented as optional instructional tactics for the teacher as well as the multiple approaches to instruction contained within each component. The major components of the curriculum include instructional guides and correlated activity books for the directed instruction of mathematics topics, a verbal problem solving component that provides instruction and practice in mathematics through practice in information processing, and a laboratory component that extends mathematics learning into the area of application in social problem solving contexts.

The instructional guide component includes directed activities in six major areas (strands) of mathematics learning: Sets, Patterns, Geometry, Numbers, Fractions, and Measurement. Each strand contains a careful developmental sequence of mathematics concepts carefully selected to balance the integrity of mathematics content system with the mathematics needs of handicapped children. Thus, topics which are unessential to the logical development of mathematics understanding and socially irrelevant for handicapped children were omitted. Topics deemed essential but difficult because of present usage of terminology or symbols were carefully revised in order to reduce unnecessary complexity, but the essential mathematics concepts were retained.

The Interactive Unit

For each concept within a strand, differentiated instructional tactics are articulated through a system for specifying instructional objectives. This system has been labeled the Interactive Unit. An early version of the Interactive Unit has been presented by Cawley and Vitello (1972) and was subsequently revised based upon the field test of Project MATH materials. The Interactive Unit focuses independently upon instructor and learner behaviors. All instruction is classified according to one of four instructor behaviors and one of four learner behaviors. The four instructor behaviors are construct, present, state, and graphically symbolize. The four learner behaviors are construct, identify, state, and graphically symbolize.

Construct behaviors imply the active manipulation of pictures or objects (or personal movement) to create the primary instructional stimulus for the child or to define the primary response mode of the child. Present behaviors imply the presentation of a fixed visual display of pictures or objects, where the manipulation of that display is not crucial to defining the stimulus for the task. Present behaviors essentially deal with nonverbal stimulus materials. The teacher creating an instructional situation using a set of pictures in a book, a fixed display of objects on a table, or the presentation of picture cards would be in all cases engaging in present behavior.

Identify behaviors imply making an instructional response by choosing the correct answer from a range of possible choices. Identify responses can be made by marking, pointing, or vocalizing (e.g., by reference to position) the correct response. Identify behaviors essentially are made in response to nonverbal stimulus materials. State behaviors imply the creation of primarily an oral stimulus to the instructional task or the requirement for an oral response to a problem. Graphically symbolize behaviors are inclusive of most written or drawn instructor and learner actions. They are also extended to include (on the instructor side) written or symbolically drawn text material or such work as might have been previously prepared on a blackboard. Graphic symbolic responses would also include multiple-choice responding where the choices were primarily verbal or graphic in nature.

Space does not permit elaboration of the implicit set of rules or procedures developed by Project MATH developers to code various instructional tasks to the Interactive Unit. The operationalization of the Interactive Unit became a process of trading off elegance in the description of instructional interactions for simplicity and usability in curriculum development and instruction. This author fondly remembers the many hours of debate over interpretations of the Interactive Unit. The point of these observations is that the Interactive Unit is a heuristic device of organizing instructional objectives. Its usefulness must be judged primarily by the effectiveness of its organizing structure for the differentiation of instructional tactics.

The four instructor behaviors and the four learner behaviors form a matrix that yield 16 unique combinations of instructional interactions. For example, if the mode of instructor behavior is construct, combining the four modes of learner response yields four unique patterns of instructional interaction: construct-construct, construct-identify, construct-state, and construct-graphically symbolize. Each pattern of instructional interaction provides the basis for development of the mathematical concept using a different instructional tactic. In other words, for each concept the Interactive Unit facilitates the potential development of 16 alternative objectives (tasks) for instruction.

Project MATH Assessment Needs

Project MATH instructional guides, being developed off the Interactive Unit, encourage the teacher to conceptualize her programming at two distinct levels of analysis. At the strategic level, the teacher must determine the concepts within the strands that she should select for instruction for any particular child. Children who have educational handicaps differ widely in their specific instructional needs. Many of these children receive special education assistance quite late in their educational experience. For many children there simply may not be enough time to develop the full range of mathematics concepts that the child might have been initially capable of mastering. For other children, specific areas for instruction (e.g., computational skills) may have been overlearned, but attention must now be directed toward the development of supporting concepts.

Superimposed over such strategic considerations are the tactical questions as to which instructional strategies should be adopted for a particular child. Proponents can be arrayed on either side of the argument as to whether a child should be instructed to his weaknesses or from his strengths. Perhaps certain patterns of interaction should be selected because of their effect upon the affective development of the child in addition to the usual cognitive determinations. The Interactive Unit does not prescribe tactics; it merely exposes the options systematically to facilitate teacher decision-making.

Project MATH Concept Inventory

To assist the teacher in the determination of strategic questions regarding the selection of concepts for instruction, Project MATH has included a criterion-referenced instrument called the MATH Concept Inventory (MCI). The concept inventory includes one item to assess the major concept outcome for the series of instructional guides that have been developed for each mathematic topic in the curriculum.

Specifically, the inventory is intended to serve two major purposes:

1. It may be used as a *screening device* to assist with the placement of children in the curriculum.

2. It may also be used as a *mastery test* to evaluate student progress *after* a sequence of instruction has taken place.

Since the instrument is both criterion-referenced and an inventory, a significant amount of teacher flexibility is incorporated in its administration. The teacher may elect to begin assessment with any item. Additionally, the teacher might elect to give some or all of the items, in one sitting or over several sittings. The constraints of formal test administration, necessary to ensure the validity of norm-referenced instruments, are unessential when individual child mastery information for specific concepts is being sought.

In terms of its use in the strategic decision-making process, the inventory is but one tool for the teacher. It is not designed to be a replacement for teacher judgment. Unfortunately, many teachers look to assessment instruments for rigid prescriptive rules in an effort to replace the need for effective decision-making. This is especially dangerous in regard to instructional planning for handicapped children. Handicapped children have such diverse patterns of cognitive and affective needs that linear systems for making programming decisions are not sufficiently comprehensive for effective and efficient instructional planning.

In respect to the MCI, when a child "fails" an item, this information is prescriptive for placing the child at some point in the corresponding sequence of instructional guides. However, when a child "passes" an item, several reasons might still compel the teacher to place the child in that sequence of instructional guides. Social and language outcomes are also important goals of instruction with Project MATH. Often, instructing a child who has little difficulty with the mathematics concept being developed in the guides allows the teacher to emphasize equally important nonquantitative cognitive and affective outcomes.

Additionally, because the items for the concept inventory were designed as multiple-choice items, the items reflect only the use of the six cells of the Interactive Unit that provide for that manner of responding. Specifically omitted were any items that would require a construct behavior on the part of the teacher or construct or state behaviors on the part of the child. Thus, although great care was taken in the selection of an item that was representative of the concept, the child might yet encounter some difficulty when performance would be required in alternate cells of the Interactive Unit.

Lastly, teachers operate in many instructional environments. Even if the teacher had an instrument with ultimate levels of precision in directing instruction, the teacher may determine the necessity for instruction within groups. This determination could be a result of teacher choice in regard to overall strategy, or it might be forced upon her by the environment that creates logistical problems to totally individual programming. For such teachers, grouping decisions become trade-offs between diversity in performance among individual children and a general level of achievement among a group of children. Thus, certain children might have to participate in instruction over concepts that they have demonstrated mastery in order to maintain instructional groups. This author does not view this tactic as inherently "bad," provided the teacher uses this opportunity for enhancement of other learning outcomes with these children.

One might raise the question as to the comprehensiveness of the strategy of designing only one inventory item for each concept. Certainly, reliability of performance on any single concept is severely impacted by this decision. However, in instrument design one is constantly faced with the choice between designing an instrument with enough items to ensure reliable performance and creating an instrument that is compact enough not to be a burden to either teacher or child. When designing the concept inventory, it was felt that unreliable performance would most probably impact our confidence in whether the child really has mastered the concept. Since nonmastery was the more prescriptive of the possible outcomes for any item and the teacher was already cautioned regarding the prescriptive limitations of item mastery performance, the damaging impact of potential unreliability of item performance was minimized.

Project MATH Instructional Evaluation Items

While the concept inventory assists in decision-making at the level of strategy, an additional assessment tool is built into Project MATH for tactical decision-making. Each instructional guide, which has been developed to reflect a unique mode of teacher-pupil instructional interaction from the Interactive Unit, contains its own instructional evaluation item or items. These items assess the mastery of the instructional activities in the instructional guide within the same pattern or mode of teacher-pupil instructional interaction.

Figure 1 displays a facsimile of a Project MATH instructional guide. For this guide, the content strand is Numbers, the area is Cardinal Property of a Set, and the concept is Fewer Number/Greater Number. The input and output modes of the Interactive Unit are present and state. They are graphically depicted in the upper right hand corner of the guide. The behavioral objective is a simple description of the behavioral exchange summarizing information from both the Interactive Unit and the content descriptors.

The reader will note the consistency of the activities suggested on the guide in reference to the pattern of instructional interaction. Similarly, the evaluative items for this lesson guide reflect the same pattern of teacher-pupil interaction.

A record keeping system is provided for the teacher that allows her to record achievement for individual instructional guide evaluations as well as the concept mastery inventory performance for each sequence of instructional guides. Careful attention to such record keeping would allow the teacher to observe consistent trends in the effects of tactical changes in instruction. For example, a child may consistently demonstrate failure on all instructional guides that require a construct response. For such a child, the teacher *might*

Figure 1
INSTRUCTIONAL GUIDE* N 122

STRAND	Numbers and Operations
AREA	Cardinal Property of a Set
CONCEPT	Fewer Number/Greater Number

INPUT	OUTPUT

BEHAVIORAL OBJECTIVE	INSTRUCTOR	LEARNER
	Presents Pictures of Sets.	States whether a set has the same number, a greater number or a fewer number of items than a standard set.

ACTIVITIES

The instructor seats one or more learners on the floor or around the table. The instructor presents pairs of pictures of sets. The instructor asks the learner(s) to state if this set (holds one set higher) has the same number as this set (holds the second set up). If the response is no, the instructor asks, "Does it have a fewer number or a greater number?" The learner(s) responds in complete sentences, e.g., "That set has the same number". The position of the sets can then be changed and the questions repeated. Sets of different cardinal properties are used.

The instructor holds up pictures of sets of different objects. The instructor states that she can make up a story about the pictures (e.g., set of three boys, set of two baseball bats. There are a greater number of boys than baseball bats; there are a fewer number of bats than boys). The instructor then holds up two different pictures and asks the learner to tell a story. If the learner has difficulty doing this, additional examples should be given by the instructor.

The instructor includes instances when she holds up one picture of three balls and ask the learner if she has a greater number or a fewer number of balls. The learner must realize that greater number and fewer number are only meaningful in terms of two or more sets - they are comparison terms.

MATERIALS: Pictures of Sets

SUPPLEMENTAL ACTIVITIES: 122 a, b

EVALUATIVE CRITERIA

1. Use two pictures - one of five children; one of four ponies. Hold the picture of the ponies at a higher level than the picture of the children. Tell the learner to state which picture has the greater number. Switch levels of the pictures and tell the learner to state which picture has the fewer number.

2. Use the same pictures as above and tell the learner to make up a story about the two pictures. (Try to elicit a story that deals with the greater number of children in relation to the fewer number of ponies).

*Reprinted with the permission of the publishers, Educational Sciences, Inc., Wallingford, Conn., 06492 decide to delay instruction on all such instructional guides until some point later in the child's instructional program. Alternatively, the teacher might wish to plan more time for instruction for that child on such instructional guides. The diagnostic significance of the consistent use of such an assessment-record keeping system should be obvious.

Many writers have suggested elaborate strategies for the development of criterion referenced test items (e.g., Hively et al, 1973). Most suggestions focus upon the definition of domains from which items may be sampled. Evaluation items for Project MATH instructional guides follow a rather simple set of procedures. These will be shared in the view that they might be helpful to the teacher who might wish to develop her own assessment program.

First, the item should represent the terminal performance of any sequence of instructional activities on a particular guide. Second, the item should be consistent with the mode of teacher and learner instructional interaction reflected in the instructional guide. Additionally, items were viewed as reflective of two basic types. Type I items would sample the range of possible activities, where the set of those activities was finite. For example, if the activities were organized to practice addition of single digit numbers whose addends were less than ten, the items would be limited by the bounds of those activities. From that pool, a set of addition problems could be selected.

Type II items would assess those activities whose range of possible examples were infinite. For example, if the child (in fractions) were to be required to recognize a whole from the display of its parts, a variety of tasks or examples could be used. Evaluative items would use a different example from those examples in the activities, which shared all relevant and/or salient features. In fact, many items will share both Type I and Type II characteristics.

The validation of criterion-referenced assessment items requires (1) the careful selection of items related to any constraints imposed by the nature of the instructional objectives or the resultant instructional activities (similar to those imposed by the Project MATH Interactive Unit) and (2) the confirmation by the teacher that her impressions regarding student achievement during instruction are validated by item performance. This latter requirement, if not met, would require the teacher to review closely the item to determine whether unique features of the item are causing the discrepancy, resulting in a revision of the item.

It is recognized that the development of criterion-referenced assessment items and instruments may prove to be a difficult task for a great many teachers. This fact should only raise our commitment level toward the inclusion of such training in both preservice and inservice teacher education programs.

Assessment Directly from Task Matrices

One other assessment approach manifested by the Verbal Problem Solving Component of Project MATH should be briefly discussed. Cawley (1970) and Goodstein (1974a, 1974b) have suggested that certain instructional tasks may be organized in such a manner that their organizational structure provides for both instruction and assessment to occur concurrently. For example, if verbal problems have been developed in such a manner that the various factors or parameters that combine to describe a problem have been controlled, organizational matrices can be used for retrieval of problems for both instruction and assessment.

For example, if a set of verbal problems has been developed from prescribed word lists at various levels, has defined information processing requirements, and has computational difficulties assigned to the problems in a systematic manner, any problem should be capable of description in relation to those three factors. An organizing three-dimensional matrix that arrayed reading difficulty levels, information processing requirements, and computational difficulty levels would provide a means of sampling problems for assessment as well as instruction. Unfortunately, at present there exist few subject matter domains where enough basic knowledge exists regarding the interaction of various subfactors upon performance to construct such management matrices.

THE NEED FOR A NEW DIAGNOSTIC MODEL

Earlier in the paper this writer alluded to the development needs in the area of diagnostic assessment in mathematics for the handicapped. Lepore (1974) reports a substantial percentage of bizarre or aberrant computational algorithms or approaches to the solution of computational problems among both mentally retarded and learning disability children. Many of these bizarre algorithms result in consistent failure on computational problems. This probably confirms the experience of countless special education teachers.

This has led to discussion among the Project MATH staff of the expansion of the current content X mode analysis model to include algorithm as a third parameter. Such a model would allow for more differentiated analysis or diagnosis of mathematical disability among children with severe mathematics disabilities. To this author's knowledge no current diagnostic assessment instrument attains this level of diagnostic prescription.

Additionally, what is needed to complete the assignment is a set of remedial modules which would be referenced to particular cells of this enlarged content X mode X algorith analysis model. Thus, once a child's idiosyncratic pattern of behavior has been identified, the teacher would be directed to use a particular module for remediation of the identified disability. The development of such a diagnostic instrument with its associated remedial modules remains one of the greatest current challenges to our development expertise.

SUMMARY

In review, this author has attempted to provide a philosophic base to the discussion of mathematics assessment and programming for the handicapped. Issues in the development of instructional objectives and criterion-referenced assessment were reviewed. A brief survey of current diagnostic tests and norm-referenced approach to assessment was presented and critically reviewed. Examples of a system of criterion-referenced assessment for both strategic and tactical decision-making were provided drawing from the author's experience in the design of the Project MATH curriculum system. An alternate assessment approach for use with highly structured content domains, such as verbal problem solving, was briefly discussed. And, finally, suggestions for an area of great challenge and promise in the further development of assessment instrumentation were outlined.

In conclusion, this author wishes to reaffirm his belief that regardless of the precision obtained in the development of assessment instruments, it must be the classroom teacher who will remain the ultimate instructional decision-maker. Assessment merely organizes the data in a systematic manner. The weighing of the alternatives for instruction must remain with the classroom teacher who is ultimately responsible for the management of instruction. The effective training of teachers to become master decision-makers remains the great challenge of our teacher education systems.

REFERENCES

Bruner, I. S. *Studies in cognitive growth.* New York: Wiley, 1966.
Buswell, G. T., & John, L. *Diagnostic chart for individual differences: Fundamental processes in arithmetic.* Public School Publishing Co., 1925.
Cawley, J. F. Teaching arithmetic to mentally handicapped children. *Focus on Exceptional Children*, 1970, 2(4).
Cawley, J. F. Designing a multiple option arithmetic curriculum for the mentally handicapped. *Education and Training of the Mentally Retarded*, 1972, 7, 151-6.
Cawley, J. F., Goodstein, H. A., Fitzmaurice, A. M., Lepore, A., Sedlak, R., & Althaus, V. *Project math: A program of the mainstream series.* Wallingford, CT: Educational Sciences, Inc. (P.O. Box 771, 06492), 1975.
Cawley, J. F. & Vitello, S. A model for arithmetical programming for handicapped children: A beginning. *Exceptional Children*, 1972, 39, 101-110.
Connolly, A. J., Nachtman, W., & Pritchett, E. M. *Key math.* American Guidance Service, Inc., 1971.
Cronbach, L. G. *Essentials of psychological testing.* New York: Harper & Row, 1970.
Eisner, E. W. Educational objectives: Help or hindrance? *School Review*, 1967, 75, 250-260.

Frostig, M., & Maslow, P. *Learning problems in the classroom*. New York: Grune & Stratton, 1973.

Gagne, R. *The conditions of learning*. New York: Holt, Rinehart & Winston, 1964.

Glaser, R. Instructional technology and the measurement of learning outcomes. *American Psychologist*, 1963, *18*, 519-521.

Glaser, R., & Nitko, A. J. Measurement in learning and instruction. In R. L. Thorndike (Ed.), *Educational Measurement*. Washington: American Council on Education, 1971, 625-670.

Goodstein, H. A. Individualizing instruction through matrix teaching. *Education and Training of the Mentally Retarded*, 1974, 9 187-190.(a)

Goodstein, H. A. Solving the verbal mathematics problem: Visual aids and teacher planning equals the answer. *Teaching Exceptional Children*, 1974, *6*, 178-182.(b)

Goodstein, H. A., Kahn, H., & Cawley, J. F. The achievement of educably mentally handicapped children on the Key Math Diagnostic Arithmetic Test. *Journal of Special Education*, in press.

Hively, W., Maxwell, G., Rabehl, G., Sension, D., & Lunden, S. Domain-referenced curriculum evaluation: A technical handbook and case study from the MINNEMAST Project. In M. Alkin (Ed.), *CSE monograph series in evaluation* (vol. 1). Los Angeles: UCLA Center for the Study of Evaluation, 1973.

Johnson, D., & Myklebust, H. R. *Learning disabilities. Educational principles and practices*. New York: Grune & Stratton, 1967.

Jones, R. Accountability in special education: Some problems. *Exceptional Children*, 1973, 39, 631-642.

Lepore, A. A comparison of computational errors between educable mentally handicapped and learning disability children. The University of Connecticut, 1974 (mimeo).

Lerner, J. *Children with learning disabilities*. New York: Houghton-Mifflin 1971.

Mager, R. F. *Preparing instructional objectives*. Palo Alto: Fearon Publishers, 1962.

Nofsinger, T. (Ed.). *Behavioral objectives for "program models for EMR students."* Ohio ESEA Title III Project #45-71-207-2. Menter Exempted Village Board of Education, 1972.

Popham, W. J., & Husek, T. R. Implications of criterion-referenced measurement. *Journal of Educational Measurement*, 1969, *6*, 1-9.

Riesman, F. K. *A guide to the diagnostic teaching of arithmetic*. Columbus, OH: Charles E. Merrill Publishing, 1972.

Schonell, F. J., & Schonell, F. E. *Diagnosis and remedial teaching in arithmetic*. Oliver and Boyd, 1957.

Jobes and Hawthorne emphasize the shift from total reliance on psychological norm referenced testing to increased emphasis on teacher assessment. The basic model suggested is behavioral in nature; it involves initial assessment of learner tasks and environmental components and, secondly, modification of learning tasks and environment to observe changes. Emphasis is given to assessment concurrent with instruction. Methods for recording data and determining when learning has occurred are stated in terms that teachers should be able to adopt and follow. The authors provide a practical example for the reader's use, to demonstrate how informal methods of assessment can be utilized to improve performance.

Informal Assessment for the Classroom

Nancy K. Jobes and Linda White Hawthorne,
Georgia State University

In recent years attention has been shifting away from traditional psychometric evaluation of exceptional children toward teacher evaluation. Concurrently, contemporary authors have stressed the need for a closer alignment between instructional goals and assessment procedures. Numerous movements within special education have precipitated these changes:

1. A decreased emphasis on the labeling and categorizing of exceptional children (Reynolds & Balow, 1972).
2. The need to hold teachers accountable for specifying instructional objectives and measuring pupil progress toward those objectives, as mandated by the Education for all Handicapped Children Act (P.L. 94-142).
3. The trend toward stating instructional objectives in precise, measurable

terms—a trend that has lent itself to the use of criterion-referenced measures (Drew, Freston, & Logan, 1972).
4. An emphasis on assessing and serving the severely handicapped, regardless of the severity of the handicap or the availability of appropriate assessment instruments (Haring, 1975).
5. Lack of empirical support for instructional programs based upon process deficits identified by standardized diagnostic tests, such as the ITPA (Hammill & Larsen, 1974).
6. A recognized need to assess variables required for academic success; e.g., verbalization of a response, as opposed to supposed correlates of academic success; e.g., auditory perception (Keogh & Becker, 1973).
7. Dissatisfaction with pupil evaluations done without regard for critical environmental variables within the academic setting (Adelman, 1971).
8. A growing trend among special educators to assess environmental variables which precede and follow pupil performance (Lovitt, 1967).

These concerns suggest the need for a model of assessment which is broad enough to encompass assessment of relevant environmental characteristics and can serve as a basis for effective instructional planning, as well as satisfying accountability demands by measuring pupil progress toward instructional goals.

The behavioral assessment procedure proposed to meet these requirements (see Figure 1) is composed of two basic stages: Initial assessment of learner tasks and a survey of environmental components to reach instructional objectives. Following such a two-stage procedure enables the teacher to identify a variety of variables within the environment which may affect learning, and then to validate the effects of selected variables during the teaching process. The on-going assessment that takes place during the teaching process will attest to both the accuracy of the initial assessment and the effectiveness of instruction. Since classroom behaviors and academic skills are considered to be learned and to be appropriate realms for teacher assessment and instruction, both will be considered.

INITIAL ASSESSMENT

Initial assessment involves identifying the following: Appropriate learner tasks; events in the environment which "set the stage" for learning to occur (i.e., antecedent or stimulus events); and the consequences available as contingencies for desired behavior (Lovitt, 1967). This initial assessment should be conducted prior to beginning formal instruction. Ideally, the assessment should be done by the same person who will be responsible for instruction. Such an arrangement would provide for continuity between initial assessment and on-going assessment.

Informal Assessment for the Classroom

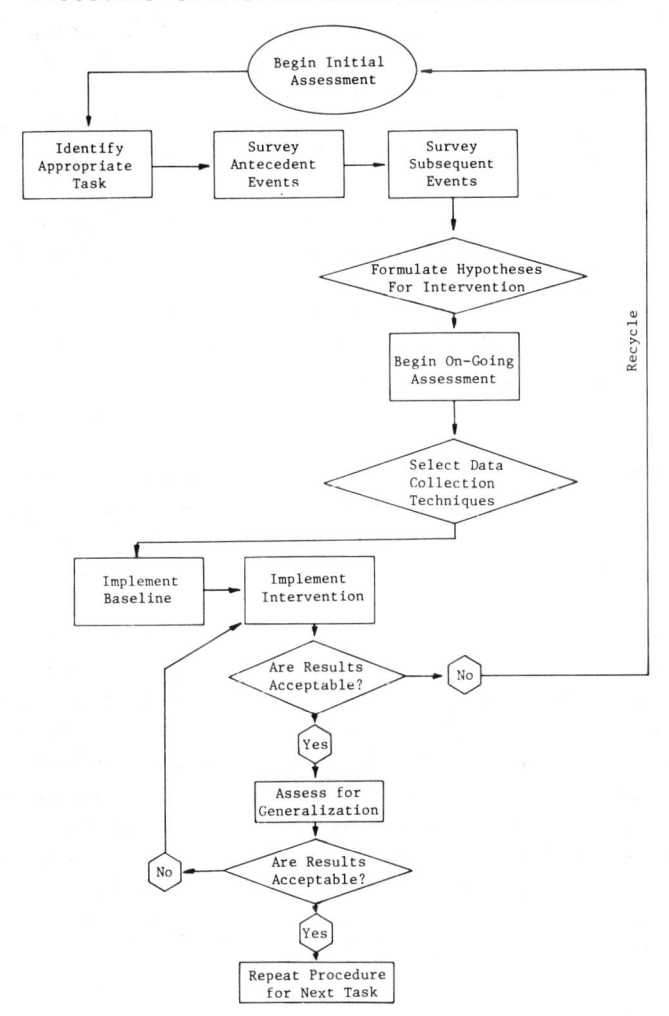

**FIGURE 1
Procedure for Informal Classroom Assessment**

```
                    Begin Initial
                    Assessment
                         │
    ┌────────────────────┤
    │                    ▼
┌─────────┐      ┌──────────┐      ┌──────────┐
│Identify │      │ Survey   │      │ Survey   │
│Appropri-│─────▶│Antecedent│─────▶│Subsequent│
│ate Task │      │ Events   │      │ Events   │
└─────────┘      └──────────┘      └──────────┘
                                         │
                                         ▼
                              ╱Formulate Hypotheses╲
                              ╲  For Intervention  ╱
                                         │
                                         ▼
                                 ┌───────────────┐
                                 │Begin On-Going │        R
                                 │  Assessment   │        e
                                 └───────────────┘        c
                                         │                y
                                         ▼                c
                                ╱Select Data ╲            l
                                ╲ Collection ╱            e
                                 ╲Techniques╱
                                         │
                ┌────────────────────────┤
                ▼                        ▼
         ┌──────────┐            ┌──────────────┐
         │Implement │───────────▶│  Implement   │
         │ Baseline │            │ Intervention │
         └──────────┘            └──────────────┘
                │                        │
                │                        ▼
                │                 ╱Are Results ╲────[No]──┐
                │                 ╲ Acceptable?╱          │
                │                        │                │
                │                      [Yes]              │
                │                        ▼                │
                │                ┌──────────────┐         │
                │                │  Assess for  │         │
                │                │Generalization│         │
                │                └──────────────┘         │
                │                        │                │
                │                        ▼                │
                │                 ╱Are Results ╲          │
                └────[No]─────────╲ Acceptable?╱          │
                                         │                │
                                       [Yes]              │
                                         ▼                │
                                 ┌───────────────┐        │
                                 │Repeat Procedure│       │
                                 │  for Next Task│        │
                                 └───────────────┘        │
                                                          │
(Recycle loop returns to Begin Initial Assessment)────────┘
```

Identifying Appropriate Tasks

The first step in the initial assessment is to identify tasks at the appropriate level of difficulty for the student. In fact, in education one of the most trite but important comments often said and heard by teachers is, "Teach the child at the appropriate level." Several assumptions are implicit in that statement: skills taught in schools are in levels (i.e., they are sequential); those skill sequences are identifiable; and to effectively teach a student, it is

53

Instructional Planning for Exceptional Children

necessary to determine what skills in various skill sequences he or she has mastered and which skills are lacking.

If teachers had to determine a sequence of skills for each academic or behavioral area they teach, the task would be overwhelming. Fortunately, such information is provided for the teacher in thousands of curriculum guides, skills and behavior checklists, criterion-referenced measures, and standardized tests. The teacher's task during this initial assessment phase is to utilize existing resources in either choosing or constructing a general task sequence that will closely approximate the sequence used for instruction in a particular area. During the on-going assessment phase, the teacher may have to do a detailed task analysis of a particular skill; e.g., determine prerequisite skills for adding one-digit numbers with sums less than ten. However, during this initial assessment the teachers should check to see if the student can perform the task without concern for assessing prerequisite skills. Such an in-depth analysis will be done during on-going assessment.

Numerous sources of information are available to the teacher who wants to identify task sequences. To select an appropriate one and make optimal use of it, the following procedures are suggested.

—When planning instruction in an academic or social area, review skill sequences developed in that area; e.g., scope and sequence charts accompanying basal series, criterion-referenced measures, standardized tests, or developmental sequences.

—Put the task sequence selected or developed into a simple, usable format. At this point, do not attempt to state the skills as complete behavioral objectives. State the task, but do not be concerned about specifying detailed conditions or standards. For instance, a task might be: "Orally count by two's to 50." In such cases, conditions remain flexible. You can tell the child to count by two's to 50 or listen to the instructions on tape, etc. Likewise, standards are somewhat flexible in that no time limits are imposed and no references are made to such factors as fluency while counting.

—In specifying the task, approximate those responses required during instruction. For example, if, in the classroom, the student is required to count to 50 by two's aloud, he or she should not be required to write the response during assessment.

—If you have previously worked with the student being assessed and have some knowledge of his or her performance, you should take advantage of it. There is no need to ask the child to count to 50 if it is already known that he or she can do it.

—If you think the student is reaching a frustration point during the assessment, but you still desire to assess more difficult tasks in the sequence, it is appropriate to take a break or switch to an easier level before proceeding to more difficult ones.

—No rules govern at what point in the sequence assessment should begin, nor how many steps in the sequence should be assessed. However, we suggest that you begin assessment at a point at which the student is likely to experience success, proceed to more difficult items, and discontinue testing at the point at which it appears unlikely that the student will be able to respond correctly to further items.

Identifying Antecedent or Stimulus Events

The second step in the initial assessment requires that you survey antecedent or stimulus events that appear to affect student behavior. Antecedent or stimulus events are those variables within the environment which occasion the behavior of students. They include the great number of stimulus materials, instructional methods, and classroom settings which "set the stage" for the child to respond to the task you have chosen. You select materials, arrange student seating, give instructions, group children, etc. It is vital, therefore, that you carefully survey the many antecedent events that may affect learning and performance if you hope to control such events to facilitate optimal student performance.

Research has been conducted to validate the efficiency of various stimulus materials, classroom settings, and instructional methods. Regretfully, the results of this research indicate trends for groups of students, but give teachers little or no information for teaching individual students. You must, therefore, identify within your own teaching environment the antecedent or stimulus events which allow for optimal performance of individual students.

Through observing and interacting with the student, you can begin to gather information concerning the child's preferences for various stimulus events. For example, if given as opportunity, would the child select a programmed text over a traditional basal, an isolated quiet area over a group activity, a model over verbal direction? Under what conditions does he or she seem to perform best? With information obtained by observation, you can formulate hypotheses regarding the stimulus events which may occasion the desired response from the child.

As an aid in determining which events facilitate student's learning and performance, a checklist, the Initial Assessment and Planning Form, has been provided as a guide (see Figure 2). The checklist enumerates stimulus events under the following headings: Mode of instruction, stimulus materials, type of instructor, rate of instructions, and setting for instruction. You may check the variables in each of the categories which seem to be most beneficial for a particular student. Obviously, the list is not inclusive, but only a beginning point in identifying stimulus events which should be considered in assessing

Instructional Planning for Exceptional Children

the total instructional environment. Add to the list other variables you find to be important.

Identifying Subsequent or Contingent Events

Although you can facilitate student performance by presenting appropriate tasks and "setting the stage" in an optimal manner, you must go one step further if you expect to obtain desired performance from your students. To state it simply, you must arrange subsequent or contingent events *as a result of* student behavior. Therefore, part of your task during the initial assessment will be to identify those events following student behavior which seem to be effective in managing future behavior.

Principles of managing behavior have been derived from learning theory. When events that follow behavior are effective in increasing or maintaining that behavior, they are called *reinforcers*. They are called *positive reinforcers* when presentation of them maintains or increases behavior, and *negative reinforcers* when removal of them maintains or increases behavior. If presentation decreases behavior, the events are called *punishers*.

For instance, a student raises his hand before asking a question, and you praise him. In the future, the student continues to raise his hand before asking a question. Teacher praise is then considered a contingent positive reinforcer. If, after being praised, the student does not continue raising his hand, teacher praise would not be considered a reinforcer. Since it did not increase or maintain behavior but decreased it, praise served as a punisher. Likewise, if you had begun frowning whenever the student raised his hand, and the student had stopped raising his hand or raised it less often, frowning would be considered a punisher. As in the previous example, if there had been no change in the amount of hand-raising behavior, your frowns would not have been considered a punisher. If, when the student raised his hand more often, you stopped frowning, frowning would be considered a negative reinforcer because it removed an average stimulus.

Two important points are illustrated in these simple examples: Events or stimuli cannot be designated as reinforcers or punishers until their effect upon behavior is evaluated; and, in order for the subsequent events or consequences, whether reinforcers or punishers, to have maximum effect upon student behavior, they must be arranged in a contingent manner. That is, the consequences received by the student must be made dependent upon the occurrences of the student responses.

As was the case with antecedent or stimulus events, an innumerable number of subsequent events exist or can be provided in a typical classroom setting. Generally, determining which of these many events will serve as potential reinforcers or punishers can best be done by observing the student in several settings or by asking his or her parents. By observing the child, you

Informal Assessment for the Classroom

can easily note his or her free-time preferences for objects or activities and can later employ these events as contingent consequences when trying to obtain desired behavior.

Another procedure that can be employed to determine subsequent events which affect the behavior of individual students is reinforcer sampling (Ayllon & Azrin, 1968). This procedure allows the student to sample the object or event before it is used as a possible reinforcer. Using such a procedure, you can determine which events have potential reinforcing properties. After the sampling period, the child may not appear to desire the object or continue the activity. You can then assume that the event's lack of reinforcing power is not due to the child's lack of familiarity. Thus, observing the student and experimenting with several events which may increase or decrease behavior are probably the best ways to initially assess the effectiveness of subsequent events.

The lists of subsequent events provided in Figure 2 may be used as a starting point when attempting to identify events that may serve as reinforcers or punishers. During the initial assessment, check those positive and negative events you think are most likely to be so desirable or undesirable to the child that they may be effective in managing his or her behavior. Although the lists include numerous consequences that might serve as positive reinforcers, you should be highly selective, checking only those consequences you think will be most likely to increase or maintain behavior.

Keep in mind that the verbalizations and physical demonstrations of approval have the strongest reinforcing properties when they are given by people important to the student. Also note that although many of the negative consequences listed may serve as either negative reinforcers (if removed) or punishers (if presented), many of them are not recommended for use because of their possible negative effects upon the child, such as escape, avoidance, and aggression. Those consequences *not* recommended are listed so that you may check to make sure you are not unwittingly using them. If you are using them, you might consider modifying your own behavior.

It is recommended that when negative verbalizations are used, they relate to specific behaviors and, when necessary, indicate exactly what is expected of the student. Sometimes it is important to give corrective feedback. The child must be told what the correct response is; e.g., "No, you spell cat c-a-t." Physical demonstrations of disapproval should be used only when the student understands what behavior is an acceptable substitute for the one he or she is using.

ON-GOING ASSESSMENT

After completing the initial assessment, you are ready to begin the second stage in the process—on-going assessment. Assessment is considered

Instructional Planning for Exceptional Children

FIGURE 2
Complete Initial Assessment and Planning Form

1. LEARNER TASKS: 1. 92 *sight words* 2. Use of "k" in initial position
   3. Use of "p" and "f" in *final* position 4. Use of *short vowel*
   sounds 5. Use of *blends* and *digraphs* "th," "sp," "br," and "cl."

2. ANTECEDENT EVENTS:

Mode of Instruction	Mode of Input	Rate of Instruction
✓ directions	✓ visual	fast
questions	auditory	moderate
cuing	tactile (touch)	✓ slow
prompting	olfactory	
✓ modeling	kinesthetic (movement)	

Stimulus Materials	Time of Instruction	Setting for Instruction
✓ textbooks	✓ morning	classroom
one worksheets	afternoon	play area
✓ pictures	period:	special rooms:
chalkboard		library
graphs		media center
films	Attributes of Material	resource room
filmstrips	small	other:
✓ flashcards	medium	cubicle
manipulatives	large	quiet area
games *not group ones*	✓ colored	interest center
tape recorder	black & white	✓ open area *carpeted*
other:	✓ simple	desk *area*
	complex	table
	many items *beside*	other:
Type of Instructor	✓ few items *desk*	
✓ male	sequential	✓ one to one
✓ female	✓ other: *materials*	small group *maybe*
✓ teacher	*until picture*	✓ large group
aide		
peer		
auxiliary		
personnel		
other: *student teacher*		

3. SUBSEQUENT EVENTS:

Verbalizations	Physical Demonstration of Approval	Token Rewards
Good!	✓ smile *be careful*	✓ stars
Great!	*our* pat *good*	checkmarks
That's right!	wink *touching*	points
Nice job!	✓ touch	tokens
You're doing fine!	hug	tickets
Much better!	thumbs up	chips
other: *way to go*	✓ nod	✓ grades
	other:	other:

Food	Toys	Activities & Privileges
candy	clay	leading group
fruit	puzzles	running errands
raisins	dolls	exempting a test
cheese	✓ balls	caring for class
cereal	✓ games	pets, flowers
soft drinks	✓ books	representing group
ice cream	✓ models *car*	free-time
other:	✓ other: *magazines*	listening to records
		pass to library,
Awards		gym, snack bar
citations		omitting an assignment
plaques		smoking
"Good Deed" charts		field trip
report cards		✓ visit with desired
letters		person *student teacher*
recommendations		✓ other: *time for leaving*
other:		

Verbalizations

✓ corrective feedback
Stop talking.
Pay attention.
Be quiet and sit down
Turn your desk around and face......
other:

Physical Demonstration of Disapproval

frown
stare
hands on hip
shake of head, finger
other:

Negative

Verbalizations (not recommended)

Think for a change!
You don't understand because you don't listen.
Act your age!
Can't you do anything right?
You should be ashamed.
Who do you think you are?
You're making me a nervous wreck!

Physical Demonstrations of Disapproval (not recommended)

curl of lip
shaking fist
gritting of teeth
spanking

Informal Assessment for the Classroom

to be an integral part of instruction. Many educators (Gronlund, 1971; Wallace & Kauffman, 1973) view it as a dynamic, on-going, even cyclical process. When viewed in such a manner, it is obvious that although the initial assessment of learner tasks, antecedent events, and subsequent events provide valuable information, it is inadequate to insure optimal learner performance across time and tasks. Only through a process of on-going assessment can you validate the hypotheses derived during initial assessment or systematically manipulate environmental variables until student objectives are achieved.

The on-going assessment process is comprised of three basic phases: Assessment during baseline, assessment during intervention, and assessment of generalization (Lovitt, 1967). Accurate baseline data provide you with a clear picture of the student's skills, knowledge, or behavior in a particular area prior to the initiation of an intervention program; it defines a starting point. Data acquired during intervention will provide the information necessary to assess the effectiveness of the instruction or intervention program. Finally, generalization data, acquired after the completion of intervention, will allow you to assess the extent to which the student's learning is transferred from one setting to another, and from one behavior to another.

In order to assess behavior during each of the described phases, you must select and use some form of systematic data collection. If data are not collected systematically, the effectiveness of instruction cannot be assessed. There are numerous procedures which can be employed to measure behavior. In deciding which of these to use, take into account the frequency, nature, and topography of the behavior, and the amount of time available to the observer (see Figure 3). Various measurement techniques will be described briefly. For a further description and instructions on implementing these procedures, see Axelrod (1977), and Cooper (1974).

Data Collection Techniques

Direct measurement of permanent products. This is measuring products which are the direct result of a student's performance. With such a procedure, you can measure tangible results of a student's behavior, either as it occurs or at a later time. This procedure is used continuously in the classroom. Examples include counting the number of correctly written arithmetic problems, spelling words, or sentences; the number of beads on a string, completed pegboard puzzles, sharpened pencils, or stacked blocks. Direct measurement of permanent products is an important measurement procedure because it is convenient and gives accurate data of a child's performance which can be evaluated and reevaluated at will.

Observational recording. Some behaviors do not result in a product which is left in the environment. These behaviors occur, but are transitory, and leave no physical evidence of their occurrence. Examples of these be-

Instructional Planning for Exceptional Children

FIGURE 3
Selection of Data Collection Techniques

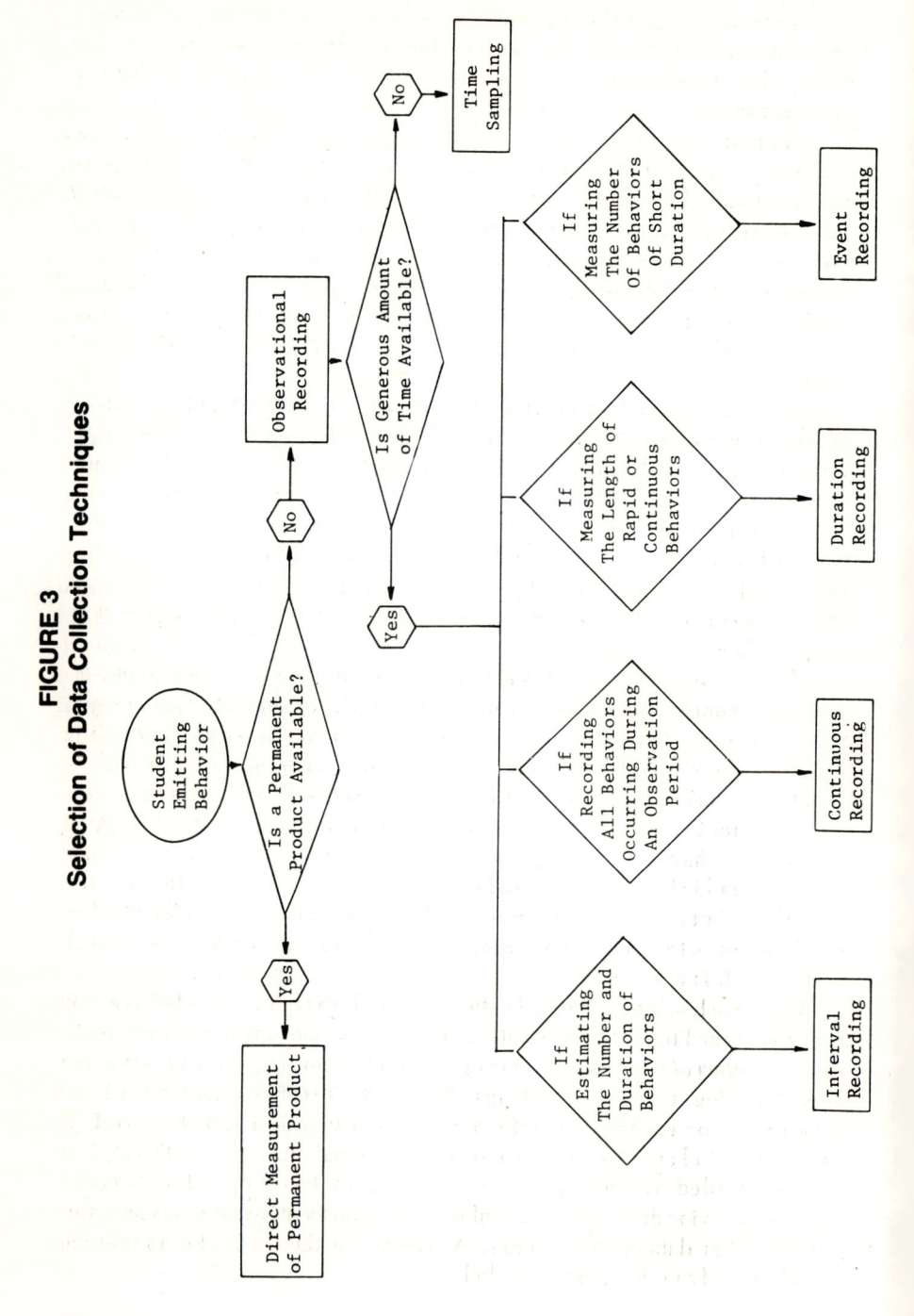

haviors are shouting, fighting, thumbsucking, orally reciting number facts, and talking out. Since no product results from these behaviors, they are measured by observational recording techniques. Several of these observational procedures are discussed.

When an attempt is made to record in detailed behavioral terms the behaviors of a person, it is called *continuous recording*. Those recordings are sometimes called anecdotal records. When appropriate, they include actual dialogue and descriptions of settings. If done properly, the anecdotal record will provide a "verbal picture" of a student and his or her behavior in a particular setting. Obviously, this technique is extremely time-consuming. It should be used prior to determining or targeting a specific behavior to be measured, or used to observe the effects of antecedent and subsequent events.

The observational measurement technique most frequently used by teachers is *event recording*. This procedure requires that you make a tally each time a targeted behavior occurs across a period of time. The technique is particularly applicable in measuring discrete behaviors of short duration. Sometimes paper and pencil are used, and the behavior occurrence is noted by a hash mark. Creative teachers have employed tape on the wrist and colored pencils, or the transference of paper clips. Teachers also have reported the convenience of wrist counters in recording behavior while they were teaching.

When a behavior continues for a period of time (e.g., attending, out-of-seat), or is composed of actions which are difficult to separate into discrete behaviors (e.g., head-banging, tantruming), an observational recording technique known as *duration recording* is appropriate to measure the behavior. This technique measures the occurrence of behavior across time (i.e., seconds, minutes, hours). It allows you to record how long a student engaged in a specific behavior. Thus, if you want to know how long Sue remained in her seat, you would check the clock and record the time she began sitting and the time she got out of her seat. Subtracting the times would give you the number of minutes of "sitting behavior." Since this procedure measures time, a clock or stopwatch is a necessity.

If you wish to have some indication of both the frequency of a behavior (as in event recording) and its duration, the appropriate meassurement technique is *interval recording*. During interval recording, you observe the student during a time interval, usually 10 to 30 seconds, and record the presence (+) or absence (−) of the targeted behavior during that interval. If the targeted behavior occurs once or several times during the interval, it is usually recorded by one notation (+). Although interval recording typically samples behavior during intervals of seconds, consecutive intervals are sampled to gather data across minutes. A typical raw data sheet for an interval record of studying behavior is as follows:

Instructional Planning for Exceptional Children

10″	20″	30″	40″	50″	60″		10″	20″	30″	40″	50″	60″
+	−	−	+	+	+		−	+	+	−	+	−

Since interval recording requires you to observe the behavior during the entire interval, its use in the classroom is frequently impractical and inconvenient. As this procedure also deals with time, a clock or stopwatch is needed.

An observational measurement procedure which is convenient and practical for teachers and which provides a record or student performance is called *time sampling*. With this procedure, you note only the occurrence or nonoccurrence of the targeted behavior at the end of a time interval, usually minutes. For example, if you want to determine how frequently Bill worked on his seat assignments while you conduct a reading group, you could teach for five minutes, note Bill's behavior, teach for another five minutes and observe again, etc. A time sampling record of such behavior would be as follows:

Minutes	5	10	15	20	25
Behavior	+	−	+	+	−

This record indicated that at the end of 5, 15, and 20 minutes, Bill was working. At the end of 10 and 25 minutes, he was not. Using time sampling, it does not matter what the child was doing immediately before or after the specific time of measurement. If the student has no knowledge of the length of the interval, a more accurate sample of behavior can be obtained across time. Since an interval of time is used in time sampling, a clock, a watch, or a timer is needed for data collection.

The recording methods discussed are appropriate for use in each phase of on-going assessment—assessment of baseline, intervention, and generalization. Proper collection of data using the appropriate procedure is crucial during on-going assessment.

Assessment During Baseline

Assessing behavior prior to intervention involves collecting baseline data. These data will provide information about the student's starting point; that is, his or her level of performing the targeted behavior before you attempt to change it. At this point, you must operationally define the behavior of interest and write a behavioral objective encompassing conditions, behavior, and criteria. During the baseline phase of assessment, you measure the behavior of interest under normal classroom conditions continuously over a period of time. Since behavior varies from day to day, only through assessment across time can you accurately determine a student's present level of performance on a task. During the baseline phase, you take data on the behavior, using one of the data collection procedures described, until the behavior appears stable, neither increasing nor decreasing as much as 50% above or below the mean.

The conditions during baseline assessment should be like those under which the behavior would normally occur. If the targeted behavior, as defined in the behavioral objective, is an academic one, you should present the task using only those antecedent events necessary for its presentation. Instructional techniques, praise for correct responses, or corrective feedback should not be provided. Likewise, you should not use other subsequent events considered to be reinforcers or punishers. If the target behavior is a social one, you should take data on the behavior as it normally occurs in the classroom, without giving any special attention or treatment to the student. The purpose of baseline assessment is to provide a basis for comparing a student's performance as it presently exists with his or her performance in a setting where antecedent and subsequent events are being controlled.

Assessment During Intervention

Following the baseline phase, conduct assessment while you intervene on the behavior. During this intervention phase, program the behavior, using the antecedent and subsequent events which you decide during the initial assessment procedure would obtain the desired behavior. If the targeted behavior is an academic task, you may choose as the antecedent events a worksheet, teacher instructions, and demonstrations of the desired response. When student responses occur, you may choose praise and corrective feedback as contingent subsequent events. If the desired behavior is social in nature (e.g., hand-raising), you may choose verbal questions as the antecedent event and calling on the child when appropriate hand-raising occurs and ignoring talking out when appropriate hand-raising does not occur as the contingent subsequent events.

Employing the antecedent and subsequent events identified in initial assessment, continue to collect data on the targeted behavior identified as the learner task. If the behavior of interest increases or decreases in the desired manner in comparison to its occurrence under baseline conditions, the change in student performance will be observed in the data generated. If the behavior is changing at the rate and in the manner you desire, you may continue employing the antecedent and subsequent events selected until the desired criterion is met. If the behavior is not changing as it should, you must reevaluate the hypotheses generated during initial assessment and decide what changes are needed.

Instructional Planning for Exceptional Children

Changing intervention techniques is common in teaching. Frequently, strategies based upon developed hypotheses do not have the expected effect on a student's behavior. As a rule of thumb, if a behavior has not begun to change in the desired direction after three to five days of intervention, a change in intervention tactics is needed. The question that arises is, "What components of the intervention phase need to be changed?" There are no easy answers to such a question. Basically, you must recycle through the procedures of the initial assessment process.

The first step would be to check the learner task to determine its appropriateness. For instance, a previous skill may need to be mastered before the targeted behavior will be acquired. If this is the case, you may need to conduct a formal task analysis (Thiagarajan, 1971). If you determine that the learner task is indeed appropriate, the next step is to review the antecedent events. Changing the mode of instruction, stimulus materials, mode of input, or rate of instruction may be necessary. Deciding on a variation of the same antecedent events or on others is a decision you can best make by observing the child during the intervention phase. The child's responses during that phase are usually cues that a change is needed. After reviewing the antecedent events, you should evaluate your selection of subsequent events. Perhaps the subsequent events you have chosen, although assumed to be positive, are not reinforcing to the child. Other events should be chosen. Based on a reevaluation of the components of initial assessment, you should develop new hypotheses to be employed in another intervention phase. Sometimes multiple intervention phases are needed before the criterion of student performance desired is met.

When the desired criterion is met, you may wonder whether the components you selected actually caused the behavioral change, or whether other variables within the environment produced the desired behavior. To empirically validate the effects of the intervention strategy, one of two experimental designs usually is employed—the reversal design, or the multiple baseline design (Axelrod, 1977; Baer, Wolf, & Risley, 1968; Cooper, 1974). The reversal design is one in which baseline conditions are reinstated after the desired change has occurred during intervention. If the behavior returns to the levels emitted during baseline conditions, evidence (although insufficient) is provided that the tactics employed during intervention caused the change in behavior. Following reinstatement of baseline conditions, the previous intervention strategy is again instituted. If improvement again occurs, additional evidence is provided, and you have demonstrated that the intervention strategy you employed caused the change in the student's behavior.

If reversing a desired behavior is dangerous, or the behavior is unlikely to reverse, or reversing it is otherwise undesirable, a multiple baseline design can be used. A multiple baseline design may be employed across students, across behaviors, or across settings. This design requires behavioral measurements to be taken on one behavior of two or more students, on two or more similar behaviors of the same student, or on one behavior of a given student in two or more different environmental settings. In using this design, baseline is first taken on all students, on all behaviors, or in all settings. Then, intervention is implemented on only one of the students, behaviors, or settings while baseline is continued for the remaining ones. When a behavioral change occurs by the first intervention, the same tactic is applied to the second student, behavior, or setting. Following the change generated by the second intervention, the same tactic is applied to the third, and so on. As was the case with the reversal design, the multiple baseline design allows the teacher to validate the effectiveness of her intervention strategy. In the multiple baseline design, the second and third student, behavior, or setting serve as controls to attest to the effect produced by the intervention strategy. If behavioral change occurs when and only when intervention has been implemented, you have increased your confidence that the tactics employed produced the behavioral change, rather than resulting from coincidence or other uncontrollable factors.

Assessment of Generalization

After a student has acquired a desired behavior in one situation or setting, it is frequently important that the behavior occur in other situations. In addition, it may be desirable for the child to exhibit other responses similar to the one just acquired, without needing additional instruction. In both cases, generalization is needed. Two basic types of generalization are expected by teachers—stimulus generalization and response generalization (Axelrod, 1977; Baer et al., 1968; Kazdin, 1975; Lovitt, 1967).

Stimulus generalization refers to the occurrence of a behavior in a different setting or situation than the one in which it was learned. For example, when a student learns to add and subtract number facts in school and later computes the amount of additional allowance needed to acquire a new baseball, stimulus generalization from a school experience has occurred. Stimulus generalization is an important part of learning, but since it may occur automatically, it should be assessed across a variety of situations and settings. Stimulus generalization may be assessed in numerous ways. For example, you may check the use of words learned during spelling as the student writes a language arts composition, or you may check the use of subtraction facts during multiplication computation. It is important that generalization be assessed so that program modifications can be made as needed. Research has indicated that stimulus generalization is more likely to occur if the new situation or setting is similar to the one in which the desired behavior was first learned (Kennedy & Thompson, 1967; Patterson, 1965; Walker & Buckley,

Instructional Planning for Exceptional Children

1968). Therefore, if generalization has not occurred, you need only restructure the situation to reinforce the new behavior in the present situation.

Response generalization refers to the occurrence of responses not previously acquired but similar to the one previously learned (Kazdin, 1975). For example, you may teach regrouping of two-digit addition problems and hope that the acquisition of this behavior will generate to three-digit numbers. Teachers depend more heavily on response generalization than upon stimulus generalization. Without response generalization, instruction would be a tremendously tedious and overwhelming task requiring teachers to teach all instances of a response. Although response generalization does occur, exceptional children experience more problems in this area than do other children (Lovitt, 1967).

You must assess the occurrence of response generalization and systematically program instruction to insure its occurrence. Research has indicated that the reinforcement of a response will increase the probability of other responses which are similar (Skinner, 1953; Buell, Stoddard, Harris, & Baer, 1968; Lovaas & Simmons, 1969). Therefore, when response generalization does not occur, you should point out similarities between the learned response and the new response and reinforce the occurrence of the new behavior. If response generalization does occur across response classes, you then know that the child has acquired a similar behavior, and you may begin teaching the next behavioral sequence.

Assessment of generalization is an integral part of instruction. Without it, you may needlessly teach a learned behavior, or you may fail to teach a skill which has not generalized. Through assessment of generalization, you can obtain the data needed to increase the efficiency and effectiveness of instruction. As has been aptly stated, "Generalization should be programmed, rather than expected or lamented" (Bauer, et al., 1967, p. 97).

APPLIED EXAMPLE

The following example illustrates the assessment procedure we have described. Ms. Edwards, a resource teacher in an elementary school, received a new referral, Charles. Charles is a nine-year-old third grader, referred by his regular teacher, Ms. Horton, because of his academic difficulties, particularly in reading. He also exhibited occasional behavior problems.

After discussing Charles' problems with his regular teacher, Ms. Edwards decided to observe Charles in his room for several days and to allow him to come to her resource room one hour each day. During the hour he was with her, she began informally assessing his reading skills, using a combination of several skill sequences which accompanied the basal readers used in her school.

In the regular classroom, Ms. Edwards observed Charles during the

Informal Assessment for the Classroom

morning for several days. She paid particular attention to his reactions to the many antecedent and subsequent events which occurred in his classroom. She noticed that when directions were given by Ms. Horton, Charles appeared to pay attention for a brief period, but began work prematurely before the instructions were completed. When working, he responded in spurts, and stopped working completely before the period was over. On observation, Ms. Edwards also noted the following:

1. Frequently, Ms. Horton came to Charles' desk and showed him what to do.
2. He worked longer on assignments in his workbook than those presented on the chalkboard.
3. Charles appeared to be interested in the colored pictures in his textbook, and often took out paper and drew figures similar to those in his book.
4. He scribbled on the margins of his language worksheets, and often failed to complete them.
5. He had difficulty following directions given to the entire class. He followed Ms. Horton's instructions when they were given directly to him, and usually responded to her in a positive manner. It was noted that when talking to Charles directly, Ms. Horton spoke slower than when talking to the class.
6. Several times he asked if he could work with a male college student who was doing his student-teaching in the class.
7. No differences were noted in his responses to auditory and visual stimuli.
8. On rare occasions when he finished his work, he would select a magazine about cars from the bookshelf and take it to a small carpet in the back of the room, where he would sit and look at the picture in the magazine.
9. Occasionally, his teacher patted him on the back while praising him. He withdrew from her touch.
10. When she responded to him by saying, "Way to go," he smiled and continued his work.
11. When Ms. Horton was busy with other students, Charles went to the student teacher to show him a paper on which he received a check (√), an indication of acceptable work.
12. During reading group, Charles had great difficulty with word attack skills, and appeared to use contextual clues and pictures to guess at the words, frequently calling them incorrectly. He was reading in a second grade basal, which seemed too difficult for him.

On several afternoons, Ms. Edwards again visited Charles' class. She noticed he appeared to be cross and irritable. She further noted that he used abusive language with the other students five times, and each time it was soon after lunch. During the afternoon recess, Charles played alone, refusing to

Instructional Planning for Exceptional Children

participate in a game of kickball. Instead, he bounced a basketball on a concrete area nearby. On two occasions during inclement weather, Charles played a lotto game with other students. Both times, he had a disruptive argument with one of the other students, and Ms. Horton removed him from the game. When he was removed, he frowned, walked to a bookcase, got a deck of multiplication flashcards, went to his desk, and began reciting them to himself.

During the time Charles spent with Ms. Edwards in her resource room, she began assessing his reading skills. He responded in a positive manner to her direction and praise but had great difficulty reading sample first-grade paragraphs. However, he was able to answer many comprehension questions about what he read. Ms. Edwards decided to limit her assessment to word recognition skills, since Charles' comprehension skills were far superior to his skills in word recognition. She began by showing him sight words on flashcards and asking him to say the words. The words consisted of those given for grades one and two in her curriculum guides. Charles responded correctly to 108 of the 200 words presented. A segment of the sight word checklist follows (√ = correct; × = incorrect):

√	after	√	were	√	once
√	has	√	over	×	pretty
×	let	×	put	×	yes
×	know	√	keep	√	now
√	may	√	round	×	thank

Then Ms. Edwards checked Charles' use of consonants in the initial position by having him read words and nonsense words formed by adding the consonants to the letters *ad*. (She knew that Charles could pronounce *ad*.) A segment of this checklist follows:

√	cad	√	jad	√	gad	√	yad
√	dad	×	kad	√	had		

Ms. Edwards continued through the checklist, assessing Charles' knowledge of other first and second grade skills, such as final consonants, use of the silent *e*, use of *y* as a vowel, knowledge of syllabication, digraphs and dipthongs, phonograms, etc. Upon completion of the checklist, she noted that he had mastered some skills taken from the first grade curriculum and a few second grade skills. She then noted on the Initial Assessment and Planning Form those skills which she felt would be high priority for such instruction. These she listed as learner tasks in Figure 2.

Having selected learner tasks and observed Charles in the classroom,

Informal Assessment for the Classroom

Ms. Edwards completed the remainder of the Initial Assessment and Planning Form. She checked both antecedent and subsequent events which appeared to facilitate Charles' performance. As she completed the form, Ms. Edwards began to develop hypotheses concerning certain antecedent and subsequent events which might increase Charles' reading skills. Not only did she check specific events, but also made notes concerning her observations which would aid her in establishing hypotheses.

Having completed the initial assessment form, Ms. Edwards began planning for instruction and the on-going assessment process. First, she selected increasing Charles' sight vocabulary as the learner task. She defined the target behavior as a correct vocal response or pronunciation of each sight word presented on flashcards. She selected 15 of the words Charles was unable to read during initial assessment. Next, she wrote the following behavioral objective: Given three sets of five sight words, Charles will pronounce each word correctly (100% accuracy) within five seconds on initial presentation for three successive days.

Reviewing the data collection procedures and the experimental designs, Ms. Edwards chose to collect data using event recording, and to test the effectiveness of her hypotheses through a multiple baseline design. Making these decisions, Ms. Edwards began taking data on Charles' pronunciation of the three sets of sight words. During baseline, she presented each word of each set in random order to Charles for five seconds without providing praise or correction feedback. She recorded the number of correct responses Charles emitted and graphed the results (see Figure 4). After five days, Charles' reading skills were neither increasing nor decreasing. He read only one or two words correctly each day.

When a stable state was obtained, Ms. Edwards began her intervention strategy. Based on her observations, she decided to use a modeling procedure to teach Charles the words and verbal praise as a contingent subsequent event. That is, when she presented each flashcard to Charles, she told him the word and asked him to repeat it. When he repeated it correctly, she provided verbal praise. When he responded incorrectly, she told him the word again. At the end of each 20-minute teaching session, Ms. Edwards again probed Charles' reading of each word in each set and tallied the correct responses (see Figure 4).

After five days, Ms. Edwards decided that Charles' progress was not satisfactory. Therefore, she again reviewed the appropriateness of the task, the antecedent events, and the subsequent events. Based on her observations of Charles in his classroom, she hypothesized that his correct responses might be increased by changing the subsequent events. As a result, she implemented a new intervention strategy. She informed Charles that from now on he would receive a checkmark for each correct response during the probe

Instructional Planning for Exceptional Children

FIGURE 4
Charles' Sight Word Acquisition

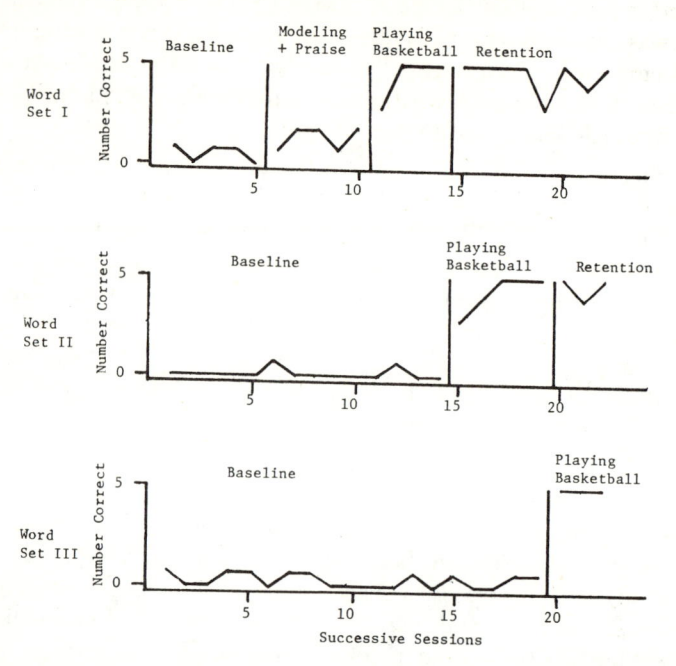

session. As a backup reinforcer, Ms. Edwards arranged with Ms. Horton to allow Charles to play basketball with the student teacher at the rate of two minutes per checkmark. Using this formula, if Charles read each word of the teaching set correctly, he would earn five checkmarks redeemable for 10 minutes of basketball. Following implementation of the new intervention tactic, Charles reached criterion on the first set of words in only four days (see Figure 4).

When criterion was reached on the first set, Ms. Edwards intervened with the same antecedent and subsequent events on the second set of words. When criterion was met on the second set, she intervened in a like manner on the third set. By the seventeenth day of instruction, Charles had reached criterion on all three sets of words, and Ms. Edwards had demonstrated that the antecedent and subsequent events employed were effective in teaching Charles to read the sight words. Having taught the 15 words to Charles, she proceeded to the next task identified during initial assessment.

Like most resource teachers, Ms. Edwards was concerned about generalization. She wanted to know whether Charles would read the learned words when he returned to Ms. Horton's classroom. Therefore, she gave Ms. Horton a list of the 15 words Charles had learned to read and asked her to take

70

data on the number of learned words he read correctly in the basal reader used in her class. Before taking generalization data, however, Ms. Edwards and Ms. Horton agreed that the basal reader in which Charles was presently reading was too difficult for him and an easier one would be more appropriate. After placing Charles in a first grade basal, Ms. Horton began to take generalization data. She reported that Charles generalized the words he had learned in Ms. Edwards' room (see Figure 5).

FIGURE 5
Charles' Sight Word Generalization

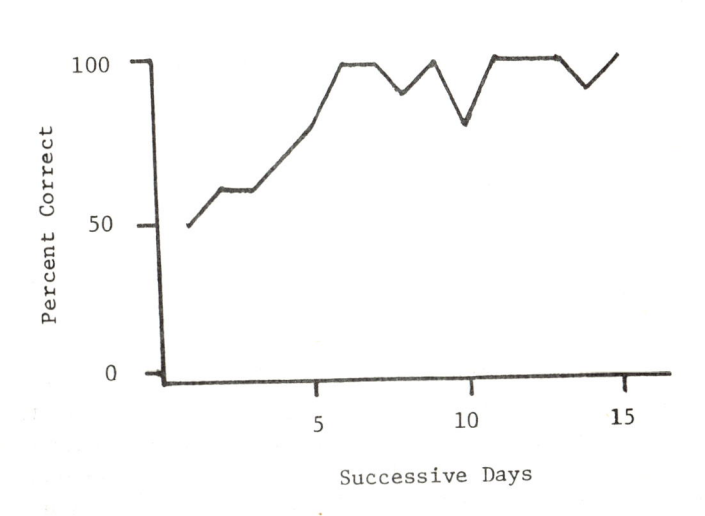

SUMMARY

If the proposed assessment procedure is followed, it will satisfy the requirements previously set forth for a viable informal assessment procedure for the classroom. It will allow you to assess relevant environmental characteristics by examining and evaluating effects of antecedent and subsequent events during both initial and ongoing assessment. It will serve as a basis for effective instructional planning. Pre-instructional planning will be based upon on-going assessment data. Finally, the assessment procedure will satisfy accountability demands by providing clear statements of instructional objectives and precise data documenting progress toward those objectives.

REFERENCES

Adelman, H. Learning problems: An interactional view of causality (Part I), *Academic Therapy*, 1970-71, *6*, 117-123.

Axelrod, S. *Behavior modification for the classroom teacher*. New York: McGraw-Hill, 1977.

Ayllon, T., & Azrin, N. H. *The token economy: A motivational system for therapy and rehabilitation*. New York: Appleton-Century-Crofts, 1968.

Baer, D. M., Wolf, M. M., & Risley, T. R. Some current dimensions of applied behavior analysis. *Journal of Applied Behavior Analysis*, 1968, *1*, 91-97.

Buell, J., Stoddard, P., Harris, F., & Baer, D.M. Collateral social development accompanying reinforcement of outdoor play in a preschool child. *Journal of Applied Behavior Analysis*, 1968, *1*, 1967-73.

Cooper, J. O. *Measurement and analysis of behavioral techniques*. Columbus, OH: Merrill, 1974.

Drew, C., Freston, C. W., & Logan, P. R. Criteria and reference in evaluation. *Exceptional Children*, 1972, *4*, 1-10.

Gronlune, N. E. *Measurement and evaluation in teaching* (2nd ed.). New York: Macmillan, 1971.

Hammill, D., & Larsen, S. The effectiveness of psycholinguistic training. *Exceptional Children*, 1974, *41*, 5-14.

Haring, N. Educational services for the severely and profoundly handicapped. *Journal of Special Education*, 1975, *9*, 425-433.

Kazdin, A. E. *Behavior modification in applied settings*. Homewood, IL: Dorsey Press, 1975.

Kennedy, D. A., & Thompson, I. Use of reinforcement techniques with a first grade boy. *The Personnel and Guidance Journal*, 1967, *46*, 366-370.

Keogh, B., & Becker, L. D. Early detection of learning problems: Questions, cautions, and guidelines. *Exceptional Children*, 1973, *40*, 5-11.

Lovaas, I., & Simmons, J. O. Manipulation of self destruction in three retarded children. *Journal of Applied Behavior Analysis*, 1969, *2*, 143-57.

Lovitt, T. Assessment of children with learning disabilities. *Exceptional Children*, 1967, *34*, 233-239.

Patterson, G. R., An application of conditioning techniques to the control of a hyperactive child. In L. P. Ullman and L. Krasner (Eds.), *Case studies in behavior modification*. New York: Holt, Rinehart, and Winston, 1965.

Reynolds, M. C., & Balow, B. Categories and variables in special education. *Exceptional Children*, 1972, *38*, 357-66.

Skinner, B. F. *Sciences and human behavior*. New York: Free Press, 1953.

Thiagarajan, S. *The programming process: A practical guide*. Worthington, OH: Charles A. Jones, 1971.

Walker, W., & Buckley, N. K. The use of positive reinforcement in conditioning attending behavior. *Journal of Applied Behavior Analysis*, 1968, *1*, 245-250.

Wallace, G., & Kauffman, J. M. *Teaching children with learning problems*. Columbus, OH: Merrill, 1973.

The authors propose a dynamic process-oriented assessment scheme which involves the parents, careful observation in the home environment, and the use of formal and informal measures. They emphasize the importance of establishing sound rapport. Special emphasis is placed on the analysis of failure to reach its cause. The teach-test-teach paradigm is likewise employed.

Assessing Severely Handicapped Children

Rebecca F. DuBose, Mary Beth Langley, and Vaughan Stagg, *George Peabody College*

Public Law 94-142 mandates the nationwide provision of special education and related services for all handicapped children, *regardless of the severity of their handicap*. More specifically, children must be assessed, and individualized education plans must be provided. Each plan must specify: (a) the child's present levels of educational performance; (b) annual goals, including short term objectives; (c) educational services to be provided; (d) the dates for initiation and anticipated duration of services; and (e) appropriate objective criteria and evaluation procedures for determining whether instructional objectives are being achieved (Section 602 [4] [19]).

Across the country, school systems are feeling the strain on available resources. Particularly alarming is the scarcity of trained manpower to meet the special educational needs of severely handicapped children. Sailor, Guess and Lavis (1975) proclaimed "an immediate need to provide a cadre of competent, qualified teachers with allied personnel and resources to deliver an effective and functional educational program for severely handicapped" (p. 201).

During the past four years, attention has focused on the immediate shortage of trained teachers and the critical factors that constitute necessary teacher competencies for directing the educational program of severely and multiply handicapped children (Altman & Meyen, 1976; Brown & York, 1974; Meyen, 1975; Sailor, Guess, & Lavis, 1975; Sontag, Burke, and York, 1973). These concerns are being addressed by staff members of teacher-training institutions singly and in concert with personnel in other training programs.

Little has been done to train allied personnel to fill effectively their assigned roles in services to severely impaired children. The substantive knowledge of testing and measurement included in the training of diagnostic personnel has proved to be inadequate. Generally, such procedures have been concerned with norm-referenced testing and have not included task analyses, criterion-referenced measures, or special adaptations for use when serious impairments notably affect performance. Clearly emerging are needs for (a) diagnosticians whose training has included a heavy emphasis on the concerns of severely handicapped children, and (b) a workable model for planning, executing, and evaluating and educational service system that can be expected to make a difference in the behavioral expressions of severely impaired children. This article will concentrate on a portion of the latter concern and present a paradigm for the analysis and instruction of severely handicapped children.

THE PROBLEM AS RELATED TO SEVERELY HANDICAPPED PERSONS

Severely and profoundly handicapped children are newcomers to public schools. Their behaviors and needs are disparate from those of their age-mates. Sontag, et al. (1973) offered a behavioral description of severely and profoundly handicapped children:

> those who are not toilet trained; aggress toward others; do not attend to even the most pronounced social stimuli; self mutilate; ruminate; self stimulate; do not walk, speak, hear, or see; manifest durable and intense temper tantrums; are not under even the rudimentary forms of verbal control; do not imitate; manifest minimally controlled seizures; and/or have extremely brittle medical existences (p. 21).

Persons manifesting the behaviors described have been traditionally labeled as "untestable." At best, interview scales provided the referring agent with a label or score but little or no additional information. The possibility of intensive programming to teach the person new skills lay dormant.

Examiners were trained in the administration of traditional mental measures and knew little about the assessment of preacademic children. Few of them were skilled in the assessment of physically and sensorily impaired persons. Additionally, examiners had not been trained to render assessments leading directly into classroom programming. Thus, both the person assessed and the examiner responsible for the assessment have been relative strangers to each other.

THE PROBLEM AS RELATED TO THE TASK

With the passage of mandatory education legislation, assessment of severely handicapped children via norm-referenced instruments has become the target of consistent criticism (Hunt, 1975; Jedrysek, Klapper, Pope, & Wortis, 1972; Keogh, 1972; Knobloch & Pasamanick, 1974; Mann & Suiter, 1974; Meier, 1975). Intervention agents relying on information from evaluations based on norm-referenced testing have frequently received only *confirmation* (in the form of a statistical abstraction) that a child was delayed. Rarely do evaluations based on such information supply the agent with insights into how the child learns or where to proceed next in the intervention process. As Haywood, Filler, Shiffman and Chatellant (1975) noted, a normative approach results in comparisons with respect to the acquisition of products. In addition, this approach has led to a static classification of children.

The most defensible use of normative assessments is for policy makers and researchers. Because of the impact of public policy decisions on large numbers of children, group data are necessary for the formulation of those decisions. Researchers, as well, have a justifiable interest in normative techniques, as they need to apply the same criteria across children and relate their performance to consensually accepted quantifiable standards. Product-oriented measures can play an important role by providing a starting point in the diagnostic process, as well as a picture of the strengths and weaknesses of the child's learning strategies across a variety of learning situations. This is necessary, but it is not enough. Knowledge of the child's success or failure in mastering different skills or associations is needed following a determination of his strengths and weaknesses; one must discover the amount of teaching or intervention required for the child to reach a particular developmental goal or, in other words, the discovery of the degree of modifiability. This information can best be assimilated through a process-oriented approach.

THE PROCESS-ORIENTED MODEL

An alternative to the product-oriented approach, a process-oriented approach (see chart), allows one to capture the sources associated with the behavioral, social, physical, and mental deficiencies that characterize the severely handicapped child. Such deficiencies are multidimensional in nature and are dynamic developmental phenomena rather than static states. A dynamic view of the problem associated with severely handicapped children creates a different set of concerns with respect to assessment. Proponents of a process-oriented approach make the following assumptions:

Instructional Planning for Exceptional Children

PARADIGM FOR ANALYSIS AND INSTRUCTION OF SEVERELY HANDICAPPED CHILDREN

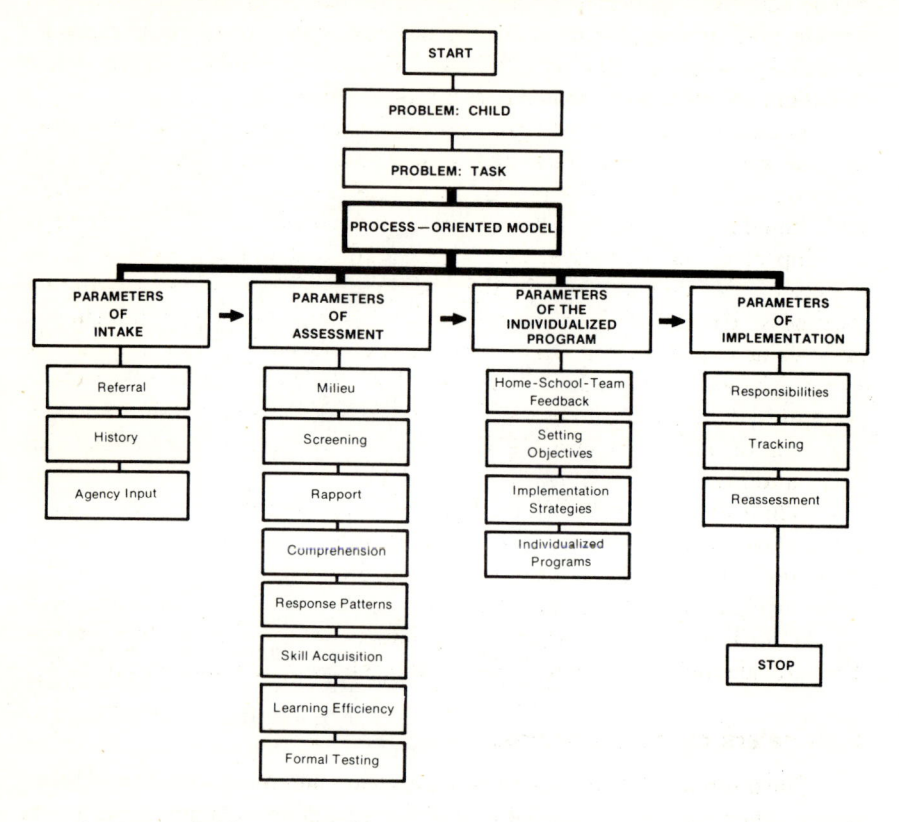

```
                    START
                      |
               PROBLEM: CHILD
                      |
               PROBLEM: TASK
                      |
           PROCESS—ORIENTED MODEL
   _____|_____
   |            |              |            |
PARAMETERS  PARAMETERS    PARAMETERS    PARAMETERS
    OF          OF         OF THE          OF
  INTAKE    ASSESSMENT  INDIVIDUALIZED  IMPLEMENTATION
                          PROGRAM
   |            |              |            |
Referral     Milieu      Home-School-Team  Responsibilities
                            Feedback
History     Screening       Setting       Tracking
                           Objectives
Agency      Rapport      Implementation   Reassessment
Input                     Strategies
         Comprehension   Individualized
                           Programs
         Response Patterns
         Skill Acquisition
         Learning Efficiency          STOP
         Formal Testing
```

1. Every child, regardless of his level of functioning, is an active agent operating on his environment, and this activity can be measured.
2. Assessment determines the child's needs in psychological, educational, and social domains, both independently and in relation with one another.
3. The learning processes employed by the child can be identified, measured, and modified within the assessment milieu.
4. The child's performance on a series of learning tasks is the most appropriate criterion for determining modifiability of learning processes.

A number of investigators have found process orientation to be a functional approach. Haeussermann (1958) advocates an adaptive-capacity approach concerned with a qualitative analysis of a child's performance. Successes and failures are explored in terms of the sensory, experiential, motivational perspectives or other aspects of the child's psychological organization.

Schucman (1957) found a test-teach-test model more sensitive than traditional testing methodology for determining the educability of severely mentally retarded youngsters. Budoff (1973) and Feuerstein (1970) found a similar paradigm effective with higher functioning children.

As mentioned previously, the severely handicapped child himself poses an assessment dilemma since he has passed the most optimum time for learning skills in all developmental areas. Before one can determine why a child functions on a specific level, one must understand the dynamic interrelationship of motor, cognitive, language, social, and self-care skills and the effects on the development of the child passing the period of optimum readiness. The thrust of the assessment process must be on the interaction of abilities across all skill areas. Emphasis on isolated learning incidents or previously acquired products does not allow the examiner to observe the dynamic interchange among skills that facilitates the integration of experiences or to observe where the breakdown is occurring that inhibits this integration and, thus, the learning sequence.

While static, product-oriented measures can supply information in the initial stages of the assessment process, a dynamic, process-oriented approach provides a description of the intervention procedures designed to modify learning processes in order to enhance learning efficiency. Such an approach would not lead to a categorization of products or children that characterize typical evaluation reports which many authors have called "litanies of failure."

Parameters of the Intake Process

The interview/intake process provides team members with an opportunity to gather information crucial in the planning of an evaluation. Such data can be used to anticipate difficulties that may be encountered, to schedule team members so as to maximize their time and skills, and to determine relevant agencies to be contacted.

Referral. The agency referring the child to the diagnostic team will serve in an initial contact and liaison role. The agency must get a report from the team and, if possible, should participate in the team evaluation.

History. A thorough developmental history should be gathered at this point, and data regarding pre- and perinatal status should be obtained. Information regarding the sensory, physical, language, and self-care milestones experienced by the child can be ascertained. Particular attention should be given to real-life behaviors in the home and school that reflect these domains.

Parents should be made aware that they are considered to be an integral part of the assessment process. They possess far more knowledge about many aspects of the child than any team will ever know, and their views and opinions deserve respect. The use of family members as participant-observers in the assessment process provides them with an opportunity to pose questions and receive feedback, and allows team members to note family reactions and priorities that must be given serious consideration in formulating subsequent programming.

Agency input. The families of handicapped children often have had contact with a variety of medical, social and educational agencies. Agencies that parents have contacted for previous evaluations or services should be noted for later contact. One should also obtain an estimate of the parents' knowledge of agency findings. Information from these agencies can supply the evaluation team with pertinent information. Such information needs to be integrated into the programming that eventually is recommended for the child and family. As such agencies are often involved in supporting the family in the community, they need information that is pertinent to their services. Provisions should be made for continuous communication with such support services so that a coordinated plan of intervention can be implemented.

Parameters of the Assessment Process

The assessment milieu. The impact of the context in which behavior takes place has been documented by various investigators (Barker, 1968; MacDonald, 1976; Sroufe, Waters, & Matas, 1974). Bruner (1973) stressed the necessity of focusing on the interaction of the child with the environment rather than concentrating on either the child or the environment as independent entities. Bortner and Birch (1970) noted that glaring differences occur in estimates of potential when alterations are made in performance conditions. Their review indicated that levels of concepts and skills are reflections of the interaction between potential and actual circumstances of training and task requirements.

The use of cross-situational assessment procedures provides a means of distinguishing performance from capacity. Such an approach leads to a conceptualization of the goodness of fit between the child and his learning situation. Certain kinds of child/environment fit will produce directions of behavior and the successful expression of selected aspects of the child's capacity. Changes in the environmental context may facilitate other types of performance that reflect different capacities.

Throughout the assessment process, the examiner must be attuned to behaviors other than those specifically being assessed. An excellent opportunity to observe language skills exists during motor testing. Fine-motor abilities are best evaluated during functional activities, such as those required for self-care.

The interrelationship of skills becomes even more critical when assessing the cognitive and social interaction skills of a child functioning within the first half of the sensory-motor period. Observing how the nonambulatory child moves to obtain a preferred object, searches for a dropped pacifier, and uses his upper extremities to manipulate and discriminate the functions of rattles, cups, bottles, and spoons alerts the examiner to the child's concepts of object permanence, object concept, construction of objects in space, imitation, causality, and means-ends relationships, as well as to the child's awareness of his environment and the people in it. The child's social interaction with significant others can be viewed in isolation and contrasted with his performance in different contexts, and with strangers.

Screening

Before planning extensive assessment procedures, each participant on the evaluation team should gather valuable screening information that will help in selecting the appropriate formal and informal tools that will yield the best data on the child. The primary purpose of screening is to identify strengths, weaknesses, and significant developmental deficits within the total behavioral complex at a particular time in a child's development (Banus, 1974; Friedlander, 1975). As the child enters the evaluation setting, the examiners can informally begin to acquire screening information needed to address the following areas of the child's development: (a) understanding and awareness of surroundings; (b) visual, auditory, and physical means of exploring surroundings; (c) abilities to operate on surroundings; (d) responsiveness to various stimuli; and (e) reaction when reinforced through different means.

Frequently used formal screening instruments include the Denver Developmental Screening Test (Frankenberg, Fandal, & Dodds, 1970), the Developmental Screening Inventory (Knobloch, Pasamanick, & Sherard, 1966), and the Developmental Profile (Alpern & Boll, 1972). A recent addition to this field, the Developmental Activities Screening Inventory (DASI) (DuBose & Langley, 1977), has been adapted for use with both nonverbal and visually impaired children.

Benefits of screening are numerous. Information derived from screening visual, auditory, and physical abilities is critical to all aspects of assessment. Screening can identify the most advantageous size, form and intensity of materials, the best means of presenting tasks to the child, and the most effective arrangements to be used during the assessment. Decisions can be made regarding the use of reinforcements, either tangible or social. Formal tests or parts of them that will be most appropriate for the child will emerge from screening. When initial screening information can be shared with other members of a multidisciplinary team, all examiners are better prepared for eliciting from the child optimal responses for maximizing his performance.

Assessment of rapport. Establishing a working rapport is the examiner's responsibility. The tone of the assessment depends upon the physical and sensory impairments of the child, chronological age, developmental level, and emotional status. While the examiner must be flexible in his approach, and sensitive to the child's total behavioral repertoire, he must maintain control of the testing situation.

Very young children will optimally respond after several minutes of close physical contact during which the examiner rocks, tickles, and babbles to them. Rapport may be maintained by placing the child on a large mat or pillow and letting him first manipulate materials there rather than immediately sitting him at a table. Often, a cooperative relationship with an older child can be created if the examiner leaves on the table a manipulative toy for the child to examine.

The severely handicapped child who refuses to comply with task demands, throws materials, and is physically abusive to both self and the examiner must first undergo behavior management training within the testing situation. Techniques found most effective have been ignoring inappropriate physical or verbal behaviors, responding through social or tangible reinforcement to desirable responses, rewarding performance of less desirable behaviors with highly preferred activities, differential reinforcement of other behaviors, and physically manipulating the child through the task.

Patience and time are of utmost importance, as some children may require several days before developing a readiness to comply with demands. How quickly the child adapts to limits placed upon his behavior and establishes a working rapport with examiners is a critical issue to consider when recommending placements and teaching strategies.

Assessment of comprehension. Before the examiner can begin to assess the child's acquisition of cognitive, language, motor, and social skills, he must first be able to communicate expectations of demands on a level the child understands. A major difficulty encountered in testing severely handicapped children is deciding whether an inappropriate response resulted because the child lacked the conceptual basis of the task or because he failed to comprehend the examiner's directions. Too often the severely handicapped child is declared untestable as his lack of response is interpreted as a lack of ability.

Haeussermann (1958) stressed that realization of the child's readiness for developing a mode of communication depends on observations of the child's performance that, in turn, indicate his level of comprehension. Banus (1974) pointed out that often the child knows the answer to a problem but the directions for eliciting the expected performance are too difficult for the child to understand. Altering the level of directions required to convey task demands will often evoke a successful performance. Imposing more structure by eliminating the number of stimuli and by offering verbal, visual, or physical cues are among the most common means of adapting tasks so that the demands are more comprehensible.

Assessment of response patterns. The quality of the child's response to tasks reveals information about his thinking processes and generalization abilities. Carrow (1972) enumerated the most common types of responses required by testing instruments. The child's approach to task demands indicates whether a response was motoric or conceptual and how he seeks information, in addition to identifying possible factors inhibiting a successful performance.

Minimal responses are exhibited by children who indiscriminately mouth or bang materials. Frequently, severely handicapped children impulsively begin to manipulate task media, performing an appropriate motoric task rather than attending to cognitive or linguistic demands. Perseveration is not uncommon, and often children respond automatically to a task set, demonstrating the effects of previous repetitive interactions with similar or identical material or contexts. Children in whom generalization concepts are emerging may solve tasks through trial-and-error approaches. The child who spontaneously self-corrects a response is demonstrating his ability to compare and contrast his own performance with task demands.

Once a behavior is well established within a child's repertoire, he will consistently approach the task in the same way, carefully scanning all possible solutions before responding. Brown, Nietupski, & Hamre-Nietupski (1976) implied that a skill is not really developed unless the child performs it in three different natural settings, to three different sets of materials, and to three different appropriate languge cues. One way of eliminating "chance" responses is having the child repeat tasks throughout the assessment to meet with the above criteria. Thus, a process-oriented approach and a multidisciplinary team are essential.

The examiner must determine the reason for failure of test items, as the developmental potential of a child is influenced more significantly by the basis of failure than by the failure itself (Haeussermann, 1958). Responses of a child reaching his limits will be erratic in contrast to the consistency and cooperativeness of his responding when items were within his developmental level. Failure on a task yields data regarding salient features of tasks on which the child is focusing and gaps within his behavioral repertoire, as well as effects of the child's impairments on his perceptual, cognitive, and motoric abilities.

The functional linkage between impairments and the child's response must be investigated to determine why the child functions as he does. Through sequential probing, comparison of skills, and the process of elimination, the examiner can determine the underlying basis of failure. If a child with efficient eye-hand coordination and grasp fails to string beads, the examiner can eliminate motoric involvement as a contributing factor to the failure. Cognitive processes can next be analyzed. In bead stringing, a child who does not realize that the string is still present inside the bead lacks an awareness of object permanence and cannot remember the sequence of

Instructional Planning for Exceptional Children

movements necessary to complete the task. His lack of this ability will significantly affect his acquisition of buttoning skills, requiring him to be dependent upon an adult for dressing needs. Through comparison of the types of responses the child exhibits and the relationship of those responses to functional skills, the examiner may begin to draw conclusions regarding the basis of the failure and how the child uses available information.

Assessment of skill acquisition. An eclectic process-oriented approach stemming from Piagetian tasks (Uzgiris & Hunt, 1975) and from the works of Gesell and Amatruda (1947), and Bayley (1969), as well as Haeussermann's (1958) structured interview have permitted examiners to identify developmental levels of severely handicapped children across all skill-acquisition areas. Through creative adaptation of materials, administrative procedures, and developmental expectations, the examiner can determine where in a skill hierarchy the child can succeed.

For example, if a child fails to meet criterion on the Merrill Palmer Scale of Mental Tests (Stutsman, 1948) for nesting four cubes, one cannot assume that the child lacks awareness of serial and spatial relationships. Administration of a downward progression of tasks tapping these concepts will reveal the level at which the child has acquired these skills. The examiner should then arrange a hierarchy of performance situations that will allow the child to demonstrate where his concepts lie in the domain of spatial reasoning. If the child cannot nest four cubes through visual comparison, the examiner should observe whether he can do so through a trial-and-error process. If the child has difficulty with the graduated sizes, the examiner should then investigate whether the child can match box lids with the correct boxes. The child who picks up an inverted cup demonstrates his recognition of the object despite its unusual spatial orientation. Having knowledge of ages at which specific behaviors normally occur, of developmental sequences, and of how to tap the acquisition of skills through adapted media, the examiner can employ a wide range of commercially available materials as supplementary diagnostic tools for determining developmental potential.

Assessment of learning efficiency. A test-teach-test model of assessment permits one to observe the child's potential abilities by assessing his efficiency of acquiring new skills. This area of assessment is especially essential when surveying prevocational abilities of older severely handicapped children. Questions within this realm of adaptive behavior that can be answered through a test-teach-test model concern the child's attention span, the number of trials required to attain a skill, how long he can retain it, and whether he can apply the new skill in another situation or under a different set of variables.

Media found most useful in determining how a child learns new skills are some of the commercially available preschool teaching toys. One such example is Mattell's *The Farmer Says*, which produces animal sounds when its string is pulled. Repeatedly guiding the child to search for and locate the string, grasp the handle, and pull, gradually fading the prompts, enables one to see how many trials including physical guidance are necessary before the child assumes the initiative for activating the toy. Once he independently operates the toy, insight into his generalization processes can be obtained by giving him a toy operated on the same basis as *The Farmer Says*. Observations should focus on how quickly the child realizes the mode of activation of the toy and how efficiently he recalls and initiates the previous learning experience to complete the motoric sequence required for activation of the toy. The test-teach-test model affords the examiner not only a means of assessing learning efficiency but also allows him to predict what the child is capable of doing.

Formal Assessment

The selection of formal assessment instruments for use with the severely handicapped has been a frustrating task for professionals in this field. No single assessment instrument exists that can adequately tap the potential of all severely handicapped children or that serves all examiners' purposes. Following are characteristics found to be most desirable in instruments used in assessing severely handicapped children.

1. They should be easily obtained and simply scored.
2. They should possess adequate validity and reliability.
3. The items should be primarily manipulative in nature.
4. Scoring should be minimally dependent upon the child's speed of performance.
5. The items should be adaptable across all handicapping conditions.
6. The instrument should yield data immediately transferable into sequentially planned developmental activities for educational programming.

The following table contains a condensed compilation of instruments which the authors have found to be the most functional in assessing all developmental domains of severely handicapped children. Individually, none of these tests possesses all the desirable characteristics, but judicious selection of several instruments or parts of them provides the examiner with a powerful battery for determining current functional abilities.

PARAMETERS OF THE INDIVIDUALIZED PROGRAM

Families and teachers have experienced disappointment because traditional psychological reports have failed to specify what could be done in the

SELECTED ASSESSMENT INSTRUMENTS FOR USE
WITH SEVERELY HANDICAPPED

Developmental Activities Screening Inventory Teaching Resources 100 Boylston St. Boston, MA 02116	6-60 months	Screening	A teacher-administered screening instrument to determine general cognitive-adaptive functioning levels, accompanied by developmental activities suggestions.
Haeussermann's Developmental Potential for Preschool Children Grune & Stratton 111 Fifth Avenue New York, NY 10003	2-6 years	Screening	An instrument designed primarily for cerebral palsied children as an assessment of cognitive abilities. Materials include objects from everyday environment.
Bayley Scales of Mental Development The Psychological Corp. 757 Third Avenue New York, N.Y. 10017	Birth-30 months	Cognitive	Similar to Cattell although more standardized and reliable. Also contains motor and social scales.
McCarthy Scales of Children's Abilities The Psychological Corp. 757 Third Avenue New York, N.Y. 10017	2½-8½ years	Cognitive	An instrument to measure general cognitive functioning, as well as the child's strengths and weaknesses in verbal and perceptual performances. Quantitative, memory, motor development, and laterality skills also are examined.
Merrill-Palmer Scales of Mental Development Stoelting Co. 1350 S. Kostner Ave. Chicago, IL 60623	18-71 months	Cognitive Development	The scales assess not only the child's cognitive abilities, but expressive and receptive language and fine and gross motor skills. Comprised largely of performance items, some of which are timed. Provision is made for a child's refusal of an item.
Ordinal Scales of Psychological Development Uzgiris, I. C., & Hunt, J. McV.	Birth-24 months	Cognitive Development	Series of 6 ordinal scales based on Piagetian observations of sensory-motor schemas. Concerned with the hierarchical interrelationship of achievements at different levels. Six scales

Selected Assessment Instrument (Cont.)

Assessment in infancy: Ordinal scales of psychological development. Urbana, IL: University of Illinois Press, 1975			include visual pursuit and permanence of objects, development of means for obtaining desired environmental events, development of vocal and gestural imitation, development of schemas for relating to objects, development of operational causality, and construction of object relations in space.
Receptive-Emergent-Expressive-Language Scale Anhinga-Press Route 2, Box 513 Tallahassee, FL 32301	Birth-36 months	Language Development	Primarily an interview scale, the REEL assesses the child's comprehension and expression of early language skills. The scale reveals any differences that may exist between the infant's CA and his combined receptive-expressive age.
Environmental Pre-Language Battery The Nisonger Clinic Ohio State University 1580 Cannon Drive Columbus, OH 43210	Early Language Development	Language Development	Designed for use by parents, paraprofessionals, and teachers in assessment of the child's comprehension, verbal and gestural imitation ability, and expression of one- and emerging two-word constructions.
Environmental Language Inventory The Nisonger Clinic Ohio State University 1580 Cannon Drive Columbus, OH 43210	One- and two-word utterance level	Language Development	Intensive assessment of the child's application of semantic grammatical rules in two- and three-word utterances. The child's expressive language is assessed in imitation, conversation, and play as he is provided with contextual and non-linguistic cues.
Inner Language Scale Child Study Center Peabody College Box 158 Nashville, TN 37203	Birth-24 months	Language Development	The way in which a child responds to objects and environmental stimuli is assessed on this scale, based on Piagetian theory.
Test for Auditory Comprehension	3-7 years	Language Development	Measures auditory comprehension of language structures and permits assignment of the child to

Instructional Planning for Exceptional Children

Selected Assessment Instruments (Cont.)

Learning Concepts 2501 W. Lamar Austin, TX 78705			a developmental level. Performance of items requires only a pointing response, and scales assess morphology, semantics, and syntax.
Fiorentino Reflex testing methods for evaluating CNS development, Springfield, IL: Charles C. Thomas	Reflex level-walking	Motor Development	Provides guidelines for looking at reflexive behaviors in children. Photographic examples are included within the text of normal and abnormal reflex development.
Cerebral Palsy Assessment Chart Semans, et al. *Physical Therapy*, 1965, 45, 463-468	Reflex level-walking	Motor Development	Chart from which the cerebral palsied child's postural control may be assessed for the purpose of rehabilitative planning. The level which should next be emphasized is indicated in the scale.
Fokes, Developmental Scale of Motor Abilities Stephens, W. B. *Training the Developmentally Young*, New York, N.Y. John Day, 1971	Birth-7 years	Motor Development	Provides height, weight, and characteristic behaviors of children of each level assessed. Assesses skills of upper and lower extremities, such as locomotion, climbing, jumping, balance, reach, grasp, release, manipulation, throwing, writing, and perceptual-motor abilities.
Peabody Developmental Motor Scales Monograph #25 IMRID Publications George Peabody College, Nashville, TN 37203	Birth-7 years Birth-6 years	Motor Development	An instrument for use in assessing gross and fine motor development. The scoring section allows the child credit for minimum success rather than a pass or failure. The scales are accompanied by developmental activities for each area assessed.
Adaptive Behavior Scales American Association on Mental Deficiency, 5201 Connecticut Ave NW Washington, DC 20015	Preschool-Adult	Social Development	Social scale standardized on mentally retarded children; divided into two sections: independent functioning and aberrant behavior. Criterion referenced checklist is most helpful in determining whether a child has coping skills to exist outside an institutional setting.

Selected Assessment Instrument (Cont.)

Lakeland Village Adaptive Behavior Grid Lakeland Village Medical Lake, WA 99022	Birth-16 years	Personal-Social	Allows the evaluator to derive developmental levels for areas such as eating, grooming, dressing, mobility, recreation, socialization and behavior control, all of which are task analyzed.
Maxfield Buchholz Scale of Social Maturity for Preschool Blind Children American Foundation for the Blind, Inc. 15 West 16th St. New York, N.Y. 10011	Birth-6 years	Social Development	Adaptation of the Vineland Social Maturity Scale for blind children. This scale of social development evaluates children in areas of general motor development, dressing, eating, locomotion, socialization, communication, and occupation.

home and school to facilitate change in the child's behavior (Keogh, 1972; Moran, 1976). If assessment data are to be translated into home and classroom programs, parents and teachers must be involved in the assessment process and in planning the individualized program.

Home-School-Team Feedback

At the conclusion of the assessment, the multidisciplinary team should report to parents regarding where their child is in comparison with other children of the same chronological age and with similar handicaps, and suggest which form of instruction would be most beneficial considering his state of readiness (Beller, 1970). Team members can report their observations of the child's attention span and performance under various conditions, the level of assistance he needs to succeed in learning skills, and the characteristics of instructional materials or methods to which the child most consistently attends. Parents can relate to the multidisciplinary team which reinforcers are most effective with their child, the people within the family constellation to whom the child is most responsive, and the environmental and material constraints of the home. Recommendations from the team are more meaningful to parents if team members formulating a practical teaching plan can relate availability of family time and materials to the plan.

Teachers of severely handicapped children frequently find their time, funds, and assistance within the classroom very limited. The teacher must share with the assessment team the general format and routine of the class, the daily schedule, time allotted for each child, materials available in the class, and the teaching style used. This information will assist the team in formulating recommendations that consider these restraints.

Setting objectives. A result of assessment using a process-oriented paradigm is the data from which one can draw when formulating goals and objectives. When the objectives are formulated by all responsible agents, they are likely to be personal and specific. The *objectives* are most functional when they describe the skills to be taught in the next six months; *goals* may be set for a longer period of time.

Developing implementation strategies. Following each objective, the program should note who should teach the task, the materials to be used, and the steps to follow in the instructional plan. Again, the extensive data available through the process-oriented model permits the examiner to incorporate all salient variables that are likely to produce success.

Designing the individualized program. The individualized program must be multifaceted, to include:

1. Concrete measurable data that can be used to compare the child's performance to a past or future performance or to a performance target.
2. The child's behavioral repertoire.
3. A detailed prescriptive program outlining goals and objectives for establishing behaviors.
4. A suggested teaching plan.
5. A projected timeline for accomplishing the objectives.

The plan indicates how each person or agency interacts with the child and delineates responsibilities. The plan allows for program changes as the caregiver sees the need but, at the same time, keeps others abreast of changes.

PARAMETERS OF IMPLEMENTATION

Assignment of Responsibilities

Implementation of the assessment data is as critical as gathering the data. Implementation concerns include how the information is conveyed to parents and agencies; agreement on goals, objectives, strategies, and evaluation; agreement on responsibilities; provisions for a feedback mechanism; and, ultimately, the responsibility of case management.

If rapport with parents has been well established and a trusting bond exists from the beginning of the assessment, conveying results to parents does not have to be a traumatic and shocking experience, but a time of synthesizing information and planning a course of action that permits parents to fulfill their natural role as teachers of their child. They can formulate their own role in the individualized plan and in doing so are more likely to fulfill their assignments.

Agencies having a role in the implementation of the assessment data should be participants in the planning of future strategies. They know their own responsibilities, their limitations and possibilities. Without their cooperation in planning the intervention, the assessment becomes another product, and the process terminates.

Tracking progress. The use of a tracking form for gathering implementation data has proven successful (DuBose, Langley, Bourgeault, & Harley, 1977). The form should meet the needs of the agencies and persons directly involved with the implementation. Measured progress on goals and objectives in the assessment report is reflected on the tracking form. The form offers an opportunity to redirect strategies as needed or set new goals and objectives. The case manager is responsible for determining when and how frequently the tracking form should be used (three to six months is usually sufficient). The value of information shared through tracking forms is that all agencies report their implementation progress in a concise, uniform manner that adds continuity to the assessment process.

Reassessment. Reassessments are scheduled when (a) data indicate the individual plan has been completed, (b) data indicate the plan needs numerous alterations, as the objectives are not being met and minor alterations were not sufficient to adjust the program to a workable level, (c) a time lapse of 12 to 18 months has occurred, or (d) major changes in the child's condition suggest needed change in the instructional program. Reassessment usually takes place within the same setting as the previous assessment so those familiar with the case can continue to participate in the process. Tracking forms are used to monitor progress, and the cycle continues. By using the process-oriented model, the child's needs are continually identified and prioritized; the environment's ability to respond to those needs is noted, and a carefully planned program is developed for bringing about changes that will facilitate learning in the child.

SUMMARY

Assessment of severely and profoundly handicapped persons cannot be a unilateral act culminating in a product filed away and used only for extracting data from which labels and classifications can be assigned. The authors advocate a dynamic process-oriented model that begins with problem identification, provides the means for including all relevant persons and data, and can be used to explore in depth the parameters of the behaviors of the person and of the milieu in which he lives. The model presented here provides specific plans and the procedures for implementing those plans, and culminates in follow-through to assure that targeted objectives are being accomplished.

REFERENCES

Alpern, G. D., & Boll, T. J. *The developmental profile.* Aspen, CO: Psychological Development Publication, 1972.

Altman, R., & Meyen, E. Public school programming for the severely/profoundly handicapped: Some researchable problems. *Education and Training of the Mentally Retarded*, 1976, *11*(1), 40-45.

Banus, B. S. *The developmental therapist: A prototype of the pediatric occupational therapist.* Thorofare, NJ: Charles B. Slack, 1974.

Barker, R. G. *Ecological psychology: Concepts and methods for studying the environment of human development.* Stanford, CA: Stanford University Press, 1968.

Bayley, N. *Bayley scales of infant development.* New York: The Psychological Corporation, 1969.

Beller, E. K. The concept readiness and several applications. *Reading Teacher*, 1970, *23*, 727-765.

Bortner, M., & Birch, H. C. Cognitive capacity and cognitive competency. *American Journal of Mental Deficiency*, 1970, *74*(6), 735-744.

Brown, L., Nietupski, J., & Hamre-Nietupski, S. Criterion of ultimate functioning. In M.A. Thomas, *Hey don't forget about me!* Reston, VA: Council for Exceptional Children, 1976.

Brown, L., & York, R. Developing programs for severely handicapped students: Teacher training and classroom instruction. *Focus on Exceptional Children*, 1974, *6*(2).

Bruner, J. S. Organization of early skilled action. *Child Development*, 1973, *44*, 1-11.

Budoff, M. Learning potential and educability among educable mentally retarded. (Progress report, Grant OEG-0-8-08056-4597 from National Institute of Education, HEW). Cambridge, MA: Research Institute for Educational Problems, 1973.

Carrow, E. Assessment of speech and language in children. In J. E. McLean, D. E. Voder, & R. L. Schiefelbusch (Eds.), *Language intervention with the retarded: Developmental strategies.* Baltimore, MD; University Park Press, 1972.

DuBose, R. F., & Langley, M. B. *The developmental activities screening inventory.* Boston: Teaching Resources, 1977.

DuBose, R. F., Langley, M. B., Bourgeault, S. E., & Harley, R. K. The model vision project: Assessment and programming for blind children with severely handicapping conditions. *Journal of Blindness and Visual Impairment*, 1977, *71*(2), 49-53.

Feurstein, R. A dynamic approach to the causation, prevention and alleviation of retarded performance. In H. C. Haywood (Ed.), *Social cultural aspects of mental retardation.* New York: Appleton Century Crofts, 1970.

Frankenberg, W. K., Fandal, A. W., & Dodds, J. B. *The Denver developmental screening test.* Denver, CO: University of Colorado Medical School, 1970.

Friedlander, B. Z. Notes on language: Screening and assessment of young children. In B. Z. Friedlander, G. M. Sterritt, & G. E. Kirk (Eds.), *Exceptional infant* (Vol. 3: Assessment and intervention). New York: Bruner/Mazel, 1975.

Gesell, A., & Amatruda, C. S. *Developmental diagnosis* (2nd ed.). New York: Paul B. Hoeber, 1947.

Haeussermann, E. *Developmental potential of preschool children.* New York: Grune & Stratton, Inc., 1958.

Haywood, H. C., Filler, J. W., Shiffman, M. A., & Chatellant, G. Behavior assessment in mental retardation. In P. McRaynolds (Ed.), *Advances in psychological assessment* (vol. 3), 1975.

Hunt, J. M. Psychological assessment in education and social class. In B. Z. Friedlander, G. M. Sterritt, & G. E. Kirk (Eds.), *Exceptional infant* (Vol. 3: Assessment and intervention). New York: Bruner/Mazel, 1975.

Jedrysek, E., Klapper, Z., Pope, L., & Wortis, J. *Psychoeducational evaluation of the preschool child: A manual utilizing the Haeussermann approach.* New York: Grune & Stratton, 1972.

Keogh, B. K. Psychological evaluation of exceptional children: Old hangups and new directions. *Journal of School Psychology*, 1972, *10*, 141-145.

Knobloch, H., & Pasamanick, B. *Gesell and Amatruda's developmental diagnosis* (3rd ed.) Hagerstown, MD: Harper & Row, 1974.

Knobloch, H., Pasamanick, B., & Sherard, E. S. A developmental screening inventory for infants. *Pediatrics*, 1966, *38* (part II), 1095-1104.

MacDonald, J. D. Environmental language intervention. In F. B. Winthrow & C. J. Mygren (Eds.), *Language, materials, curriculum management for the handicapped learner.* Columbus, OH: Charles Merrill, 1976.

Mann, P. N., & Suiter, P. *Handbook in diagnostic teaching: A learning disabilities approach.* Boston: Allyn & Bacon, 1974.

Meier, J. H. Screening, assessment, and intervention for young children at developmental risk. In B. Z. Friedlander, G. M. Sterritt, & G. E. Kirk, (Eds.), Exceptional infant (Vol. 3: Assessment and intervention). New York: Bruner/Mazel, 1975.

Meyen, E. *Preparing personnel for the severely and profoundly mentally retarded.* Paper presented at the Conference on Education of Severely and Profoundly Retarded Students, New Orleans, April, 1975.

Moran, M. R. The teacher's role in referral for testing and interpretation of reports. *Focus on Exceptional Children*, 1976, *8*, 1-16.

P.L. 94-142. An Act to amend the Education for all Handicapped Children Act to provide educational assistance to all handicapped children and for other purposes. Sec. 602 (4) (19).

Sailor, W., Guess, D., & Lavis, L. Training teachers for education of the severely handicapped. *Education and Training of the Mentally Retarded*, 1975, *10*, 201-203.

Schucman, H. *A study in the learning ability of the severely retarded; a method for obtaining a quantitative index of the educability for severely mentally retarded children.* Unpublished dissertation, New York University, 1957.

Sontag, E., Burke, P., & York, R. Considerations for serving the severely handicapped in the public schools. *Education and Training of the Mentally Retarded*, 1973, *8*, 20-26.

Sroufe, L. A., Waters, E., & Matas, L. Contextual determinants of infant affective response. In M. Lewis, & L. A. Rosenblum (Eds.), *The origins of fear.* New York: John Wiley, 1974.

Stutsman, R. *Merrill Palmer scale of mental tests.* Chicago: Stoelting Co., 1948.

Uzgiris, I. C., & Hunt, J. McV. *Assessment in infancy: Ordinal scales of psychoeducational development.* Urbana, IL: University of Illinois Press, 1975.

This article on the subject of nondiscriminatory testing provides an excellent review of concerns expressed in the literature, especially regarding minority children. The authors suggest four possible approaches to overcoming cultural bias. Encouragement is still held out for the development of nondiscriminatory tests, at the same time pointing out that tests are inherently built to discriminate between and among people. The goal, however, is to discriminate on variables of intelligence and achievement rather than culture.

Innovative use of adaptive behavior scales which do not appear to be discriminatory, as well as prescriptive teaching techniques which emphasize how a person learns, are offered as encouraging approaches. Alley and Foster also examine certain assessment devices used with the severely handicapped, and their apparent freedom from bias.

Nondiscriminatory Testing of Minority and Exceptional Children

Gordon Alley and Carol Foster, *University of Kansas*

"When is Washington's Birthday?" If you are of the majority culture, you probably would answer "February 22." This response would be scored correct according to the Wechsler Adult Intelligence Scale scoring criteria (Wechsler, 1955, p. 34). If, however, you were to respond "April 5," your response would be scored as incorrect, using that scoring criteria. The implication is that you must associate *George* rather than *Booker T.* with *Washington*. This item could be classified as culture-biased (example provided by Williams, 1974, p. 16).

In like manner, a visually handicapped child might be asked, "What should you do if you see a train approaching a broken track?" This handicapped child might have to reorient his or her learning strategy and problem solving skills to parallel those of a sighted group in giving a "correct" response such as, "Wave a handkerchief."

Nondiscriminatory Testing

These examples are not a condemnation of the Wechsler measures. Similar examples are found on most measures. The examples are representative of items that have caused at least one group of psychologists to advocate calling a moratorium on administration of conventional psychological tests to minority groups (Position Statement of the Association of Black Psychologists, adopted at a meeting of the Association in Washington, DC, August 1969).

Concurrent to this position statement, the judicial branch of the U.S. Government was hearing the *San Antonio Independent School District* v. *Rodriquez* case (1973). The ruling included an explicit statement that traditional assessment measures are unsatisfactory when used as a side measure to identify exceptional children who represent minority groups.

The Civil Rights Act of 1964, Title VI, require(s) that "there be no discrimination on the basis of race, color, or national origin in the operation of any programs benefiting from Federal financial assistance" (Memorandum for Chief State School Officers and Local School District Superintendents, DHEW, Washington, DC, August 1975, p. 1). Other legislation (Title IX of the Civil Rights Act, 1964 (1972); PL 93-380, which amended Part B of the Education of the Handicapped Act (PL 91-230) (1969); and PL 94-142 (Education for All Handicapped Children Act of 1975) followed.

Title IX of the Civil Rights Act requires that no program shall discriminate against a person because of sex. Overinclusion or underinclusion of children of either sex in any special program category can suggest noncompliance. In addition, using criteria or methods of referral, placement, or treatment which in effect discriminate because of sex also can constitute noncompliance.

Public Law 93-230 includes specific standards relating to testing and assessment. The following two standards are included as part of the requirements for state plans:

1. Failure to adopt and implement procedures to ensure that test materials and other assessment devices used to identify, classify, and place exceptional children are selected and administered in a manner which is nondiscriminatory in its impact on children of any race, color, national origin or sex. Such testing evaluation materials and procedures must be equally appropriate for children of all racial and ethnic groups being considered for placement in special education classes. In that regard procedures and tests must be used which measure and evaluate equally well all significant factors related to the learning process, including but not limited to consideration of sensorimotor, physical, sociocultural and intellectual development, as well as adaptive behavior. Adaptive behavior is the effectiveness or degree with which the individual meets the standards of personal independence and social responsibility expected of her or his age and cultural group. Accordingly, where present testing and evaluation materials and procedures have an adverse impact on members of a particular race, national origin, or sex, additional or substitute materials and procedures which do not have such an adverse impact must be employed before placing such children in a special education program.

Instructional Planning for Exceptional Children

2. Failure to assess individually each student's needs and assign her or him to a program designed to meet those individually identified needs (p. 3).

The most explicit standards to assure nondiscriminatory testing of exceptional children are included in the regulations provided for compliance of PL 94-142. Both the evaluation procedures and placement assessment are covered in these regulations:

121a532 Evaluation procedures.
State and local educational agencies shall insure, at a minimum, that:
  (a) Tests and other evaluation materials:
    (1) Are provided and administered in the child's native language or other mode of communication, unless it is clearly not feasible to do so;
    (2) Have been validated for the specific purpose which they are used; and
    (3) Are administered by trained personnel in conformance with the instructions provided by their producer;
  (b) Tests and other evaluation materials include those tailored to assess specific areas of educational need and not merely those which are designed to provide a single general intelligence quotient;
  (c) Tests are selected and administered so as best to insure that when a test is administered to a child with impaired sensory, manual, or speaking skills, the test results accurately reflect the child's aptitude or achievement level or whatever other factors the test purports to measure, rather than reflecting the child's impaired sensory, manual, or speaking skills (except where those skills are the factors which the test purports to measure);
  (d) No single procedure is used as the sole criterion for determining an appropriate program for a child, and
  (e) The evaluation is made by a multidisciplinary team or group of persons, including at least one teacher or other specialist with knowledge in the area of suspected disability.
  (f) The child is assessed in all areas related to the suspected disability, including where appropriate, health, vision, hearing, social and emotional status, general intelligence, academic performance, communicative status and motor abilities (*Federal Register*, August 23, 1977, pp. 42496-42497).

CURRENT APPROACHES TO NONDISCRIMINATORY TESTING

To evaluate the various alternatives which have been suggested to be nondiscriminatory, one initially must present specific criteria for such an evaluation. First, we offer the following definition of a nondiscriminatory measure to be used in our evaluative task:

A nondiscriminatory measure is one which results in similar performance distributions across cultural groups. These cultural groups may differ with respect to any or all of the following:

1. language/dialect
2. value system

3. information
4. learning strategies.

Regardless of the purpose of a test *or its validity for that purpose*, a test should result in distributions that are statistically equivalent across the groups tested in order for it to be considered nondiscriminatory for those groups. If different groups' performances result in different distributions, the test discriminates among groups.

For some variables, such as height and weight, the measures that have been used have been demonstrated to have such high validity, reliability, and little error in measurement that differences occurring among populations are considered *real* rather than flaws in the measurement device.

For other variables, especially psychological ones such as intelligence and achievement, the measures have had much lower validity, reliability, and fairly significant measurement error, resulting in less confidence. When minority groups produce performance distributions that vary from the majority group distribution, a strong tendency is to assume that the differences are in precision of the measurement and that these differences are not *real* between the groups. Because of the many problems in measuring intelligence and achievement, this seems to be a most parsimonious explanation.

If we accept that intelligence and achievement tests are discriminatory across various cultural groups, we must then ask, "How can we measure intelligence and achievement in all of those groups so that we are not discriminatory?"

Using the criteria described above, one can evaluate testing and assessment procedures that have been popular in their use as nondiscriminatory methods. Four popular procedures have been advocated; namely:

1. Translating traditional tests from the majority language directly to the minority language;
2. Norming traditional tests on specific groups of minorities;
3. Using a minority examiner to test minority children; and
4. Identifying majority group competencies required for minority group children to survive in the majority culture, then evaluating the minority child's achievement of these competencies, and, finally, teaching the child the unattained competencies.

All of these procedures appear satisfactory when given cursory attention. A critical evaluation of these procedures however, yields information that may discourage their use in approaching nondiscriminatory testing.

First, consider procedure 1, literally translating the Stanford-Binet, Raven, Peabody Picture Vocabulary Test, etc. into the native language of a minority group, say, Spanish-speaking children. This procedure appears to be a simple and efficient method of equating the language difference of majority group children with minority group children. In fact, PL 94-142 specifically states that this procedure meets one of the requirements of nondiscriminatory testing. But language differences are *not* equated by this procedure when one considers the complex language idioms, colloquialisms, words with multiple meanings, and words of similar but not identical meanings that characterize all languages.

Garcia (1976) provided an excellent example of problems associated with literal translation. On one test, a question in English contains the words, "hot dog." Thus term translated literally into Spanish means "a female dog in heat." The structure of the translated statement was changed to the extent that the children did not know how to respond to such a nonsensical statement. In addition to the above problem the translation procedure does not equate for the differing cultural information, learning strategies, and value systems when the test items are not changed to reflect these factors as they occur among the different groups.

Procedure 2 suggested to fulfill nondiscriminatory testing evaluation criteria appears more satisfactory. When normative data are available on children of a minority group, this permits better comparisons of one minority child's performance to the performance of other children of the same minority group. Several alternatives of this procedure have been suggested for use (Mercer, 1973; Thorndike, 1974; and Williams, 1974).

Thorndike (1974) stated that some test users consider a measure to be nondiscriminatory if there is no difference in mean scores and/or variability of two culturally different groups on a test, and/or if the regression equation developed on one cultural group neither overpredicts nor underpredicts another cultural group's performance on the test. He argues that difference in means and/or variance per se does not constitute discriminatory testing; rather, "one must examine the correlates of those differences" (p. 37). On one hand, if there is *no relationship* between a *criterion* variable (e.g., highest grade attended in school) and *predictor* variable (e.g., score on a test), one has no basis for judging the nondiscriminatory qualities of the measure. Conversely, if the relationship of the two variables is established, the test score is obviously discriminatory for the measure defined—i.e., low scores on test are related to highest grade attended.

Thorndike provides an excellent example of a discriminatory intelligence test. A situation exists in which only students obtaining IQ scores of 100 or above were selected for clerical positions; the test is obviously unfair to minority groups.

> . . . if it were found that, given certain conditions of adaptive and remedial instruction, a group of culturally deprived youngsters with a mean IQ of 85 (predictor) could be brought

to the same level of proficiency in a clerical position (criterion) that was displayed by an unselected sample with an IQ of 100 . . . (p. 40).

Thus, the group IQ score discriminates fairly between the two groups of youngsters, given no job training is provided. If job training is provided to the selected applicant(s), the group IQ score discriminates unfairly between the two groups of applicants.

Thorndike provides two definitions of nondiscriminatory use of tests. The first is appropriate to this discussion. It provides that both the majority group and the minority group have the same opportunity for selection to special services (criterion) as would be represented by the proportion of the group falling below critical score on the test of academic performance in the regular classroom (predictor). This definition can be implemented by setting a critical score on the achievement test (predictor) for the majority group, based on the percentage found to benefit from special services in the past (criterion). *Independently*, one must set a critical score on the achievement test for the minority group, based on the percentage found to benefit from special services in the past (criterion).

This procedure requires that one have specific information related to performances of the minority group on both the predictor variable (achievement test) *and* the criterion variable (beneficial effects of special services). This procedure, however, does not consider intraminority group differences. Garcia's (1976) statement is particularly relevant here:

> Make no assumptions about the bilingualism of Mexican-American or other linguistically-different students. *Some* may be fully literate in two languages. *Others* may speak only English (p. 2).[1]

Mercer (1973) has attempted to meet this criticism. She suggested the use of pluralistic norms for interpreting the meaning of a test score (e.g., IQ to predict mental retardation status). She stated that it is not possible to consider blacks or Mexican-Americans as homogeneous social categories or to ". . . hold sociocultural factors strictly constant by controlling only for ethnic group (p. 248)."

Pluralistic norms ". . . evaluate the . . . (performance) of a person only in relation to others from similar sociocultural backgrounds (p. 248).[2] She provided an excellent example of use of the pluralistic approach:

> . . . if he is a Mexican-American child and manages to achieve 75 on an intelligence test when he comes from an overcrowded, Spanish-speaking home in which the father has less than an eighth grade education and was reared in a rural area, and his mother does not expect him to finish high school, he would be diagnosed as having normal ability (p. 249).

---
[1] Italics added for emphasis.
[2] Information in parenthesis added by authors for contextual clarity.

With reference to the pluralistic approach, the reason this child is classified as normal and not to be considered for special education services is that he scored within one standard deviation of his sociocultural modality group. His low score on the intelligence test reflects his lack of opportunities rather than a general learning deficit. Mercer (1973) suggested that the pluralistic approach may be used with other minority groups. The only requirement is that the predictor test score is interpreted within the framework of each minority modal grouping. One also might note that ". . . nothing happens to anglo rates when pluralistic norms are applied" (p. 254).

This second procedure of obtaining pluralist normative data on children of minority groups, however, contains several severe limitations. Thorndike (1974) lists three limitations:

— relevancy
— reliability
— bias.

Relevancy, according to Thorndike in describing criterion variability which has been unaccounted for by the test, is only partially attained on tests of either prediction or criterion. For example, achievement test measures are not constructed to measure *all* aspects of school performance. Therefore, one can only guess whether the unmeasured aspects of school performance will enhance or handicap a minority child. In addition, no school achievement test accounts for 100 percent of the variance of actual school achievement. Even if the test accounts for 81 percent of the variance (r = .90), which is generally higher than typically occurs in practice, one cannot account for 20 percent of the variance. Thorndike aptly states, "It becomes impossible to be sure what adjustment in critical score, if any, is appropriate for minority group members" (p. 45) to yield a true measure of achievement. This same argument holds for majority group members.

If the measure is unreliable, one must make an estimate of the true criterion performance. Thorndike provides a rationale and statistical procedure to obtain an estimation of the true criterion difference based on means, standard deviations, and reliability coefficient of both the majority and minority groups to provide statistical fairness. One then must decide if this statistical fairness provides a socially fair test. Resolution has not been made to the satisfaction of the present authors.

Finally, "if the criterion measure is itself biased in an unknown direction or degree, no rational procedure can be set up for the 'fair' use of the test" (p. 44). That is, the criterion performance must mean the same thing to both majority and minority children. School success is a good example of criterion performances. To some children, in both the majority and minority groups, school success is not measured by academic performances (e.g. grade in automotive repair). For these children, a criterion test of only academic performance is biased and discriminatory to their value systems.

Williams (1974) provided the reader with the lead question of this article. He considered the response "George Washington" as a biased estimate of the black child's knowledge. Williams constructed the Black Intelligence Test Counterbalanced for Honkies (BITCH) (Williams, 1974). All items were obtained from black culture, and the test ". . . is biased in favor of black people (p. 16). He developed this measure to emphasize the need to revalidate conventional tests to responses of black persons on "white-oriented" tests (p. 17).

Alley (1976) provided a fourth limitation of the procedure of obtaining normative data on children of minority groups on conventional measures, stating that the procedure solidifies the status quo of minority children. Using Mercer's (1973) example of the Mexican-American child scoring an IQ of 75, Mercer interpreted this performance to be normal functioning for the sociocultural modality group of which he was a member; i.e., children from that particular sociocultural modality group or any other such group would "*always perform poorly* and that no attempt would be made to find the child's areas of strength or to search for defects in the test."

On the basis of the four criteria of equality, this second procedure tangentially considered the information of the minority group child from the majority group's standards (Mercer, 1973). It does not consider the child's value system as it relates to the criterion performance (Thorndike, 1974). This procedure also does not consider either the language structure of the items or the learning strategies of the minority children (Garcia, 1976).

Williams (1974) contends that ". . . there is a white psyche and a black psyche" (p. 17) and that "white psychiatrists, white psychologists, white social workers, and other white mental health workers cannot successfully treat the black psyche" (p. 18). The reason that white mental health persons cannot treat most black persons is that they do not understand what Williams calls "niggerosis"; i.e., being black, being called "nigger and being told you are unintelligent when you are intelligent." His solution is to train more black professionals to treat the black psyche. This contention and solution also are advocated by Garcia (1974) for bilingual children in his suggesting this third procedure to obtain nondiscriminatory test results. He recommends:

> Be skeptical about utilization of standard diagnostic instruments when used to identify the learning behaviors and capabilities of bilinguals. Instead, utilize bilingual clinicians to assist in the identification process (p. 3).

Most persons would agree that many white teachers and other white professionals associated with minority group children neither understand nor communicate well with these students or clients.

The solution of providing a minority group examiner to administer a test to a minority child, however, is simplistic. Three conditions have been overlooked by persons advocating this procedure. First, the attitudes of one person toward another may reflect social class differences to a greater extent than racial or ethnic differences. In Wagner (1972), Clark provides one reason not to use some minority group examiners to test minority group children:

> Many of today's scholars and teachers came from (culturally deprived)[3] backgrounds. Many of these same individuals, however, when confronted with students whose present social and economic predicament is not unlike their own past tend to react negatively to them, possibly to escape the painful memory of their own prior lower status (p. 131).

Wagner (1972) provides a second reason, characterizing some persons' attitudes as, in essence:

> "I came from a neighborhood like this, and I pulled myself up without all the help which is being provided you; you can pull yourself up too," and (then they) drive away to their suburban homes (p. 440).

The present writers believe that the key word of persons advocating this third procedure is *empathy*.

Third, is empathy enough? The authors would suggest that choice of examiner, whether the examiner represents any one of several sociocultural modality groups, racial or ethnic minorities, is not enough to assure nondiscriminatory testing. Excellent as this procedure may appear to be, the examiner must be provided with more than the conventional, culturally-biased tests. Even in the hands of the most competent and empathic examiner, regardless of his or her group membership, the minority child cannot display competence on these conventional tests. Thus, the third procedure will obtain nondiscriminatory results only if the selected minority examiner is provided with alternative measures that more appropriately evaluate the child's competence.

This third procedure *assists* in obtaining nondiscriminating testing if the examiner possesses similar language, value system, cultural information, and learning strategies as those of the child. If the examiner is to administer the *conventional* discriminatory tests, however, administration of the test will be frustrating to both examiner and child.

The fourth and final procedure to obtain nondiscriminatory testing is to identify and teach competencies required to survive in the majority culture. This procedure is analogous to teaching "cram courses to servicemen who were selected for duty in countries with a language and socioculture value systems different from their own." The courses did teach the servicemen minimal language competence, but generally did not consider the differences in value systems, cultural information, and learning strategies of the people.

---
[3]Information in parenthesis is added by author for contextual clarity.

The result was that these serviceman could ask some questions and minimally converse, but they required more experiences to become integrated into the sociocultural milieu of the country.

The experience of one of the present writers in Japan and Korea permitted him to witness the integration of some servicemen into these countries' sociocultural systems. Many of the servicemen who become integrated into the societies were neither completely knowledgeable of the country nor proficient in the country's language, but they shared common experiences with the people and did not permit cultural differences to alienate them from the people. This personal experience has been corroborated by reports from Peace Corps volunteers who reported sustaining friendships with persons, irrespective of language or sociocultural differences, when they shared experiences common to each other.

The point inherent in the above two reports is that the fourth procedure arbitrarily and explicitly places a higher value on the majority group's language and cultural information. Implicit to the procedure, but explicit to the child, is that the language, value system, cultural information, and learning strategies of the minority group are inferior. Stacker (1967) suggests that the result of this procedure on the Mexican-American student is ". . . that his culture is no good and therefore assumes that *he* is no good and grows up with this attitude, completely denying his own culture and value system" (p. 439). Coleman (in Wagner, 1966) reported that his committee found that parents stopped reinforcing the child's positive attitudes toward school as instruction content became irrelevant to the parents. Williams (1974) stated that the black child has had to leave both verbal and cultural skills outside the classroom because these skills are not rewarded in the middle-class classroom.

We have questioned the conventional use of nondiscriminatory or "fair" testing. Thorndike has stated that this conventional usage ". . . is based on predicted criterion performance (*survival in the majority sociocultural system is set by one who is almost always the test constructor*)[4] at some level or standard of predicted criterion performance as the requirement for acceptance, and would apply this *majority group* standard to both majority and minority groups (p. 43).

All four procedures to obtain nondiscriminatory testing have serious flaws inherent in their rationale and/or use. Two options remain: First, one could follow the lead of Williams and the Association of Black Psychologists in calling for a moratorium on conventional psychological tests until truly nondiscriminatory tests are available for use; or, second, one might seek innovations that may prove more productive in the search for nondiscriminatory tests and testing.

Messick and Anderson (1974) provide the consequences of choosing the

---

[4]Parenthesis are the authors.

first option. They suggest that examiners then would turn to subjective appraisals in which the likelihood of discrimination of minority groups inevitably would increase. A second consequence would be that data generally would be gathered unsystematically. A third consequence would be increased parochialism without benefit of regional or national norms. The three consequences are not of equal importance, in these authors' opinion, but the sum and substance of the results would suggest that one choose the second option.

ADVANCES IN NONDISCRIMINATORY TESTING

Recently, several innovative assessment procedures have yielded optimistic results that may have provided direction toward the development of nondiscriminatory tests and testing practices. These assessment procedures have sought to focus on the competencies of exceptional children rather than on their deficits, and appear to result in more equal performances of sociocultural subgroups of the majority and minority groups.

The first procedure is *clinical teaching* (Lerner, 1976). Clinical teaching does not tap what a child has learned, but rather provides experiences for children to actively involve themselves in problem solving. Budoff and Hutton (1972) provide the learning potential procedure to probe for competencies among minority group members who are considered to be exceptional. Budoff uses a testing measure that is less culturally-biased and language-oriented than traditional measures of problem solving—Raven's Progressive Matrices. He has found that some children viewed as poor problem solvers apparently have not profited from majority group cultural information. Using Raven's Progressive Matrices, 50 percent of those children scored at or above the average range when the task was changed to a less majority-biased learning format.

Even more dramatic, Budoff and Hutton found that if they provided only one hour of structured experiences in problem solving to children who initially scored low on the Raven's, 50 percent of these low performing children scored at the 50th percentile or above on the posttest given after this short training. The latter group, "gainers," overrepresented minority groups. Platt (1976) and Swanson (1976) found a similar result with learning disabled children. This is a major assessment breakthrough in the identification of exceptional children, particularly of exceptional children representing minority groups.

Working independently of Budoff, Flavell (1975) has been studying the learning strategies of preschool and primary grade children. He found that nonhandicapped children who could state strategies to retrieve information performed better at memory tasks than those who could verbalize no strategy to retrieve this information. Anderson (Anderson & Alley, 1977), using a similar approach with a problem solving discrimination task and using matched age mentally retarded and normally functioning children, found that the label of MR or nonhandicapped was not as important to success on this task as was the ability to verbalize a strategy to solve the problem. These findings suggest a second approach to assessing the competencies of exceptional children.

A third procedure that has been studied for a long time but has been given little practical attention by school psychologists, counselors, and teachers is the importance of the child's adaptive behavior. Adaptive behavior refers to the extent to which a child meets the cultural and societal demands in her or his environment (Mercer, 1973). Such activities as self-help skills, language, personal and social relationships, and vocational competencies are measured with academic competence. Using this broader base of information, one can judge the exceptional child's competencies in total living skills rather than only a narrow cognitive area (e.g., knowledge of fractions).

Nondiscriminatory Testing with the Severely/Profoundly Handicapped

If we examine the issue of discriminatory testing with regard to the severely and profoundly handicapped, we must ask if the individuals, when grouped according to cultural backgrounds, produce different distributions. To the authors' knowledge, this question has not been answered. On intelligence tests for the general population, few, if any, included severely handicapped individuals in their population for developing norms, and they measure grossly at the low end of the scale. Nevertheless, a high correlation ($r = .88$) exists between individuals being classified at various levels of intelligence tests and a clinical psychologist's classification of adaptive behavior (Leland, Nihira, Foster, Shellhaas, & Kagin, 1966). Therefore, although these tests may not make fine discriminations (at least if one accepts a clinical classification as a useful referent for validity), they do seem to be related to general functioning.

The question of whether they make these distinctions equally well independent of cultural background is still unclear. Mercer (1973) found that the tests had a heavy cultural bias when dealing with mildly retarded individuals. This discussion concludes with the authors' observation that this is an empirical question which has not been adequately approached, but that limited evidence seems to indicate that it is not seen as much of a problem.

Sailor and Horner (1976) examined the same issue with regard to tests designed specifically for the severely and profoundly handicapped. Their focus is on global educational assessment devices which can be used to assess individuals and describe their current skills and skill deficits. Older tests had the goal of determining how "retarded" an individual was but, with the change in emphasis to educational programs, the newer assessment tools were used more to prescribe the individual's educational prescriptive program.

The scales reviewed by Sailor and Horner include the Vineland Social Maturity Scale (Doll, 1947), the Cain-Levine Social Competency Scale (Cain, Levine, & Elzey, 1963), the AAMD Adaptive Behavior Scale (Nihira, Foster, Shellhaas, & Leland, 1974), the Balthazar Scales of Adaptive Behavior (Balthazar, 1971a, b, c, d; 1973), the Camelot Behavioral Checklist (Foster, 1974), the Portage Project Checklist (Shearer, Billingsley, Frohman, Hilliard, Johnson & Shearer, 1970), the Pennsylvania Training Model: Individual Assessment Guide (Somerton & Turner, 1975), the APT (Pennhurst Assessment/Program Tool, 1976), and the TARC System (Sailor & Mix, 1975). Many other assessment devices are aimed at this population, but these provide a good overview and will be used as the basis for this discussion.

One way in which most of these assessment devices differ from standardized intelligence tests is that they either consist of checklists or involve direct observation of individuals performing specific behaviors. The interest of the evaluator is in that behavior per se, and not in that behavior's theoretical relationship to some global characteristic for which it is assumed to be a measure, such as intelligence. Here, the emphasis is on identifying whether or not an individual has a certain skill. If she or he lacks that skill, it needs to be taught. If she or he possesses that skill, no further inference is necessary about intelligence or functioning level—the conclusion is merely that this skill does not have to be included in an educational program for this individual.

Assessment of procedures with severely handicapped individuals appears at first glance to be one area in which tests and evaluation instruments are relatively nondiscriminatory; i.e., one has little reason to assume that the effects of one cultural background versus another would produce deviations in the results of the tests large enough to be even noticeable, when compared to the differences that the tests measure which are consistent across almost all cultures. For instance, although cultures may differ widely on the techniques an individual uses to dress or feed her or himself, they all are in fairly close agreement that one should be able to dress or feed oneself.

Because most of the assessment instruments are geared more toward the grosser assessment of skills, variations in skills related to a specific cultural background are of little importance. Individuals across a wide variety of cultural backgrounds would be scored fairly similarly on assessment devices for the severely handicapped, and individuals who scored significantly lower on the devices generally would be considered to have major impairments, regardless of cultural backgrounds. For instance, if an individual has no expressive language and little receptive language, she or he would be considered impaired for adaptation to any culture. Also, little error would be found in diagnosing a deficit at this level, as opposed to assessing someone who has a fair amount of language skills embedded in a culture different from the one of the test or of the test giver.

One characteristic common to all these devices is that they assess over a large number of skills in many different domains. They almost all look at the following areas, at least: self-care, cognitive or academic, language, motor skills, and vocational. Because they examine an individual across such a broad base, and it is generally assumed that skill deficits will occur across all of them, if individuals are low on only one of these areas, they would be subjected to much more extensive assessment before a determination of diagnosis or program is made. This procedure is one of the safeguards against improper diagnosis and misuse of assessment instruments for the severely handicapped.

Another safeguard is that the responsible professionals typically do not depend upon one sample of the individual's performance which can be adversely affected by a large number of variables such as illness, medication, attitude, etc. Most of the devices (e.g., the Adaptive Behavior Scale, the Vineland, and the Camelot Behavioral Checklist) are scored by someone who knows the individual quite well, and who rates the individual's typical performance. Since these checklists and scales almost always refer to observable behaviors, scoring of them can be done fairly quickly and reliably (e.g., inter-observer reliability for the Adaptive Behavior Scale, pp. 71 to 92, for Part I which measures adaptive skills, and for the Camelot Behavioral Checklist, p. 93).

Even this assessment is seen as preliminary for checklists which are prescriptive instruments (e.g., the Portage Project Checklist, the Pennsylvania Training Model, and the Camelot Behavioral Checklist). After the checklist is completed, instructions are provided for determining what specific skill training programs the individual should have. The first step of the training is a preassessment which involves direct observation of the individual attempting to perform the task in question. If the individual demonstrates the skill, the next skill in the sequence is tested. This procedure continues until the pretest indicates that the individual cannot perform the task. A few checklists (the Balthazar Scales of Adaptive Behavior; the Pennhurst Assessment/Program Tool) utilize direct observation of the individual for completing the entire assessment. This can be done if one is interested in investing a great deal of time in assessment or if one assesses small segments of performance in detail.

One other emphasis of this area of assessment which frees it from being discriminatory is the degree to which most of the instruments avoid labels and static diagnoses. Instead, they emphasize assessment of specific skill deficits, which leads to a specific educational program to promote that skill. Here, the reason for assessment is strictly to determine what skills an individual requires

Instructional Planning for Exceptional Children

to adapt to the general demands of society, and then proceeds directly to teaching that skill.

In general, then, one can conclude that assessment procedures of severely handicapped individuals are not subject to discrimination on the basis of cultural biases because:

1. They assess behaviors which are generally similar across cultures;
2. They assess the individual in ways that are not influenced by specific temporary states of the individual;
3. They assess a wide range of skills, and individuals who have deficits in only one area would be treated differently from those who lack skills in all areas;
4. They emphasize prescriptive educational programs, sometimes to the exclusion of labels or diagnoses;
5. They depend on direct observation of the individual performing or failing to perform certain skills either during the assessment itself, or as a backup to initial assessment.

These factors combine to produce assessment instruments which are valid for the purpose of discriminating individuals who are severely handicapped from those who are not. Although some problem is presented in discriminating borderline cases, of course, this provides no basis for concluding that the devices are discriminatory along any cultural or ethnic basis.

One problem of these assessment instruments, however, relates to their relative inadequacy to determine specific handicaps which may affect habilitation programs. According to the Bureau of Education for the Handicapped, the term *severely handicapped* refers to:

From title 45 Public Welfare
   Chapter 1—Office of Education, Dept. of HEW
   Programs for the Education of the Handicapped
   Part 121—Definitions, General Provisions

Severely handicapped children are those who because of the intensity of their physical, mental, or emotional problems, or a combination of such problems, need educational, social, psychological, and medical services beyond those which are traditionally offered by regular or special educational programs, in order to maximize their full potential for useful and meaningful participation in society and for self-fulfillment.

(a) The term includes those children who are classified as seriously emotionally disturbed (including children who are schizophrenic or autistic), profoundly and severely mentally retarded, and those with two or more serious handicapping conditions, such as the mentally-retarded blind and the cerebral palsied deaf.

Severely handicapped children (1) may possess severe language and/or perceptual-cognitive deprivations, and evidence normal behaviors such as (i) Failure to respond to pronounced social stimuli, (ii) Self-mutilation, (iii) Self-stimulation, (iv) Manifestation of intense and prolonged temper tantrums, and (v) The absence of rudimentary forms of verbal control, and (2) many also have extremely fragile psychological conditions.

Because this definition is so broad, it encompasses many specific disabilities. Individuals applicable to this definition are all similar in that they have extensive skill deficits in many different areas, but an individual who is blind-deaf, is of normal intelligence, and has had a relatively poor education program may appear the same on the assessment instrument as an individual who has severe retardation and an orthopedic impairment. These two individuals may have identical assessment profiles, and may have the same skills targeted as their next educational goals. Nevertheless, they must be treated quite differently beyond this point. If they are both to be taught skills of self-feeding, one child may need equipment adapted for orthopedic impairments, and might be taught through modeling and verbal instructions; the other may be taught using regular eating utensils, with physical guidance being faded out. For these two individuals, similar results on prescriptive assessment devices should result in totally different programs.

The above example may seem purely academic since few professionals would train an individual who was obviously visually impaired and deaf the same way they would train a severely retarded orthopedically handicapped individual. Handicapping conditions, however, are not always obvious. Procedures for determining intelligence, blindness, deafness, range of motion, language skills, and so on among the severely impaired are not well validated. Procedures for audiometric evaluation of the severely retarded through operant techniques are fairly well standardized (Fulton, 1971), but they are used in few instances; and the technology for assessing other physical attributes (e.g., visual acuity) is still under development (Spellman & DeBriere, 1976).

The impact is that, although assessment devices for the severely impaired do not appear to be discriminatory on cultural or ethnic bases in describing the individual's current ability to adapt to society, they may result in all severely handicapped individuals' being treated in the same way. This may result in inappropriate training strategies or goals to be used if information on the associated handicaps is under development (Fulton, 1971; Spellman & DeBriere, 1976; Foster & Barnes, 1977), it does not appear to have had the same impact as that of assessment instruments used for prescriptive programming.

CONCLUSIONS

Tests are built to discriminate among individuals—If everyone scored exactly the same, the test would be useless for any purpose. Tests, however, should discriminate *only* along the variables they were designed to measure (e.g., intelligence, achievement), and not along other measures such as cultural background, sex, or value systems.

Although the use of nondiscriminatory test measures is characterized as being problem-wrought for the teacher/psychologist/administrator and the child being evaluated, some reasonable guidelines are suggested for application, along with a list of research questions which must be addressed so the problems do not remain the same or worsen in the future.

The authors make the following recommendations for individuals responsible for administration, interpretation, or decision making on the basis of test results.

Recommendations Related Specifically to PL 94-142 and Nondiscriminatory Testing

1. If one has reason to believe that a test may be discriminatory with a given child, use a large test battery and apply the best results in making any decision based on this testing. Do not make any decisions on the basis of one test alone. *This recommendation relates specifically to Section 121a 532(d).*
2. Validate the results of any evaluations by observations of behavior in natural settings. That is, if a child appears to be below norms on measures of intellectual functioning, does this appear to be substantial in all other situations? Does the child do better in some classes than could be expected from the test results? Are his or her social skills quite high? Is the child fairly competent in language skills, even though the language is dependent upon cultural background? If routine observation results in one's questioning results of the assessment, assessment results should be examined more closely before making decisions based on them. Also, certain alternative procedures, such as testing by a selected person representative of that minority culture, may prove useful. *This recommendation relates specifically to Section 121a 532(a).*
3. The IQ provides a general estimation of a child's performance. As such, this measure of global functioning has minimal relevance to instructional planning. Measures of specific educational domains are most relevant to educational planning and should be included in the assessment process; educational domains include academic, performance, vision, hearing, social and emotional status, and communication skills. Within each domain are major sub-domains. The *Federal Register* (November 29, 1976) suggests major subdomains to be assessed when identifying children with learning disabilities; namely:
— Verbal (oral) expression;
— Listening comprehension;
— Written expression;
— Basic reading skills;

— Reading comprehension;
— Mathematics calculation;
— Mathematics reasoning; and
— Spelling.

This recommendation is Specifically related to Section 121a 532(b) and (f).

4. In evaluating a child with a suspected disability, PL 94-142 (Section 121a 532(e)) *requires* the use of a multidisciplinary team or group, which must *include* either a teacher or *specialist* with knowledge in the area of the suspected disability. The authors recommend this group process with several reservations. A group is superior to an individual when accomplishing intellectual tasks (Davis, 1969). This superiority is based upon the group providing a higher frequency of judgments, more opportunities to correct errors, and a greater chance for one of the group members to possess the skills to solve a complicated task. PL 94-142 has contributed to a high probability of group success by stating that the composition must include a specialist (Middlebrook, 1974). But several reservations are in order:

   a. The group may subject members to intense social pressure to conform and subvert individual efforts—i.e., "group-think" (Janis, 1972), "risky shift phenomenon" (Tubbs & Moss, 1974), and group cohesiveness.
   b. The task may require a sophisticated and high degree of coordination and organization. If so, an individual may be more effective than a group.
   c. The specialist or member who is highly talented in identification of the suspected disability may be more effective individually in making evaluation judgments than would be a group not containing a highly gifted member making similar judgments (Middlebrook, 1974).

5. An agenda assists in increasing the effectiveness of the assessment team. Tubbs and Moss (1974) describe the *Single Question Form* as an agenda which seems to best meet the spirit of agenda of PL 94-142. It is:

   a. What is the single question, of which the answer is the only thing the group must know to accomplish its purpose?
   b. What subquestions must be answered before we can answer the single question we have formulated?
   c. Do we have sufficient information to answer confidently the subquestions? (If yes, answer them; if not, continue below.)
   d. What are the most reasonable answers to the subquestions?

Instructional Planning for Exceptional Children

e. Assuming that our answers to the subquestions are correct, what is the best solution to the problem? (Larson, 1969, p. 453).

Recommendations Related to Nondiscriminatory Testing

1. Examine placement recommendations of decisions for biases. Administrators of programs should examine their placement records. If the records indicate that individuals placed appear to be predominantly from certain cultural, ethnic, or sex groups, procedures for determining those placements should be examined carefully for cultural biases, and should be changed if biases are discovered.

   If the assessment procedures appear to follow the best guidelines but biases still appear to exist, perhaps other possible causes should be examined. Are the individuals responsible for actually acting on the placement recommendations arranging for placement of some children before others? Are some children recommended for returning to regular classes at a higher rate than others? If one can find no bases for bias in placement after careful search, one at least will have examined the situation thoroughly and be able to justify the existing placement procedures.

   Additionally, teachers may wish to examine the records for their own history of referring individuals for special class placement. If they had referred a statistically higher percentage of minority students, they perhaps should try to determine the basis upon which these recommendations were made.

2. Use test items that reflect the content of the curriculum. If the tests being used predict the probability that individual students will be able to succeed in school, one should determine if those tests are truly related to success. Although this is generally a research issue to be addressed in other situations, one can grossly determine such a relationship by face validity.

   For instance, if attempting to predict probability of success for an individual's completing a vocational education program, using a test which has been validated for predicting success of individuals in college preparatory programs, such a test probably is not useful for the first purpose. The style and content of test items for the two predictions probably would be quite different. If one suspects from examining a test that it is invalid for a particular purpose, one should check the manual to determine if the test has been used before for the current intended purpose. If data are unavailable, assume that the measure probably is not appropriate.

3. Results of an assessment battery should yield measures of both

standardized and optional performance, and should indicate both competencies and lack of competencies. Many tests do not measure students' behavior under the best circumstances; this factor needs to be considered, and followed by any modifications needed. Results of the assessment should indicate not only what diagnosis is most appropriate, but also the individual strengths, discrepancies between standardized and optimal performance that may be important, areas of growth that should be targeted, etc.

4. Realize that a test samples only a small part of the child's behavioral repertoire. On any given behavior tested, one is measuring a small part of the child's total behavior. Thus, one is drawing inferences about the child's total condition on the basis of a small part, and this can lead to gross errors. The smaller the item sampling, the more likely there is item bias.

5. Motivational factors may affect a child's scores adversely, but inflating children's test performance through motivational factors is unlikely. Behaviors can be prompted, and the scores inflated, but motivation will be due to consequent events. A child's scores, however, may be much lower, because of motivation, than that of which she or he is capable. Therefore, motivation does need to be taken into account in interpreting test results adequately. If extrinsic reinforcers are used in a testing situation of standardized tests, however, they may well affect the results, since testing conditions were not standard.

6. Periodically evaluate your own empathy toward minority vs. majority groups. If you have either strongly positive or negative bias toward some group, you would do well to question your test results, or possibly check them with other testors.

7. If errors occur in placement decisions, they should be in the direction of least-restrictive placement. That is, if questionable or borderline cases arise, decisions should be made toward regular school class placement, followed by frequent monitoring to ensure that the placement is not affecting the child adversely. Additionally, children placed in special education classes should receive continuous monitoring, to be able to recognize sufficient improvement allowing for placement in a less restrictive class.

8. Make explicit criteria for placement in special classes, and evaluate how good these criteria are for making decisions.

9. One way to resolve the dilemma of minority children appearing to perform poorly on standardized tests is to set up new norms that would allow a child's raw score on the test to be translated to an appropriate IQ score with a mean of 100 and the same standard deviation as the majority form of the test. In this way, a child scoring

75 on majority norms would achieve an IQ of 100 on the norms for the minority group represented by that child *if* the performance represents normal functioning for a child in that sociocultural modality group. Using this system, the norms would be set up differently for each minority group in the same way that they currently are set up for children of different ages and sexes.

This procedure, however, does not provide for analysis of defects in the test nor does it provide the opportunity for minority children to demonstrate excellence in abilities, information, and problem solving strategies that may be stressed within their sociocultural group but not in the majority's.

RECOMMENDATIONS FOR FUTURE RESEARCH

The above recommendations for practitioners are intended as usable guidelines which can be followed until researchers approach the necessary questions systematically. After a solid data base has been developed on nondiscriminatory testing, the recommendations proposed here can be examined in light of the new data, and be accepted, modified, or rejected. Until those data are available, the authors hope the suggestions in this article will be helpful to those who are faced with immediate problems in educational assessment.

To facilitate development and implementation of the necessary research efforts, the authors have developed sampling questions that need to be addressed, and further suggest that the field would be enhanced greatly if these questions were addressed systematically by some group or agency. This research project could be a useful funding priority for the Bureau of Education for the Handicapped, Office of Education.

The research questions which seem essential to development of effective nondiscriminatory testing are:

1. What minimum common skills are necessary for survival in both majority and minority cultures, and how can these skills be measured? If these skills can be determined, can they beneficially be used as a predictor of the need for special education services?
2. How reliable are existing tests that have been developed or modified from older tests when they are used as suggested? If the tests are reliable, how valid are they for the intended purposes?
3. How are the norms of existing tests affected when these tests are restandardized on other minority cultures, or on the current majority culture? What validity do these tests have for predicting certain educational outcomes (such as failure in regular classes, but success with special services)?

4. What is the effect of using minority examiners on test results when controls for empathy and testing procedures are introduced? Do they affect the interpretation of results? Of overall norms?
5. What performance standards are most appropriate with various tests, including criterion-referenced measures?
6. Are there theoretically-oriented differences between cultures that affect test results? (For example, do all cultures progress through the same development sequence? Would a Piagetian developmental test be equally appropriate for all cultures?)
7. What is the efficiency of PL 94-142 on nondiscriminatory placement and testing?

These questions represent a small part of what must develop into a major effort before nondiscriminatory testing becomes a reality. The authors hope that this effort is imminent.

REFERENCES

Alley, G. R. *Methods of assessing the performances of exceptional children who represent minority groups.* Paper presented at Regional Problems of Exceptional Children Meeting, Regional USEO and GAC, Kansas City, MO, June 1976.

Anderson, J. E., & Alley, G. R. *A comparative study between educably mentally retarded and nonhandicapped children on visual-motor tasks and metamemory self-report performances.* Manuscript submitted for publication, 1977.

Balthazar, E. E. *Balthazar scales of adaptive behavior, Part 1: Handbook for the professional supervisor.* Champaign, IL: Research Press Co., 1971. (a)

Balthazar, E. E. *Balthazar scales of adaptive behavior, Part 2: Handbook for the rater technician.* Champaign, IL: Research Press Co., 1971. (b)

Balthazar, E. E. *Balthazar scales of adaptive behavior, Part 3: The scales of functional independence.* Champaign, IL: Research Press Co., 1971. (c)

Balthazar, E. E. *Balthazar scales of adaptive behavior, Part 4: Workshop and training manual.* Champaign, IL: Research Press Co., 1971. (d)

Balthazar, E. E. *Balthazar scales of adaptive behavior II: Scales of social adaptation.* Palo Alto, CA: Consulting Psychologists Press, 1973.

Budoff, M., & Hutton, L. The development of a learning potential measure based on Raven's Progressive Matrices. *Studies in Learning Potential,* 1972, *1* (18).

Cain, L. F., Levine, S., & Elzey, F. F. *Manual for the Cain-Levine social competency scale.* Palo Alto, CA: Consulting Psychologists Press, 1963.

Davis, J. *Group performance.* Reading, MA: Addison-Wesley, 1969.

Doll, E. A. *Vineland social maturity scale–Manual of directions.* Minneapolis: American Guidance Service, Inc., 1947.

Flavell, J. H. Developmental studies of mediated memory. In L. P. Lipsitt & H. Reese (Eds.), *Advances in child development and behavior* (Vol. 5). New York: Academic Press, 1970.

Foster, R. W. *Camelot behavioral checklist manual.* Parsons, KS: Camelot Behavioral Systems, 1974.

Foster, R. W., & Barnes, K. *Range of motion checklist.* Unpublished assessment instrument, 1977. (Available from Ray Foster Project LGARN, Kansas Neurological Institute, 3107 West 21st Street, Topeka, KS 66604).

Fulton, R. T., & Spradlin, J. E. Operant audiometry with severely retarded children. *Audiology,* 1971, *10,* 203-211.

Garcia, R. L. *Unique characteristics of exceptional bilingual students.* Paper presented at regional meeting of USOE and GAC, Kansas City, MO, June 9, 1976.

Janis, I. Groupthink. *Psychology Today*, 1971, 5. 43-46, 74-76.

Larson, C. Forms of analysis and small group problem solving. *Speech Monographs*, 1969, 36, 452-455.

Leland, H., Nihira, K., Foster, R., Shellhaas, M., & Kagin, E. Conference on Measurement of Adaptive Behavior: II. Parsons, KS: Parsons State Hospital and Training Center, 1966. (Monograph)

Lerner, J. W. *Children with learning disabilities: Theories, diagnosis, teaching strategies* (2nd ed.). Boston: Houghton Mifflin Co., 1976.

Mercer, J. R. *Labeling the mentally retarded.* Berkeley, CA: University of California Press, 1973.

Messick, S., & Anderson, S. 2. Educational testing, individual development and social responsibility. In R. W. Tyler & R. M. Wolf, *Crucial issues in testing.* Berkeley, CA: McCutchan Publishing, 1974, pp. 21-34.

Middlebrook, P. N. *Social psychology and modern life.* New York: Alfred A. Knopf, 1974.

Nihira, K., Foster, R., Shellhaas, M., & Leland, H. *AAMD adaptive behavior scale manual.* Washington, DC: American Association of Mental Deficiency, 1974.

Platt, J. S. *The effect of the modified Raven's Progressive Matrices Learning Potential Coaching Procedure on Raven's posttest scores and their correlation value with productive variables of learning disabilities.* Unpublished doctoral dissertation, University of Kansas, 1976.

Sailor, W., & Horner, R. D. Educational assessment strategies for the severely handicapped. In N. G. Haring & L. J. Brown (Eds.), *Teaching the severely handicapped* (Vol. 1). New York: Grune & Stratton, 1976.

Sailor, W., & Mix, F. J. *The TARC assessment system* (user's manual). Lawrence, KS: H & H Enterprises, 1975.

San Antonio Independent School District v. Rodriquez. 410 U.S., 93 S. Ct. 1278, 36 L. Ed. 2d 16 (1973).

Shearer, D., Billingsley, J., Frohman, A., Hilliard, J., Johnson, F., & Shearer, M. *The Portage guide to early education: Instructions and checklist* (Experimental ed.). Portage, WI: Cooperative Educational Service Agency No. 12, 1970.

Somerton, E., & Turner, K. *Pennsylvania training model: Individual assessment guide.* King of Prussia, PA: Regional Resources Center of Eastern Pennsylvania for Special Education, 1975.

Spellman, C. R., & DeBriere, T. *Research and development of subjective visual acuity assessment procedures of severely handicapped persons* (BEH Grant No. G0076 02 592). Parsons, KS: Parsons State Hospital and Training Center, 1976.

Stacker, J. Se habla Espanol. *American Education*, May, 1967, 17-18.

Swanson, J. E. *Learning potential as a predictor of behavioral changes in learning disabled elementary students.* Unpublished Master's thesis, University of Kansas, 1976.

Thorndike, R. L. 3. Concepts of culture-fairness. In R. W. Tyler & R. M. Wolf, *Crucial issues in testing.* Berkeley, CA: McCutchan Publishing, 1974, pp. 35-45.

Tubbs, S. L., & Moss, S. *Human communication: An interpersonal perspective.* New York: Random House, 1974.

Wagner, H. Attitudes toward and of disadvantaged students. *Adolescence*, 7 (28), 1972, 435-446.

Wechsler, D. Manual for the Wechsler Adult Intelligence Scale. New York: Psychological Corp., 1955.

Williams, R. I. 1. Black pride, academic relevance and individual achievement. In R. W. Tyler & R. M. Wolf, *Crucial issues in testing.* Berkeley, CA: McCutchan Publishing, 1974, pp. 13-20.

Probably the most common instructional problem presented by handicapped children relates to the skill of reading. Blake presents a straightforward discussion of problems related to testing reading achievement among handicapped children. In the process, she differentiates between norm-referenced and criterion-referenced measures and speaks to the discriminatory factors which frequently enter into the evaluation process. The selection does not present an extensive discussion of reading skills; rather, it addresses the teacher's role in the assessment process. Reading teachers, particularly, will find this selection helpful in improving their attempts to individualize instruction through the collection of meaningful, usable evaluation data.

Testing the Reading Achievement of Exceptional Learners

Kathryn Blake, *University of Georgia*

The term *testing* sometimes has been used to refer to the actual administering of instruments, with *assessment* or *evaluation* referring to the problem solving process. The author, however, uses *testing* to denote the entire process of collecting evidence and using that evidence in creative problem solving, specifically, to reach the decisions necessary for the student's individual education plan. In this context, the challenge is to decide how best to teach reading to exceptional learners. *Approaches to this challenge must be creative because there is no single answer— each student requires different solutions.* The task, then, is to discover the best possible solution for each learner.

We may consider four steps in creative problem solving:

1. Generating questions;
2. Collecting evidence to answer the questions;

115

Instructional Planning for Exceptional Children

3. Assuring that the evidence is accurate and nondiscriminatory; and
4. Answering the questions and making decisions.

GENERATING QUESTIONS

Decisions in teaching reading pertain to identifying the scope and sequence of reading instruction, actually teaching the reading, and managing reading instruction (Blake, 1974). Additionally, we may wish to identify a pupil's position in a norm group for reading achievement (Blake, 1976).

Questions In Identifying the Scope and Sequence of Reading Instruction

Scope refers to what reading skills we teach. *Sequence* refers to the order in which we teach those skills. A layout of particular reading skills in a particular order—*a scope and sequence chart*—can be obtained from publishers of reading materials, or a person can develop one; either way, one must decide the scope and sequence appropriate for the students being taught. To make this decision, one must answer the following questions:

1. *Scope*: What reading skills should be taught?
   — What reading skills does the student need to get along in society?
   — What reading skills is the student potentially able to learn?
   — What reading skills should a student learn in preparation for learning more complex skills?
2. *Sequence*: In what order should the reading skills be taught?
   — How should the skills be arranged for presentation within a given category of skills (e.g., phonics)?
   — How should the skills be arranged for presentation across categories of reading skills (e.g., phonics, structural analysis, literal comprehension, interpretation)?

Norm-referenced intelligence tests can be used to gather evidence in determining what reading skills the student potentially is able to learn; task analyses provide evidence to answer the remaining questions.

Questions In Teaching Reading

Figure 1 gives three steps in the teaching process: Step 1 deals with *what* instructional objectives (or content) should be taught; Step 2, with *how* the instructional objectives are taught (methods and materials); and Step 3, with *how long* an instructional objective is taught (pacing).

Figure 1
Steps in the Teaching Process

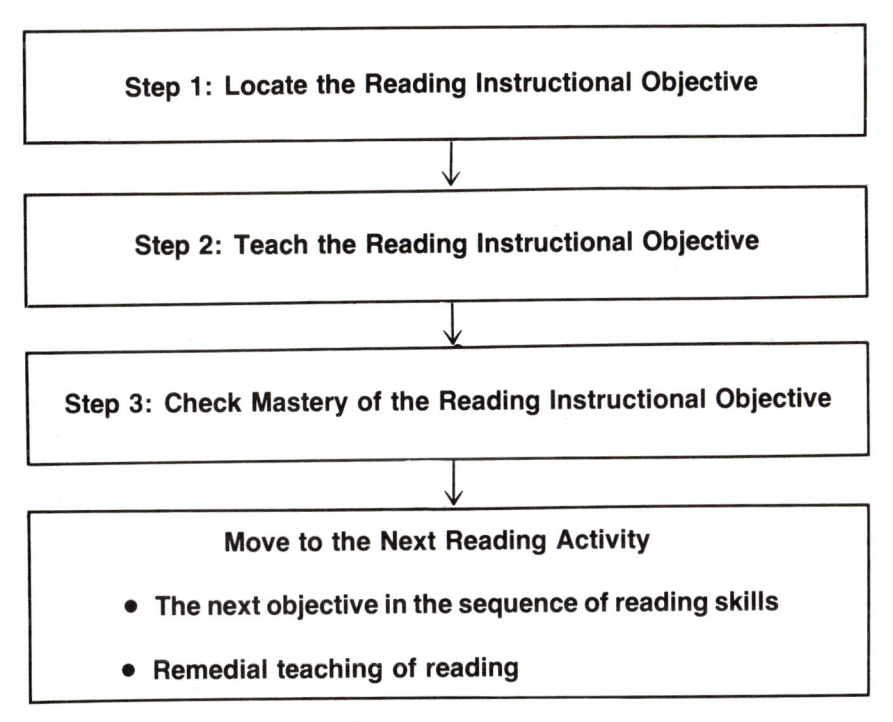

Step 1: Locate the Reading Instructional Objective

↓

Step 2: Teach the Reading Instructional Objective

↓

Step 3: Check Mastery of the Reading Instructional Objective

↓

Move to the Next Reading Activity

- **The next objective in the sequence of reading skills**
- **Remedial teaching of reading**

Step 1–Locate the Reading Instructional Objective

The leading question is: *What reading instructional objectives should the student be taught to master?*

— What are the possible reading skills the student can work on?
— What skills on the reading scope and sequence chart has the pupil mastered? What skills remain to be learned?

The scope and sequence chart used for reading instruction provides information to answer the first question. The second should first be addressed by consulting the pupil's cumulative educational record, to be able to make judgments on what skills the pupil has under firm control and also to project the skills not learned. A second source of information is the criterion-referenced test (discussed in more detail under the heading "Types of Tests"), keyed to the instructional objectives sought; this information, combined with and checked against inferences based on the pupil's educational history, should lead to answers concerning the skills learned and not learned.

Instructional Planning for Exceptional Children

Step 2—Teach the Reading Instructional Objective

This teaching consists of two parts: providing direct instruction to the student; and having the student engage in independent practice. The leading question is: *What reading methods and materials are most appropriate for a particular reading instructional objective and a particular student?* To answer the first part of the question, one must examine methods and materials with the following questions in mind:

— Do the methods and materials address the content behavior specified in the instructional objective?
— Is the information conveyed to the pupil accurate?
— Are the methods and materials easy to use?
— Do the methods and materials have a reasonable cost?
— Do the instructional materials have a clear, open format?
— Do I (the teacher) like the instructional materials?

Information to answer all these questions comes from the materials themselves, and from the publishers' catalogs.

Given a set of instructional methods and materials appropriate for the objective, which ones, then, are appropriate for the student? One should ask:

— Does the student have handicaps that could interfere with using the methods and materials?
— Will the pupil like the methods and materials?

Observation is the primary source of information and, secondarily, reports by physicians, audiologists, speech clinicians, and tests assessing special abilities. Physical handicaps, visual deficiencies, hearing impairments, speech and language disabilities are the most obvious areas of search, but handicaps also may be manifested in special abilities like perception, visual sequencing, and conceptualization, and in distractibility, or handicaps in focusing attention on something for a sustained period. As to whether or not the pupil will like the methods and materials, information will derive from the teacher's acquiring knowledge about the pupil's interests.

After determining the methods and materials appropriate for a particular student, one needs to ask:

— How many sets are needed to give the student the number of repetitions of direct instruction and independent practice necessary to master the instructional objective?

Two sources offer information about how fast the pupil learns: norm-referenced intelligence tests, and criterion-referenced reading achievement tests keyed to the instructional objective. The first allows one to make "guesses" and the second verifies if the guesses are correct. (These are the tests used in the following step.)

Step 3—Check Mastery of the Reading Instructional Objective

After the student has been taught—received direct instruction and independent practice with the methods and materials—the teacher assesses how well the student has benefited from instruction and if the skill is mastered. The leading question is: *Has the pupil reached criterion for mastery in the instructional objective?* A criterion-referenced test keyed to the instructional objective provides information to answer this question.

Finally, the teacher must decide what to do about the next reading activity. If the student has reached mastery, he or she should move on to the next instructional objective in the reading scope and sequence chart, and the three-step process outlined in Figure 1 is repeated with the next instructional objective. If the pupil has not reached mastery, the teacher undertakes to find out *why*. This requires remedial teaching of reading.

Questions In Managing Reading Instruction

These questions pertain to the organization of students and teachers and the deployment of space, furniture, materials, equipment, and other facilities. Deciding how to organize students and teachers essentially requires answers to the questions of who works with whom at what times. More specifically:

— What pupils are working on the same instructional objectives? Can these pupils be taught as a group?

— What pupils are working on instructional objectives that no one else is working on? Can these pupils be tutored individually?

— At what time during the school day do I (the teacher) work with each group and with each individual?

— Do I need a helper (e.g., a teacher aide or a peer tutor) to supervise some pupils' independent practice while I provide direct instruction to other pupils?

— Do I need to work with a team teacher (e.g., a resource teacher) to give the pupil direct instruction? That is, do the instructional objectives the pupil is working on differ so much from those that other pupils are working on that I do not have time to give all the instruction needed? Does the pupil have problems that I do not have the expertise to deal with?

Instructional Planning for Exceptional Children

Criterion-referenced tests keyed to the instructional objectives lead to answers to the first two questions. The last three questions can be answered on the basis of the number of groups and individuals to be worked with and the time available for reading instruction.

Space, furniture, materials, equipment, and other facilities should be organized to most effectively accommodate the unique needs of pupils and teachers. For example, independent learning centers might be established if a lot of individual work is appropriate; a reduced stimulation area might be most appropriate for the peer instruction of a distractible pupil.

Questions In Identifying the Pupil's Position in a Norm Group

So far, the questions have pertained to a pupil's attainment of particular reading instructional objectives considered appropriate to teach. In addition one might ask: How well does the pupil achieve in reading in relation to other pupils of the same chronological age? This might refer to the others in the pupil's class, school, school system, or state—generally called *local norms*. Other pupils of the same chronological age in the entire Unites States are referred to as *national norms*. Information about local and national norms is used in classifying exceptional students in those areas where deficits in adaptive behavior are one criterion for categorizing diagnostic groups (e.g., in the AAMD system for classifying pupils as mentally retarded). Norm-referenced tests are used to derive information about the pupil's position in a norm group.

COLLECTING EVIDENCE

Types of Tests

Both criterion-referenced tests and norm-referenced tests are used to gather evidence to answer questions about teaching, management, and the student's position in a norm group for reading.

Criterion-Referenced Tests

To reiterate, criterion-referenced tests are used to gather evidence for these questions:

— What skills on the reading scope and sequence chart has the student mastered?
— Given reading instructional methods and materials appropriate for

the pupil, how many sets do we need to give him or her the number of repetitions of direct instruction and independent practice necessary to master the instructional objective?
— Has the student reached the criterion for mastery in the instructional objective?
— What students are working on the same instructional objectives? Can these pupils be taught as a group?
— What students are working on instructional objectives that no one else is working on? Can these pupils be tutored individually?

A criterion-referenced test is designed so that a pupil's test responses are expressed in relation to the instructional or therapeutic objectives for an area being tested. Instructional objectives contain, or are accompanied by, a statement of content and behavior and a criterion for mastery. For example, an instructional objective for one reading skill can be expressed this way:

| The pupil will differentiate between facts and opinions in argumentative discourse. | Given 10 paragraphs written in the argumentative mode, some containing fact and some containing opinion, the pupil will identify which components are facts and which are opinions, with 90% accuracy. |

If the pupil performs nine items correctly, he or she is considered to have mastered the objective; if seven items are performed correctly, the student has not reached mastery. *Criterion-referenced tests do not make reference to how well other pupils have performed*; the emphasis is on the pupil's status vis a vis an instructional objective.

Informal test often is used synonymously with *criteron-referenced test*. This usage developed before psychometric theory had advanced to the point of including criterion-referenced tests. Generally, a *formal test*, in contrast, was equated with standardization groups and standard procedures for administration, scoring, and interpretation.

Norm-Referenced Tests

In summary, norm-referenced tests are used to answer the following questions:

— What reading skills is the pupil potentially able to learn?
— Given reading instructional methods and materials appropriate for the pupil, how many sets do we need to give the number of repetitions of direct instruction and independent practice necessary to master the instructional objective?
— How well does the student achieve in relation to other students of the same chronological age? (Local norms? National norms?)

Instructional Planning for Exceptional Children

In a norm-referenced test, a pupil's responses are expressed in relation to a group's performance. (*Norm* comes from the word *normal*.) It is a standard of performance that shows the normal or average response of pupils in a group defined in a certain way. A norm group defined by chronological age is termed an age norm; by school grade, a grade norm.

For example, suppose a student's test performance leads to a grade placement score of 4.2 on the reading portion of a grade norm instrument such as the *Metropolitan Achievement Tests*. The score is interpreted to mean that the student is reading at a level attained by pupils in the norm group at the second month of the fourth grade.

Norm-referenced tests do not make reference to how well the pupil has mastered given content; the emphasis is on the pupil's status vis a vis a norm group. Norm groups sometimes are called standardization groups—groups with a particular status or characteristics that can influence performance on the test; e.g., chronological age, brightness, socioeconomic background, educational background, etc. Norms usually are based on samples of students from throughout the country; in addition, for most tests, norms can be set up for a state, a school district, a school, or a class. The procedure is to define the characteristics of a group, administer tests, figure average levels of performance, and express these averages as scores.

Most test authors try to norm their tests on a cross-section of the population. The more the norm group represents the total population, the more widely the test results can be generalized; in other words, the more individuals the pupil can be compared to.

Constructing Tests

Constructing a Single Criterion-Referenced Test

Constructing a criterion-referenced test is straightforward. Two basic procedures are involved: designing the test, or planning its contents and structure; and preparing the test, or getting it ready to use with students.

Designing the Test. The three essential components of design are: specifying the instructional objective, developing the test, and checking to see if it is accurate for the intended use.

1. Specify the instructional objective the test is to measure. Accompany this objective with a statement of the criterion behavior, including:
    a. The behavior the pupil should show;
    b. The level of mastery he or she should reach;
    c. The content involved; and
    d. The given conditions under which the student should show the behavior.

2. Develop the test.
   a. Write test items that sample *behavior* specified in the instructional objective; for example:
      The pupil will supply . . .
      The pupil will recognize . . .
      The pupil will choose . . . (among options).
      Be sure the test samples the behavior it is intended to sample. For testing pupils' recognition of sounds in words, for example, the test cannot have real words because pupils may read them by sight; instead, use made-up words.
   b. Write test items that sample the *content* specified in the criterion statement. If the statement specifies that the pupil will recognize certain consonant sounds, for example, have items sampling each consonant sound listed.
   c. Write test items that parallel the *given conditions* in the criterion statement. If the criterion states, for example, "Given 20 words pronounced orally . . . , the test items should involve 20 words pronounced orally.
   d. Construct the *number of items* called for in the criterion statement in the instructional objective. If the criterion statement says, for example, "19 of 20 times, use 20 items; if the criterion statement specifies 95% accuracy, use items with a multiple of 5.
   e. Use foils as needed; that is, in recognition tests (e.g., true-false, matching, multiple choice), combine both positive and negative items that pupils must respond to differentially; otherwise, pupils may respond mechanically without really attending to each item.

Preparing the Test. Four steps are involved in getting the test ready for use with pupils.

1. Assemble the test items.
2. Write the directions. Be sure they are easy to understand. Allow ample time.
3. Design the test format. Arrange the items in an uncrowded, easy-to-read manner. Allow pupils ample space to respond.
4. Reproduce the test. Type the items or write them legibly. Be sure they reproduce clearly. On oral tests, enunciate clearly.

Constructing an Ordered Series of Criterion-Referenced Tests

Sometimes, a teacher wishes to establish a pupil's position in a given sequence of instructional objectives. (An *informal reading inventory* is an

Instructional Planning for Exceptional Children

example.) Constructing an ordered series of tests is a simple procedure, requiring these three steps:

1. Select the topic to be sampled.
2. Do a task analysis of the topic.
   a. Identify the skills involved in that topic.
   b. Put the skills in order according to some dimension; e.g., complexity, grade level at which they are conventionally taught, etc.
3. Construct a single criterion-referenced test for each skill in the sequence.

Teachers also may want to identify the grade level at which a pupil is working. One can go "piggy-back" by working with a publisher's series of graded material (e.g., the Scott Foresman series), in which the teacher chooses a publisher, receives the series, selects an instructional objective and corresponding material from the respective levels of the series, and builds the test around the instructional objective and material.

Establishing grade level in this manner is fine as long as teachers do not overgeneralize. Grade level is not absolute or real; it is something a publisher sets up arbitrarily. As a result, grade levels differ among publishers. One publisher may use one grade level and another publisher may use another grade level to locate a particular skill; for example, the rule in structural analysis about the omission of the final *e* before a suffix beginning with a vowel (e.g., safe / saf*est* / safe*ty*).

Constructing Norm-Referenced Tests

Constructing norm-referenced tests in a way to yield an adequate instrument is a complex, expensive undertaking. Most people will never do it. Teachers can use norm-referenced tests more intelligently, however, after understanding how they are built. The following is an overview of the major steps:

1. Define the reading behavior to be sampled. Give the theory or other rationale for that definition.
2. Specify the target population; i.e., describe the characteristics of the group for whom the test is intended, or designed to generalize to.
3. Select test items for sampling the reading behavior defined. (Here, *test items* means questions, materials, directions, etc.)
4. Design the test format. Prepare the test package.
5. Try out the test. Revise it as necessary.
6. Select the standardization sample. Demonstrate that the sample

adequately represents the population for which the test is designed to generalize.
7. Collect the standardization data. Express these data in the form of the derived scores chosen for use (e.g., percentiles, grade placement scores, normalized standard scores).
8. Select the samples to use in getting data for demonstrating reliability and validity.
9. Collect the reliability and validity data. Express these data in the statistics chosen for use.
10. Develop interpretive materials (e.g., profiles).
11. Package the test. Include the tests, the administrator's manual with directions, scoring criteria, and interpretive materials; the technical manual with the behavior definition, the theory or rationale, descriptions of the standardization and reliability/validity samples, and data for standardization, reliability, validity, and interpretation.

Selecting Tests

Many reading achievement tests already have been developed and are available. The teacher's task is to select tests appropriate for a *particular* pupil and a *particular* decision to be made.

Available Reading Tests

Buros (1972, 1974) has published a directory and an analysis of reading tests in print. Publishers including Scott Foresman, Ginn, American Guidance Service, McGraw-Hill, and many others have extensive catalogs containing such tests. Figure 2 lists selected tests, their intended grade levels, and publishers.

The Selection Process

Picking the right test is a complex undertaking, and a crucial one. A teacher should consider the following steps in selecting the appropriate test for a *particular student for a particular decision to be made*:

1. State the question to be answered. (Refer back to the question about the teaching process, management process, and identifying a pupil's position in a norm group. Which of these questions do you want to answer?)
2. Locate some possibly appropriate tests. Consult the local test library, publishers' catalogs, Buros' materials. Find tests that look like they will provide evidence for the question. Construct your own tests if no

Instructional Planning for Exceptional Children

Figure 2
Examples of Available Reading Tests

Test	Grade Levels	Publisher
California Achievement Tests: Reading	1-14	CTB/McGraw-Hill
Comprehensive Tests of Basic Skills Reading	Kgn-12	CTB/McGraw-Hill
Gates-MacGinitie Reading Tests	1-9	Teachers College Press
Gates-MacGinitie Reading Tests: Survey F	10-12	Teachers College Press
Iowa Silent Reading Tests	4-16	Harcourt Brace Jovanovich
Metropolitan Achievement Tests: Reading Tests	2-9	Harcourt Brace Jovanovich
Nelson-Denny Reading Test	9-16 & adults	Houghton Mifflin
Primary Reading Survey Tests	2-3	Scott, Foresman
Sequential Tests of Educational Progress: Reading	4-6, 7-9, 10-12, 13-14	Educational Testing Service & American Printing House for the Blind
Stanford Achievement Test: Reading Test	1, 5-9	Harcourt Brace Jovanovich
Classroom Reading Inventory, Second Ed.	2-10	William C. Brown
Diagnostic Reading Scales, Revised Edition	1-6 & retarded readers 7-12	CTB/McGraw-Hill
Diagnostic Reading Test: Pupil Progress Series	1.9-2.1, 2.2-3, 4-6, 7-9	Scholastic Testing Service
Gillingham-Childs Phonics Proficiency Scales	1-12	Educator Publishing Service
Group Phonics Analysis	1-3	Drier Educational Systems
LRA Standard Mastery Tasks in Language	1, 2	Learning Research Associates
McQuire-Bumpus Diagnostic Comprehension Test	2.5-3, 4-6	Croft Educational Services
Phonics Criterion Test	1-3	Drier Educational Systems
Prescriptive Reading Inventory	1.5-2.5, 2.0-3.5, 3.0-4.5, 4.0-6.5	CTB/McGraw-Hill
Reading Diagnostic Probes	2-5, 3-9	American Testing Company
Silent Reading Diagnostic Tests	2-6	Lyons & Carnahan
Sipay Word Analysis Tests	2-12	Educators Publishing Service
Stanford Diagnostic Reading Test	2.5-4.5, 4.5-8.5	Harcourt Brace Jovanovich
Test of Phonic Skills	Kgn-3	Harper & Row
Wisconsin Tests of Reading Skill Development: Word Attack	Kgn-2, 1, 1-3, 2-4, 3-6	NCS Interpretive Scoring Systems
Woodcock Reading Mastery Tests	Kgn-12	American Guidance Service
Botel Reading Inventory	1-4, 1-6, 1-12	Follett
Durrell Listening-Reading Series	1-2, 3-6, 7-9	Harcourt Brace Jovanovich
Instant Word Recognition Test	1-4	Drier Educational Systems
National Test of Basic Words	1-5	American Testing Company
Oral Reading Criterion Test	1-7	Drier Educational Systems
Reading Miscue Inventory	1-7	Macmillan
Analysis of Readiness Skills: Reading and Mathematics	Kgn-1	Houghton Mifflin

An Inventory of Primary Skills	Kgn-1	Fearon
Lippincott Reading Readiness Test	Kgn-1	J. B. Lippincott
Macmillan Reading Readiness Test, Revised Edition	1 gr. entrants	Macmillan
Pre-Reading Assessment Kit	Kgn-1	CTB/McGraw-Hill
Preschool and Kindergarten Performance Profile	Preschool & Kgn.	Educational Performance Associates
Reading Inventory Probe 1	1-2	American Testing Company
Basic Reading Rate Scale	3-12	Revrac Publications
Comprehensive Tests of Basic Skills: Study Skills	2.5-4, 4-6, 6-8, 8-12	CTB/McGraw-Hill
Wisconsin Test of Reading Skill Development: Study Skills	Kgn-1, 1-2, 2-3, 3-4, 4-5, 5-6, 6-7	NCS Interpretive Scoring Systems

possible appropriate tests are available or if the available tests exceed the budget.

3. Judge whether or not the test(s) will yield accurate and nondiscriminatory evidence.

ASSURING ACCURATE AND NONDISCRIMINATORY EVIDENCE

Errors from Tests

Testing is fraught with error. When we use tests to sample reading behavior, many things can keep us from getting a true picture of what the student actually can do in reading. For example:

> A pupil may know prefixes and suffixes and understand how to apply them in unlocking word meanings but not be able to demonstrate that knowledge and skill because perceptual problems interfere with recognition of the graphemes.

> A pupil may be able to grasp main ideas in discourse read aloud to him or her, and yet be unable to demonstrate that skill in silent reading because of an inadequate sight vocabulary or poor word recognition skills.

> A pupil may be a fluent reader but not be able to demonstrate that achievement on a test because of test anxiety.

> A seven-year-old pupil may be able to read material usually given to twelve-year-old pupils but may not demonstrate the knowledge because the test administered has a ceiling at what is called the third grade level.

Instructional Planning for Exceptional Children

Inaccurate evidence from tests leads to inaccurate answers to questions which, in turn, leads to inaccurate decisions about pupils' reading instruction and placement. This result is profoundly serious; for example:

Erroneous information can lead to erroneous decisions about content, methods, and timing when individualizing the pupil's instruction and related services.

Erroneous information can lead to the wrong decisions about placement in the least restrictive environment.

Erroneous information in a pupil's record can lead to wrong decisions later, about matters like college or job preparation.

Wrong decisions can cause losses of time and opportunity in a student's life—losses which are difficult or impossible to make up. Also, such wrong decisions can harm the pupil's cognitive, emotional, and social well-being—harm which is hard to remediate. In addition, wrong decisions can cause a waste of teacher time and a waste of school materials and facilities; these types of waste, of course, translate into a waste of taxpayers' money.

Sources of Error

Detailed discussions of sources of error can be found in Blake (1976) and Newland (1971). This information is highlighted here, with respect to criterion-referenced tests and norm-referenced tests.

Potential Error In Criterion-Referenced Testing

Inappropriate criteria are one source of error in criterion-referenced tests. The assumption in using criterion-referenced tests is that the student received the test items under the stated conditions as given in the instructional objective and that the student made the response specified. If that assumption is not met, the test items may become easier or harder than the instructional objective. At least, they become different.

Sometimes, pupils' handicaps prevent their responding to the test items in the way specified under the conditions given in the instructional objective. A blind pupil could not respond to items based on an instructional objective that required sight reading and writing. If this pupil were given the material in oral form, the items would be harder than in the written form. In such situations, the tests are not appropriate because the reference standard is not appropriate. Thus, the test materials and procedures are discriminatory and unfair.

Potential Error In Norm-Referenced Testing

Inappropriate norms are one source of error in norm-referenced tests. Two assumptions are made in using norm-referenced tests; teachers must meet these assumptions if the norm-referenced test is to be appropriate for use with the pupil:

— That the pupil being tested and the pupils in the norm group had the same directions, responded in the same way, and generally received the test under the same conditions. If all of this uniformity does not occur, the norms no longer apply. The test may be easier or harder for the pupil being tested than it was for the pupils in the norm group.

— That the pupil being tested had the same chance as pupils in the norm group to learn the language used in the test and to learn how to use materials similar to those in the test items. If the pupil being tested has had restricted learning experiences, the test items are not good ways to sample the behavior they are supposed to sample.

Three sets of pupil characteristics can interfere with meeting these assumptions for norm-referenced tests:

Some pupils come from language backgrounds different from pupils in the norm group. They may not understand the language involved in the test directions and the test items. Using the tests with these pupils would violate the first assumption.

Some pupils have physical, sensory, or language handicaps. They cannot use the same directions or make the same responses as pupils in the norm group. Using the tests with these pupils would violate the first assumption.

Some pupils come from cultural backgrounds different from pupils in the norm group. They do not have an opportunity to experience the kinds of materials and situations involved in the tests. Using the tests with these pupils would violate the second assumption.

When the assumptions are violated in these ways, the tests are not appropriate because the reference standard is not appropriate. Again, the test materials and procedures are discriminatory and unfair.

Another source of error with norm-referenced tests relates to the process of sampling behavior and making inferences. Behavior sampling and inferring depend upon tests that are highly reliable, have a low standard error of estimate and are highly valid indicators of the characteristic they purport to measure.

Public Policy and Testing Exceptional Students

Errors in testing and decision making represent an area of tremendous concern. The critical literature is extensive. As an example, one can examine the series of papers in the *National Elementary Principal* entitled "Standardized Testing in America I and II (1975a & b). Protecting pupils in testing has become a matter of public policy. The legal bases for this protection are primarily in the equal protection and due process provisions in the fourteenth amendment to the U.S. Constitution, and secondarily in the sixth and eighth amendments. The particular protections are codified in the common law, the statutory law, and the tort law. Those pertaining to equal protection in evaluation, periodic reevaluation, due process in evaluation, confidentiality, and program effectiveness are included in PL 94-142, *The Education for All Handicapped Children Act of 1975*. To summarize:

Equal Protection in Evaluation. The requirements for equal protection in evaluation essentially mandate that tests must be technically sound, nondiscriminatory, valid, and reliable. (Section 121a.430)

Periodic Reevaluation. The prescriptions for reevaluation are aimed at: checking whether the original decisions about instruction, therapy, and placement were correct; and checking whether the instruction and placement are effective in producing the desired effect and, if not, what changes should be made. These prescriptions are made through requirements for examining and revising the Individual Education Plan. (Section 121a.222, 255(e), 433)

Due Process. Due process procedures essentially provide that: the parents (or their surrogates) *must* give consent for the evaluation, they *may* have access to all evaluation results, they *may* challenge any evaluation results and have redress, and they *must* participate in decision making based on evaluation data. This is a profound innovation. (Section 121a.400, 401, 402, 403, 404, 406, 407, 408, 409, 411, 412, 413, 414)

Confidentiality. Three concerns about test data—either erroneous or accurate—are: that they will not be available to the pupil and his/her parents; that they will be available to people who have no business seeing them; and that they will be kept and will jeopardize the pupil later in school and in getting admitted to college, getting a job, or in such activities as getting financial credit. The Privacy Act of 1974 has stringent regulations about confidentiality. These regulations were incorporated into PL 94-142 to protect the confidentiality of the exceptional pupil. The regulations pertain essentially to access, challenge and redress, safeguards, and destruction of data. (Section 121a.400, 451, 452, 453, 454, 455, 456, 457, 458, 459, 460, 461, 462, 463)

Program Effectiveness. The prescriptions for checking program effectiveness require checking whether the treatments are facilitating a pupil's progress, to insure that the special education and related services provided do not become dead ends for the pupil. (Section 121a.255)

Observing Legal Protections

Due Process for Evaluation Requirements

Due process for evaluation requirements assures that tests given to the student are necessary, appropriate, and accurate. Figure 3 is a sample guide for monitoring due process requirements.

Equal Protection in Evaluation Requirements

Equal protection in evaluation procedures assures that tests are technically sound and nondiscriminatory. To decide about soundness and fairness, one should bring together and weigh information about the pupil's characteristics and information about tests from the Buros Mental Measurements Yearbooks and the technical manuals supplied by the publishers. Figure 4 is a guide for judging whether the requirements for equal protection in evaluation have been met.

Confidentiality Requirements

Confidentiality procedures assure that the evidence in the pupil's records is accurate. They also assure that only duly qualified people have access to the evidence. Figure 5 is a guide for examining whether the requirements have been met.

ANSWERING QUESTIONS AND MAKING DECISIONS

Decisions about reading instruction must be made within the context of the individualized education plan. To review, the IEP includes a statement about:

- the pupil's present levels of educational performance

Instructional Planning for Exceptional Children

Figure 3
Guide For Monitoring Due Process Requirements

1. Advocate:
   a. Is the pupil old enough and competent to participate? (Explain)
   b. Are the parents/guardians competent and willing to participate? (Explain)
   c. If parents refuse to participate, document reasons and procedures used to satisfy their objections or other reasons.
   d. Is a surrogate necessary? If so, what is his/her name?
   e. What is the advocate's native language?
   f. Does the advocate have a sensory impairment?
   g. If a translator/communicator is needed, give his/her name.
2. Information about procedures and rights:
   a. Was information about the individualized education plan, the assessment process, and due process communicated to the advocate orally and in writing, and in terms appropriate to his/her apparent level of understanding?
   b. Is there evidence that the advocate apparently understands the procedures and the pupil's rights?
3. Permission:

   Has the advocate's permission been obtained for each procedure used?
4. Information about results:

   Has the advocate been informed about the results of the evaluations?
5. Independent assessments:

   Has the advocate been informed about the right to obtain independent assessments?
6. Appeal:
   a. Does the advocate have objections to the assessment procedure or the results?
   b. Have appeal procedures been established and followed?

Figure 4
Guide For Monitoring Equal Protection In Evaluation Requirements

A. *Characteristics of the Pupil*

1. Native Language:
   a. What language is predominantly spoken in the pupil's home?
   b. Does the pupil need a translator?
2. Speech:
   a. Is the pupil's speech intelligible?
   b. If not, how does he or she communicate responses?
3. Hearing:
   a. Does the pupil have a hearing impairment sufficient to interfere with understanding of test directions?
   b. If so what means of communication can be used?
4. How mature is the pupil's understanding and use of language (i.e., syntactical functions and vocabulary meanings)?
5. Vision:
   a. Does the pupil have a visual impairment severe enough to interfere with understanding of test directions and responding to test materials?
   b. If so, what adjustments need to be made?
6. Hand use:
   a. Does the pupil have sufficient control of his or her hands to manipulate test items that must be moved?
   b. If not, what adjustments need to be made?
7. Head and postural control:
   a. Is the pupil able to maintain a reasonably upright sitting/body position and head position?
   b. If not, what adjustments need to be made?
8. Sociocultural and experience background:

   Has the pupil been in an environment where he or she may not have had experience with activities like those used in the test items?

B. *Technical Soundness of the Test*

Identification

1. Name of test or test battery:

2. Acronym used to label test, if any:

3. Publisher:

4. Copyright or publication date:

5. Target group:

6. Source of content or objectives sampled:

7. Sources of information:

Information Specific to Criterion-Referenced Tests

(Do the following for each objective)

Instructional objective:

1. Do all of the test items sample the behavior specified in the instructional objective? Yes _____ No _____

2. Does the test include the number of items called for in the criterion statement? Yes _____ No _____

3. Do all of the items sample the content specified in the instructional objective? Yes _____ No _____

4. Do the test items parallel the given conditions in the criterion statement? Yes _____ No _____

5. Are the directions easy to understand? Yes _____ No _____

6. Is the test format satisfactory? Yes _____ No _____

7. Are the foils, if used, appropriate? Yes _____ No _____

(Continue through all objectives)

Information Specific to Norm-Referenced Tests

1. Detailed description of the standardization group:

2. Procedure for establishing validity:

3. Evidence about validity:

4. Procedures for establishing reliability:

5. Evidence about reliability:

6. Types of scores used and their interpretations:

C. *Fairness of the Tests*

For All Tests

_____1. Are the test items free from errors and ambiguities?

_____2. Is the pupil free from health problems or emotional problems that could interfere with test performance?

For Norm-Referenced Tests

_____1. Are the norms appropriate? (To answer *yes*, be sure that the pupil does not have any cultural differences, language differences, or handicaps which make him or her different from the norm group.)

_____2. Is the reliability coefficient sufficiently high and the standard error of measurement sufficiently low?

_____3. Is the test validity sufficiently high?

_____4. Are the test ranges sufficient for the pupil being tested?

For Criterion-Referenced Tests

_____1. Does the test meet the standards for criterion-referenced tests?

_____2. Are the criteria appropriate? (To answer *yes*, be sure that the pupil does not have any handicap which could prevent his/her responding to test items in a way specified under the conditions given in the instructional objective.)

Figure 5
Guide For Monitoring Confidentiality Requirements

Name of information maintained:

1. Notice:
   a. Has notice been given for all activities—data collection, data use, etc.?
   b. Were the notices published in the native language of the groups involved?

2. Access Rights:
   a. Are parents and, when appropriate, the pupil given access to the data?
   b. Have they been informed of the right of access?

3. Hearing Rights:
   a. Are parents and, when appropriate, the pupil given a hearing about any change they request?
   b. Is the hearing scheduled at a reasonable time?
   c. Is this hearing in the parents' native language or, if needed, is an interpreter present?
   d. If their request is denied, is their rebuttal filed in the pupil's records?

4. Consent:

   Is the parents' consent or, if appropriate, the pupil's consent requested for wider disclosure of data?

5. Safeguards:
   a. Who is responsible for insuring confidentiality of data?
   b. What employees have access to the data?
   c. Have these employees' names been published?
   d. Have these employees been given proper training in procedures for protecting confidentiality?

6. Destruction:
   a. Does the agency have procedures for destroying data?
   b. Are parents and, when appropriate, pupils informed of their rights to copies of data before they are destroyed?

- annual goals, including short-term instructional objectives
- the specific educational services to be provided to the pupil (i.e., instructional services, nonacademic services, related services, and services to insure the procedural safeguards)
- the extent to which the pupil will be able to participate in regular education programs
- the projected date for initiation and anticipated duration of the services
- appropriate objective criteria and evaluation procedures
- a schedule for determining, at least annually, whether instructional objectives are being achieved.

In addition, the IEP must be done within the requirements for the student's legal protection—i.e., periodic reevaluation, due process in testing, equal protection in testing, and confidentiality.

Specifically, the test evidence used in the IEP and the decisions that evidence is used for are:

— To answer questions about *teaching reading*, to make decisions about the pupil's present levels of educational performance; annual goals, including short-term instructional objectives; specific educational services to be provided to the pupil; and appropriate objective criteria and evaluation procedures.
— To answer questions about management or reading instruction, to make decisions about the extent to which the pupil will be able to participate in regular education programs.
— To assure the accuracy of evidence, to meet the requirements of the several legal protections.

REFERENCES

Blake, K. A. *Teaching the retarded*. Englewood Cliffs, NJ: Prentice-Hall, 1974.
Blake, K. A. *The mentally retarded: An educational psychology*. Englewood Cliffs, NJ: Prentice-Hall, 1976.
Buros, O. K. *The seventh mental measurements yearbook*. Highland Park, NJ: Gryphon, 1972.
Buros, O. K. *Reading tests in print*. Highland Park, NJ: Gryphon, 1974.
Newland, T. E. Psychological assessment of exceptional children and youth. In W. M. Cruickshank (Ed.), *Psychology of exceptional children and youth*. Englewood Cliffs, NJ: Prentice-Hall, 1971.
Standardized testing in America I—Intelligence Testing. *National Elementary Principal*, 1975, 54 (4). (a)
Standardized testing in America II—Achievement Testing. *National Elementary Principal*, 1975, 54 (6). (b)

Part 2

Instructional Planning

Edward L. Meyen, *University of Kansas*

The learning characteristics of exceptional children and youth translate into a wide range of instructional challenges for classroom teachers. While some instructional needs are met through minor modifications in materials, scheduling changes, or through corrective devices, most instructional needs require a major investment in instructional planning by teachers and support personnel.

Until recently, instructional planning as a basis for special education programming has been something for which educators acknowledged the need, but something which was accomplished rarely. At the least, relatively little evidence is apparent of systematic instructional planning on behalf of exceptional children and youth. Certainly, some planning has been carried out—but not at a level that many would consider sufficient. The reasons for this omission range from a failure by administrators to provide teachers with time for planning to a lack of planning skills on the part of teachers. In some situations, administrators have been content merely with recruiting a teacher to teach exceptional learners, with no real expectancy of effective instructional planning.

Today, circumstances have changed greatly. Experiences derived over the past 10 years in implementing the resource room model, in which two or more teachers are involved in coordinating a child's instructional program, have necessitated more precise planning. An even more important change has been the evolvement of the individualized education program (IEP) requirement of PL 94-142. By mandating the development and maintenance of IEPs for handicapped students, the need for resources in the area of instructional planning has become essential. Implications of this requirement extend far beyond the roles of special education personnel. Most regular classroom teachers also must become participants in the planning process.

Although Public Law 94-142 specifies the content of IEPs and the conditions under which they are to be developed, the law does not propose a planning technology. The rudiments of a planning technology exist in the literature and to the degree teachers employ planning procedures approximating a technology. But little progress has been made in relating instructional planning to the IEP process. For the most part, districts are preoccupied with designing IEP forms and complying with the basic requirements for completing IEPs on handicapped students.

As the emphasis shifts from mere compliance to developing more systematic approaches to IEPs in the context of instructional planning, attention must be given to some rather specific skills on the part of teachers and other participants in the IEP planning process. If the IEP process is to be optimally successful, teachers must be skilled in planning procedures, observing pupil behavior, conducting educational assessments, interpreting evaluation information, applying task analysis, specifying behavioral stated objectives, and monitoring pupil performance related to specific objectives.

The selections appearing in this section include an emphasis on the roles of parents and teachers in the planning process, specific planning strategies, the application of instructional planning to subject matter areas, and the involvement of paraprofessionals in instructional planning. The reader is encouraged to review the IEP requirements of Public Law 94-142 as a frame of reference for making maximum use of the material which follows.

Few educational mandates have caused as much activity, and in some cases concern, on the part of educators as the required individualized education program (IEP) for each handicapped child. Instructional planning is not new—but development of instructional plans, inclusive of specific objectives and conferences with parental participation, is a new approach. The challenges in implementing this requirement go far beyond assisting teachers in acquiring the skills necessary to develop IEPs; they center on effective involvement of parents, provision of time for teacher participation, and techniques for evaluating effectiveness of the IEP process. The authors provide a state-of-the-art review of what is occurring in implementation of the IEP process. The article is highly appropriate for individuals at the public school with responsibilities for developing and administering IEP systems, as well as teacher/trainers involved in preservice or inservice education.

Implementation of IEPs: New Teacher Roles and Requisite Support Systems

Nancy D. Safer, Martin J. Kaufman, and Patricia A. Morrissey, *Bureau of Education for the Handicapped;* Linda Lewis, *Nero & Associates*

The Education for All Handicapped Children Act of 1975 represents a unique and innovative piece of legislation in that it addresses not only administrative and fiscal concerns, but also deals directly with instructional programming. Through its provisions that every handicapped child must have an Individualized Education Program (IEP), the law essentially legislates an individualized, child-centered approach to educating handicapped children.

Certainly, the concept of child-centered, individualized programming for children is not new to special education. If special education instructional literature of the past decade has had a focus, this has been it (Johnson, 1967; Reger, Schroeder & Uschold, 1968; Hammill, 1971; Cartwright, Cartwright, & Ysseldyke, 1973; Herrick, 1972; Minskoff, 1973). A predominant concern in special education has been to avoid dealing with children in terms of labels, focusing instead on each child's unique qualities, carefully determining his or her educationally relevant strengths and weaknesses, and devising an appropriate educational program for the child based on those strengths and weaknesses. In special education, this generally has been referred to as the *diagnostic/prescriptive approach* to teaching. Because the IEP component of PL 94-142 requires the child's current level of functioning to be determined and used as a basis for establishing goals and objectives, it represents a formalization of the diagnostic/prescriptive approach to education.

Since the IEP provisions of PL 94-142 are basically consistent with a predominant trend in special education, implementation of the law would seem to be almost a routine matter for special education teachers and administrators. Passage of the law, however, was greeted with confusion, speculation, and consternation in many instances—much of this centering on the IEP. One likely reason for this reaction was suggested by Gotts (1976): Widespread adoption of the diagnostic/prescriptive approach has never occurred at the classroom level. Despite extensive literature, heavily promoted curriculum materials, and reoriented teacher training programs, individualized educational programming in many instances remains a concept rather than an operational reality.

Thus, actual implementation of individualized educational programming necessitates major changes in the provision of instructional programs and services to handicapped children. Furthermore, since the special education teacher has been identified as the person most appropriately involved in prescriptive aspects of the individualized educational planning process (Fenton, Yoshida, Maxwell, & Kaufman, 1977), implementation of individualized educational programming can be expected to particularly change the role or job requirements of the special education teacher.

IEP PROVISIONS OF PL 94-142 AND THEIR IMPLICATIONS

PL 94-142 requires that every child receiving special education services must have an IEP developed in a meeting attended by a representative of the local educational agency, the child's teacher(s), parents of the child, and, when appropriate, the child. The individualized education program plan is to contain statements of the child's current level of performance, annual goals and short-term objectives, the specific special education services to be provided to the child, the extent to which the child will be able to participate in regular education programs, the expected dates for initiation of services and projected duration of services, and the objective criteria by which progress toward the short-term objectives will be measured, as well as a schedule for reviewing (at least on an annual basis) the IEP.

The spirit of PL 94-142, then, is one of assuring that handicapped children receive special instructional services which are planned and implemented in keeping with their individual needs. This intent is in keeping with the concepts of diagnostic/prescriptive teaching—assessment of educational needs and determination and implementation of a program on the basis of those needs. Though unintentional, the language of the law can be interpreted as extending these basic tenets of diagnostic/prescriptive teaching somewhat in the direction of *precision teaching* (Kunzelmann, 1970; Haring, 1971; Gentry & Haring, 1976), or *data-based instruction* (Hall, 1975; Lilly, 1977). It does this by specifying that short-term objectives will be written, accompanied by objective criteria by which progress in meeting the short-term objectives will be measured. The terms *short-term objectives, objective criteria,* and *progress measured* all are reminiscent of these more behavioral, accountability-oriented teaching approaches.

From the provisions of the law, several types of changes seem necessary if individualized education is to be implemented. First, planning or developing individualized education programs requires that certain tasks be carried out. These tasks include administering educational assessments, meeting and working with parents, developing annual goals and short-term objectives for individual children, and measuring and keeping careful records to substantiate progress toward attaining annual goals and short-term objectives.

Second, implementation of individualized education programs may require a reorientation of the classroom because each child will be working on different goals and objectives. In many instances, large group instruction will be replaced by more individualized activities. Work centers may be established and freshly equipped each day with self-instructional materials and worksheets appropriate for each child. Aides, volunteers, and student tutors may have to be drawn into the classroom and their activities coordinated and supervised.

Finally, the authority and responsibility for decisions related to instructional programming will be shared by special education teachers, regular education teachers, parents, principals, support personnel, and in some instances, handicapped students. At the same time, greater accountability is implied in assuring that each student's instructional program is in accordance with the IEP document generated by the group.

Changes such as these will be far-reaching in scope and will have particular impact on the special education teacher. To some extent, the nature of the role of special education teacher will change from one of being primarily a provider of instruction to one of being more like an instructional manager. Thus, special education teachers in particular have expressed apprehensions concerning the implementation of individualized educational programming for handicapped children.

A Framework for Looking at Changes

The work of Dan Lortie (1975) provides a framework for looking at these apprehensions which suggests that changes in teacher role are more than just interesting sociological phenomena—they can have very real consequences in terms of job satisfaction and teacher morale. In his book *School Teacher* (1975), Lortie lists three types of rewards a career can offer: (1) extrinsic rewards such as income, prestige, and power; (2) ancillary rewards such as security, hours, or cleanliness; and (3) psychic or intrinsic rewards. The structure of teaching, he suggests, emphasizes psychic rewards. According to Lortie, teachers report "reaching a group of students" or the joy of teaching as their major source of satisfaction in the profession. Teaching is viewed from a service orientation, and as such is rewarded by the culture which extols the "dedicated teacher." Because the primary rewards in teaching are psychic, Lortie says, teachers value and assign priority to aspects of the job in which such rewards are likely to occur—activities in which they either are working directly with students or performing closely related tasks such as lesson preparation or counseling. Teachers also devalue and resent noninstructional activities such as clerical duties or duties outside the classroom; they perceive such activities as detracting from their potentially productive time instructing students.

Lortie also refers to the cellular nature of schools with their multiple self-contained classrooms and low task interdependence among teachers. Throughout the history of schooling in this nation, he points out, teachers have worked relatively independently, assuming specific areas of responsibility without assistance from others. Thus, traditionally, teachers have enjoyed primary responsibility for and control of activities in their classrooms. Related to this independence is the feeling among teachers, as reported from a survey by Lortie, that teaching effectiveness can best be judged by the teacher from observations and interaction with students. Though many teachers expressed occasional difficulties in assessing teaching effectiveness, they did not believe that outside agents or even tests could assess the effectiveness of teaching as well as the teacher herself or himself.

Lortie's work suggests that because the primary rewards of teaching are derived from tasks associated with the role, rather than from extrinsic sources such as salary level, changes in the teaching role must be considered in terms of their effect on job satisfaction and feelings of personal fulfillment among teachers. Changes perceived negatively by teachers might result in lowered morale, dissatisfaction and, ultimately, in a rapid turnover rate among teachers. The information presented by Lortie suggests that several types of role changes might be perceived particularly negatively by teachers. Three of these will be given particular emphasis later in this chapter: (1) less time for direct instruction of children because of increased noninstructional tasks; (2) shared responsibility for classroom activities; and (3) increased accountability to outsiders. The instructional programming changes necessitated by implementation of individualized education seem likely to result in all of these role changes for special education teachers. Thus, there is a need to identify and clarify some of the potential major changes in the role and job requirements of the special education teacher.

Project IEP

The federally funded Project IEP was designed to identify and clarify perceptions related to roles in the IEP process. An open-ended interview procedure was used in 31 school districts in four states—Alabama, New Jersey, Washington, and Wisconsin. Teachers from two cohorts of districts were identified and interviewed. The first cohort of districts was selected on the basis of three criteria: (1) the degree to which an individualized educational programming process similar to that required by PL 94-142 was already required by the state; (2) national geographic representativeness; and (3) willingness to participate in the study. Similar criteria were used in selecting districts within states. In addition, efforts were made to maintain representative urban/suburban/rural and socioeconomic distributions within a state.

The project called for open-ended interviews with representatives of various groups affected by the individualized education process, such as administrators, regular and special education teachers, personnel from institutions, support personnel, parents, and advocacy groups. Initial interviewing took place in three cycles, with many respondents being interviewed more than once so information could be gathered on points that had come to light during previous interviews. Although a consistent set of general questions was used with all respondents, the format of each interview varied. Further, because the intent was to elicit as much in-depth information as possible on topics with which the respondents were most familiar or which were most important to them, varying amounts of information were obtained from respondents on different topics.

The processes used by the four states varied in their similarity to the IEP process required by PL 94-142. In two of the states, a system similar to requirements of PL 94-142 was utilized. In one of these states, however, a statement of short-term objectives was required, although parents did not necessarily participate in its development. In the other states, a statement of objectives was suggested but not required, parents and teachers were not necessarily involved in the IEP meeting, and there was some variance in review schedules. In a third state, a multidisciplinary team approach to diagnosis and placement was used, and a statement of long-range goals for the special education career of the child was one product of this process. No statement of annual goals and short-term objectives was required by this state, and parents and teachers were not necessarily included in team meetings. In the fourth state, placement decisions were made by a committee, but no provisions were made for anything resembling an IEP process. Within all four states, as much or more variation was found among the districts within a particular state as between states. Thus, even the states with requirements similar to those mandated by PL 94-142 had districts in which there was essentially no effective IEP process in operation. Furthermore, within states that did not already require an IEP process at the state level, some districts had implemented many elements of the mandated IEP process at the district level.

From the first cohort, 133 special education teachers were interviewed. Of these teachers, 94 taught at the elementary level, and 39 taught at the secondary level; 51 of the teachers were resource teachers, and 82 were teachers of self-contained classes. With only a few exceptions, these teachers taught children with some type of cognitive impairment (retardation or learning disability) or emotional impairment. *Throughout this article, this sample of teachers will be referred to as the first group of teachers.*

Special education teachers interviewed in the four states expressed apprehensions and concerns about changes in their roles resulting from implementation of individualized educational programming or from additional requirements posed by PL 94-142. Further, although teachers in some districts in each of the states seemed comfortable with the role changes, their lack of apprehension was not related necessarily to the degree of implementation of a similar process at a district or state level.

To discover the factors that related to lack of teacher apprehension, a second cohort of school districts was selected. The second cohort was much smaller, consisting of four districts in the state of Washington. One of the four districts also was included in the first cohort of school districts. Fifteen special education teachers from the second cohort were interviewed. One third of these teachers taught at the secondary level, and slightly more than half were resource teachers. These teachers primarily taught cognitively or emotionally impaired children. *Hereafter, these teachers will be referred to as the second group of teachers.* In addition, directors of special education and support personnel in each of these districts were interviewed to provide further information.

Since the purpose of the second cohort was to obtain an initial impression of conditions, policies, and practices that result in high teacher morale and job satisfaction, school districts were selected for: (1) practices similar to those required by PL 94-142 that had been in effect for a year or more; and (2) indications that teachers were relatively comfortable with those practices. For the most part, the four districts served middle class children. Three of the districts were located in suburban settings, and the fourth encompassed both a small city and rural population.

The first and second groups of districts may have differed in systematic ways. For example, the background and training of teachers, district resources, the composition of groups interviewed—or even information collection procedures—may have differed. Thus, no direct comparisons between the groups should be made. Nevertheless, although direct comparison of factors affecting the two groups is prohibited by the study's methodology, the teachers' and other interviewees' ideas and concerns about the new requirements are rich in useful information. Also, though it was believed that use of an open-ended, less structured interview technique would produce more in-depth, accurate information, this technique also makes the reporting of findings in terms of percentage of respondents virtually impossible. Thus, statements referring to teachers may be interpreted here as referring to a majority of teachers in the designated group unless otherwise indicated. Comments of particular teachers or district directors of special education also are included to exemplify or further explore certain points.

CHANGES IN THE SPECIAL EDUCATION TEACHER'S ROLE AND JOB REQUIREMENTS

Interviews in the four states confirmed that special education teachers expected the implementation of individualized educational programming to affect their role as teachers substantially and alter some of the requirements of their job. Teachers were apprehensive about changes in their role, although many were enthusiastic about the potential effects of individualized education for their students. Many of the perceptions and concerns expressed by teachers centered on the three critical role changes suggested by Lortie's work (1975). This section considers teacher perceptions and reactions related to each of these three areas of role change, as well as two other anticipated changes—demands on personal time and new skill requirements—suggested by the teachers themselves.

Less Time for Direct Instruction of Children

In all four states, the first group of special education teachers expressed concerns that the IEP component of PL 94-142 would result in less teacher time being devoted to direct instruction of children. By direct instruction, these teachers seemed to refer to a teacher/pupil interaction in which the goal is the pupils' acquisition of some skill or concept. The first group was virtually unanimous in the belief that a decrease in teacher contact time would be harmful for students' learning. In addition, teachers predicted that their jobs would be less satisfying with a decrease in instructional activities. Teachers reported that they selected their careers to teach children, not to keep records and arrange meetings.

Two elements of providing individualized educational programming appeared to teachers to be most likely to result in less time for direct instruction of children. The first stems from the additional noninstructional planning tasks and the second from the anticipated reorientation of special education classrooms to provide for implementation of individualized education programs.

Additional Noninstructional Planning Tasks

The first group of teachers feared that requirements of the IEP component of PL 94-142 would necessitate spending a greater proportion of their time and effort in activities that would be noninstructional in nature. Teachers cited their increased involvement in administering informal educational assessments, writing annual goals and short-term objectives, notifying parents of program changes and obtaining their consent, attending IEP meetings, and keeping records of pupil progress, as examples of time consuming, noninstructional clerical tasks they would have to perform. Teachers clearly saw these as "add on" tasks to their original job descriptions, and essentially saw no alternative to cutting instructional time in order to carry them out. In two states, teachers recounted their experiences following implementation of state legislation with certain documentation requirements similar to those of PL 94-142. For example, one communication disorders specialist stated that because of the state legislation, she has had to cut the services provided to children in order to participate in program development activities. A resource room teacher reported that when faced with the pressure to document his work with children, he often has to choose between working with a child and record keeping.

Clearly, the component steps of the IEP process—assessing current performance, writing objectives, and evaluating and recording progress—were not viewed as elements of instructional planning by many of the teachers in this study. This is somewhat surprising since Lortie (1975) found that teachers included similar activities related to lesson planning within the domain of "potentially productive time." This category included instruction and activities closely related to it, and was distinct from "inert time" such as that spent in clerical tasks.

According to Shavelson (1976), instructional planning or lesson planning can be seen to include four elements: (1) specifying the outcomes that are to result from instruction in terms of observable student behaviors; (2) determining the student's present educational level; (3) designing an instructional sequence to move the student from her or his present level toward the outcome; and (4) determining a means of evaluating the outcomes. These elements seem virtually identical to the statement of annual goals, statement of present level of functioning, statement of short-term objectives, and statement of objective criteria by which progress will be measured as required by PL 94-142 in each IEP document.

It would appear, then, that the information contained in the IEP documents should feed directly into the information required for lesson planning, whether that planning is for groups or for individuals. That is, in individualized lesson planning, the outcomes specified for the lesson could be the same as or a derivative of a short-term objective from the IEP document for the child. The present educational level of the learner could be determined from the statement of present level of functioning in an IEP document, updated by any records of progress in meeting that objective. For a group lesson, the outcomes specified for the lesson could still correspond to some aggregate of short-term objectives from the plans of the children to be taught. Thus, although the individualized education program plan for a handicapped child maps out an annual program for a child, there would seem to be some potential that the information contained in that plan could guide teachers as they go about their daily lesson planning.

Many teachers in the first group did not, however, share this perspective. Though these teachers reported spending a good deal of time planning lessons and preparing materials, they did not see the information required in the IEP plan as a part of or even particularly useful to that process. Basically, a number of teachers stated that their lesson plans came from their instincts about the group. They reported that after a few weeks with a child they "knew that child" as a function of teaching her or him—and that knowledge or gestalt guided their planning.

Teachers in the second group, on the other hand, spoke strongly of the key role the individualized educational programming process played in their instructional planning. They reported that the process required them to think about and analyze their teaching. Carrying out assessments, they stated, focused their attention on the student, while writing goals and objectives structured their thinking about where they were going during the year and

Instructional Planning for Exceptional Children

what they wanted to accomplish. These teachers stated that the individualized educational programming process actually saved them time during the year in planning lessons. The program plan, they said, provided the goals of instruction as well as the means of evaluation, so that it was necessary only to plan the "how"—the activities or materials that would foster the particular goal. Thus, lesson planning became almost automatic.

The teachers in these districts also believed that the IEP document served to keep them on target during the year. Several teachers stated that as the year progressed, it was easy to lose sight of the goals of instruction and to get caught up in activities. Having written goal statements helped prevent this. They also found the daily or weekly records of progress extremely helpful. One teacher stated that without regular record keeping, several days might pass before the teacher was aware that children were bogged down. Other teachers said that instincts can be misleading and cited instances in which the teacher "felt" a lesson or a sequence of lessons had been on target and gone very well only to find out later that the students hadn't learned the skills and concepts presented.

These teachers also found systematic record keeping useful in motivating pupils. They reported that if an objective was written in measurable terms and shared with the student, pupils enjoyed evaluating their daily or weekly progress toward that objective, and would strive to improve their performance. Several of the teachers mentioned that although regular data collection or record keeping was important, it was sometimes a problem finding time to review the data and determine its implications for pupil programming. One teacher suggested that specific objectives and daily records be kept in only one or two subject areas, such as reading and math.

When asked how their teaching would change if no federal, state, or local requirements mandated individual assessment, stated objectives, and records of progress, virtually all of the teachers in the second group of districts reported that it would change very little. Referring to the IEP process, one teacher said, "I can't overstate how useful it is."

Clearly then, special education teachers in the second group found the IEP process an integral part of their teaching. The teachers interviewed, however, came primarily from university training programs which emphasized data-based instruction along with a diagnostic/prescriptive approach. Similarly, all of these teachers were teaching in school districts oriented to some degree to a perspective, data-based approach. The IEP process mandated by PL 94-142 seems to be highly compatible with such an approach, in many instances modifying only slightly the ongoing procedures already positively viewed by the teaching staff.

Data-based instruction and precision teaching, with their emphasis on assessment, task analysis, specific measurable objectives, and continual record keeping, stem from a particular approach to learning: *behaviorism*. Although behavioral approaches to teaching have received much attention in special education in recent years, other viable approaches to education exist. We do not know, for example, whether a teacher with a Piagetian approach to education, who might be more concerned with creating learning environments that would help a child move from one cognitive stage to another, would find the IEP process as compatible or ultimately as useful as did the teachers in the second group. Thus, some of the teachers in the original survey who were pessimistic about the usefulness of the IEP may have felt that way because they adhered to a nonbehavioral educational philosophy.

The degree to which teachers' actual lesson planning approximates Shavelson's (1976) ideal sequence is also unclear. Some work by Morine (1976) suggests that in writing lesson plans, teachers tend to state nonbehavioral goals and fail to state the present level of the students or the procedures to be used in evaluating the lesson. These, of course, are the elements of instructional planning for which the IEP process seems to have the most potential relevance. Thus, if teachers are not including these elements in their lesson planning, one should not be surprised that they do not perceive the IEP as facilitating their task. (Morine does point out, however, that the fact that teachers don't address the level of the students or evaluation procedures in their written plan doesn't necessarily mean they don't consider these issues mentally.)

The second group of teachers expressed some hope that the IEP requirement would force more teachers to do the type of planning and record keeping that these teachers believed was necessary for effective instruction. To date, no research has been conducted which validates the superiority of a diagnostic/prescriptive, data-based approach or the effects of instructional planning on teaching performance (Morine, 1976). Despite these cautions, findings from the second group of districts suggest that once an efficient IEP process is underway, it will prove to be instructionally relevant to at least those special education teachers who favor a diagnostic/prescriptive, precision approach.

Reorientation of Special Education Classrooms

A second factor seen as affecting the time teachers spend in working directly with students is an anticipated reorientation of special education classrooms to provide for the implementation of individualized education programs. Although individual instruction is not required by PL 94-142, many of the first group teachers assumed that a great deal of individualization would be necessary to provide appropriate educational activities for children having various goals and objectives. Individualization frequently means establishing work stations where individual pupils or small groups of pupils

Instructional Planning for Exceptional Children

can work on appropriate self-instructional materials. Teacher time then must be expended in supervising—circulating among work centers to make sure students are on task, checking pupil progress, recording pupil progress, and locating materials for the next day's objectives.

Individualization also frequently brings aides, volunteers, or student tutors into the classroom to work with individual students or small groups. Teacher time, then, also must be spent directing the activities of these other persons—assigning and explaining tasks to them, supervising tasks, and coordinating their schedules. Although the addition of other persons to the class may increase the interaction individual students have with adults, teachers generally are convinced that these supporting persons cannot provide the same quality of instruction as a trained teacher. Thus, from the teachers' perspective, an amount of their potential instructional time is taken up supervising persons who cannot provide the same high quality of instruction.

Interviews in the second group of districts confirmed both an expanded job description for teachers and a trend toward individualized instruction within the classroom. These teachers reported performing regular informal assessments, writing goals and objectives, conferring with parents, and keeping records of progress toward goals and objectives. The teachers also reported a high level of individualization in their classrooms, at least for the basic skill subjects of reading, math, and spelling. All of the teachers interviewed in the second group had established at least a few work centers and used tape recorders, individual folders, or clipboards to inform students of their day's activities. Work centers were predominant in resource classes, but even teachers in self-contained classes reported establishing some work centers and spending part of the day (generally the part of the day devoted to basic academic skills) using an individualized instructional format. Students moved through the centers working on their assigned activities, generally worksheets or a set of exercises in a programmed text. Upon completing an assignment, students were checked for progress by the teacher, an aide, or sometimes checked themselves, then moved on to the next center.

Most of the teachers interviewed in the second group of districts reported spending considerable amounts of time checking and recording pupil progress, supervising students at their work centers to make sure they were on task, writing new short-term objectives, and locating or developing appropriate materials for accomplishing individual objectives. Several teachers reported using their aides to keep records, check progress, and help locate materials. Almost all teachers interviewed in the second group had aides and/or volunteers at least part of the day. Though teachers were grateful for the additional support, they also spoke of their feelings of frustration at having to take time "from the children" to explain assignments or procedures to the aides or volunteers.

Thus, reorientation of the classroom is confirmed somewhat by the second group of teachers. Clearly, each pupil spends less time in direct interaction with the teacher. Not only must teaching time be divided among the number of pupils or groups in the class, but a very real factor seems to be that teachers do have to engage in programming, record keeping, and supervisory activities that were not formerly a part of their role. Several of these teachers, particularly at the secondary level, appeared to be spending almost all of their time in such activities, with virtually no time remaining for instructing students directly.

The benefit or harm of such circumstances for students seems to depend in part on whether the education provided by carefully selected self-instructional materials such as programmed texts or worksheets is equal in quality to the education received through more direct, intense teacher interactions. A director of special education in the second group of districts indirectly addressed this issue. In reporting his district's experiences over a period of several years, he spoke of a tendency, when initially instituting an individualized prescriptive system, to overrely on self-instructional materials and work centers to the detriment of educational quality. This tendency stems, in his opinion, from the noninstructional demands placed on teachers which, without appropriate support from the district, can be awesome. Although this district initially had experienced this situation, teachers estimate that they now spend 50 minutes of every hour directly teaching children—attributed both to the emphasis that the district placed on direct instruction and to the administrative support provided to teachers.

Although many teachers in the second group of districts were spending a great deal of time assessing students, planning programs, keeping records, or supervising instead of directly instructing, none of the teachers expressed dissatisfaction with these aspects of the job. Furthermore, they gave no indication that they thought their students were receiving less than quality educational experiences. All of the teachers interviewed, however, had received their special education training in institutions stressing a diagnostic/prescriptive, precision approach to special education. This then may account for their satisfaction with their current classroom role.

The director of special education interviewed stated that as state and district policies had moved toward greater accountability and a diagnostic/prescriptive approach, some special education teachers had left the system. Presumably, these teachers were less satisfied with certain aspects of their changing role. Thus, some caution must be used in generalizing the positive attitude of teachers interviewed in the second group of districts to other teachers.

Shared Responsibility for Classroom Activities

In each of the four states, special education teachers expressed concern that they would lose some amount of control in the pupil planning process as a result of the specification in PL 94-142 that a child's educational program plan be developed at a meeting attended by the parent and an LEA representative. Teachers in this first group viewed the inclusion of others in program development as meaning that classroom planning which previously had been handled primarily by the teacher would now be a shared responsibility. As one district director of special education noted, bringing others into the planning process to discuss and plan for classroom instruction makes many teachers feel that what they have been doing has not been adequate. In addition, many of these teachers resented the fact that persons not responsible for classroom instruction would now have a role in planning for it. Some predicted that parents might insist on setting objectives inappropriate for a child or that a psychologist, unfamiliar with classroom instruction, might recommend objectives in line with results of an assessment but beyond the scope of the classroom setting. The teacher then would be obligated to teach unrealistic objectives.

Most teachers in this first group stressed that the teacher, trained to instruct and knowledgeable about the functioning of the child in the classroom, is best able to determine objectives and select instructional materials and strategies. Though not denying the value of input from parents or other professionals, teachers clearly believed they should have the ultimate say in determining an educational program. Teachers viewed PL 94-142 as potentially reducing their autonomy in determining educational programs and classroom activities by mandating the participation of other persons in the planning process.

In contrast, teachers in the second group of districts reported that sharing responsibility in the pupil planning process has not resulted in a loss of control over either the development of educational plans or the provision of classroom instruction. They reported that they still exercise primary control over the goals and short-term objectives they will teach to in the classroom. The one change they mentioned was simplifying their language to better communicate the nature of the objectives to parents. They reported, however, that parents generally viewed the parental role in planning as providing input and approving the educational program plan. None of these teachers reported that parents used their expanded role in program development to make unreasonable demands. As pointed out by parents and some school personnel in the initial interviews, most parents consider the teacher and other school personnel, because of their training, best prepared to determine the specifics of the child's program.

In one of the districts, the problem of other school personnel contributing unreasonable goals and objectives to the child's program plan was handled by assigning responsibility for working on the goal or objective to the person suggesting it. If another staff member suggests a goal or objective, the teacher includes it in the plan only if he or she is in agreement with it or if the other staff member agrees to take responsibility for it. In the other districts, teachers said the IEP process had not resulted in conflicts between them and other staff members over decisions related to program development and classroom instruction. In fact, they said the group process often facilitated staff interactions that produced qualitatively better information in the planning process.

There are obvious limits to the extent to which the experiences of the second group of districts can be expected to foreshadow the experiences of other districts in other states which may have quite different circumstances. The experiences of the second group of teachers, however, are consistent with a survey from the State of Connecticut which found members of placement teams to share the perception that the special education teacher was the most appropriate person to suggest students' subject matter needs, suggest instructional methods for students, and to set evaluation criteria for students' academic performance (Fenton, Yoshida, Maxwell & Kaufman, 1977). This certainly implies, as was found in the second group of districts, a continuing, predominant role for the special education teacher in planning the education of handicapped students.

Increased Accountability to Outsiders

Many of the first group of teachers thought that with the implementation of PL 94-142 they would be monitored by outsiders and be held more accountable for pupil progress because of the specificity of the individualized education plan and the collection of extensive data implied by the law. These concerns seemed to stem from two sources. On the one hand, some teachers believed that any federal law implies more accountability on the part of persons whose functions are affected by its mandated provisions than would a state or local regulation. In the case of PL 94-142, teachers in the first group assumed that federal regulation of certain elements of educational planning and programming would mean actual monitoring, perhaps even federal monitoring, of the teaching function and the teacher. On the other hand, teachers viewed the law's provision that measurable evaluative criteria be included in the educational program plan to mean that continuous measurable progress for each child was expected, an expectation they thought put unreasonable pressure on them as teachers. They pointed out that factors over which the teacher has little or no control, such as the home situation, available resources, or the child's physical or emotional condition, often interfere with teaching efforts and slow the child's progress, necessitating substantial revision of goals or objectives.

Many teachers were concerned that the IEP would be used by parents and school administrators to measure teacher performance, or by the state or federal government to monitor a district's compliance with the law. They had many reservations about such people's knowledge or awareness of the actual classroom situation. Consequently, they considered setting general objectives in the child's plan as preferable to the risk of being seen as a failure or being held liable. (One should note that the regulation governing PL 94-142 states that the IEP document is not a legal contract and, therefore, teachers and school districts cannot be held liable for a child's failure to attain a specified objective.)

In summary, concerns of teachers in the first group focused on their perception that under PL 94-142 they would be charged with producing continuous measurable progress toward goals and objectives with which they might not fully agree and, furthermore, that their success in so doing would be the sole criteria used by persons unfamiliar with the classroom situation or the child's functioning in that classroom in judging teaching effectiveness.

The issue of accountability was difficult to pursue in the second group of districts, because teachers virtually dismissed as impossible the idea of being monitored by unknowledgeable outsiders. These teachers viewed accountability not as a threat in the sense of liability, but from a personal perspective, as a function of the teaching job. To them, acceptance of the job meant also the acceptance of personal responsibility for facilitating pupil progress.

Thus, all the teachers interviewed in the second group saw the continual measurement of pupil progress as helping them monitor their own teaching effectiveness on an ongoing basis. Each stressed the importance of data collection and detailed record-keeping in enhancing their ability to continuously monitor pupil progress and to respond quickly and effectively to the child's learning needs. Without accurate, up-to-date records on each child, teachers questioned how they could identify current levels of performance, plan for the next step in any given area, or determine what materials and methods to employ. They found the extensive documentation to be so useful that, even without being required to do so, they claimed they would continue it as part of their teaching.

While teachers in the first group were concerned that a child's failure to meet a goal or objective set out in the IEP might reflect negatively upon them, teachers in the second group of districts expressed no such concern. On the contrary, they said that a child's failure to attain a particular objective provides them with important information. They use their records on the child to help determine an approach that might work better in teaching the objective or perhaps to select another, simpler objective.

These teachers in the second group expressed a similar attitude about projecting a child's expected progress. They did not think that missing one of their projections reflects on them personally. Their attitude was that a goal or objective is at best an estimate of where the child is going and that everyone involved accepts that view. These teachers essentially had confidence in their ability to effect pupil progress and viewed accountability in terms of their own responsibility toward the child rather than in terms of potential personal or district liability.

This attitude undoubtedly derived from the tone set at the district level. Clearly, these teachers never had been "brought to task" for failing to promote progress with a child or to attain a goal or objective. Although teachers in two of the districts met regularly with district personnel to discuss pupil progress and teachers in all of the districts met regularly with parents, the sessions were viewed as problem solving sessions, not checks on the teacher. These teachers also expressed confidence that if a parent should ever charge a teacher with not meeting a goal or objective that had turned out to be unfeasible, the teacher would receive full support by the district.

As PL 94-142 is implemented nationally, one can expect that a district's posture toward group planning and teacher accountability will affect its teachers' attitudes. In districts where the IEP conference and review sessions are perceived by all involved as cooperative, problem solving sessions rather than checks on the teacher, teachers' experiences and perspectives hopefully will be positive. On the other hand, in districts where an atmosphere of distrust prevails among staff members or between parents and school personnel, teachers may indeed feel they are being put on the defensive.

Demands on Personal Time

Teachers interviewed in the first group of districts expressed concern that carrying out the tasks associated with individualized education programming would place extraordinary demands on their already overcommitted time. Teachers reported that they presently were working long hours preparing lessons, developing materials, and keeping records. They believed that to carry out informal assessments, write annual goals and short term objectives, coordinate with other professionals, and meet with parents, they would have to commit increasing amounts of their personal time to fulfilling their teaching functions. Though a number of teachers in the first group stated that they already were individualizing instruction in their classroom, teachers were still apprehensive about the time required to prepare individualized learning activities for their students, as well as the time required to keep detailed records of progress for each student. Teachers expressed fears that the additional time would be at the expense of their families, professional development, or other outside interests.

Instructional Planning for Exceptional Children

One of the supposed benefits of a teaching career has been the shorter working day (Lortie, 1975). Surveys have suggested, however, that although teachers spend fewer than the standard 40 hours in classroom instruction, their other job-related activities add considerable time to the total. A National Education Association survey (1967), for example, found that elementary teachers worked an average of 46.5 hours per week, and secondary teachers worked 48.3. A similar survey by New York Teacher's Association (cited in Anderson, Christin, Hunsberger, 1974) found that elementary teachers spent 47.8 hours in school related activities, and secondary teachers spent 50.3 hours. Breaking down the figure for elementary teachers, this survey reported that 36.7 hours were spent in the classroom, 9.6 hours in preparing lessons and grading papers, and 1.5 hours in professional activities.

Special education teachers interviewed in the four states in the Project IEP study stated that they worked even longer hours than their regular education counterparts, a viewpoint that principals and directors of special education tended to confirm. Assuming that the special education teachers interviewed were spending only the average number of hours reported in the national survey for elementary teachers, it is hardly surprising that they would be concerned about the assignment of other potentially time-consuming responsibilities.

Formally developed individualized education programs are a relatively new and little studied innovation. Further, IEP development time can be expected to vary depending on grade level, type of handicap, local procedures, and whether the IEP is for a current special education student or a new referral. One recent study found that the average amount of time a teacher spends collecting data and writing an IEP for each preschool handicapped child was 10.9 hours, and the median was 5.0 hours (Davis, 1977). (The author of that paper suggests that because of extreme scores, the median is a more accurate estimate than the mean.) Even the more conservative figure, multiplied by the number of children in the average special education resource or self-contained class, results in a considerable number of potential hours.

In the second group of districts, most teachers confirmed the heavy time commitment required of teachers in writing and implementing individualized education programs for handicapped children. In three of the districts, the estimated number of hours spent per week in job-related activities ranged from 55 to 67 hours among the teachers interviewed. These teachers reported spending time before and after their instructional day locating or developing materials for individual pupils, writing short-term objectives, keeping records, conferring with other teachers and support personnel, and assessing and developing IEPs for new referrals. Most teachers stated that they had to spend even more time in the fall and spring in administering informal assessments, writing goals and objectives, contacting parents, and attending conferences for each student they instructed.

When asked about the length of time usually required to actually complete an IEP, these teachers estimated 5 to 6½ hours for a new referral and 2 to 4 hours for a student currently in the program. For new referrals, teachers reported spending 2 to 3 hours assessing the child, 1 to 2 hours writing goals and objectives, ½ hour arranging the conference, and 1 to 1½ hours in the IEP conference. In reviewing the plans of current students, teachers may spend up to 2 hours assessing the child, ½ hour writing goals and objectives, ½ hour arranging the IEP conference, and 1 hour in the conference. None of the districts in the second group compensated teachers in any way for hours spent beyond contract time.

Teachers in these districts, though adamant in their support for individualized, data-based instruction, nonetheless spoke with some discouragment about the time involved. One teacher spoke of the frustrations she felt in spending more than 55 hours a week at her job and still not being able to get everything done. "It's hard," she said, "never getting closure." Another teacher referred to the long, uncompensated hours by saying, "It's worth it, but it's not right."

Teachers, directors of special education, and a principal in the second group of districts referred to teacher "burn out" when extraordinarily long hours are required just to get the job done. Several teachers wondered aloud how long they would be able to keep up the pace before they would give up and quit. One director of special education actually reported that the district anticipated that teachers would have "two to three good years" and then move on to something else.

Data from three of the four districts in the second group, then, essentially confirmed the legitimacy of concern for personal time that was expressed by the first group of teachers. An issue emerging from interviews with all of the teachers focuses on the amount of time and energy that can justly be demanded of special education teachers without compensation. Some have suggested that the IEP requirements of PL 94-142 in some sense formalize the heart of special education—diagnostic/prescriptive teaching—but can any system of teaching be valid if it is at the expense of special education teachers?

Experiences of three of the districts in the second group suggest that, at present, implementation of individualized education programming relies to a great extent on the good will and dedication of special education teachers, not on the provision of adequate resources. But the resulting phenomenon of special education teacher "burn out" cannot be ignored. A turnover of teachers, say, every three to five years would be a waste of both training and valuable experience. Equally disturbing are the potential effects on students of "burned out" teachers who decide to stay.

Persons interviewed in the first group of districts suggested that implementation of individualized education would require more planning time for special education teachers. Suggestions included: providing additional support staff to assist in noninstructional tasks, hiring additional specialists such as art, music, or physical education teachers to relieve special education teachers by allowing them free periods during the day, compensating teachers for work after hours, moving to 12-month contracts for special education teachers, and designing forms, procedures, and support systems that facilitate the tasks of the teacher.

Most of the suggestions, of course, require increased fiscal commitment by the local education agency. For the most part, the directors of special education interviewed in the second group of districts stated that they were unable to make such a fiscal commitment, although they tried in every way possible to continually increase aide time available to teachers. Because of fiscal limitations, the directors primarily attempted to alleviate the tasks of special education teachers by streamlining forms and procedures and developing resource systems for support.

That district planning and effort expended in this way could be effective was particularly demonstrated in one of the four districts included in the second group. The planning procedures, forms, and available resource support system in this district were perhaps the most elaborate and comprehensive of the districts in the second group. Teachers interviewed in this district expressed obvious enthusiasm for their jobs. For the most part, these teachers stated they spent only 5 to 10 hours per week beyond contract time, giving them a 40 to 50 hour work week. The exception they cited was during the period of IEP development or review, when parent conferenes required them to spend more time before or after school.

New Requisite Skills

A final area of concern expressed by special education teachers in the first group of districts centered on their feelings that they might not have the skills necessary to carry out all the tasks required or implied by individualized educational programming. Some teachers believed that to adequately fulfill the provisions of the federal law, they would need training in performing educational assessments, identifying and projecting appropriate goals and objectives, writing annual goals and short-term objectives, collecting data, managing individualized classroom instruction, and communicating with parents.

Both teachers and administrators in the first group agreed that much in-service training would be necessary to inform teachers of the new policies and procedures and to provide training in required skill areas in which deficiencies existed. Persons interviewed, however, did not specifically state the skills they thought teachers would lack or the extent to which the special education teaching population could be expected to need additional training.

All the teachers interviewed in the second group of districts reported that although they had needed more information about new procedures when state or federal regulations were introduced, they had developed most of the requisite skills for implementing individualized education programs during their university training courses. Directors of special education in the second group agreed that, in most instances, teachers who had received their special education training in the last few years needed little additional training except for learning specific district policies and procedures. Two of the directors stated that they had avoided the need for additional training to a great extent by careful hiring practices during the past few years; in both districts, virtually all of the teachers who remained in the system had received extensive training in diagnostic/prescriptive teaching as part of their university program. In the remaining two districts, directors and teachers reported the necessity of providing training beyond an explanation of new policies and procedures to some, although not most, of the teachers in the district.

Directors and teachers in the second group of districts stated that learning to project goals and objectives for a specific period of time and matching appropriate materials with goals and objectives tended to cause teachers the most problems. All agreed that while some training in these skills could be useful, they developed primarily from experience; that is, these teachers believed that familiarity with materials, understanding curricular sequences of objectives, and ease in using alternative instructional methods developed after a few years of actually planning for and instructing handicapped children.

In contrast, many teachers believed that writing goals and objectives could be taught successfully in a workshop format. In one district, teachers referred to in-service training sessions they had held in which participants developed actual goals and objectives for children, then critiqued each other's work. Although those involved thought this format was successful, they expanded on their statements by suggesting that much on-the-job practice must follow if the writing of behavioral objectives is to become automatic. This district also had presented several workshops in various curricular areas that focused on developmental sequences of skills, since they had found that many teachers have difficulty in sequencing goals and objectives. Their experience seemed to be that this was a useful way to spend in-service time, although it was still necessary for teachers to have continual access to various curriculum guides and objective banks.

Although interviews in the second group of districts confirmed the need for in-service training, interviewees seemed to think that need was less critical

Instructional Planning for Exceptional Children

and seemed less concerned about the scope and amount of in-service training required. In part, this opinion may stem again from the fact that almost all of the teachers in these districts had received special education training at either a bachelor's or master's level within the past five years and, further, that they had received this training from institutions stressing the skills needed to provide individualized education programs. Unfortunately, we do not know how typical this situation is. Certainly, we have reason to believe that the trend toward diagnostic/prescriptive teaching in special education is reflected increasingly in special education training programs. Thus, we may expect that teachers trained within the last five years would, at a minimum, be able to perform educational assessments and write behavioral goals and objectives. The issue is, then, what percentage of teachers this might include.

Information from one recent study, Project PRIME, showed that 42 to 43 percent of special education teachers had been teaching five years or less (Baker, Safer, & Guskin, 1977). One may reasonably assume that at least some of the teachers with more years of teaching experience would have pursued master's degrees in special education or would have switched from regular to special education and taken college classes since the beginning of their teaching careers. This assumption still leads to the conclusion that, despite the experience of the second group of teachers, a sizeable number (though probably not a majority) of special education teachers in many school districts across the nation may be lacking certain skills necessary for providing individualized education programs to handicapped children.

Information from the second group of districts does suggest that although some skills, such as writing goals and objectives, can be taught relatively easily in a workshop format, other skills, such as learning to project annual goals, simply may require experience in doing the task. Much evidence suggests that before launching a major in-service training program, districts should assess carefully the percentage of teachers who actually lack requisite skills, the specific skills lacking, and whether those skills can be acquired by training.

Comment on Perceptions of Changes in Teacher Role and Job Requirements

Special education teachers interviewed during Project IEP confirmed that the impact of implementation of individualized educational programming would be to change the nature of their role as teacher from that of providers of instruction to instructional managers. Essentially, they saw some *basic* changes to their role. The work of Lortie (1975) suggests that role changes, particularly ones that affect the reward system offered by a job or career, can have a major impact on job satisfaction or morale. Among the types of role changes that could particularly affect the "psychic rewards" received by teachers were: less direct instruction by teachers because of noninstructional activities, loss of teacher control over classroom activities, and increased accountability to outsiders.

In examining the perceptions of teachers in the first group, the Project IEP study found that they perceive implementation of individualized educational programming as changing their roles in exactly these ways, as well as placing inordinate demands on their time and requiring skills they don't have. Thus, they gave reason to believe that the anticipated changes are important in terms of teacher role—changes that could affect their satisfaction with teaching and their morale.

A different perspective characterized the second group of teachers. Although the changes in teacher role anticipated by teachers in the first group were confirmed, teachers in the second group did not perceive those changes negatively. Most of the second group teachers did report spending a lot of time supervising, preparing materials, writing objectives, and keeping records rather than directly instructing pupils; but they saw these tasks as related to instruction and an integral part of their teaching. In addition, these teachers saw themselves as still controlling the educational program in their classrooms and as having most of the skills they needed to implement individualized education programs. Instead of fearing liability from monitoring, the second group of teachers considered the detailed records they kept to be primarily a tool that helped them monitor their own teaching effectiveness rather than evidence that others would use in judging them. The only real concern expressed by teachers in the second group dealt with the extraordinary amount of time they had to spend to adequately carry out the various tasks associated with their role.

The discrepant pictures painted by the two groups of special education teachers raise a question: Will the concerns expressed by the first group, concerns which Lortie's work suggests could be serious, simply disappear given greater experience with the IEP process? Several factors suggest that, at least in some instances, they won't.

When teachers and directors of special education in the second group of districts were asked why they thought implementation of individualized educational programming had worked in their districts—how they had avoided many of the problems anticipated in other districts and other states—they touched on several common themes. Essentially, these related to the ways in which changes were undertaken and facets of administrative support which the districts offered to teachers. Maybe districts that did not approach change in the same way or did not offer teachers adequate administrative support would experience many more of the anticipated problems.

Of possibly even greater significance in explaining the divergent perspectives may be that most of the teachers interviewed in the second group of districts had received their special education training within the past five years from institutions focusing on a diagnostic/prescriptive approach to special education combined with elements of precision or data-based instruction. The IEP process mandated by PL 94-142 has been interpreted as closely following the tenets of diagnostic/prescriptive, data-based teaching; teachers thoroughly trained in this approach, therefore, would be more inclined to perceive implementation of individualized educational programming not so much as changing their role as bringing it in line with special education teaching as they believe it should be. Since rapidly increasing numbers of training programs have adopted a diagnostic/prescriptive approach over the past few years, a growing number of teachers across the country will likely deemphasize the role changes associated with individualized educational programming as, at most, a problem of logistics.

At the same time, one must remember that diagnostic/prescriptive, data-based teaching is only one of several potentially valid approaches to teaching children. To teachers holding other educational philosophies or perspectives, the role changes associated with implementation of federal and state regulations indeed may seem major. To these teachers, the IEP process may appear to be no more than a series of clerical tasks, pulling them away from teaching children, decreasing their control over their classroom programs, and ultimately resulting in lowered morale. Certainly this is a perspective of which to be cognizant.

IMPLEMENTATION STRATEGIES AND ADMINISTRATIVE SUPPORT TO TEACHERS

When asked why their systems worked as well as they did, directors of special education and special education teachers in the second group of districts cited two significant factors: the *implementation strategies* used when individualized instruction was initiated, and the *support systems* available to teachers.

In reviewing the research on implementation of new curricula and instructional methods, Fullan and Pomfret (1977) suggest four strategies that are important in the successful implementation of innovations. These are: *participation in decision making, in-service training, resource support*, and *feedback mechanisms*. It was interesting to note that the practices described by administrators and teachers in the second group of districts fell into these four categories.

Participation in Decision Making

In three of the second group districts, administrators involved teachers from the beginning in planning for implementation of individualized educational programming. Either as individual consultants or as members of task force committees, teachers worked with administrators in comparing current practices with future goals and new mandates to determine the specific areas in which changes would have to be made. Also, they suggested strategies for facilitating the required changes in district policies, procedures, responsibilities, and forms, and identified the skills and knowledge teachers would need in order to assume new responsibilities. Further, they designed in-service training directed toward acquisition of those new requisite skills for implementing individualized educational programming. Teachers and administrators emphasized that this joint planning fostered an accepting attitude toward the changes that extended beyond the few who participated in the planning effort.

Since newly identified responsibilities and procedures reflected teachers' concerns for educational relevance and instructional utility, they were more readily accepted than if they simply had been imposed by administrators. In two of the districts, other school personnel such as psychologists and education specialists were included in the planning efforts because of the interrelationship of functions and responsibilities associated with providing individualized education programs to children with handicapping conditions. Those interviewed agreed that consideration of multiple perspectives resulted in development of a system responsive to the concerns of all who would be involved in its implementation. Therefore, the inclusion of teachers and other staff members in determining district policies and practices related to individualized educational programming was reported as a critical factor to successful implementation in all of the second group of districts.

In-Service Training

As mentioned previously, all of the districts in the second group had used in-service training sessions to acquaint teachers with new policies and procedures, and to teach skills such as writing behavioral objectives and sequencing goals and objectives when necessary. All four directors of special education and most teachers emphasized the important role that in-service training had played in the success of implementation. In addition, two of the four directors said that in-service training has become an integral part of their special education program. Workshops in these districts are held on a regular basis, about twice a month after school. The topics presented are selected largely on the basis of teacher suggestions. Additionally, teachers proficient in particular skill areas often plan and conduct the in-service training sessions, which reportedly are well received.

Beyond workshop-type in-service training, one of the second group of districts used a mentor system to orient new special education teachers. In this district an educational specialist is assigned to each new teacher for the first month of school. Citing the complexity of individualized educational programming, and particularly of this district's IEP system, the director and teachers said it usually takes a year of experience before a new teacher feels comfortable managing all the tasks and responsibilities associated with the teacher role. To facilitate the new teacher's entry into the system, the educational consultant is available both during and after school hours and serves as a resource for any areas in which the teacher needs help. All those interviewed believed this approach to be an important supplement to the usual in-service activities.

Resource Support

Teachers and administrators in the second group of districts identified ways in which teachers were receiving support in carrying out their planning and instructional responsibilities. The teachers found this support critical to providing effective individualized education. Resource support included: provision of assessment systems, sequences of objectives, adequate materials cross-referenced to objectives, standardized forms, aides, and consultative assistance.

Each district was found to employ practices that effectively reduced the amount of teacher time and effort to complete tasks associated with planning. Three of the districts had adopted a standard battery of assessment instruments which was quickly and easily administered and thought to be particularly useful in determining the child's level of functioning in various skill areas. Two of these districts actually had developed their own assessment instruments; these instruments allowed a child's performance on a particular scale to be translated immediately into specific objectives from an objectives sequence.

Availability of sets sequences objectives in at least the basic skill areas of reading, math, and spelling also was cited as extremely useful in formulating individualized education plans. In three districts, the objectives sequences had been developed by the teachers and tested in the district for at least a year. According to those interviewed, objectives are stated simply, are highly specific, and are accompanied by appropriate evaluation criteria. Once the child's current level of performance in a skill area has been determined, the teacher automatically selects an appropriate objective from the continuum of skills and attaches a copy of the sequence to the child's program plan.

Since statements of objective criteria accompany each objective, little teacher time is devoted to determining appropriate evaluation measures. Teachers and administrators both pointed out that sequenced objectives stated with the evaluation component were particularly helpful to newer teachers not yet experienced either in sequencing tasks or in determining appropriate measurement criteria. Several teachers said that sequenced objectives in basic subject areas meant that teachers did not have to "reinvent the wheel" and could devote their time to other things.

Resource support in the area of materials was another important feature listed by special education teachers in the second group of districts. In three of these districts, teachers had access to numerous commercially-produced or teacher-generated materials at either the building or district level or both; nonetheless, they reported spending considerable time searching for materials appropriate for particular objectives or developing materials themselves.

In one of the districts, however, teachers indicated that their resource system in the area of materials was particularly helpful and supportive. This district, which operates with district-generated sequences of objectives in basic skill areas, has materials cross-referenced to objectives in such a way that teachers can easily select an appropriate commercial material for a particular objective. Several choices are listed whenever possible so that teachers may use the materials they prefer and so that alternatives are available to meet the needs of different children. This district also maintains a highly organized materials center, which includes teacher-generated and tested materials organized both by objective and subject area. Thus, in this district, the process of determining an objective, identifying appropriate materials to teach it, and procuring the materials is relatively simple and, teachers reported, not time consuming. Teachers said they still develop new materials as they see the need for them, but they do not have to devote continual attention to the task.

A final type of support identified as essential to facilitating the planning function was a rational set of forms for planning and record keeping. Teachers and the directors of special education in three districts of the second group agreed that the outstanding features of the system of forms used in their districts are that they parallel the planning process, feed directly into one another, and are useful to teachers for both long-range and daily instructional planning. While the forms differed in format from one district to another, they all enabled teachers and other staff to easily and concisely record all essential planning data related to assessment, goals, objectives, and evaluation, and to record pupil progress for each objective on a continuing basis. In each of the three districts, the forms used in the IEP process had been designed to support teachers' information needs so that further documentation in the form of daily lesson planning or record keeping was not necessary.

While stressing the importance of support to teachers in carrying out their planning tasks, teachers and administrators in the second group of districts believed that individualized education was possible only in conjunction with *classroom* support. To varying degrees, these districts provided such support.

In each district, teachers reported having three to four hours daily of teacher aide time. In addition, student or community volunteers or student interns were assigned to assist teachers in the classroom. Depending upon their experience and training, these people were given such responsibilities as instruction, data collection, record keeping, and preparing student folders. Teachers said that, although coordination of additional personnel is sometimes difficult, the assistance they provide is invaluable. Two of the four district directors of special education said they deemed aide assistance so important in carrying out individualized instruction that they commit their scarce resources to it at the expense of other budget items.

In addition to assistance in the classroom, one of the second group of districts was experimenting with a rather innovative approach referred to as the *teacher advisor model*. This model assigns either a psychologist, communication disorders specialist, or education specialist to work on a continuing basis with each special education teacher. Twice weekly the advisor visits the classroom, either to observe, experiment with a new instructional strategy, or to work with a child in need of special help—in general, to be of whatever service the advisor and teacher agree to. The two of them meet once a week for discussions about changes in individual programs and classroom activities. Teachers said this model is a source of continual feedback to them on their teaching, and considered it a particularly supportive approach.

Feedback Mechanism

No formal feedback mechanism was discussed in any of the second group of districts. At the same time, it was apparent in talking to teachers and administrators that informal feedback is a continuous process in these districts. In all four districts, policies and practices concerning individualized educational programming had changed over a period of time as teachers and other staff members determined what seemed to work or didn't work. Two of the districts reported almost weekly meetings with the entire special education staff of the district to exchange information and discuss various practices. The critical function of feedback seemed to be adequately served in these districts on an informal basis.

Comment on Implementation Strategies and Support to Teachers

Information from the second group of districts suggested that successful implementation of individualized programming depended in part on the implementation strategies and support systems adopted by the district. Fullan and Pomfret (1977) suggested four strategies and tactics important to the successful implementation of innovations—participation in decision making, in-service training, resource support, and feedback mechanisms. The critical practices and policies described in the second group of districts fit into these strategy categories. Fullan and Pomfret also suggested that the four types of strategies or tactics are interactive in the sense that the absence of any one reduces the effectiveness of the others. Though the information from the Project IEP study is not such that this interactive effect can be examined, some evidence indicated that the degree of comprehensiveness in the implementation strategies and support system offered by a district had a cumulative effect on teacher morale and satisfaction.

For example, one of the second group of districts had developed an assessment battery leading directly to objective sequences which, in turn, were cross-referenced to materials. This same district was experimenting with the mentor in-service approach for orienting new teachers, as well as the teacher advisor model. Although teachers in all four districts expressed satisfaction with their role as special education teacher, teachers in this particular district were the most enthusiastic, stating that even the time demands were reasonable. And when asked what made their role so satisfying, all of the teachers interviewed in this district replied that the system of support offered by the district essentially freed them to teach in a way they believed in and thought personally fulfilling. Thus, the implementation strategies and systems of support developed by the second group of districts seem to be critical in implementing individualized educational programming for handicapped children.

SUMMARY AND IMPLICATIONS

Potential role changes and changes in job requirements for special education teachers related to the implementation of individualized educational programming include less direct instruction because of teacher resources expended on noninstructional tasks, shared responsibility for classroom activities, increased accountability to outsiders, demands on teacher time, and new requisite skills. Though all of these changes were confirmed by interviews in the second group of districts, they did not necessarily result in low morale and decreased job satisfaction. Three factors seemed critical in determining whether changes resulted in decreased satisfaction—teacher beliefs and style, time, and district implementation strategies and support to teachers.

Teacher Beliefs and Style

One crucial factor related to teacher morale and job satisfaction appears to be the degree to which the model of individualized education selected by an LEA or state is flexible enough to accommodate varying teacher beliefs and styles.

The four districts in the second group had selected models of individualized education that were data-based and behaviorally oriented. This selection was compatible with the orientation expressed by teachers in these districts, many of whom had been trained in a precision-teaching model; thus, these teachers were satisfied with the model of individualized educational programming they were using.

The language used in PL 94-142 tends to lend itself to a similar data-based, behaviorally oriented interpretation, although that may or may not have been the lawmakers' intent. An example of such an interpretation is given in an article by Lilly (1977), which stresses highly specific, performance based objectives, quantitative evaluative criteria, collection of baseline data, and frequent (twice weekly) measurement and recording of progress. This orientation may not be compatible with all teaching styles and beliefs. For instance, a teacher oriented toward a Piagetian style of teaching might be interested in helping a child move from one cognitive stage to another. The process of considering the child's current level, where the child should be going, how to move toward that point, and signs indicating that the child has reached the new stage should be useful to such a teacher. However, stipulating highly specific objectives and quantitative criteria may not be as useful in this case as stating less specific objectives and some qualitative signs as criteria. Further, frequent measurement actually may interfere with the type of learning environment the teacher is trying to establish. If forced to use a highly specific, data-based model of individualized education, the teacher may feel that he or she is wasting time planning and record keeping. Such feelings could result in frustration and low morale.

If evidence existed that a behavioral, data-based orientation to planning and instruction resulted in greater achievement for handicapped children, one would have good reason for insisting on such an approach to individualized educational programming. Such evidence, however, does not exist at present. Furthermore, the regulations to PL 94-142 do not require that objectives be written in performance terms, that evaluative criteria be quantitative, or that measurements of progress take place more than once a year.

In establishing policies and procedures for individualized educational programming, then, districts should consider carefully the orientation and flexibility implied by those procedures. A decision to require highly specific behavioral objectives, quantitative criteria, and frequent record keeping should reflect a conscious and articulated decision to orient special education to a precision-teaching, data-based approach.

There also is a need to explore the individualized educational programming process to determine alternative ways it can be structured both to meet federal and state regulations and to be relevant to teachers with differing beliefs and styles. Likely, provisions of the federal law can be interpreted more flexibly than they often are. For example, a list of *qualitative* signs that indicate achievement of an objective should be considered as valid as *quantitative* criteria. Also, one could contend that "objective criteria" simply means the judgment of persons other than those directly working with the child. Then, agreement of the IEP committee, including the parent or outside observers, that a child has "a more positive self concept" or is "less hyperactive" might serve as sufficient evidence that an objective is being met.

A similar need exists for exploring the instructional options for individualized educational programming. Although it has been assumed that much more individual instruction will now take place within the classroom, *individualized education is not synonymous with individual education.* Work stations with individual assignments are certainly one option for providing individualized educational programming, but other options such as teaching a group lesson at several different levels to meet the needs of different children, also exist. For example, a teacher conducting a group discussion following a science demonstration might expect some children to name only the materials used (vocabulary building), others to express themselves using complete sentences, and still others to make certain inferences related to the demonstrated concepts. Certainly, much creative thinking should be devoted to determining a wide range of viable instructional options for providing individualized educational programming.

Time

Information from the second group of districts suggested that most teachers were spending extensive amounts of time carrying out their planning and instructional tasks. Concerns were expressed that teacher "burn out" is becoming an increasing problem in special education because of the greater time demands placed on special education teachers.

Although most teachers in the second group of districts clearly were spending much more than their contract time, how much of this time was related in individualized educational programming is difficult to determine. No figures were gathered in the initial interviews in the four states, but special education teachers in those states suggested that they too spend considerably more time each week than their contract called for. Previous surveys suggest that special education teachers in general easily could be spending 50 hours or more a week in instructionally related tasks, a figure only slightly less than that reported in the second group of districts. To the degree, then, that tasks associated with individualized educational programming replace or facilitate other teacher tasks, the additional time attributed to individualized education actually may be minimal. This suggests a need to streamline the IEP process to make it useful and compatible with other teaching functions, presumably at the LEA level, in conjunction with teachers. In addition, resource support provided by the district to teachers is critical in reducing teacher time associated with individualized educational programming.

Beyond the time demands imposed by individualized educational programming, however, information from both the first and second groups of districts suggests a more basic issue related to the inordinate demands on teacher time that seems to be a general function of special education teaching. In some ways, the implementation of individualized educational programming may be serving as a focus for time-related concerns and dissatisfaction that probably existed prior to any of the current changes. This suggests a possible need for some basic changes in the educational system, to alleviate the inordinate demands on teacher time.

Several areas appear to have potential for change and deserve exploration. First, there may be a need to change the ways time is viewed and allocated. The concept of modular scheduling, in which time is a variable changing day by day and week by week, might be one alternative. Under modular scheduling, a student, for example, might go to the resource room one day for three hours during some weeks rather than going every day at ten o'clock for one hour. The group in the resource room at the same time might also vary on different days with grouping and regrouping occurring constantly on the basis of the children's needs. Modular scheduling, then, might allow needed flexibility, as well as eliminate a certain amount of redundance in preparation and instruction on the teacher's part.

There also may be a need to reconsider the roles of various personnel. Within the second group of teachers, all were highly involved in both individualized educational planning and instruction. Creating special roles such as master teachers or educational specialists to carry out many of the planning functions could free other teachers to devote their time to instruction. A problem with this approach, however, was suggested by Lortie's work (1975): It would increase the likelihood of teachers' feeling they were not controlling the activities in their classrooms—that many classroom activities were determined by other persons.

Also, new ways of grouping students might be necessary to reduce the number of separate preparations required. One approach might be departmentalization within schools to reduce the number of subject areas for which any one teacher is responsible. Team teaching might reduce preparation time by providing a larger pool of students from which groups could be formed on the basis of similar educational needs. Ideally, such groups would be flexible, changing from skill to skill. Again, however, Lortie's work (1975) suggests that, given the traditionally cellular nature of schools, teachers may not be familiar with cooperative teaching arrangements. So new interaction patterns among teachers may have to be developed if such arrangements were to succeed.

Obviously, none of these concepts is new. They are intended only as examples of potential areas of change in the structure of education that might prove fruitful in solving an important and complex challenge currently facing special educators.

Implementation Strategies and Support Systems

Discussions with teachers and directors of special education in the second group of districts suggested that the way in which individualized educational programming is implemented and the support the district provides teachers are critical factors in successful implementation. To maximize the effectiveness of implementation of individualized educational programming as an innovation, the requirements and procedures of a school system should not only be rational but also should be designed to be compatible with the instructional approaches of teachers in the district. Involving teachers in planning for implementation assures that, to the extent possible, the emerging system is responsive to their concerns and reflective of their educational beliefs. Teacher involvement in planning may further engender a sense of commitment among the teaching staff toward successful implementation of individualized educational programming in their classrooms.

The experience of the second group of districts suggests another strategy important to implementation. A district needs to carefully design in-service training, to explain the new system and to teach requisite skills teachers may need to carry it out. Skill training should be based upon careful assessment of the new skills teachers will need. Some indications are that in-service training may be more effective if it is provided on a systematic, ongoing basis rather than as a one-time workshop, and if district personnel rather than "outside experts" are involved whenever possible in planning or conducting the sessions.

A third strategy to consider during implementation is the use of a feedback system at the district level which enables administrators to maintain close contact with teachers so problems in the system can be identified and worked out as they arise.

A final factor that seems crucial to the way individualized educational programming is implemented reflects the key role of the district administrator. Clearly, administrators have a responsibility to demonstrate a positive attitude toward implementation and to establish a productive atmosphere in which it can take place. When sharing responsibility for development and review of educational programs with others is new, the district can foster a positive attitude among teachers by approaching the planning meetings as cooperative problem-solving sessions rather than reviews of teacher performance. In the same way, the administrator is in a unique position to promote open communication among school staff and between staff and parents, who also share in the program planning process.

District planning to develop a support system also seems critical to successful implementation of individualized educational programming. It is especially important that the various components of program planning be linked to one another. For example, assessment batteries that quickly translate into instructional goals and objectives should be made available. Access to references of objectives in various skill areas reduces demands on teacher time. Having materials cross-referenced to goals and objectives also seems to save teachers' planning time as does having numerous materials readily accessible. Above all, the forms used to document elements of the child's program must be rational and parallel to the planning process so the teacher is not continually completing multiple forms for different but overlapping purposes. Building the required record keeping information into the forms is particularly helpful in that little, if any, rewriting or paper shuffling is necessary.

The experience of the second group of districts clearly indicates a need for the district to provide as much in-class assistance as possible. Teachers need aides—as many and for as long as resources permit. Teachers also may benefit from having access to consulting personnel on a regular basis. If aide time is limited, volunteers may need to be brought into the classroom, and experimentation with such strategies as peer tutoring may prove valuable. In exploring options for classroom assistance and then planning for other provisions, however, districts must recognize that the addition of someone to the class does not cut the teacher's job proportionately. Untrained persons do not have the same instructional skills as the teacher, so their help in the classroom may be limited to certain activities. And teacher time is required to supervise and coordinate the activities of others in the classroom, as well as to provide some training to new assistants.

CONCLUSION

The concept of individualized educational programming for handicapped children clearly is not new in special education. Previous efforts to achieve implementation at the classroom level on a widespread basis, however, have not been successful. These efforts have been conceptual (calls for reorienting special education instruction), curricular (proposed individualized curricula), and educational (reorientation of teacher training programs) in nature. The commonality is that they all have focused on the teacher and have attempted to change teacher behavior. Findings from Project IEP, however, suggest that to change teacher behavior is not enough. Even the most highly motivated teachers cannot truly implement individualized instruction without great personal sacrifice unless carefully planned administrative support is available at the district level.

PL 94-142 provides a new impetus, this time in the form of a legislative mandate, to implement individualized educational programming. Will this effort succeed where previous efforts have failed? Several factors related to the legislative mandate might favor implementation. First, PL 94-142 places the responsibility for providing individualized educational programs on the LEA and the state—not on the teacher. Thus, districts have greater incentive to assure implementation. To the degree that implementation requires systematic administrative planning and resource support to teachers, the legislative focus on districts' responsibility may assure these efforts. Refocusing attention to the district may promote the needed administrative attitudinal and fiscal commitments.

A second factor relates to the undeniable costs associated with implementing individualized educational programming. This is a time of limited resources for education in general. Special education is constantly placed in competition with other programs in obtaining critical dollars, including dollars for individualized education. The existence of a federal mandate for individualized educational programming may give special education administrators some of the influence they need in obtaining funds for requisite resources from dollar-conscious school boards and legislatures.

The history of individualized educational programming for handicapped children cautions against excessive optimism that the day of implementation is here. The required changes in teacher role are major, the dangers of lowered morale and dissatisfaction exist, and the requisite resource systems are comprehensive and complex, but at the same time, there is some reason to believe that the legislative mandate provided by PL 94-142 may cause local and state special education administrators to join with special education teachers in searching for viable policies, practices, and resource systems for implementing individualized educational programming at the classroom level. Clearly, the best and only chance for widespread implementation depends upon the cooperation and shared responsibility of all special educators. Perhaps then, the new legislative impetus, in conjunction with reoriented university training programs and curricular innovations, will allow school districts and teachers to make individualized educational programming a reality rather than a goal.

REFERENCES

Anderson, B., Christin, J., & Hunsberger, K. *A study of the utilization of teacher times free of students during the day.* South Bend, IN: Indiana University at South Bend, 1974. (ERIC Document Reproduction Service No. ED091316)

Baker, J. L., Safer, N., & Guskin, N. The participant composition. In M. Kaufman, J. Agard, & M. Semmel, *Mainstreaming: Learners and their environments.* Baltimore, MD: University Park Press, 1978.

Cartwright, G., Cartwright, C., & Ysseldyke, J. Two decision models: Identification and diagnostic teaching of handicapped children in the regular classroom. *Psychology in the Schools,* 1973, *10,* 4-11.

Davis, F. *Planning time: Summary of preschool individualized education program plans.* Unpublished manuscript, 1977. (Available from CONNECT, 1-A North Progress Ave., Harrisburg, PA 17109).

Fenton, K., Yoshida, R.K., Maxwell, J., & Kaufman, M.J. *Role expectation: Implications for multidisciplinary pupil programming.* Washington, DC: U.S. Office of Education, Bureau of Education for the Handicapped, Division of Innovation and Development, State Programs Studies Branch, 1977.

Fullan, M., & Pomfret, A. Research on curriculum and instruction implementation. *Review of Educational Research,* 1977, *47,* 335-397.

Gentry, D., & Haring, N. Essentials of performance measurement. In N. Haring & L. Brown (Eds.), *Teaching the severely handicapped* (Vol. 1). New York: Grune & Stratton, 1976.

Gotts, E. The individualized education program: Potential change agent for special education. In Division of Personnel Preparation and Division of Media Services, Bureau of Education for the Handicapped, U.S. Office of Education, *Conference summary on Public Law 94-142.* Washington, DC: Roy Littlejohn Associates, 1976. (Available from RLA, 1328 New York Ave., NW, Washington, DC 20005)

Hall, R. Responsive teaching: Focus on measurement and research in the classroom and the home. In E. Meyen, G. Vergason, & R. Whelan (Eds.), *Alternatives for teaching exceptional children.* Denver: Love Publishing Co., 1975.

Hammill, D. Evaluating children for instructional purposes. *Academic Therapy,* 1971, *6.*

Haring, N. A strategy for the training of resource teachers for handicapped children. In M. Reynolds & M. Davis (Eds.), *Exceptional children in regular classrooms.* Reston, VA: Council for Exceptional Children, 1971.

Herrick, M. Developing individualized instruction is the difference. *Journal of Special Education,* 1972, *5,* 552-559.

Johnson, D. Educational principles for children with learning disabilities. *Rehabilitation Literature,* 1967, *28,* 317-322.

Kunzelmann, H. *Precision teaching: An initial training sequence.* Seattle: Special Child Publications, 1970.

Lilly, M. Evaluating individualized education programs. In S. Torres (Ed.), *A primer on individualized education programs for handicapped children.* Reston, VA: Council for Exceptional Children, 1977.

Lortie, D. *School teacher.* Chicago: University of Chicago Press, 1975.

Minskoff, E. Creating and evaluating remediation for the learning disabled. *Focus on Exceptional Children,* 1973, *5,* 1-11.

Morine, G. *A study of teacher planning* (Beginning Teacher Evaluation Study, Special Study C). San Francisco: Far West Laboratory, 1855 Folsom St., San Francisco, CA 94103, 1976.

National Education Association. *The American public-school teacher, 1965-1966.* Washington, DC: Research Division, 1967. (Research report 1967-R4)

Reger, R. Schroeder, W., & Uschold, K. *Special education: Children with learning problems.* New York: Oxford University Press, 1968.

Shavelson, R. Teachers' decision making. In N. Gage (Ed.), *The psychology of teaching methods.* Chicago: University of Chicago Press, 1976.

Assessment of pupil performance always has been an important ingredient in instructional planning. Until recently, however, teachers assumed a secondary role in carrying out assessment and interpreting assessment results. Educational diagnosticians and school psychologists played major roles in the evaluation process. However, we are now experiencing a major movement toward teachers' assuming more responsibility in the design of assessment strategies, as well as in determining the nature of evaluations to be conducted on children who are experiencing learning problems. Moran views evaluation in the context of a prescriptive process. The article is a valuable resource for the classroom teacher and as a reference in preservice and inservice training.

Nine Steps to the Diagnostic Prescriptive Process in the Classroom

Mary Ross Moran, *University of Kansas*

Sophisticated systems of evaluative-diagnostic remedial services in the schools have accompanied the movement toward individualizing instruction. Teachers can refer a child to the school psychologist, the reading specialist, the methods and materials consultant, or other ancillary personnel to obtain diagnostic information and recommendations for remediation. The resulting emphasis upon testing by experts has led to an assumption that intervention by the teacher must await evaluation by a diagnostic specialist. Since delays of several months are common, the referral system results in loss of valuable time. The more critical loss, however, is the lack of involvement of the classroom teacher in the diagnostic process.

Since the ultimate responsibility for instructional decisions rests with the classroom teacher who must carry out any special program regardless of who designs it, there are many reasons to utilize the unique skills of the teacher at all stages of the evaluative-diagnostic-remedial continuum. This can be accomplished through teacher development of instructional prescriptions, with evaluation and remediation centered in the child's own classroom.

There are usually two reasons offered by teachers who hesitate to undertake the role of a diagnostic-prescriptive specialist in the classroom. First, they believe they must be trained to administer and interpret standardized tests in order to evaluate a child intensively. Second, they feel they cannot design a program for a child unless they know his level of intellectual functioning.

It is helpful to remind teachers that standardized tests are developed as short cuts, as controlled samples of behavior upon which the clinician relies because he can spend little time with a single child. The clinician who gives a well-selected battery of standardized instruments which are carefully interpreted can indeed learn a great deal about a child in two hours. But the classroom teacher who has access to unlimited samples of behavior over time can be taught to interpret these data just as carefully to yield information which is more directly applicable to instruction. In general, standardized norm-referenced tests designed to provide variability and to distinguish between children have limited usefulness in planning an individual instructional program for a specific child.

Perhaps the only relevance of the IQ for prescription development is the possibility that a child whose intellectual functioning is below average will require more trials to reach criterion. As this will become obvious through informal testing and initial teaching, there is no reason to await an IQ before planning a program. If IQ were indeed necessary to plan instruction, there is evidence that teachers are good estimators of IQ. Studies which have involved the use of deliberately inflated IQ have revealed that teachers can distinguish inflated scores from true scores (Fleming & Anttonen, 1971).

The requirements for a teacher who would undertake the diagnostic-prescriptive process in the classroom do not then include the skills of a clinician. Instead, they encompass abilities already present in a good teacher's instructional practices. Prescription development does require that certain points of view be cultivated.

First the teacher must become skills-oriented. This means that she must look at a child primarily in terms of specific academic strengths and weaknesses, rather than concerning herself with etiology or diagnostic labels. For purposes of preparing prescriptions, the relevant information is precise isolation of specific task behaviors as exhibited by an individual child.

Second, the teacher must become a systematic observer of behavior. She must learn to examine task performance closely. Observation tells a teacher whether the child is impulsive or deliberative, a planner or a trial-and-error learner, highly verbal or action-oriented, dependent upon aid or able to work alone, a risk-taker or afraid to chance failure. Such characteristics have implications for instructional decisions, and the teacher must be alert to the child's problem-solving style as well as his absolute skill performance.

Third, the teacher must be flexible enough to engage in trial teaching. This term is similar in meaning to clinical teaching (Lerner, 1971) or remedial diagnosis (Beery, 1968); it is here used to describe systematic modification of methods and materials in response to the child's reactions to them in the actual instructional situation. The diagnostic-prescriptive process is dynamic, not static. The prescription is not engraved in stone; instead it is a working guide which is revised to correspond to new information yielded by the instructional interaction over time.

Following are nine major steps to be undertaken toward a systematic approach to the diagnostic-prescriptive process in the classroom.

1. EVALUATE PRIOR DATA

An investigation of available background information in school records can be useful in developing hypotheses prior to informal testing.

Cumulative Records of Grades and Test Results

The cumulative record can answer the following questions: Which academic skills areas are relatively low as indicated by letter grades? What was the time of onset of lower grades? What is the absence record? Have test results corresponded to classroom performance?

In preparing an informal assessment, it is important to focus on critical skills while avoiding unnecessary testing. The relative achievement described by letter grades aids in planning the emphasis of informal testing by revealing which skills areas are comparatively intact and which are in need of remedial attention.

The second contribution of the cumulative record is to establish the time of onset of academic problems. Patterns of development appear. For example, if the record shows that low grades began in first grade and continued, the problem is likely to involve deficits in the correlates of learning such as motor, perceptual, or language abilities so that basic readiness skills may not be established. If, instead, the child earned average marks in the first few grades but began to break down in third or fourth grade, he is probably intact in terms of prerequisite subskills but may demonstrate an uneven profile of skills deficits at higher levels. This information is helpful in determining whether one is dealing with developmental disabilities or secondary problems manifested in low achievement.

The absence record should be compared to the time of onset of problems.

Instructional Planning for Exceptional Children

If a child missed thirty days of school in first grade, inadequate continuity of instruction is as suspect as is developmental lag to explain lack of readiness skills. The absence record is reviewed for length of absences, the time of year when they occurred, and the grades which followed. Frequent absence over years suggests serious health or family problems, while absence only during the winter quarter may indicate chronic upper respiratory infections and possible conductive hearing loss. The record may show that a child has missed enough instruction to account for failure to master specific skills.

Standardized test results should be investigated beyond a global percentile or grade-equivalent score. For children who are not achieving, the total score is the least important piece of information to a teacher who should instead be alert to these questions: Did the child respond in a way which indicates that he misunderstood test directions? Did he miss relatively easy items while answering more difficult ones correctly? Did he respond randomly or were errors systematic.? Did he complete as many items as classmates, or did he overdeliberate or refuse to attempt items?

Answers to these questions require access to the test booklet completed by the child. If available, this is the best source of information. However, the computer printout provided by a scoring service does show relative performance, and a blank test booklet can reveal the demands which were placed on the child.

The most important point for a teacher to keep in mind when evaluating standardized test results including IQ is that a child cannot do better than the level of which he is capable but he can do a great deal worse if he is anxious or unsure of directions. It is useful to consider such test scores as a minimum point on the child's range, with his true score occurring somewhere above that level. Another factor to remember is that the test-retest reliability of a subtest is lower than that of the global test. For this reason, a profile should be viewed as an indicator of relative strengths and weaknesses while little weight is given to the absolute score of any single subtest. Furthermore, the standardized conditions prohibit modifications such as extending time, altering stimulus or response mode, limiting choices or other changes which might make it possible for a child to perform. Thus standardized tests offer no clues to compensatory behaviors of which a given child might be capable.

Anecdotal Teachers' Reports

Such records offer insight into behavior patterns and social interactions. For example, comments to the effect that the child does not follow directions, does not complete work, engages in repetitive motor activity, or gets lost in the building may be clues to the disorganized behavior associated with developmental disabilities. Comments about social withdrawal, aggressive acts, complaints of frequent illness or extreme reactions to ordinary events suggest unusual emotional stress. Such information is helpful in planning motivational strategies and in determining how much structure a child needs. If a teacher believes that such comments may prejudice her view of a child, it is a good idea to meet a new child informally to gain original impressions before consulting the records.

Health Record

The school nurse may have been alerted to a physical problem which affects learning, or she may know that medication is administered before a child comes to school. A sweep check may have indicated that a full hearing evaluation should be conducted, but there may have been no follow up on the referral. Or the record may show that the child once wore glasses although the teacher notes that he is not now wearing them. Indications that visual or auditory acuity should be evaluated are frequently uncovered by checking the health record.

2. CONDUCT INFORMAL CLASSROOM ASSESSMENT OF SKILLS

Informal testing can be structured to fit into a regular daily routing or scheduled during planning time or after school. Many teachers prefer at least one individual session to enable them to focus on a single child without distraction. This permits close observation and responsive modification of test activities. After basic skills are tested on a one-to-one basis, tasks which require further investigation can be given while other children are in the room. By observing the child under both situations, the teacher can assess the child's ability under optimal conditions and in the setting which approximates the day-to-day conditions under which he is expected to work.

For prescriptive planning, the testing of choice is criterion-referenced rather than norm-referenced, diagnostic rather than survey, and administered in a flexible, responsive atmosphere rather than under standardized conditions. The purpose of informal testing is to sample behaviors which are as close as possible to the criterion or outcome behaviors. This is accomplished by using for testing the same materials which the child will use in class. Maximum information is extracted from such informal testing by systematically altering task demands so that the child's ability to use compensatory mechanisms or to use specific input-output mode combinations can be investigated.

The ideal test battery consists of an informal reading inventory drawn from the basal series adopted by that school, supplemented by a skills test drawn from the series' scope and sequence chart; a spelling test based on sight words read by the child in the informal inventory; a writing sample encompassing words and sentences read by the child; a sample of oral language based on retelling of a story; and an arithmetic sample drawn from the scope and sequence chart for the classroom series.

Reading Assessment

Following the general practice of testing down, so that terminal behaviors are sampled to learn which subskills must be tested, it is best to begin with an informal reading inventory which requires recognition of both flashed and untimed words in isolation, followed by paragraph reading, a comprehension check, a listening capacity test, and finally a skills inventory selected from the results of the word and paragraph reading. There are several good sources of information on developing an informal reading test from the basal reader (Otto & McMenemy, 1966; Kress & Johnson, 1965; Betts, 1957).

Both silent and oral paragraph reading should be followed by at least four comprehension questions prepared in advance. One question should request a definition of a word in the passage, a second should require recall of a fact, a third should ask the child to draw an inference from the facts presented, and the fourth should request the main idea of the passage. To test sequencing ability as well as recall, ask the child to retell one or two passages in the order in which events occurred.

After the paragraph reading is completed, compute the error percentage for each oral passage to determine the child's independent reading level 99% word recognition; 100% comprehension), and instructional reading level (95% word recognition, 75% comprehension). Beginning at the point just above the instructional level, read the higher level passages to the child and follow with comprehension questions. This will establish the child's listening capacity level (75% comprehension).

Though it involves a considerable amount of preparation, the informal reading inventory drawn from the basal series can be reused to test every child in the class, with each child in a different range along the continuum of graded selections. The inventory yields answers to a number of questions.

First, what is the child's potential instructional level? This is determined on the basis of the discrepancy between the child's expectancy level, as computed by a standard formula (Lerner, 1971), or the child's listening capacity level and his present instructional reading level. For purposes of prescriptive planning, the listening capacity level of the informal reading inventory is considered a good estimate of a child's potential instructional level because he has the vocabulary and linguistic competence to understand material at that level although he cannot comprehend it visually due to word recognition problems. If a child comprehended material read to him with 75%

accuracy at a 5.2 level but his instructional level is 3.1, the 5.2 reader is a realistic goal to work toward in planning remedial instruction.

Second, what is the relationship between the flashed word recognition score and the untimed word recognition score? This yields information on the child's ability to utilize word attack skills. If there is no difference between his flashed and untimed scores, he lacks word analysis cues since he cannot improve his score by taking time to decode an unknown word. If there is a difference between the two scores, an item-by-item analysis can detail the subskills to be tested more intensively.

Third, what is the pattern of oral reading errors? This is determined by computing a simple frequency percentage of the different types of errors. For example, a given child may exhibit 50% substitutions, 25% mispronunciations, and 25% insertions. This is quite a different picture from the child whose error profile shows 50% omissions, 25% examiner pronunciations, and 25% substitutions. The first child is willing to experiment; he is probably a context reader who guesses on the basis of meaning and his comprehension may be quite good although he lacks word attack skills. The second child will not attempt to analyze a word if he does not recognize it on sight, and he has not learned to predict a probable word on the basis of the sense of the passage; however, his precision will be an advantage in learning word attack skills. Thus error patterns can reveal the child's reading "personality." A more intensive analysis of errors, such as the types of substitutions, offers greater precision. Does the child substitute on the basis of configuration cues, initial consonant, the meaning of the passage, or following any other system? Are the words he substitutes real words or nonsense approximations to English words? Does the substituted word fit or violate the sense of the passage? Answers to these questions are useful in selecting subskills to be further investigated.

Fourth, what is the relationship among types of comprehension questions answered and missed? A child who correctly answered 100% of the factual questions but missed all of the inference questions and 50% of the vocabulary questions is quite different from the child who answered only 50% of the factual questions but 100% of the vocabulary and main idea questions. The first child is a literal reader whose recall is good but who cannot build on or bring problem-solving techniques to bear on the facts he knows. The second child is not sufficiently attentive to detail, but he can develop the meaning of words from context and he can grasp the important ideas of a passage. This type of analysis can be used to develop study guides or other aids to comprehension for specific children.

Fifth, what is the relationship between oral reading rate and silent reading rate? In a mature reader, silent reading rate should be a great deal faster than oral rate. Even in a developing reader, this relationship should

Instructional Planning for Exceptional Children

show up. If silent rate is not faster, there are several possibilities. Perhaps the child is overanalyzing words rather than processing them as units. Sometimes an overemphasis upon phonics instruction results in a reader who uses word attack skills for familiar words which he should know at sight. Slow silent rate can also be an indication of a word-by-word reader, who plods along rather than making predictions and monitoring his reading against the sense of the passage.

Sixth what is the relationship between oral reading comprehension and silent reading comprehension? Children who are slow silent readers are likely to exhibit low comprehension scores as well. They may regress and reread the same line a number of times in an attempt to understand or remember it, or they may be subject to intrusive thoughts when the auditory reinforcement of oral reading is not available to them. The child who demonstrates poor silent comprehension is not a likely candidate for lengthy independent seatwork; he should be kept actively involved in tasks by multisensory approaches in order to anchor his attention to the stimulus materials. All these pieces of information gained from the informal inventory have implications for planning an instructional program.

The next part of the reading evaluation is the subskills test based upon the scope and sequence chart. This is a diagnostic test which draws on specific skills listed on a scope and sequence chart to isolate the child's deficits. The instrument is drawn up to specify first the skill, second the task which will sample the skill, third the identification of stimulus and response modes, fourth the correlative abilities or subskills which are presumed to underlie the skill. A sample test drawn from primary levels of the scope and sequence chart might include the items presented in Figure 1.

In addition to presenting the items as given in the task section, the input and output modes should be altered if the child cannot perform. For example, a verbal response as required by the blending task may not be possible, but the child may be able to point to the correct word if it is presented to him in print as a multiple choice task. Tasks should be presented in a variety of ways so that different combinations of visual, auditory, and motor responses are required.

Spelling

A single exception to using classroom texts is made in testing spelling. A teacher-constructed spelling test based on the results of the informal reading inventory is preferred over the classroom spelling text because the text is likely to contain stimulus words which are not in the child's reading vocabulary. Since the child has just read a list of words from a graded basal reader, this list identifies words which are in the child's reading vocabulary. Selecting

Nine Steps to the Diagnostic Prescriptive Process

Figure 1

SKILL	TASK	S-R MODES	CORRELATES
1. Blending of consonant and vowel sounds to form a meaningful word.	Given orally a series of up to three individually pronounced sounds which form a word in the child's oral vocabulary, the student will blend these sounds into a word.	Auditory-Verbal	Auditory Discrimination Auditory Sequential Memory Vocal Encoding
2. Identifying like and unlike words in print.	Given a list of Dolch sight words in primary type in random order, the student will match pairs of duplicated words by pointing to the matching word when the teacher points to a stimulus word.	Visual-Visual Motor	Visual Discrimination Form Constancy Gross Motor Coordination
3. Recognition of long vowel sounds in words.	Given orally a series of words containing long vowel sounds, the student will identify by circling with a pencil the corresponding letter presented in random order in primary type.	Auditory-Visual Motor	Auditory Discrimination Visual Discrimination Auditory-Visual Association Fine Motor Coordination
4. Associating consonant sounds with corresponding grapheme in initial position.	Given a set of words orally, the student will point to the initial consonant of each word when presented in random order in primary type.	Auditory-Visual Motor	Auditory Discrimination Auditory Memory Auditory-Visual Association Visual Discrimination Visual Memory Gross Motor Coordination

words which have been read by the child is an effective way to ensure that spelling skills are being isolated from word recognition skills.

Ten to twenty words should be selected from the child's reading vocabulary, at the highest level of word recognition skill. Individual stimulus words should be selected in such a way that a variety of initial and final consonants, consonant clusters, blends and vowel patterns are represented. A balance should be sought between words which are phonetic for spelling and words which are not phonetic.

In addition to isolating spelling problems as distinguished from word recognition problems, it is important to separate spelling from recall or memory factors and from impairments of motor execution. In order to accomplish this isolation, the same spelling words are presented in three ways.

Instructional Planning for Exceptional Children

First the child is asked to write the words spontaneously to oral dictation. Then, the words which were not spelled correctly in that way are dictated to the child a second time and he is asked to spell them orally. Finally, words which have not been correctly spelled in either way are presented a third time printed on paper as a multiple choice task which requires the child to select one of three alternate spellings.

The oral spelling test has proved to be effective in identifying children who have visual memory or motor execution problems which interfere with written spelling, but who can recall the auditory sequence of a word. The multiple choice task is useful for the child who has motor problems, but it usually identifies the child who has memory or recall problems, such as the child with auditory memory or sequencing deficits who nevertheless recognizes a correct visual representation of the word. Figure 2 outlines how the task is set up.

Figure 2

SKILL	TASK	S-R MODES	CORRELATES
1. Writing spelling words to dictation.	Given a series of dictated words which are in the child's sight vocabulary, the student will write them in cursive script in a vertical list.	Auditory-Visual Motor	Auditory Discrimination Auditory Memory Auditory-Visual Association Visual Memory Visual Sequential Memory Fine Motor Coordination
2. Orally spelling words to dictation.	Given a series of dictated words which are in the child's sight vocabulary, the student will verbally state in order the letters which appear in the words.	Auditory-Verbal	Auditory Discrimination Auditory Memory Auditory Sequential Memory
3. Identifying a correctly spelled word in print.	As the teacher pronounces a word, the student will point to the one of four words printed in primary type which is a correct spelling of the stimulus word.	Auditory-Visual Motor	Auditory Memory Visual Memory Auditory-Visual Association Visual Discrimination Gross Motor Coordination

By presenting the same materials in three ways, the teacher gains a good sample of the child's spelling strengths and weaknesses in a very brief testing. Error analysis can answer questions such as these: Do letter substitutions appear to be related to auditory similarity, such as /t/ for /k/, or to visual similarity, such as /b/ for /h/? Are vowel substitutions phonetic? Are there indications of overreliance on auditory cues such as "shur" for "sure" or "lisen" for "listen"? Are correct letters placed in transposed order as in "fram" for

Nine Steps to the Diagnostic Prescriptive Process

"farm"? Are these reflections of faulty pronunciation as in "liberry" or "pichur"? Does the child demonstrate any knowledge of rules such as changing /y/ to /i/ before suffixes or doubling consonants? It is informative to study the spelling performance in conjunction with the word recognition performance, since errors often reflect phonics problems common to both.

Writing

Because it provides a means of isolating problem areas, the writing test includes three types of tasks (see Figure 3). First the child is asked to write letters, words, or sentences spontaneously to dictation. Then he is asked to copy letters, words, or sentences from one paper on his desk to another. Finally he is to copy letters, words, or sentences from a vertical to a horizontal surface, as from the blackboard to a paper on his desk.

Figure 3

SKILL	TASK	S-R MODES	CORRELATES
1. Writing letters of the alphabet in manuscript to dictation.	Given orally a set of isolated letter names, singly and in random order, the student will print the letters in dictated order on a lined primary tablet.	Auditory-Visual Motor	Auditory Discrimination Auditory-Visual Association Visual Memory Directional Orientation Fine Motor Coordination
2. Writing letters of the alphabet in manuscript in alphabetical order.	Given an incomplete sequence of letters in pica type in uppercase form, the student will insert in manuscript the letter which belongs in each blank space.	Visual-Visual Motor	Visual Discrimination Visual Sequential Memory Directional Orientation Visual Closure
3. Copying letters of the alphabet in cursive script on a plane surface.	Given a set of letters written in cursive on a sheet of paper placed on his desk, the student will write the letters in correct sequence on a lined primary tablet.	Visual-Visual Motor	Visual Discrimination Directional Orientation Fine Motor Coordination
4. Copying letters of the alphabet in cursive script from a vertical to a horizontal surface.	Given a set of letters written in cursive on a blackboard, the student will write the letters in correct sequence on a lined primary tablet.	Visual-Visual Motor	Visual Discrimination Form Constancy Directional Orientation Fine Motor Coordination

The purpose of presenting both spontaneous writing and copying tasks is to separate the language formulation or recall problem from the motor execution problem. Many children who cannot write spontaneously demonstrate visual memory or revisualization problems. A copying task which requires the same motor activities follows the spontaneous writing, and if the child can then perform, motor impairment is ruled out. The copying task is then duplicated from another plane to determine whether that affects performance, since children with perceptual problems sometimes cannot shift from one plane to another without distorting form. By systematically altering the task, the teacher attempts to isolate areas of deficit.

To test language formulation with children who are able to write sentences, it is best to ask the child to write something undemanding in terms of memory or vocabulary requirements. If the child has just completed the information reading inventory, he might be asked to write an event he remembers from one story. Or, he can be asked to write a sentence or two about what he did the day before. This type of written sentence construction permits evaluation of word order, use of plural and tense markers, and general usage.

Oral Language Formulation

The child's linquistic abilities are usually apparent in casual conversation, but it sometimes helps to determine whether he can construct sentences by taking an informal language sample. The easiest way to do this is to present picture stimuli which illustrate stories and ask the child to tell the story. Avoid questions which constrain partial responses, such as asking what, who, when, or where. Instead, if the child hesitates, say, "Tell me more about it," or "Finish the story for me." If possible, tape-record the storytelling so that the language sample can be reviewed to answer questions such as: Are words in conventional order or is syntax confused? Are function words such as prepositions, articles, conjunctions represented in the sample? Are personal pronouns correct as to gender and case? Are plural nouns and past tense forms of verbs used? Are auxiliary verbs used? Are compound and complex sentences represented? Such a language sample on tape allows for concentration on language formulation problems or articulation defects which should be brought to the attention of the speech and language clinician. With her guidance, such structures can be included in the classroom prescription.

Arithmetic Computation and Reasoning

Again, the scope and sequence chart of the classroom text is the basis of the testing. The test specifies stimulus and response modes which are varied to provide isolation of deficits. By making the task more concrete or by

Nine Steps to the Diagnostic Prescriptive Process

eliminating the memory or recall factor, the teacher can help the child to demonstrate what he needs in order to perform arithmetic computations (see Figure 4).

Figure 4

SKILL	TASK	S-R MODES	CORRELATES
1. Writing numerals up to 10.	Given orally a whole number up to 10, the student will write the corresponding numeral on lined primary paper.	Auditory-Visual Motor	Auditory Memory Visual Memory Auditory-Visual Association Fine Motor Coordination
2. Identifying written numerals.	Given a printed list of numerals up to 10 arranged in random order in a horizontal sequence, the student will name each numeral in the order it appears.	Visual-Verbal	Visual Discrimination Directional Orientation Auditory Memory Vocal Encoding
3. Matching sets up to 10.	Given a picture of up to six sets composed of up to ten objects, the student will identify equal pairs of sets by drawing a pencil line between them.	Visual-Visual Motor	Visual Discrimination Fine Motor Coordination
4. Counting concrete objects up to 10.	Given a set of manipulative objects up to 10, the student will identify each object by naming in sequence the corresponding ordinal number.	Visual-Verbal	Visual Perception Auditory Memory Auditory Sequential Memory Vocal Encoding

When written computation on a worksheet is presented, it becomes important to distinguish spatial and directionality problems from erroneous concepts about the operation. For example, a common error in subtraction with borrowing is illustrated by: $\begin{array}{r}23\\-17\\\hline 4\end{array}$ and a multiplication error by: $\begin{array}{r}14\\\times 3\\\hline 123\end{array}$ Although these errors are likely to represent erroneous concepts about the operation, the spatial element should be ruled out by indicating the correct direction of the operation and asking the child to repeat the computation. It is also sometimes the case that the child understands the direction of the operation, but he transposes the numbers when writing his answer. Directional errors or spatial orientation problems should always be considered if answers fit such a pattern.

Instructional Planning for Exceptional Children

When word problems are introduced, it is necessary to isolate skills specific to problem-solving activities as distinct from reading problems. The child should be given a written problem and asked to read it and solve it. If he cannot do so, he should be asked to read the problem aloud. If he does not read with 95% word recognition, the problem should be read to him. The following questions should be asked: What numbers are to be used in the computation? What is the computational operation? What is an estimate of the answer? Although problem-solving ability is more difficult to assess than is computation, the child's capacity to reason to a correct procedure should be sampled in the informal testing.

The informal assessment procedures suggested above represent a considerable investment of teacher time in preparation, administration, and interpretation. Of course, the informal reading inventory and the skills tests from the scope and sequence charts can be used for any number of children once they are developed. The time and effort are justified. Only by sampling performance on the materials actually used in her class can the teacher ensure that the assessment will yield information that is specific, skills based, and relevant to the everyday tasks of the classroom.

3. SET PRIORITIES FOR REMEDIATION

When assessment has been carried out, the next task is to determine which skills are to be included in the prescription and in what order of presentation. Because it is not possible to work simultaneously on all deficits for all children, a limit must be placed on the skills to be covered by the prescription. Many teachers decide arbitrarily that they will work with the five or six most critical needs of each child initially, then add another deficit area from the bottom of the list as the higher priority items reach criterion. Such a plan calls for a systematic method of setting priorities. There are at least three considerations.

Subskills Prerequisite to Higher Skills

The major advantage of using the scope and sequence chart for skills testing is that the skills are presequenced and the teacher can see at a glance which must precede and which can come later. Thus skills which require prescriptive planning can be arranged in the order in which they appear on the scope and sequence chart, in order to ensure that prerequisite subskills will be developed before higher skills are attempted. Of course, any subskills which could be considered in the readiness range, such as letter recognition and basic concepts of size and number, are obvious prerequisites. For higher level skills, however, the scope and sequence charts of classroom series provide the best guide to priorities.

Balance of Strong and Weak Modalities

A second way in which priorities are determined is in accord with the child's need for specific stimulus restrictions. Although pure auditory or visual learners are rare, it is important to consider a child's modality preference if he has one. For example, if a child seems to be primarily a visual learner, this type of activity should take first priority over auditory tasks so that the child can gain a success experience early in his program. As he demonstrates success with highly visual materials, the priority should shift toward auditory tasks so that neglect will not further weaken that modality.

Student and Teacher Goals

Another way to set priorities is to base them on the best fit between the teacher's goals and the child's own goals. This should be handled by a frank interview at the conclusion of the informal assessment in which the child is told what his needs are and how the teacher plans to remediate skills deficits. This interpretation conference is an ideal format to elicit the child's own goals and to discuss their relationship to those of the teacher so that the two members of the team are not working at cross purposes. A good way to compromise between teacher and pupil goals is to use the child's preferred tasks as reinforcers following each performance of the teacher's priority tasks. So long as the child's wishes are being incorporated into the prescription, he will tend to view the work as a joint undertaking toward mutual goals.

4. STATE BEHAVIORAL OBJECTIVES

Clearly stated behavioral objectives allow both student and teacher to determine with precision when goals have been met. There are a number of sources of information on the preparation of instructional objectives (Mager, 1962; Kibler, et al., 1970). There are three essential elements in a behavioral objective.

Behavior Which Is Observable and Measurable

The statement must specify clearly what the student is to do to demonstrate that he has mastered the task. The child's response must be one which can be directly observed and measured. It may be useful to place overt behaviors into three classes based upon the type of activity the learner is to perform.

The discrimination objective requires the student to select from two or more alternatives by responding to differences or to likenesses. The overt activity would be matching, sorting, or choosing. The verbal objective involves providing oral spontaneous language or an imitative response. Overt activity includes naming, listing, defining, describing, repeating, spelling. The motor performance objective requires physical action, or manipulating instructional materials through gross or fine motor activity. Examples of overt behaviors are pointing, marking, drawing, copying, replacing, writing. Of course the three types of objectives can be combined in a single task, but it aids in sorting stimulus and response modes if they are considered separately.

Conditions Under Which Behavior Is to Occur

The objective must specify what the child will be given in order to make the response. List or exclude any concrete manipulative materials or any learning aids which the student may or may not use in his terminal performance. Specify any particular method which he is to follow. Identify any materials or information which will be provided, including the size, type of script, numbers of items on a page, or any other relevant stimulus information.

Criteria for Judgment of Acceptability

Define criteria for performance which will detail how rapidly, accurately, frequently he must perform or the number, percentage, or proportion of correct responses which will be acceptable. If a time limit is to be imposed, specify the period exactly. Figure 5 contains examples of instructional objectives that may be helpful.

Figure 5

DISCRIMINATION OBJECTIVE	VERBAL OBJECTIVE	MOTOR OBJECTIVE
Given a list of typewritten lower case letters including no other reversible forms, the student will correctly match by pointing to the typewritten letters b and d within the ten seconds of presentation.	Given a picture depicting an action by a boy or a girl, the student will insert into an incomplete caption read by the teacher the correct personal pronoun "he" or "she" within two seconds after the caption is read.	Given a 9 by 12 inch wooden puzzle with one irregularly shaped part removed, the student will replace the puzzle part in its proper position within ten seconds of presentation.

5. SELECT METHODS AND MATERIALS

Although an achieving child is able to work toward general objectives which cover broad content and skills areas over a long instructional period, a child with skills deficits requires more readily attainable goals presented in brief sequential units for incremental learning. Because the goal with an achiever is to maintain the task behaviors he is already using, he can be placed on a relatively lean or infrequent reinforcement schedule. A child with deficits, however, needs continuous reinforcement in order to establish new behaviors. This means that objectives should be set up so that he can reach them within a reasonable time and on a regular schedule.

Adjustment of Instructional Approaches

Success with a learning task may not be sufficient reinforcement for a child who has come to devalue school experiences. External consequences such as free time for games, classroom privileges, or even edibles may be necessary to maintain motivation. If so, such consequences should be written into the prescription.

Because of uneven skills development or a stronger visual or auditory style, other modifications may be suggested. For example, the child who cannot perform arithmetic operations with the class following oral directions may be able to do so if the teacher provides a visual demonstration; or a child who cannot work independently because he cannot read directions can do quiet seatwork if directions are put on tape and given to him through earphones. Most remedial learners will require considerable use of audio-visual aids. Some may be candidates for the multisensory systems of integrated reading, writing and spelling instruction. Decisions will have to be made in regard to providing group experiences for children on prescription, so that they do not find themselves working in isolation on seatwork activities for much of the day. Peer tutoring and paraprofessional aides have a place in prescriptive programming.

Adaptation of Published Materials

Usually, only portions of adopted basal readers, arithmetic, social studies, and spelling texts are appropriate for children with skills deficits. Texts must be supplemented by skill-building activities selected from a variety of sources, as well as by teacher-made materials. Because development of materials is often prohibitive in terms of time, many teachers find that they can adapt available materials to meet special needs.

Simple adaptation measures might include reducing the number of arithmetic problems on a page by cutting the page into four parts to be presented separately or making a task more concrete by supplementing a word problem involving addition of sets with objects which can be counted to correspond to the sets. Moderate levels of adaption could include recording word problems on tape and permitting the child to listen to rather than read them or preparing a set of questions for a page of social studies material to be studied before the page is read as an aid to comprehension. More complex adaptations are such measures as the application of readability formulas in order to match the reading level of materials in content areas to the child's instructional reading level or, alternatively, arranging for another child or an aide to put content-area materials such as social studies chapters on tape.

Teachers who are well-acquainted with a variety of materials can usually locate a published lesson which can serve a particular purpose. Just as an automobile mechanic might "cannibalize" several cars to find parts to repair one automobile, so the teacher must take apart published materials to find appropriate parts to repair skills deficits. Of course, access to a well-equipped materials center is ideal for prescriptive teaching, but it cannot substitute for a knowledge of materials and the creativity to find a new way to use a familiar material. Careful selection and adaptation of materials can mean hours of time and considerable effort conserved in prescriptive teaching.

6. DEVELOP A TIME-LINE FOR THE PROGRAM

In determining a time-frame in which to implement the instruction, at least three decisions must be made.

Estimate of the Number of Trials Required to Meet Criterion (an impression of how quickly a child might be expected to respond to instruction aids in long-term planning). If five top-priority skills are incorporated in the prescription, the teacher should know from informal testing which of these is likely to be most difficult or require the most work to meet the objective. This estimate controls the decision about frequency of presentation.

Sequence and Frequency of Task Activity. In addition to the estimate of the number of trials required to meet criterion, the priorities for remediation must be considered in determining how often tasks will be presented. Highest priority skills will be presented daily, with lower-priority skills practiced several times a week. The sequence of task activity in any given day might also be controlled by priority, with more critical skills presented early for the best learning conditions.

Time Block for Each Task. The question of whether to provide massed practice or spaced practice must be considered. For children with limited attention to task, two ten-minute sessions a day on a single skill would be preferable to one twenty-minute session. But if a sequence of concepts must be developed for a given task, a single twenty-minute session might be the time block of choice to ensure incremental learning.

7. IMPLEMENT THE PRESCRIPTION

All of the decisions made earlier culminate in the trial teaching which puts the prescription into practice. The prescription development is not complete until the methods and materials have been evaluated in interaction with the child. The teacher should plan to implement only one new prescription a day and allow extra time to devote to the target child.

Arrangement of Materials and Instructions

Materials should be placed so that the student can take them from storage and arrange them for use himself. Materials should be placed across the room from the child's desk so that he returns completed work and picks up the next task throughout the day. This serves the purpose of providing the teacher with a highly visible check on his progress through his work, since she can note his beginning and ending times for each task from any point in the room and she can note the times for computation of rate. The schedule for the day should be written for each child and taped to his desk so that he can refer to it and be independent in moving from task to task. A dittoed sheet which requires only the insertion of page numbers saves time. If the child is to work with an aide, it should be clear who will initiate the sessions. In order to avoid interruptions, the teacher should instruct the child in the operation of tapes, filmstrips, records, or other aids.

Adjustment of Physical Conditions

To permit access to electrical outlets or to limit distractions, it may be necessary to arrange work centers in the room. A screen that doubles as a bulletin board or a carrel constructed from a large packing box can reduce visual stimuli. Changing the location of a child's desk so that he faces a wall for part of the morning may serve the same purpose. Auditory distractions can usually be reduced by cuing the child in advance about the sounds he will hear while he works. If he knows that the class will be moving about for reading groups, for example, he may not find it necessary to look up when he hears them.

Demonstration of the Initial Lesson for Each Objective

Although ultimately the child takes responsibility for his own daily program, initially it is wise to involve the teacher closely in the activities of the prescription. If the teacher is to work one-to-one with the child on a daily basis, make this the first activity on the first day of the prescription so that the child gets a set for moving right into a task. If an aide is to work with him, the teacher should still introduce and observe the first lesson to endorse the aide's work and express interest. Even on independent seatwork, the teacher should demonstrate the task and watch the child respond to a few items of each activity so that the lesson gets off to a good start. The teacher's proximity and enthusiasm should set a tone of cooperative work.

8. EVALUATE THE PRESCRIPTION

Since the prescription is viewed as a dynamic rather than a static diagnostic-remedial approach, an essential part of the process is the ongoing evaluation system. There are a number of ways to determine the child's progress through the program.

Direct Product and Time Records

Appropriate for independent seatwork, this type of record allows the teacher to graph each day how much work is completed in a certain time unit. By noting the time when a student picked up a worksheet and the time at which he returned it, the teacher can estimate his rate. This enables her to judge whether a time contingency should be added, such as utilizing a kitchen timer for decreasing intervals and rewarding the child for beating the clock, or whether time should be increased as a means to improve deliberation and accuracy. The child's daily work products plus the teacher's observations of time allow for a good measure by which to adjust the daily program.

Number of Trials per Lesson

For work done with the aide or the teacher, a graph should be kept showing how many trials of a given task are presented each session. This kind of information sometimes reveals that tasks are not appropriately sequenced or that they are not in small enough steps. If a child who has been learning two new spelling words a day with five trials on the average suddenly requires ten trials each day, the teacher is alerted that an adjustment is needed.

Consumer Satisfaction

Feedback should be solicited from the child to determine how well the prescription is working. An interview between teacher and child at regular intervals, perhaps five minutes at the end of each week, can provide the format for the child's perceptions of the prescription and any adjustments he might request. Again, the child's continuing cooperation is enlisted toward joint goals.

9. MODIFY THE PRESCRIPTION

Despite the time and effort devoted to the prescription thus far, it will not succeed unless the teacher is responsive to the interaction of the child with the instructional program. Careful observation of the child's on-task behavior plus the records which are kept daily and the interviews with the child combine to yield the information necessary to make adjustments in the program. Changes might involve the type of material or the method of presentation, the stimulus or response mode, the complexity of the task or the amount of work presented in one session, the time block or the sequence of tasks, the type or schedule of reinforcement. No alteration is made without a rationale, but the flexibility to change in response to a demonstrated need is essential to the diagnostic-prescriptive process.

REFERENCES

Beery, K. *Remedial diagnosis.* San Rafael, CA: Dimensions Publishing, 1968.

Betts, E. A. *Foundations of reading instruction.* New York: American Book Co., 1957.

Fleming, E. S. & Anttonen, R. G. Do teachers get what they expect? The self-fulfilling prophecy revisited. *Childhood Education,* 1971, *47,* 451-453.

Kibler, R. J., Barker, L. L. & Miles, D. T. *Behavioral objectives and instruction.* Boston: Allyn & Bacon, 1970.

Kress, R. & Johnson, M. *Informal reading inventories.* Newark, DE: International Reading Association, 1965.

Lerner, J. *Children with learning disabilities.* Boston: Houghton Mifflin, 1971.

Mager, R. F. *Preparing instructional objectives.* Belmont, CA: Fearon Publishers, 1962.

Otto, W. & McMenemy, R. A. *Corrective and remedial teaching.* Boston: Houghton Mifflin, 1966.

Parents have long been sensitive to the power of games in influencing the behavior of children. Only recently, however, have educators recognized that games can serve instructional purposes and that the games need not be highly sophisticated nor expensive to be effective as teaching-learning devices. Thiagarajan draws on his extensive experience in instructional planning and media in presenting a succinct discussion on how to design instructional games for handicapped learners. He presents guidelines for designing and using games, as well as on adapting existing games for instructional use with handicapped children and youth.

Designing Instructional Games for Handicapped Learners

Sivasailam Thiagarajan, *Indiana University*

In recent years, the use of instructional games has increased tremendously at all levels from preschool to postgraduate classrooms. There is a corresponding increase in the use of games with handicapped children. Although a number of excellent instructional games for this type of learner are commercially available, there is still a need for many more. The major emphasis in this article is on how a teacher can design, produce, evaluate, modify, and adapt instructional games for the classroom.

WHAT IS AN INSTRUCTIONAL GAME?

The increasing popularity of instructional games is accompanied by an increasing confusion in the related terminology. The term *game* in this article is used in a technical sense to imply three essential characteristics: conflict, control, and closure. Each of these three is briefly discussed below.

Conflict. A game usually requires the players to compete among themselves to obtain certain limited resources. In chess, for example, there is a conflict to see who can trap the other player's king first; in bridge, each partnership strives to take more tricks than the other.

The element of conflict in games, however, need not always manifest itself as intense competition among players. It may be used to create a high degree of cooperation among members of a team in its competition with other teams. It is also possible to design a "cooperative" game in which all players compete against an external force (such as chance) or criterion (such as a time limit). In a solitaire game, conflict is channeled into the player's attempts to outperform the vagaries of chance or his own previous record.

Control. All games have a set of rules to control the behavior of players. Thus in chess, the king may move in any direction, but not any number of spaces; in bridge, the lowest trump may take the highest cards of other suits, but a trump may be played only under specific conditions. In addition to these explicit rules, players follow certain implicit rules of fair play. Successful play of any game depends upon the acceptance of these controls by all players. Therefore, even in the most intensively competitive game, there is an element of cooperation in abiding by rules.

Closure. The third critical element of a game is its termination. Open-ended play by children may go on forever, but games come to an end when the king is checkmated in chess or all 13 tricks are taken in bridge. One aspect of this closure is the determination of the winner. Very often, a single player wins and the others lose. However, it is possible to structure a game with multiple criteria for winning so that more than one player wins.

Conflict, control, and closure are the technical characteristics of a game. Each of them presents a number of desirable and undesirable outcomes. In a later section of this paper, we discuss how a game designer can emphasize the former and eliminate the latter type of outcomes. We also present a list of *desirable* characteristics for games for the handicapped.

While all games help players learn something new, an *instructional* game goes about it with certain deliberation. It is intentionally designed to help a specific group of learners attain a specific set of instructional objectives. In this article, we are primarily interested in instructional games for handicapped learners dealing with cognitive and affective objectives. Although instructional games are effectively used for the teaching of psychomotoric skills, their design requires a slightly different set of competencies. This article does not address itself to these competencies.

Many instructional games are also simulations. The term *simulation* implies that the rules and the materials used in the games represent some real-life objects and processes. In Scrabble where the players use letter tiles to make up high-scoring words, they are not simulating a process—they are doing the real thing. Therefore, Scrabble is not a simulation game. However, in Monopoly, where real estate is bought and rent and taxes are paid, players do simulate an outside reality. Monopoly is a simulation game. Instructional simulation games, especially those which involve roleplaying, are of special use in teaching handicapped children such skills as money management or interviewing for a job.

RATIONALE

The use of instructional games in special education goes further back in history than their use in regular education. With a few exceptions (e.g., Fink et al., 1971), very little empirical evidence exists on the effectiveness of these games. However, teachers' experiences and logical analysis suggest that instructional games have an important role in the teaching of handicapped children. A few of the salient advantages of using games with handicapped children are presented.

Games and Communication Skills. Many handicapped learners lack verbal fluency and are unnecessarily penalized for poor receptive and expressive communication skills. In games, where both stimuli and responses are very often nonverbal, success is seldom correlated with verbal ability. Many scholars believe that games mobilize intellectual competencies at the iconic rather than the symbolic level. Such games provide the handicapped learner with the ability to grasp a situation intuitively rather than analytically.

Games and Instructional Objectives. Games can enhance learning at different levels. The curriculum for the handicapped learner involves a large number of lower-level cognitive objectives such as language patterns and number facts. Though essential, this learning is not exciting. Games can add spice to these dull didactic chores. Handicapped children also need to attain a number of higher-level cognitive objectives, and games are an effective means for achievement in this area. These learners cannot handle abstractions easily; a game could make such abstractions concrete and specific. Finally, games have been proven to be extremely successful in helping learners attain various desirable attitudinal objectives. Play of games is a useful activity for learners to explore the affective domain.

Games and Instructional Feedback. Handicapped children need more frequent and immediate feedback than their normal peers in acquiring new skills and concepts. In a game, such feedback is prompt and real. It is the natural consequence of the player's performance and is related to the ultimate outcome of the game. In this way, the feedback is closer to its real-life counterpart than any other type of classroom feedback.

Games and Socialization. Piaget (1962) and others have pointed out that game experiences are essential for the development of full interpersonal capabilities and capacities of children. Classroom games provide the handicapped learner with a general orientation toward social relations and a realistic perception of life's rules. These games also require cooperation and agreement among the players for their success. Individualized instructional activities in the classroom often isolate the handicapped child. Instructional games compensate for this by encouraging peer learning and cooperation.

Games and Self Concept. Usually the labeled child has a poor concept of himself and hesitates to participate in the face of repeated failures in the classroom. Games free him to engage competitively in stimulating activities and to develop a healthy attitude toward both success and failure. As he ventures out through instructional games, the learner finds success through a combination of good luck and good judgment. This type of intermittent reinforcement keeps his learning performance at a high level and increases the number of his success experiences. There is room for more success in a game than in a lesson—an ingenious idea which might have passed unnoticed or misunderstood in a classroom discussion may make a dramatic difference in a game. The player feels that power of controlling his environment and enhances his image of self-efficacy.

Games and Motivation. Many problems in teaching handicapped children are motivational, and instructional games contribute importantly in this area. With a variety of dramatic aspects, these games involve the learner to a degree unequalled by any other instructional activity. Learning from a game is unobtrusive; useful skills are developed at the exact time the learner needs them. Thus games provide a high degree of relevance to what is being learned by the handicapped child.

DANGERS AND DISADVANTAGES

The use of instructional games with the handicapped is not without some disadvantages and limitations. In fact, many of the above advantages can be turned around to reveal a potential danger. In the following brief discussion, we forewarn the designer of some of the more salient limitations of instructional games.

Overstimulation. Instructional games could be so motivating that all other classroom activities are dull in comparison. It is important that instructional activities are sequenced in such a way that the motivating strength of games is used as a positive consequence to encourage other low-probability learning behaviors.

Ethical Considerations. Game designers are becoming increasingly worried about the incidental effects of instructional games, especially those which involve simulation of social processes. All simulations distort reality to some extent; no matter how hard the designer may try, it is impossible to keep his personal biases from coloring players' perceptions. There does not appear to be any simple way out of this dilemma.

Transfer Issues. Simulation games provide a low-risk situation where many real-life skills can be practiced. However, trying to corner the real-estate market on the basis of success in a game of Monopoly is obviously a dangerous exercise. There are many other subtle differences between even the most faithful simulation and reality which could be extremely frustrating.

Peer Pressure. While social interaction during the play of games provides many positive outcomes, it could turn out to be extremely frustrating for a slow child caught in intense competition. Repeated individual failures and blame from other members of the team may do greater damage to the socialization and the self-concept of a child than any of the traditional classroom activities.

DESIRABLE CHARACTERISTICS

At the beginning of the article, we discussed the technical characteristics of an instructional game. We are now ready to discuss the desirable characteristics of an instructional game to be used with handicapped learners. The following list of these characteristics is based upon the experiences of teachers who have successfully designed and used instructional games in their classrooms.

1. Materials and equipment for the game should be assembled into a self-contained kit, so that the children are not required to improvise anything. Materials used in the game should permit self-checking of the correctness of the responses required of the players. This eliminates the need for constant supervision by the teacher.
2. Game materials should be attractive and colorful. Whenever appropriate, they should make maximum use of nonverbal cues such as color coding. The use of three-dimensional objects for kinesthetic stimuli and physical manipulation is highly recommended. Audiotape cassettes provide interesting variation to stimulus materials used in a game. The combined use of such diverse materials permits a multisensory approach.
3. Materials used in the game should be of high personal and local relevance. The board for a map reading game, for example, may show the layout of the classrooms in the school. Polaroid pictures of children can be used as integral material for a number of games.
4. Game materials should be appropriate for use by children at a given age level. The usual dice have to be enlarged to large wooden cubes, and cards should be the size of postcards rather than the usual playing cards.
5. Each game should be of fairly brief duration and should permit

repeated replaying. In this way, the games accommodate fairly short attention spans, and the handicapped children receive the necessary redundance.
6. Games for use with handicapped children should permit equal competition among learners at different levels. This could be accomplished by prescribing different roles and objectives or by providing different amounts of resources for children at different levels. Also, elements of skill and chance may be combined in such a way that the below-average student wins from time to time.
7. Rules of the game should be simple and unembellished. They should be stated in children's own language. This will permit other teachers and parents to read them directly to the children and get them into the game with minimum delay.
8. A series of short games is preferable to a single complex game. These games may use the same materials and the same basic set of rules, but require increasingly complex skills from the players. This permits gradual shaping of the learner's behavior toward the terminal performance.

ADAPTING INSTRUCTIONAL GAMES

Although an increasing number of instructional games are becoming available for use with handicapped children, there is still a large gap to be filled through local production. The remaining portion of this article discusses various strategies for use by the special educator in designing instructional games. In addition to increasing the number of available games, this activity results in several positive outcomes.

1. Teachers of the handicapped understand the needs of their learners better than commercial game manufacturers. As a result, the games teachers design are likely to be more appropriate for use with exceptional children.
2. Teacher-designed games have more local relevance and are more smoothly integrated into the curriculum.
3. The process of translating an abstract lesson into concrete game activities provides the teacher with insights about the structure of the curriculum.

The best way to learn game-design strategies is through adapting *frame games*. A frame game is a basic game format which can be easily modified to teach new content and skills. Obviously, this is not an innovative idea—many classroom teachers frequently use such traditional frame games as Bingo to teach different skills to their children. These frame games make it easy for the

Instructional Planning for Exceptional Children

teacher to plus new instructional content into existing game formats. They are also useful from the learner's point of view because the mastery of one game permits him to play a large number of variations. Thus, children spend more time learning from the game than learning the game.

Where does one get the basic frame-game formats which are adaptable to teach different instructional content to handicapped children? The best sources are traditional children's games such as Old Maid and Dominoes. There are also some newer commercial games which can be analyzed to provide instructional adaptations. Descriptions of suitable games may be found in such game magazines as *Simulation/Gaming/News*, in teachers' magazines such as *Instructor* and *Teaching Exceptional Children*, and in specialized magazines such as *Arithmetic Teacher* and *Science Teacher*. There are also a number of books on old and new games (Bigson, 1971; Golick, 1973) which describe many useful frame-game formats.

EXAMPLES OF ADAPTING A FRAME GAME

Earlier, we mentioned the fact that many teachers use adaptations of frame games such as Bingo to help their learners attain different instructional objectives. Actual examples of these adaptations are presented below to demonstrate the process of converting a frame game into different instructional variants. For those readers who are unfamiliar with Bingo, here is a brief description of the original game.

BINGO

Equipment and materials:

1. A number of Bingo cards. These contain 5 x 5 grids with 25 random numbers from 1 to 75 arranged in a random pattern. The arrangement of numbers in each card is different from the arrangement in every other. The middle box of the grid is a "free" one; it does not contain a number.
2. A set of counters for each player.
3. A set of 75 counters for the game leader, each with an individual number from 1 to 75.

Number of players: Any number can play.

Approximate time requirement: Depending upon the draw of the counters, anywhere from 3 to 10 minutes.

Play of the game:

1. Each player receives a Bingo card and a set of counters. The player places a counter on the free box.
2. The game leader throws the number counters into a bag, mixes them thoroughly, and draws them out one at a time. He announces the number of each counter and places it on a master sheet for verification at the end of the game.
3. Whenever a new number is called out, each player checks his grid to see if it appears in any one of the boxes. If so, he places a counter on that box. During a round, more than one player may find the number in his grid; some may not find it at all.
4. Whenever a player has 5 boxes in a straight line covered by his counters, he shouts, "Bingo." These 5 boxes may be horizontal, vertical, or diagonal and may or may not include the free box.
5. The game leader verifies the placement of the counters and, if correct, declares the player to be the winner.

The purpose of the traditional Bingo game is to provide an entertaining way to persuade players to contribute to a charitable cause. Although this is hardly an instructional objective, the game can obviously be used to help children attain the skills of identifying numerals, matching oral numbers with printed numerals, scanning a field to detect the presence of a numeral, and recognizing the placement of five items in a vertical, horizontal, or diagonal straight line. More useful instruction can be achieved through an analysis of the Bingo game and adaptation to teach specific skills. Any game may be analyzed in terms of what is given to the learner and what is expected from him in terms of specific behaviors. In Bingo, the player is given an auditory stimulus (a number) and he is required to make a multiple-choice response by placing his counter on a printed version of the same number.

The first set of adaptations which follows involves giving a visual stimulus to the player and requiring him to give a visual matching response. For example, in a game for beginning readers, the teacher holds up cards with different letters. The player searches his grid for the same letter and places a counter on the box which contains that letter. The play of the game is exactly the same as in the traditional Bingo. The procedure of having the teacher (or one of the players) hold up a series of cards is also used in the adapted games listed in Figure 1.

The number of variations of this theme is obviously unlimited. In the next series of adaptations, both the stimulus given to the player and the response required of him are again visual. However, the player has to process the information given to him before he identifies the appropriate box. For example, in an arithmetic game, the teacher holds up cards with simple

Instructional Planning for Exceptional Children

Figure 1

INSTRUCTIONAL TOPIC	WHAT THE TEACHER HOLDS UP	WHAT THE PLAYERS DO
Color recognition	Different colored cards	Identify the same colored box in their grids
Picture matching	Cards with pictures of different animals	Identify a box in their grids with the same shape
Shape recognition	Cards cut into different shapes (e.g., circle)	Identify a box in their grids with the same shape

addition problems. The player has to add the numbers together and identify the sum in his Bingo grid. More adapted games along the same theme are listed in Figure 2.

Figure 2

INSTRUCTIONAL TOPIC	WHAT THE TEACHER HOLDS UP	WHAT THE PLAYERS DO
Sight reading	Pictures of various objects	Identify in their grids the word which stands for the object
Traffic rules	Pictures of different road signs	Identify in their grids a short sentence about what this sign stands for
Phonics	A short printed word (e.g., *hot*)	Identify in their grids another printed word containing the same vowel sound (e.g., *mom*)
Initial consonants	Pictures of various objects	Identify in their grids the initial letter of the name of the object
Map reading	Pictures of mountains, lakes railroad lines, etc.	Identify the appropriate map symbol in a teacher drawn map divided into a BINGO grid

In the final set of adaptations, we return to the original arrangement of the game—the stimulus is auditory, and the player responds by identifying a suitable visual. For example, in a history game, the teacher names different presidents of the United States. The players identify the picture of that president in their Bingo grid and place a counter on that box. The adaptations in Figure 3 use the same type of auditory stimuli and visual matching responses.

Designing Instructional Games

Figure 3

INSTRUCTIONAL TOPIC	WHAT THE TEACHER SAYS	WHAT THE PLAYERS DO
Initial consonants	Different words	Identify in their grids the initial letter of the word
Listening comprehension	Names of different animals	Identify in their grids a picture of the animals
Vocabulary	Different words	Identify in their grids the opposite word (antonyms)
Auditory discrimination	Different words	Identify in their grids the vowel sound in the words
Numerals	Different numbers	Identify in their grids the appropriate numeral

As you may have noticed, we have come back to the original Bingo game in our last example. This demonstration of adapted games illustrates the tremendous flexibility afforded by the frame-game approach.

MORE EXAMPLES

In this section, we present another set of sample adaptations of an instructional frame game. The original game is a teacher-developed one called Shapes.

SHAPES

Equipment and materials: A deck of fifty 3 x 5 cards, with one side blank and different shapes drawn on the other. These shapes contain examples of squares, rectangles, and triangles with variations in their size, color, and orientation. In addition, nonexample shapes which do not belong to any of these categories (e.g., pentagons, parallelograms) are also included. A bag of marbles is used to simplify score keeping.

Number of players: Two to eight. Best game is for four to six.

Appropriate time requirement: Depending upon the number of players and their skill, a game may last anywhere from 5 to 15 minutes.

Instructional Planning for Exceptional Children

Play of the game:

1. Each player is given 5 marbles. The rest of the marbles are set aside in a paper cup.
2. The teacher specifies a particular shape for the game.
3. Cards are dealt out, one by one, as far as they will go. It does not matter if some players receive one more card than the others.
4. Each player gathers up his cards and without looking at them arranges them in a neat pile with the shape sides facing down.
5. Beginning with the first player, players take turns flipping up the top card of their pile and placing it face up in the middle of the play area.
6. If the turned-up card contains the shape specified for the game, players may slap it. The first player to slap the card gets a marble from the paper cut.
7. If a player mistakenly slaps a card with a shape other than the one specified for the game, he loses a marble. He has to return one of his marbles to the paper cup.
8. The game ends when all cards have been turned up. The player with the most marbles is the winner.
9. The game is replayed with a different shape specified.

The shrewd reader may have recognized the children's card game of Slapjack as the original frame of this game. However, let us concentrate on the Shapes version as a frame game and demonstrate various ways of adapting it. As before, the first step in this process is to analyze the game in terms of what stimulus is given to the player and what response is expected from him.

What is given to the player? A card from a deck with different examples of a few closely related concepts and "nonexamples" which belong to none of these concept categories.

What is expected from the player? (1) Generalization: Slap all examples of a particular concept. (2) Discrimination: Do not slap nonexamples of that concept (i.e., examples of other concepts).

With this basic analysis, let us see how the game may be adapted to teach different instructional skills. At the first level of adaptation, the rules and the structure of the original game are retained intact; the content of the cards is changed.

Adaptation 1: PEOPLE

This game is designed to help players recognize key people in the school. Although this is not a formal part of the curriculum, the teacher thought it important for the children to know the librarian, custodian, principal, school nurse, and the bus driver. With a Polaroid camera, she took pictures of these different people in different locations and wearing different clothing. There is a total of 40 cards in the deck; at the beginning of each game, the teacher specifies a particular person (e.g., the school nurse). The play of the game is exactly the same as in Shapes.

Adaptation 2: COLORS

This is an extremely direct adaptation of the Shapes game. A piece of different colored paper is pasted on one side of a card. Six different colors are used, each on ten cards. At the beginning of the game, the players are told to look for a particular color.

Adaptation 3: LETTERS

This game is used to provide drill practice for children in recognizing letters. A deck of 50 flash cards is used in the game, each with one of the 10 different hard-to-discriminate letters. Each letter appears in slightly diffferent styles of printing. Each card contains the picture of a small smiling face on the top right corner to prevent confusion of a letter like "p" as "q," or "d" as "b." At the beginning of each round of the game, the children are told to slap a particular letter.

Adaptation 4: PARTS OF THE BODY

The deck for this game contains 10 pictures of each of the following parts of the body: face, arms, legs, chest, and back. Children are required to slap the cards with a specific body part. The pictures show a variety of child and adult, male and female bodies.

Adaptation 5: MAKING CHANGE

The cards used in this game contain pictures of different coins in various combinations. At the beginning of the game, players are asked to slap a specific total (e.g., 27¢). They can slap any combination (e.g., 2 dimes, a nickel and 2 pennies; a quarter and 2 pennies; 4 nickels and 7 pennies) as long as the coins add up to the required total.

The next two adaptations go beyond the mere substitution of the content

Instructional Planning for Exceptional Children

of the cards. The players' responses are the same, but there are some ingenious modifications in the rules which result in more exciting play and more complex skills.

Adaptation 6: BUILD A WORD

Flash cards with various letters are used in this game. A spelling word (e.g., apple) is specified at the beginning of each game. The players are required to slap the correct letters, one at a time, in the correct order. They first look out for the letter "a," then the "p," then the second "p," and so on. Thus, the game helps children learn how to spell different words.

Adaptation 7: COMMUNITY HELPERS

The deck used in this game consists of a number of pictures of such community helpers as the policeman, mailman, fireman, and milkman. The cards show these people at various appropriate tasks. There are also some cards showing the same people doing incongruous things, such as the policeman delivering milk. The children are required to spot and slap those cards which show a particular community helper (e.g., policeman) doing an unusual thing. The game is very popular with children who enjoy the comical combinations in the pictures.

In the next three adaptations, the original frame game is changed more radically. The basic operations of generalization and discrimination are still expected from the players, but the examples and nonexamples are no longer cards and the response is not limited to slapping.

Adaptation 8: DANGER

This game is designed to teach various safety rules to handicapped children. The game uses a number of color slides which are projected on a screen one at a time. Players sit in small groups of four or five and watch the screen. A wooden block painted red is placed in the middle of each play group. Children are required to pick up this block whenever they see something dangerous shown on the screen (e.g., a child walking across the street when the light is red). The first player in each group to pick up the block scores a point. After verification, this player is given a marble, and the block is replaced in the middle of the next round.

Adaptation 9: SOUND OF VOWELS

Each child has a small tile with the symbol for a short vowel on one side (e.g., o) and a long one on the other (e.g., o). A cassette tape recorder is placed in the middle of the play area. The tape presents different short words with ample pauses in between. As soon as each word is heard, *each* child places the tile with the appropriate sound symbol facing up in front of him and hides it with his hand. If the vowel sound in the word is neither of the two sounds represented on the tile, the child merely places his hand in front of him. After each player has his hand in front of him, all players raise their hands to reveal the face of their tile (or the absence of the tile). Those players who have classified the sound correctly receive a marble; those who made a mistake return a marble. The game continues until all the words recorded on the tape are played out.

Adaptation 10: MAP READING

A large map hangs on the classroom wall, and players are free to move around it. Each player has a "compass" card with the names of the four directions marked on it and movable pointer. The teacher names two locations on the map. The players locate them and determine the direction of the second relation to the first. Each player secretly sets up the pointer in his compass card to indicate the appropriate direction. When all players are ready, they reveal their response. The scoring method for the game is the same as in Sound of Vowels just described.

DESIGNING INSTRUCTIONAL GAMES FOR THE HANDICAPPED

The two sets of examples presented above strongly suggest that with a little imagination a teacher can adapt a frame game to teach new content. While a single frame game may lend itself to a number of content and structural variations, it will still involve the same basic type of learning. Thus, in order to provide for the wide variety of learning in the curriculum, the teacher-designer should have a wide base of flexible frame games.

In these adaptations, we begin with a suitable frame game and seek out those instructional topics which are amenable to it. Although very efficient, this approach lets the form determine the function. A more desirable alternative approach is to begin with an instructional objective and then design a suitable game to help handicapped learners attain this objective. Designing a game from "scratch" is more complicated than adapting a frame game. How-

Instructional Planning for Exceptional Children

ever, there is considerable overlap between these two activities; adapting frame games provides an excellent introduction to the strategies of more elaborate design.

A systematic procedure for designing an instructional game for handicapped children is outlined in the flow chart (see Figure 4). Each of the steps in the flow chart is described below.

Figure 4
SYSTEMATIC PROCEDURE FOR DESIGNING A GAME

```
┌──────────────────────────────────┐   ┌──────────────────────────────────────┐
│ Analysis of the instructional task│   │ Analysis of the handicapped learner group│
└──────────────────────────────────┘   └──────────────────────────────────────┘
                    │                                   │
                    └───────────────┬───────────────────┘
                                    │
                    ┌───────────────────────────────┐
                    │  Selection of a suitable frame │
                    └───────────────────────────────┘
                                    │
        ┌───────────────────────────┴──────────────────────────┐
        │                                                      │
┌───────────────────────────────┐   ┌──────────────────────────────────────┐
│ Specification of tentative rules│   │ Design of game materials and equipment│
└───────────────────────────────┘   └──────────────────────────────────────┘
                    │
                    ┌───────────────────────────────┐
                    │ Modification of rules and materials │
                    └───────────────────────────────┘
                                    │
                    ┌───────────────────────────────┐
                    │  Production of the prototype game │
                    └───────────────────────────────┘
                                    │
                    ┌───────────────────────────────┐
                    │     Tryout and modification    │
                    └───────────────────────────────┘
                                    │
                    ┌───────────────────────────────┐
                    │        Final packaging         │
                    └───────────────────────────────┘
```

Task Analysis. In this step, the game designer specifies the behavioral objective for his game. This main objective is analyzed into various subobjectives. The major type of learning implied by these objectives is also identified. All of these pieces of information help in the selection of a suitable frame in a later step.

Learner Analysis. An analysis of the relevant characteristics of the learner for whom the game is being designed is undertaken parallel to the task analysis. Learner analysis involves identifying relevant skills and knowledge which the player already possesses. It also identifies preferences for different types of games. Finally, various handicapped conditions of the learner (e.g., hearing impairment) and the level of his language are also determined.

Selecting a Frame. A suitable frame for the game is now selected on the basis of the earlier analyses. The structure of this frame parallels to a large extent the structure of the instructional task. The learner's entry level determines whether the game is to be used for initial learning or for providing practice. The players' game preferences for the type of game plays an important role in the final phases of this step.

Specifying Tentative Rules. All games need a closure rule which determines the winner. This is usually the first rule to be specified in the design of an instructional game. Ideally, winning the game should be directly correlated with the mastery of the main objective. The subobjectives for the instructional task usually suggest control rules for the play of the game.

Designing Game Materials and Equipment. Equipment and materials for the game are designed simultaneously with the specification of tentative rules. The frame for the game and its rules suggest what types of materials (e.g., cards and counters) and equipment (e.g., timers and spinners) are needed. These, in turn, make the tentative rules of the game more specific.

Modifying Rules and Materials. A recommended procedure for the design of an instruction game, or any other creative design activity, is to produce a rapid and spontaneous first draft, leave it aside for some time, and critically review and revise it later. The revisions and refinements are based upon the designer's hindsight, aided by notes from task and learner analysis, to ensure that the outline for the game meets the requirements of the task and the needs of the learner. The game may also be evaluated with a suitable checklist; the eight desirable characteristics of an instructional game mentioned earlier from the basis for a useful checklist.

Producing the Prototype. Once the revised outline for the instructional game is prepared at the end of the previous step, the game designer is ready to produce the prototype version. This is a suitable step for collaboration among teaching colleagues and for involving the learners themselves. The following list of practical tips will simplify this production process for the uninitiated.

1. Collect discarded games from parents and local rummage sales. Spare parts from these games make excellent components for your prototype.
2. Suitable game boards may be copies from samples found in game catalogs. Styrofoam insulation and masonite peg boards make unusual but functional game boards.
3. Your beautiful game boards can be protected with clear contact paper. Stains and thumbprints can be wiped off with a damp rag.
4. For consistent and readable lettering, use a primary typewriter. You may also want to try stencils and lettering guides for larger letters. Press-on letters come in different sizes and styles and produce a professional result.

Instructional Planning for Exceptional Children

5. Metal washers, golf tees, colorful buttons, and foreign coins make excellent pieces for different games.
6. Index cards come in different sizes and colors. The 5 x 8 card is the most suitable size for children's games.
7. Spirit duplicating masters come in different colors, too. They are handy for reproducing large numbers of cards and play money.
8. Children's coloring books and comic strips provide excellent illustrations for game materials. Larger illustrations for game boards may be obtained from discarded posters.
9. Felt markers are very useful for coloring game boards, cards, and other materials.
10. Large wooden blocks make better dice for children than the standard ones. Spots for different faces of the dice may be cut out of gummed paper.

Tryout and Modification. This is the most important step in the design of an instructional game. The most sophisticated and attractive game is of no instructional value if the children find it unplayable. Here is another set of practical tips for getting the most out of this formative evaluation/modification step:

1. Have a group of your colleagues play the game before introducing it to the children. This will help you identify and eliminate major problems in the game.
2. Use a small group of representative children. Three or four such players make a nice group.
3. Get the players into the game as soon as possible. Don't lecture them about all rules before the game. You can explain some of the rules later when the need arises.
4. Participate in the play of the game, but be sure not to dominate.
5. Help the children only if there is a serious danger of the game breaking down. Very often children come up with their own simple but practical solutions to minor dilemmas.
6. Listen carefully to children's comments and watch their reactions. You will be able to identify those sections of the game which need to be changed.
7. At the end of the game, ask children how they feel and what they learned. This debriefing will give you additional suggestions for improving the instructional and motivational effectiveness of the game.

The modified game must be tested out with a fresh group of players. The game may have to be recycled a few times through this revise-retest loop before satisfactory results are consistently obtained.

Final Packaging. When the designer is satisfied with the effects of the instructional game with handicapped children, he undertakes the final packaging. The designer may seek professional help during this step if needed, but is perhaps more effective and definitely more rewarding for him to use the skills which he used earlier for the production of a prototype. The outcome of this step will be a self-contained, student-tested game for helping handicapped learners attain specific instructional objectives.

CONCLUSION

Our experiences with successful teacher-game designers suggest that their skills were learned through three different approaches. First, designers learned and applied theoretical principles of game design. Second, they repeatedly modified the content and the structure of frame games. In this article, we have attempted to give explanations and examples for the beginning game designer consistent with these two approaches. However, the most effective way to learn game design is the third approach—to actually design a game and try it out with handicapped learners. These learners are the game designer's best teachers. Through repeated testing and modification, both individual games and the game designer's techniques become refined. We hope that the reader will find opportunities for such "on-the-game" training.

References

Fink, A. H., Sitko, M. C., Semmel, M. I., & Shuster, S. K. *The effects of games on motivational aspects of teacher-pupil interaction.* Bloomington, IN: Center for Innovation in Teaching the Handicapped, 1971.
Gibson, W. B. *Hoyle's simplified guide to the popular card games.* New York: Doubleday, 1971.
Golick, M. *Deal me in!: The use of playing cards in teaching and learning.* New York: Jeffrey Norton Publishers, 1973.
Piaget, J. *Play, dreams, and imitation in childhood.* New York: Norton, 1962.

Portions of this paper are based on developmental activities supported by contract #OEC 74-9303-Semmel from the U.S. Office of Education, Bureau of Education for the Handicapped, to the Center for Innovation in Teaching the Handicapped. Contractors undertaking such projects under government sponsorship are encouraged to express freely their professional judgement in the conduct of the project. Points of view or opinions stated do not, therefore, necessarily represent official Office of Education position or policy.

The lack of experience by public schools in providing programs for severely handicapped children has caused considerable concern on the part of administrators as they work toward implementation of Public Law 94-142. Most school districts have not previously provided services to this population, nor do they have staff members with a background in programming for the severely handicapped. In response to these circumstances, the authors provide an overview of issues related to program development, discussing curriculum planning, identification processes, the significance of early intervention, and the importance of utilizing local resources. The comprehensiveness of this article makes it a usable reference for individuals who are knowledgeable about program development, as well as those who are in early developmental stages of programming for the severely handicapped.

General Principles and Guidelines in "Programming" for Severely Handicapped Children and Young Adults

Norris G. Haring, Alice H. Hayden, and G. Robin Beck,
University of Washington

Developing programs for severely handicapped persons has become the challenging responsibility of educators. While it would be foolhardy to insist that educators alone can or should implement programs designed for severely handicapped persons, this fact remains: As a result of recent legislative mandates, court decisions, and accompanying social trends for change, educators are now on the front line in efforts to change centuries of neglect and mismanagement of severely handicapped persons. And they are the only professionals required by law to be there.

General Principles and Guidelines in "Programming"

If the challenge is immense, so are its attractions. It would be hard to imagine a more interesting set of problems to try to solve or questions to address. We have purposely chosen to use the term "program" in this paper since it emphasizes both the *process* and the *content* required in planning classes for severely handicapped pupils. "Programming" as a process requires, first, the application of principles which may be as old as time but which were first formally articulated earlier in this century and, interestingly, which were applied as long as two decades ago to the instruction of *institutionalized* severely handicapped persons. As educators have become more experienced in teaching severely handicapped children, they have become aware that the increased precision made possible by systematic arrangement of instructional cues, following the principles of programmed instruction, has powerfully increased the effectiveness of the instruction of these children and young adults.

Second, in applying these principles to educational programming in classrooms rather than in institutions, it is necessary to expand traditional practices extensively. For instance, in our curricula, we now need to include behaviors which have rarely before been included in "school" curricula, behaviors which may occur in infancy, including respondents. Moreover, there is now an additional person with a significant role in the classroom—the parent.

Third, since the severely handicapped child now entering public school programs may have many bizarre behaviors and medical problems, the educator is challenged by the need to apply the very latest tactics—or to devise new tactics— for modifying these behaviors and for managing medical problems *in the classroom.*

Finally, because severely handicapped pupils are more likely than others to have lifelong multiple problems, any programs developed for classroom application must be seen as part of a more global strategy that includes access to resources involved in the *comprehensive* management of these children. It is no accident that the authors of this paper represent more than one discipline.

PRINCIPLES OF "PROGRAMMING"

In the middle of this century, a flurry of interest in the formal principles of programming arose when Skinner and Holland, among others, applied experimental results to human learning and stimulated interest in "process" with the further development of teaching machines and programmed materials, with and without hardware. These materials have been used in government and industry, but have also been applied in instructional settings. But in 1975, programming may sound like a dated and mechanistic way of describing what happens in a classroom. Yet it is fair to say that the *principles* of programming have always been inherent in good teaching. The underlying rationale in programming, or in any systematic teaching, is that waiting for the vagaries of genetic endowment, experience, and "accidental curriculum" (or discovery") to be expressed as "learning" is *inefficient*. So it is worth reiterating that while the term programming and the automated presentation of material are no longer popular, the basic principles or rules which were developed and articulated in programming material for instructional purposes are really the basis for effective teaching and the subsequent development of an educational technology. These rules have special relevance in programs for severely handicapped children.

1. Measure entering behavior (developmental level).
2. Specify terminal behavior (the particular skill or set of skills to be learned).
3. Require an active response by the pupil.
4. Arrange small, sequential steps to achieve the terminal behavior in order to maximize the opportunities for success.
5. Build in periodic review of skills already learned (for instance, through drill and practice).
6. Withdraw discriminative stimulus systematically by shaping generalization and differential discrimination skills.
7. Systematically measure progress throughout program (precise data collection).

Classroom Application

Using the general principles noted above in programming instruction yields curriculum and measurement strategies that give the teacher immediate feedback concerning student level and rate of progress. This information is valuable because it tells the teacher what he/she needs to do next: Change the program, if that is indicated; or move the child to more elementary or more complex skills. In general, this highly individualized strategy also leads to pupils' acquiring skills at a faster rate and with fewer errors. It is important to point out that what distinguishes programming as a process for severely handicapped pupils is not anything new about the strategy but, rather, the pupils' entering behavior (which occurs at earlier and earlier developmental levels) and the need to make the individual instructional steps smaller (slicing the behavior into finer and finer pinpoints). An example of the latter can be found in the chapter "Developmental Pinpoints" prepared by Cohen, Gross, and Haring (1975).

Moving from the pinpoints—which can also be used to assess the developmental level of a severely handicapped child—to creating a curriculum for that child can open many alternatives to the teacher. However, whatever curriculum is developed and introduced must adhere to the basic principles noted above and must result in a quantified measure of change in pupil behavior. The kinds of data a teacher can collect to determine the child's progress include response rate data, trials to criterion, and other reliable measures. The basic progression is this: By using assessment data to determine what skills a child has and has not mastered and those developmentally appropriate skills he or she should master, the teacher can begin to prioritize instructional concerns. The teacher selects an appropriate target skill, slicing the instructional components as finely as is necessary for the child to master all of the target behavior's prerequisite skills. Tables 1 and 2 illustrate this process.

EARLY INTERVENTION

We have emphasized the need to develop pinpoints and curriculum appropriate for the child from birth onward for two reasons. First, it is very likely that older handicapped children newly enrolled in educational programs may be functioning at this level in at least some areas of their development; usually there is tremendous "scatter" across developmental areas. But the more critical reason for this focus on infant skills is that *one further guideline in programming for severely handicapped pupils is to have access to them at the earliest possible time.* In order for this to occur, there must be the earliest possible recognition of infants or children at risk for severe handicapping conditions by professionals responsible for their healthy development.

In order to understand the importance of early intervention and issues to be raised later concerning early identification and the development of resources for severely handicapped persons, it will be useful to review here the history of the infant, with particular emphasis on the development of the central nervous system (CNS), the substrate for educational intervention.

Infant Development

If we divide the nine month period from conception to birth into three trimesters, we can look at the major developmental events occurring during each period. During the first trimester, the form or *anatomy* is being established—that is, the shape and structures of all organs, including the brain. Insults of whatever nature (etiology) at this time may lead to abnormalities of anatomy—for instance, heart defects, limb defects, cleft lips, or abnormalities of the brain.

The second trimester can be characterized by the growth that occurs not

Instructional Planning for Exceptional Children

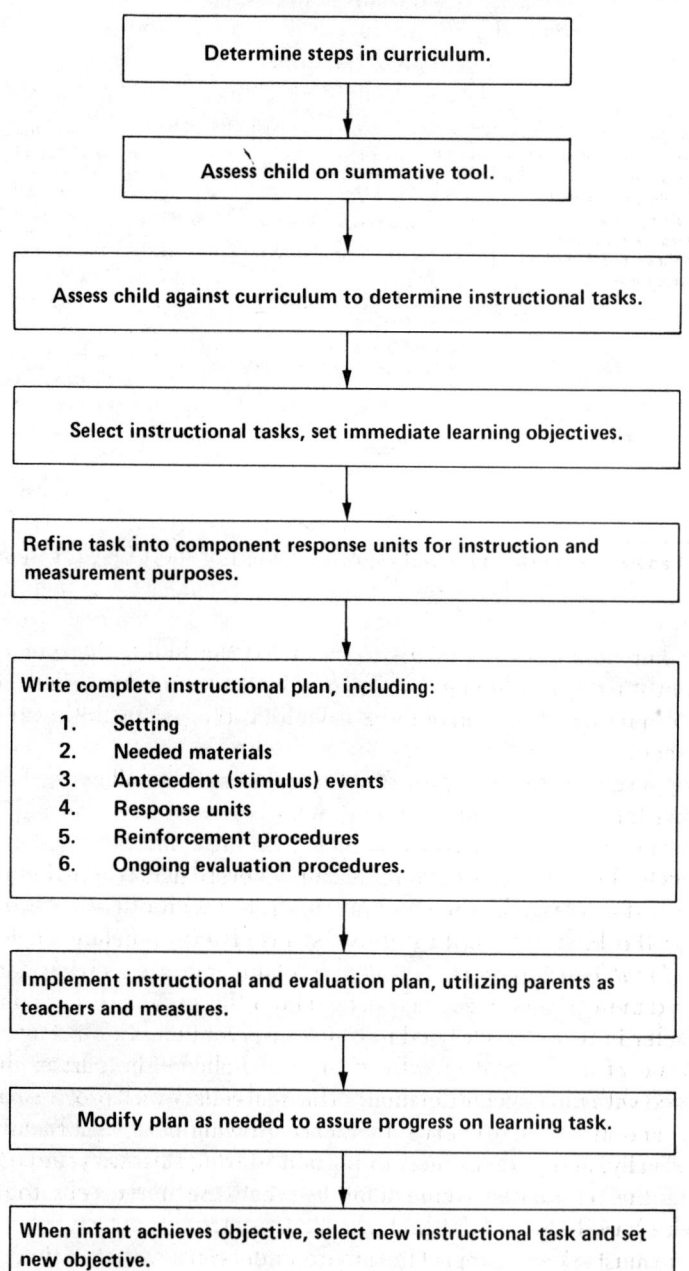

Table 1
STEPS IN THE INSTRUCTIONAL PROCESS

```
┌─────────────────────────────────────────┐
│   Determine steps in curriculum.        │
└─────────────────────────────────────────┘
                    ↓
┌─────────────────────────────────────────┐
│   Assess child on summative tool.       │
└─────────────────────────────────────────┘
                    ↓
┌─────────────────────────────────────────────────────────┐
│ Assess child against curriculum to determine            │
│ instructional tasks.                                    │
└─────────────────────────────────────────────────────────┘
                    ↓
┌─────────────────────────────────────────────────────────┐
│ Select instructional tasks, set immediate learning      │
│ objectives.                                             │
└─────────────────────────────────────────────────────────┘
                    ↓
┌─────────────────────────────────────────────────────────┐
│ Refine task into component response units for           │
│ instruction and measurement purposes.                   │
└─────────────────────────────────────────────────────────┘
                    ↓
┌─────────────────────────────────────────────────────────┐
│ Write complete instructional plan, including:           │
│     1. Setting                                          │
│     2. Needed materials                                 │
│     3. Antecedent (stimulus) events                     │
│     4. Response units                                   │
│     5. Reinforcement procedures                         │
│     6. Ongoing evaluation procedures.                   │
└─────────────────────────────────────────────────────────┘
                    ↓
┌─────────────────────────────────────────────────────────┐
│ Implement instructional and evaluation plan, utilizing  │
│ parents as teachers and measures.                       │
└─────────────────────────────────────────────────────────┘
                    ↓
┌─────────────────────────────────────────────────────────┐
│ Modify plan as needed to assure progress on learning    │
│ task.                                                   │
└─────────────────────────────────────────────────────────┘
                    ↓
┌─────────────────────────────────────────────────────────┐
│ When infant achieves objective, select new              │
│ instructional task and set new objective.               │
└─────────────────────────────────────────────────────────┘
```

General Principles and Guidelines in "Programming"

Table 2
RELATIONSHIP BETWEEN INFANT CURRICULUM STANDARDIZED ASSESSMENT, AND CLASSROOM PROGRAMMING

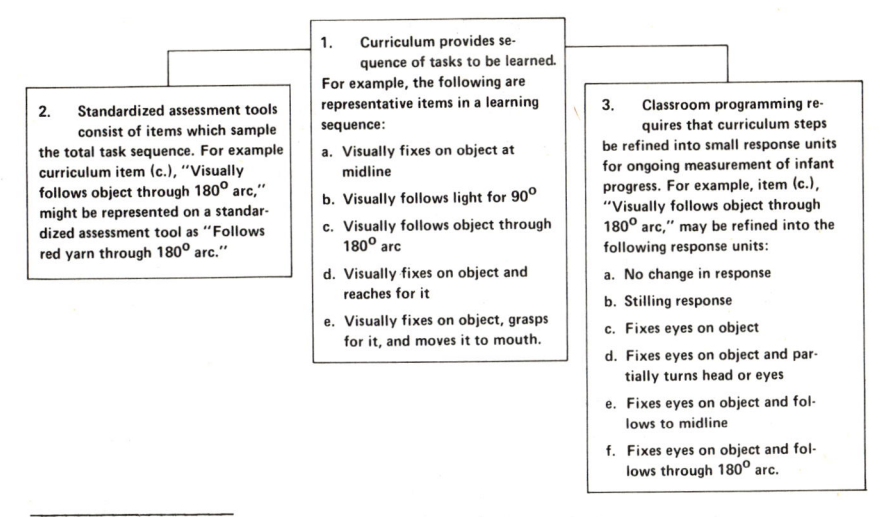

2. Standardized assessment tools consist of items which sample the total task sequence. For example curriculum item (c.), "Visually follows object through 180° arc," might be represented on a standardized assessment tool as "Follows red yarn through 180° arc."	1. Curriculum provides sequence of tasks to be learned. For example, the following are representative items in a learning sequence: a. Visually fixes on object at midline b. Visually follows light for 90° c. Visually follows object through 180° arc d. Visually fixes on object and reaches for it e. Visually fixes on object, grasps for it, and moves it to mouth.	3. Classroom programming requires that curriculum steps be refined into small response units for ongoing measurement of infant progress. For example, item (c.), "Visually follows object through 180° arc," may be refined into the following response units: a. No change in response b. Stilling response c. Fixes eyes on object d. Fixes eyes on object and partially turns head or eyes e. Fixes eyes on object and follows to midline f. Fixes eyes on object and follows through 180° arc.

Tables 1 and 2 were provided by Dr. Dale Gentry, Principal, Experimental Education Unit School.

only in numbers of cells but, particularly for the brain, the *type* of cells. Apparently in the developing human fetus, by the end of the second trimester the total number of neurons (nerve cells) that the person will ever have is established.

The final trimester is a period of further growth for all parts of the fetus including the CNS.

Beyond the prenatal period, some extremely interesting information relevant to the issue of programming for severely handicapped children is apparent—for instance, when and at what rate different tissues grow.

For the brain, the critical growth period begins before birth, but *it extends for at least two years*. Not all parts of the brain are growing at the same time, and there are some characteristics about this growth that are important to consider in planning early educational intervention. For instance, this is the period of most rapid growth of the cerebellum (the part of the brain associated with muscle coordination). The glial cells (which provide structural support and insulation to nerve fibers) are growing most rapidly during this time. Finally, and perhaps most important, during this two year period and beyond, the number of connections between the nerve cells themselves (dendrites) are being established (see Figure 1).

One must ask what impact the environment can have at this time, and the answer is very clear—a significant impact. This answer is supported by

Instructional Planning for Exceptional Children

Figure 1
CENTRAL NERVOUS SYSTEM DEVELOPMENT FROM CONCEPTION TO TWO YEARS

Conception			Birth	
Trimester 1	Trimester 2	Trimester 3	Year 1	Year 2
Anatomy	Total neuron number established	Growth	Growth of: 1. Cerebellum 2. Glial cells - Support structures and myelin 3. Dendrite proliferation	

experiments with animals and by experience with humans. Examples of the latter include the known impacts of severe malnutrition or environmental deprivation on growth—in particular, brain growth—during the first years of life and on subsequent size and intelligence. We would like to refer readers to a remarkable discussion of brain development by John Dobbing (1975) who reports some recent research with animals and its potential implications for intervention.

For the infant at risk for severe handicapping conditions (particularly retardation), the environment and the conditions under which the child grows during the first two years of life are critical. The major implication for the comprehensive management program is clear: Educators and others must have early access to these children. (For a review of early intervention, see Hayden and Haring, 1975.)

Identification

As we have noted, a critical variable in early intervention is identification. Work by researchers in various scientific fields which has contributed to the understanding of severe handicapping conditions has also permitted some important generalizations to be made with implications for early identification. (Since remediation is our concern in this discussion, we will not present the important implications for prevention that are inherent in these findings.) One extremely useful approach is to categorize severe handicapping conditions, and a method recently suggested by David Smith (1975) is to sort them according to *the probable timing of the injurious insult* to the CNS. Using the previous figure showing CNS development during fetal life, we can now superimpose a diagnostic paradigm and look at these onset categories together with what we know is happening during the different development periods (see Figure 2). Because this topic has been discussed elsewhere at length

General Principles and Guidelines in "Programming"

Figure 2
TIMING OF INSULT TO THE CNS: WHAT AREAS OF DEVELOPMENT ARE AFFECTED

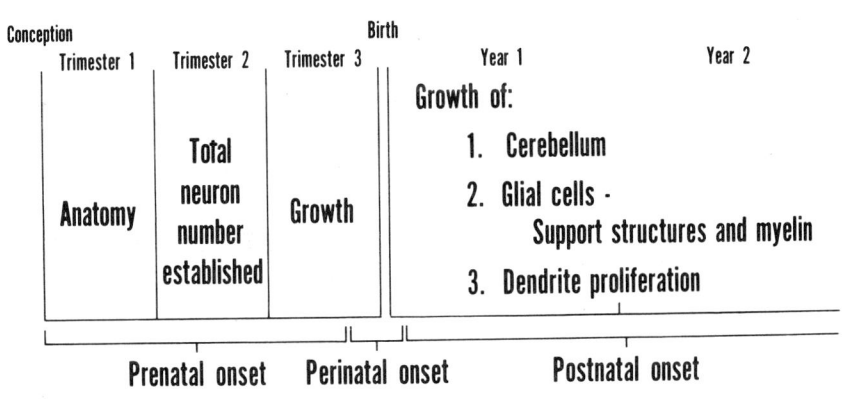

Conception			Birth		
Trimester 1	Trimester 2	Trimester 3		Year 1	Year 2
Anatomy	Total neuron number established	Growth		**Growth of:** 1. Cerebellum 2. Glial cells - Support structures and myelin 3. Dendrite proliferation	

Prenatal onset   **Perinatal onset**   **Postnatal onset**

(Smith, 1975; Beck, Adams, Chandler & Livingston, 1975), we will restrict this discussion to two categories only.

The first category—disorders with *prenatal* onset—accounts for almost one half of the number of children institutionalized with severe handicapping conditions, including mental retardation. Referring again to Figure 1, we see that in the first trimester of prenatal life the "anatomy" or structure of the developing embryo is established. Fully one-third of the children whose disorders have prenatal onset have a single malformation of the brain or CNS. The other two-thirds of the children in this category are those who may have not only abnormal CNS development but also major and minor malformations of non-CNS structures. Indeed, these malformations may be exhibited in *patterns* which have established etiologies—for instance, Down's syndrome (a cluster of abnormalities with a chromosomal or "genetic" etiology); fetal alcohol syndrome (a cluster of abnormalities related to "drug" etiology); or rubella syndrome (a cluster of abnormalities caused by an infectious agent, a virus).

During the second and third trimesters, when neuron proliferation and growth are occurring, an insult to the CNS is likely to produce abnormalities in cell number or size. Examples of infants sustaining insult in the later trimesters are those who are small at birth but who are not truly premature. These infants may have many medical complications in the newborn period, depending on the cause of the intrauterine growth failure. The subsequent development of these children is again quite variable; however, the majority will have measurable deficits in learning.

The second category of handicapping conditions, those with *perinatal onset*, comprises conditions arising from all of the complications that can occur in the birth process and the immediate newborn period, and that can adversely affect the CNS. During this critical transition period from intrauterine

Instructional Planning for Exceptional Children

to extrauterine life, the CNS can be injured by interruption of the supply of oxygen, glucose, or other metabolites necessary for maintaining neuron viability. Infections or hemorrhage of the CNS may affect later development by injury produced through the above mechanisms or by direct injury to the nerve cells and supporting tissues of the brain.

Summary

It is useful to think of the development of the CNS in devising educational interventions. Indeed, the period of development from birth to two years may be *the* most critical period for educational intervention. Early intervention for most children with severely handicapping conditions including mental retardation is a diagnostic process including a *careful physical examination* (for major and minor malformations related to timing of onset) and a *detailed history* (particularly for events which could adversely affect the CNS). This process could lead to designating as "educationally high risk" *by one month of age* as many as 50% of children who subsequently are recognized as severely handicapped, including those with mental retardation.

Two of the most important facts from the above discussion that must be basic considerations in devising educational intervention programs for severely handicapped children are these: *Most severely handicapped children can be identified early, and these children are likely to have multiple problems.* Besides needing educational programs, the children may also need to be referred to a facility such as a Birth Defects Clinic that is organized to manage the multiple medical problems of these children or a University Affiliated Facility, a center concerned with diagnosis, treatment, and basic research into the causes and prevention of mental retardation.

In the remainder of this paper, we will discuss some aspects of the educational intervention program—or classroom—for the severely handicapped pupil.

SOME SPECIAL ASPECTS OF CLASSES FOR SEVERELY HANDICAPPED CHILDREN

Once a child has been identified, a resource must be available for the educational intervention strategy from birth onward. That resource is the classroom, with input from various disciplines involved in managing severely handicapped pupils; occupational or physical therapists, speech and communication disorders specialists, psychologists, nurses, and physicians are all part of the intervention team. Classes for severely handicapped children can now be divided into two general categories. The first is the class for the older severely handicapped child who has previously had minimal educational intervention, or none. Children in these classes usually attend school daily for five or six hours. The second category is the infant class, which serves infants and children under two. Professionals in this class may have contact with the infant or child for as little as one hour a week and only rarely for more than three hours a week.

The chronological age of the pupils is the least interesting or important aspect of these programs, for both may utilize curriculum which extends downwards to early infancy. We would like to look at these two types of classes, emphasizing the special characteristics of each and the *teacher* behaviors which are different in serving this population rather than the educational technology.

The classes to be described operate within the Center for the Severely Handicapped at the University of Washington's Experimental Education Unit. In keeping with the principles of programming, ongoing review of pupil progress is a major component of the management strategy; by measuring progress continually, the staff are able to make necessary program changes instantly. In addition to daily, direct measurement, there is also periodic overall review of the group's progress in regular management team meetings and meeting between the team and parents.

Programs for Older Severely Handicapped Pupils

Two case studies of older pupils with multiple problems should help to identify the roles of the interdisciplinary classroom team, which includes not only a teacher but also the other specialists mentioned above.

Case Study #1: Jane

Jane (a pseudonym) entered this class when she was seven years old. Her history included birth abnormalities such as cleft lip and palate and abnormal findings in transillumination of the head (a diagnostic procedure). Subsequently, an abnormality in brain anatomy was diagnosed—holoporencephaly, an abnormality with prenatal onset, probably within the first trimester. Because Jane repeatedly showed high serum sodium (an indication of water depletion) when tested, physicians identified another problem—a defect in posterior pituitary function, which resulted in loss of water in her urine. Her contact with a birth defects clinic led to surgical repair of the cleft lip and palate as well as medical management of Jane's endocrine problem. Later, between her third and fourth birthdays, Jane's physicians believed that she had recovered her pituitary functions; medication for maintaining water balance was discontinued.

But Jane's history between ages four and seven was replete with hos-

Instructional Planning for Exceptional Children

pitalizations (as many as four yearly) for dehydration. The physicians responsible for her care attributed this to Jane's taking insufficient fluids. Therefore, it was necessary to monitor her fluid intake. After Jane was enrolled in the class for severely handicapped children, it became obvious that the staff could do the monitoring; and that activity became a part of her program management goals within the classroom.

When she joined the class, Jane's performance was at less than the one year level; she had no self-feeding skills, was not toilet trained, and emitted many bizarre behaviors including self-stimulation. The following immediate classroom goals were set for Jane:

1. Increase her fluid intake to meet her needs (minimum of 1000cc, or a litre, per day); and monitor her urine concentration (specific gravity).
2. Decrease Jane's self-stimulating behaviors.
3. Begin curriculum to develop self-feeding, toileting, and other self-help behaviors.
4. Increase Jane's communication skills.
5. Institute a physical therapy program for improving Jane's muscle tone and function.

The classroom staff noted that the surgical repair of Jane's cleft lip and palate was far from functional—Jane had difficulty in swallowing, with regurgitation into the nose; and her nasal passages were so narrow that she had obstruction with the slightest upper respiratory infection. Therefore, the staff added to the list of goals for Jane a referral for evaluation of the surgical repair. Further, Jane needed vigorous decongesting with any upper respiratory infection as an interim solution until surgical consultations about repair of her cleft lip and palate could be obtained.

The data collected by Jane's teacher are grouped in Figure 3. The staff observed the following: The weekly blood test performed in the classroom showed that, even with adequate water intake, Jane's serum sodium did not fall to normal levels. However, during this 3 month period Jane did not have to be hospitalized.

At this point, elective hospitalization was scheduled for reevaluation of Jane's pituitary-renal axis; indeed, Jane was found to have partial function of this feedback system. The specific recommendation of the endocrinologist was to try different oral medications to maximize the effect of her partially active feedback system.

When Jane returned to the classroom, she was placed on oral medication. The teacher in the class monitored Jane's fluid intake and measured the specific gravity of her urine during the toileting program, using a test he had been trained to perform. Further, the physician continued to draw a blood sample once each week in order to evaluate Jane's progress under this

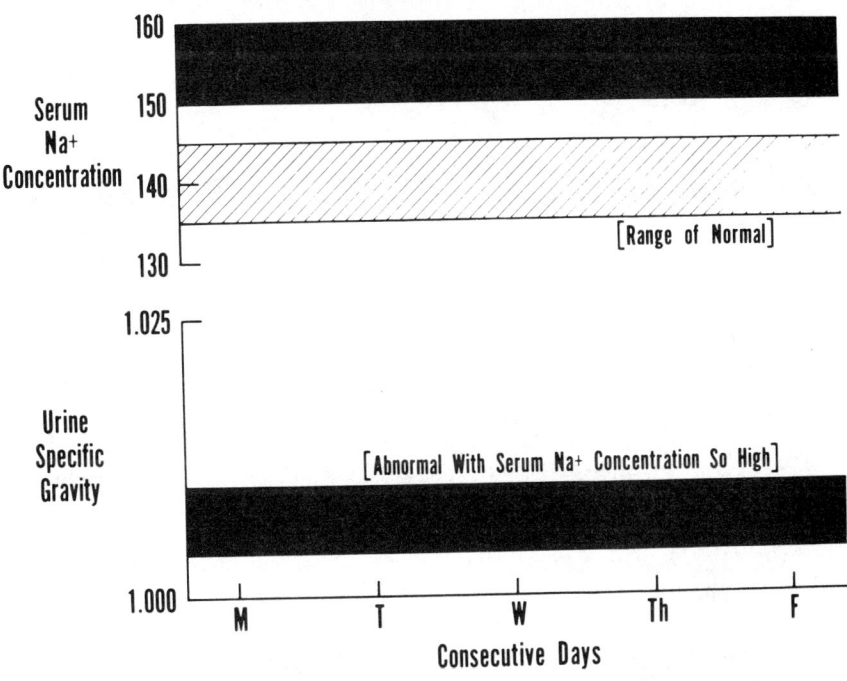

General Principles and Guidelines in "Programming"

Figure 3
JANE'S SERUM SODIUM AND URINE SPECIFIC GRAVITY WITH OPTIMUM FLUID INTAKE IN THE CLASSROOM: FINDINGS BEFORE MEDICAL TREATMENT

Normal range is indicated by shaded block; Jane's abnormal findings are indicated by black block.

program. The subsequent data collected by the teacher are shown in Figure 4.

Programs for other, more traditional educational interventions are continuing for Jane. She has not required hospitalization (other than the elective admission mentioned above) since she entered the classroom. The type, dosage, and timing of oral therapy for her endocrine problem can be closely followed in the classroom; these observations have been crucial in managing Jane's medical problem.

Comment. Jane's case illustrates quite clearly how the classroom management team can serve extremely useful functions, in addition to providing traditional educational intervention, by their observations, data collection, and monitoring of progress. It is fair to say that without the input of those who observed Jane in the natural environment of the classroom, her condition would have led to repeated bouts of dehydration and expensive hospitalizations. It is worth mentioning that, had Jane not had multiple problems, her partial pituitary-renal impairment would have been diagnosed much earlier.

Instructional Planning for Exceptional Children

Figure 4
JANE'S SERUM SODIUM AND URINE SPECIFIC GRAVITY DURING MEDICATION TRIALS AND MONITORING IN THE CLASSROOM

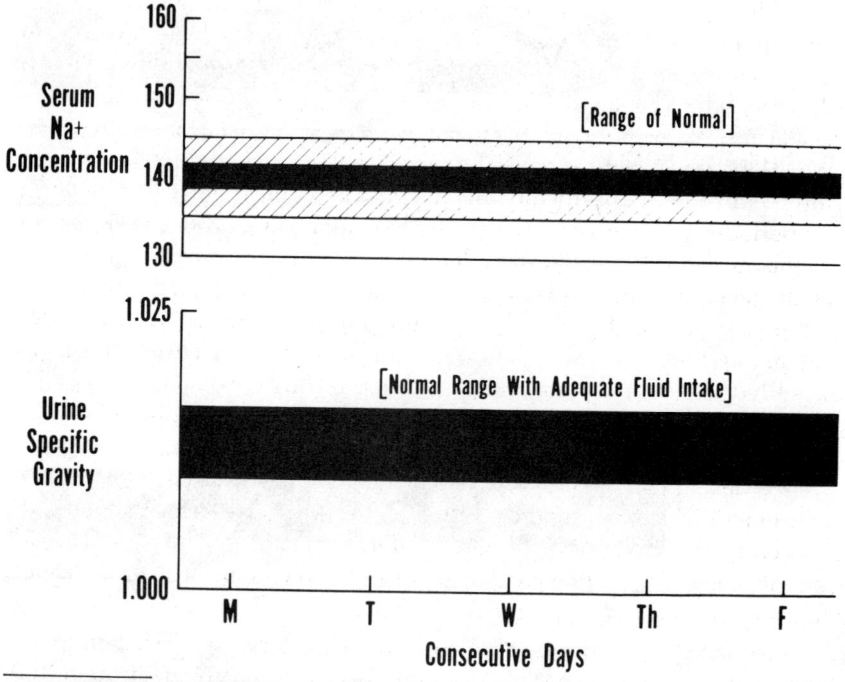

Jane's findings, indicated in black blocks, are now well within the normal range.

The precise measurement of the important variables was possible only in the classroom environment.

Case Study #2: Jackie

Other problems managed in the classroom not usually considered within the "jurisdiction" of educators, but increasingly within their province as they work with severely handicapped children, include monitoring of seizure control medications. Perhaps this problem can emphasize some of the difficulties faced by the educational program managers of severely handicapped pupils. Traditionally, control of seizures has been the management concern of neurologists, not of educators. Unfortunately, most seizure medications have side effects which may interfere with learning; and in many instances, seizure control has been possible only with the use of more than one drug, each compounding the number and type of side effects that can interfere with learning. Only through the classroom for severely handicapped children have

General Principles and Guidelines in "Programming"

we gained the precision which allows for the close monitoring of side effects *and* learning.

Jackie (a pseudonym) is another student in our class for severely handicapped pupils, and her case illustrates some of the problems involved in seizure management. She was born with multiple major and minor abnormalities and was diagnosed as having a very rare chromosomal anomaly (with prenatal onset). Jackie did not begin to have seizures until late in her first year of life. She was hospitalized for neurological evaluation, and drug therapy was instituted in order to control the seizures. Since "medical" intervention tends to be periodic, Jackie was not reevaluated for approximately one year, except for adjustments of her medication dosages as necessary to accommodate her growth. Jackie's mother, however, made some interesting observations during that year: Although Jackie clearly was not normal, she had been an active child and *had* been learning before her seizures; the side effects of seizure control led to seemingly complete cessation of this development. Jackie's mother was quite daring; she decided to stop medication. In her view, the rare occurrence of a seizure was not nearly so alarming as was Jackie's impeded developmental progress. Unfortunately, this decision led to severe chastisement of Jackie's mother by the child's physician. One cannot fault either party; the issue was really one of different priorities. The physician was primarily concerned with controlling seizures and was not so alarmed about inhibiting developmental progress.

Fortunately, Jackie was enrolled in the class for severely handicapped children at this time. The staff reinstituted seizure control medication, but within an environment where the possibilities for learning *and* for controlling seizures could be optimized. The staff had to help Jackie's mother overcome her guilt and anger about what had previously occurred, support her appreciation of the need for promoting developmental progress, and reestablish contact with those responsible for Jackie's seizure control. This time, however, Jackie's physician had the classroom data that he needed to optimize both seizure control and developmental progress.

Comment. We spoke earlier about the need for comprehensive management of severely handicapped pupils. We also mentioned that educators are in fact the only professionals who are required by law to concern themselves with this issue. It is fair to say that educators will have to lead the way in *classroom-based* comprehensive management by eliciting the support, interest, and involvement of other specialists. Jackie's case illustrates one of the most effective ways this can be done—by collecting and supplying classroom data to other professionals. In Jackie's case, the physician caring for her was first of all quite surprised and pleased that there was a resource—the classroom—available for Jackie where she would be given systematic opportunities for learning. This alleviated some of the understandable frustration he shares with many professionals who fear that they will not be able to make adequate referrals for their handicapped patients. Second, when he was shown performance data—data demonstrating that Jackie was making developmental progress—he was impressed by the kinds of learning that were occurring. But the critical information that elicited his support was presented in differential performance data; these data demonstrated clearly that Jackie's performance was impeded when she was on higher drug dosages and was either asleep or drowsy much of the time, and that she *could* make quite acceptable progress when the dosage was lowered. The physician's cooperation with the classroom management team has been an important outcome of data sharing.

Infant Programs

Development of a program for infants and children younger than two years, based on the early recognition of severely handicapping conditions or the risk of significant developmental delay, has changed the traditional concept of a classroom. We would like to discuss some of the unique features of the early intervention program.

Diagnosis and Intervention. From our earlier discussion, we know that establishing that an infant is at high risk for developmental delay should be possible from a review of the medical history and a detailed physical examination. Immediate referral of the child to a program is justified if the staff in the program carefully establish developmental pinpoints, sequence curriculum, and generate reliable performance data. What happens then is that the fine-focus "diagnosis" of developmental delay depends on infant or child performance *over time* in a program that provides appropriate intervention and a longitudinal commitment to the child and his/her family *within the community.* The classroom also provides a base for focusing the input of the interdisciplinary team whose members may be physically remote from the program. This input includes the periodic administration of developmental assessment tools (for instance, the Bayley) by appropriately trained psychologists. These assessment data can be utilized by the staff not only in curriculum development but also for monitoring the effectiveness of intervention tactics. Periodic assessment also provides information that can be utilized in establishing frequency of classroom contact and "graduation" from the program. Finally, these data also provide a means for monitoring continued development after the infant leaves the program. However, to emphasize the point we made earlier: Diagnosis of developmental delay by the administration of a "test" is *not* a prerequisite for an infant's referral to, or enrollment in, an intervention classroom.

Use of "Respondent" Behaviors. Young infants and some severely handicapped older children emit respondent behaviors which can be utilized in an

General Principles and Guidelines in "Programming"

intervention program. Some of these behaviors include the Moro reflex, rooting reflex, tonic neck reflex, stepping reflex, trunk incurvation, and placing reflex. When eliciting these reflexes, one is impressed by the variation from infant to infant in strength, duration, and the composite impression of "quality" of response. Some of these variables may depend on the state of *food deprivation*, other variables may relate to CNS function.

One may argue whether these behaviors are truly respondent or operant (for instance, the rooting reflex or behavior might be operant after a tactile discrimination stimulus). However, it is useful to consider these as respondents since the reflexes tend to change in time (components drop out the response or the response disappears) as the infant matures. This may reflect the increasing control of higher brain centers (whose output tends to be inhibitory) with maturation and is also consistent with the finding that these "reflexes" reemerge in brain-injured adults—that is, adults who sustain sudden removal of input from the "higher" brain centers.

As an intervention strategy for an infant with asymmetry of response, incomplete response, or decreased muscle tone, the elicitation of respondents may help to overcome deficits in the response as well as to improve symmetry of response and, therefore, may be part of the intervention goals.

To reiterate, all infants and some older severely handicapped children have a class of behaviors, respondents, not found in normal older children which may be utilized in the infant curriculum; and the state of food satiation may be an important variable in the timing of the classroom intervention program.

Intervention vs. Maturation. The infant program must be able to separate the effect of the intervention on behavioral change from that related to maturation of the CNS occurring during the first two years of life. This is important not only to document effectiveness of different intervention programs but also to allow economic use of teacher/parent time in program administration. For example, it may be inefficient to begin sequences designed to develop visual discrimination for color or shape before the time when the infant's visual acuity is appropriate for the task. Conversely, it might be most effective to correct *all* children's "normal" deficit in visual acuity early in the first year and to begin these sequences early (although the prospect of a class full of infants wearing glasses gives one pause). Likewise, since the cerebellum in undergoing the most rapid growth of any part of the brain following birth managers must carefully consider the timing and type of motor intervention sequences.

Parent Involvement. The infant classroom experience not only provides ongoing assessment and sequencing for the infant, but includes the development of a parent curriculum. This curriculum begins with the parent's learning to run the instructional program and includes the goal of training the

Instructional Planning for Exceptional Children

parent to use differential responding and recording of data in simple contingency management. Where reflexes and physical therapy exercises are involved, the parent can be taught instructional skills. As the parent's skills increase, new tactics are introduced. This aspect of the infant program may indeed be the most important. At present, the infant's time in the classroom may be limited to one hour per week. Therefore, it is imperative that the parent be able to run the program at home. When we look at the prognostic implications of some educational intervention, we will see that the parent curriculum may play another highly significant role.

REPLICATION OF THE BASIC INTERVENTION MODEL

The topics and examples we have discussed illustrate the diversity of problems and issues which program managers in classes for severely handicapped pupils may be expected to handle. The measurement of behavior and collection of data (whether behavioral or physiological data) reflect the tenets of "precision teaching," a systematic approach to instruction that has special relevance to the multiple problems of the severely handicapped.

The examples, however, were drawn from classes within an interdisciplinary center, one whose resources are sophisticated and where highly trained specialists bring their expertise to the management of severely handicapped pupils. It is certainly fair to ask whether the service delivery model operating in such a center is relevant to needs and resources in the "real world" outside the center. One of the guidelines in developing a program for severely handicapped pupils is that, if the model is to be at all useful to practitioners, it must "travel" well and be adaptable to many different environments. One of us (Dr. Beck) has recently had the opportunity to observe, and participate in, service delivery in a very remote community, American Samoa. We would like to discuss briefly the experience of the American Samoan government in developing programs for severely handicapped children as a model of planning and utilization of *available local resources*. Table 3 encapsulates the time and activities involved in developing this model.

The ten-day assessment period was the culmination of work carried on during the preceding two years, initiated by Dennis McRae, Director of Special Education in American Samoa. During that time, Public Health Nurses known in the villages were able to identify approximately 25 children with severe handicapping conditions by traveling to the villages and conducting a house-to-house (fali-to-fali) survey. Also during this time Samoan teachers were sent for special training to the University of Washington, equipment was ordered for the classroom, and details of transporting these children to the classroom were finalized.

On the first day of school in September, 1975, the assessment team—a

General Principles and Guidelines in "Programming"

Table 3
MODEL UTILIZING AVAILABLE LOCAL RESOURCES

TIME	MEDIC
1 - 3 years (variable)	ADMINISTRATION: Formulating plan Writing funding proposal Acquiring space and personnel with appropriate training

6 months - 1 year (concurrent with above)	FIELD:
	Public Health Nurse canvass of catchment area for severely handicapped children
	
	ADMINISTRATION:
	Finalize needs in funding proposals:
	  1. Personnel—teachers: number and training type
	  2. Space
	  3. Equipment, including transportation

6 months (approximately)
 	
10 days
	TEACHER TRAINING
	
	ASSESSMENT TEAM AND TEACHER ACTIVITIES:
	1. Establish student charts that include the following:
	    medical history
	    —physical examination
	    —goals: educational and medical
	2. Arrange for input to the classroom from speech and communication disorders specialist, physical therapist, and medical resource personnel

special educator and a pediatrician—arrived. The children were brought to the classroom in small groups, and with the teachers present the children were examined physically and educationally. The pediatrician subsequently reviewed the medical histories, including hospital records. A classroom record was begun (see Table 3) for each child. The director of special education and the assessment team then met with personnel of the Lyndon Baines Johnson Tropical Medical Center and arranged for physical therapists, public health nurses, and physicians to be involved in the classroom for severely handicapped pupils. This was accomplished with cooperative efforts on the part of the LBJ hospital staff and facilitated by the generation of precise educational and medical goals for each child in the classroom. Indeed, management of some of the children's medical problems became possible for the first time because of the children's daily attendance in a highly structured, supervised program—that is, the classroom.

The establishment of a "high risk" register to be reviewed jointly by the medical director of the Maternal and Infant Care Project and the director of special education will lead to earlier identification of children at risk and intervention through the ongoing development of the American Samoan program for severely handicapped persons.

CONCLUDING STATEMENT

Implementing *effective* comprehensive programs for severely handicapped persons, including infants and children under two years of age, with establishment of a community-based educational resource has been made possible by the precise application of an educational technology. Effective community-based programs can provide an alternative to institutionalization for many severely handicapped children by optimizing their opportunity to achieve semi-independence within the community. However, without an extended family system (as is found in American Samoa, for instance), we will never be able to close all institutions because there are times when some parents are no longer willing or able to provide care for their severely handicapped children. What *can* be accomplished through the community-based program is to optimize the educational intervention for such children, increase the age at which institutionalization becomes necessary, and plan continued educational interventions within institutions. While the above accomplishments can be defended on humanitarian grounds alone, they may well be economical too given average costs of institutional care (approximately $1,400.00 per month).

Inevitably, at many points in developing programs for severely handicapped children, one can expect to be faced with queries—even from well-meaning professionals—about the worth of such a program for a particular child who seems capable of only "vegetative" function. Physicians, for instance, have been forced to define "end-points" in many aspects of service, as the current case of Karen Quinlan so poignantly makes clear. For example, one uses 26 weeks gestation to determine viability of a fetus and the time when it is no longer possible to electively terminate pregnancy, a flat EEG for 24 hours to determine "brain death." Will we, as educators, be forced to define a "null point" or "zero rate" for determining when to end educational interventions? Fortunately, we think not. This is not only because of the precision and demonstrated effectiveness of the teaching methodology available to us, but also because of the parent curriculum we discussed earlier. To our way of thinking, it is meaningless to talk about "comprehensive management" unless a child's family are active participants. It is not only feasible but eminently desirable that parents (or surrogate parents) be trained to participate in their children's educational intervention. We believe, therefore, that no matter how severe the damage to an infant or child—damage that interferes with learning—there is still a program that parents can be trained to manage, with ongoing assistance from all of the resources mentioned earlier in this paper. Such a program involves helping the child to learn what he or she *can* learn, maintaining the child with dignity, and performing those "nursing" functions that can prevent complications of the child's condition or morbidity. There is no excuse for ending such intervention.

REFERENCES

Beck, G. R., Adams, G., Chandler, L., & Livingston, S. S. The need for adjunctive services in management of severely and profoundly handicapped individuals: A view from primary care. In N. G. Haring & L. Brown (Eds.), *Teaching the severely handicapped: A yearly publication of the American Association for the Education of the Severely/Profoundly Handicapped* (Vol. 1). New York: Grune & Stratton, 1975.

Cohen, M.A., Gross, P., & Haring, N. G. Developmental pinpoints. In N. G. Haring & L. Brown (Eds), *Teaching the severely handicapped: A yearly publication of the American Association for the Education of the Severely/Profoundly Handicapped* (Vol. 1). New York: Grune & Stratton, 1975.

Dobbing, J. Human brain development and its vulnerability. In *Biologic and clinical aspects of brain development*, Proceedings of the Mead Johnson Symposium on Perinatal and Developmental Medicine No. 6. Evansville, Indiana: Mead Johnson & Company, 1975.

Hayden, A. H., & Haring, N. G. Programs for Down's syndrome children at the University of Washington. In T. D. Tjossem (Ed.), *Intervention strategies for risk infants and young children*. Baltimore, Maryland: University Park Press, 1975.

Smith, D. W. Rational diagnostic evaluation of the child with mental deficiency. *American Journal of Diseases of Children*, 1975.

A major factor that often restricts teachers in achieving benefits from their instructional planning centers on their inability to influence the social behaviors of some students. In this paper, Rosenberg and Graubard discuss the implications of behavior modification techniques in the context of teaching students to change the behaviors of others. The authors use examples of research to illustrate the technique. Their discussion on the cases involved also serves as a meaningful frame of reference for teachers in understanding children and youth who present behavioral problems.

Peer Use of Behavior Modification

Harry E. Rosenberg, *Visalia (California) Unified School District*
Paul Graubard, *Yeshiva University*

Social deviance and maladaptive behavior can be alleviated through the use of behavior modification techniques. In the experiments reported in this paper, a novel approach was taken: The "normals" were treated to increase their tolerance for deviant behavior.

This approach developed as a result of a concern at seeing individuality and creativity suppressed in "exceptional" children, who are expected to conform to the rules of the dominant culture. These children are often tragic victims of of society. Under the mantle of "helping," society has stigmatized these children with labels such as "mentally retarded," "psychotic," and "schizophrenic." They have been subjected to loss of privacy, public ridicule, involuntary detention in training schools and hospitals, and loss of prestige and privileges. In many cases, this "help" also leads to physical abuse (James, 1969). This phenomenon is also compounded by racism and class bias. In our opinion, it is no accident that special education classes, child guidance clinics, mental hospitals, and training schools are filled with youth of minority group status far out of proportion to their actual numbers in the population.

For an understanding of the approach, first imagine that a child has absented himself for 37 days of an 80 day school term. If he is referred to a guidance counselor or clinical psychologist, the medical label (which tends to pre-empt all others) will be applied to him. He will be viewed and designated as "school phobic," "emotionally disturbed," or "sick" to some degree. A dean of discipline or a probation officer would label and treat the same child as a "juvenile delinquent," "incorrigible youth," or "youth in need of supervision." Other citizens might view this absentee behavior as "wrong" and would recommend moral lessons dealing with the rewards of virtue and respect for diligence.

In contrast, some members of a counterculture might define this same truancy as heroic behavior to be encouraged, as it seems to violate an oppressive law.

Thus, the problem of maladaptive behavior (or what is popularly called emotional disturbance) can be reasonably interpreted in the language of psychopathology, of learning theory, or of social deviancy. The social deviancy model, long popular in anthropology, has seen little use in the field of applied behavior analysis. This is unfortunate, as it is a model which carries many implications for both understanding and ameliorating behavior problems.

In 1934, Benedict noted in her study of comparative cultures the ease with which people who would be considered abnormal in America were functional in other cultures. It did not matter what kind of "abnormality" she studied—those which indicated extreme instability or those which were more in the nature of character traits like sadism or delusions of grandeur—there were still well described cultures in which these abnormals could function at ease and with honor. These people apparently functioned without danger or difficulty to their society.

If one agrees that given behaviors are not good, bad, healthy, or pathological in themselves and that any component of behavior is either adaptive or maladaptive for a specific culture, then "non-normative," "pathological," and "social deviant" become equivalent terms. Use of this conceptualization demands examination of (1) the specific behavior, (2) the perceiver of behavior, and (3) the effect of the behavior upon the perceiver.

Theories and methods generated by the field of ecology are of great value here, as they view man within the ecosystem or context of the environment. Ecologists do not conceptualize or treat "emotional disturbance." They attempt to describe behavior which is a mismatch between surroundings and individuals or groups. The implication is that behavior, behavior analysis, and planning strategies to reduce conflict can be conducted only in the originating habitat. It is the "goodness of fit" of behaviors to specific environments that must be scrutinized. Rabkin and Rabkin (1969) say that it is the interface (described as the meeting of two social systems, including the context or

Instructional Planning for Exceptional Children

background of their encounter) and the clash between cultures that is in need of change when clinical intervention is requested. The behavior of neither the behaver nor the perceiver in isolation from this interface is the target. The behaver, whether a member of a minority or majority group, should be considered with reference to culture-specific factors. This is particularly true if we take the pluralistic ideals of our society and the rights of minority groups seriously. In our opinion, aberrant behavers constitute a minority group as meaningful as groups composed of ethnically different members of the population.

In the field of mental health, we usually find one group—usually that within the dominant, established culture—which labels the behavior of individuals from another group as disturbed. Those so labeled usually come from a political or social minority. Both Szasz (1970) and Rhodes (1969) discuss the political under-pinnings of mental health labeling in current society.

The treatment of "social deviants" by "normals" cannot be extensively documented here. The theme of cruelty to underdogs runs through the social history of Western society and is extensively detailed in our literature (e.g., Chekhov's *Ward Six,* 1965), and the harassment of "deviants" can be seen on any playground as "normal" children torment a "different" child. Thus, if we work with the "goodness of fit" model, to change the behavior of "normals" may be of equal importance to changing the behavior of "deviants." Change in the interface between conflicting groups is the most significant factor.

The behavioral literature is replete with examples of how behavior modification has been used to change the behavior of the social deviant (e.g., any issue of the *Journal of Applied Behavior Analysis*). There are few examples in the literature where deviants, as part of a planned process of change, were taught to modify the behavior of normals.

We feel that it is necessary to teach deviants to change other people, not only for self-protection but also because the positive use of power leads to self-enhancement and positive feelings about the self. If children are to be more than recipients of someone's benevolence, they must learn how to operate on society as well as to accept being operated upon. Moreover, our clinical data indicate that, in the process of learning to change others, the "deviant" changes his own behavior and receives feedback and reinforcement for this change.

The experiments to be described took place in an agricultural community. "Anglos" comprise the predominant group within the town, although there is a large Chicano population and a small Black community. Each experiment describes a special approach. These experiments are reported as representative of a method, and we assume a much wider spectrum of possible applications than is illustrated here.

CHILDREN-MODIFIED TEACHER BEHAVIOR

This experiment took place in a school which had a reputation for being hostile to the special education program in general and toward adolescent minority group children in particular. Experience had shown that it was extremely difficult to reintegrate special education children into the mainstream of that particular school. It was felt that many regular class teachers scapegoated special education children. Supervisors' directives that all children, including special education children, were to be treated equally had little effect.

The goal of the special education program was to reintegrate its members into regular classes of the school. The children spent more time with each of the regular class teachers than any professional consultant or administrator could and had the greatest personal interest in changing their teachers. They were, therefore, expected to exert the most influence over their teachers, if given an effective technology.

Method

Sam's eighth grade teachers found him frightening. Only 14 years old, he already weighed a powerful 185 pounds. He was easily the school's best athlete, but he loved fighting even more than sports. His viciousness equaled his strength; he had knocked other students cold with beer bottles and chairs. Sam's catalog of infamy also included a 40 day suspension for hitting a principal with a stick and an arrest and a two and one-half year probation for assault.

Inevitably, Sam's teachers agreed that he was incorrigible and placed him in a class for those with behavioral problems. Had they known he had begun secret preparations to change their behavior, they would have been shocked.

Sam's math teacher was one of the first to encounter his new technique. Sam asked for help with a problem; when she had finished her explanation, he looked her in the eye and said, "You really help me learn when you're nice to me." The startled teacher groped for words, then said, "You caught on quickly." Sam smiled, "It makes me feel good when you praise me." Suddenly, Sam was consistently making such statements to all of his teachers. And he would come to class early or stay late to chat with them.

Some teachers gave credit for Sam's dramatic turnaround to the special teacher. They naturally assumed that he had done something to change Sam and his "incorrigible" classmates. Rather than change them, the teacher had trained the students to become behavior engineers. Their parents, teacher, and peers had become the clients.

Subjects. Seven children with an age range of 12 to 15 years were selected as behavior engineers. Two children were Caucasian, two were

Black, and three were Chicanos. Each engineer was assigned two clients (teachers), and each had the responsibility of accelerating praise rates and decelerating negative comments and punishment by the teachers.

Procedure. The class day in the school was organized into seven 43-minute periods. Special education children met with a special class teacher three periods a day and were integrated into the regular classes for four periods daily.

Instruction and practice in behavior modification theory and techniques were given during one period a day by the special class teachers. Initially, instruction was on a one-to-one basis, but later the whole class worked together on practicing their newly learned skills. The children were told that they were going to participate in an experiment. Scientific accuracy was stressed as being extremely important. Students were directed to record all the client-teacher's remarks during the pilot period of two weeks. Through consensual validation of the class and special education staff, these comments were sorted into positive or negative groups.

Techniques taught to the children included making eye contact with teachers, asking for extra help, and making reinforcing comments such as, "Gee, it makes me feel good and work so much better when you praise me" and "I like the way you teach that lesson." They also were taught to use reinforcing behavior such as sitting up straight and nodding in agreement as teachers spoke. These techniques and phrases were used contingent upon teacher performance. The pupils were also taught to perform the "aha" reaction (so notably described by Fritz Redl) as follows: When a pupil understood an assignment, he was to ask the teachers to explain it once again. In the middle of the second explanation the student exclaims, "Aha! Now I understand; I could never get that point before."

Pupils were also taught to break eye contact with the teacher during a scolding, to ignore a teacher's provocation, to show up early for class, and to ask for extra assignments. These techniques were explicitly taught and practiced repeatedly. Simulation techniques and role playing were employed. Video tapes were used extensively so that other children could monitor their performance and, under both class and teacher prompting, adjust those factors that were targets for change.

Reliability. Each of the seven students were observed in action. At various times, an observer-aide unobtrusively recorded his own version of positive and negative contacts within the teacher-student interface. These records were later compared with those of the student-participants for the same observation periods.

On positive contacts from teacher-clients, the range of correlations between student and observer records was very narrow, from a low of .815 to a high of .980. The mean correlation across seven student-observer combinations is .942.

On negative contacts, the range of correlations is from .453 for one student-observer combination to 1.00 for two such combinations. These perfect correlations reflect the fact that students were often observed well into the experiment during periods when negative contacts by teachers were few, often zero. Therefore, agreement between students and observers in the absence of negative contact for such periods is quite high. The average for the seven student-observer combinations is .957.

An interesting sidelight was that at the beginning when procedures were piloted, the observer-aides consistently differed from the children in the number of positive comments made. Closer monitoring revealed that the aides were more accurate in recording, since often the special education children were unable to recognize conventional praise phrases as such. Therefore, they consistently underestimated the amount of praise that was given to them. Teachers were experimentally naive.

Results

Data were collected during a nine week period. With seven student-engineers, each with two teacher-clients, there were, in effect, 14 replications to examine. An ABA design was employed: The first two weeks were considered baseline weeks and were followed by five weeks of intervention. During the last two weeks, students were instructed to stop all reinforcements, thereby applying extinction.

Data on positive contacts by each teacher-behavior engineer during the nine weeks were cast into a repeated-measures analysis of variance. One data point was used per student-teacher combination for each week (the average number of positive contacts during the week for that combination). The results of that ANOVA, summarized in Table 1, are fairly straightforward. There is no significant interaction between Weeks and Teacher Replications, and no significant overall effect for teachers. There is a very marked effect for Weeks (which we shall return to in our discussion briefly) and, as might be expected, a significant effect for Subjects.

A similar analysis on negative teacher-as-client contacts is summarized in Table 2. In most respects, the effects here are similar to those for positive contacts. The exception is a significant effect for Teacher Replications which, though reliable, is quite small in magnitude.

Figure 1 shows a plot of average frequency of positive contacts and of negative contacts over the nine weeks of the experiment. For positive contacts, there is a significant jump from Week 2 (a baseline week) to Week 3 (the first week of treatment). There is a general improvement in frequency of positive contacts throughout the next four weeks, all intervention weeks. With Week 8 (the first week of extinction), there is a marked and significant drop in positive contacts by teacher-clients. By Week 9, the frequency of

Table 1

ANALYSIS OF VARIANCE FOR POSITIVE CONTACTS IN STUDENT-TEACHER SHAPING AS A FUNCTION OF WEEKS AND TEACHER REPLICATION

Source	df	ms	F
Subjects (S)	6	113.83	4.8*
Weeks (A)	8	975.88	41.49*
Teacher Rep. (B)	1	6.00	1.50
A x B	8	6.00	1.68
A x S	48	23.52	
B x S	6	4.00	
A x B x S	48	3.58	

* $< .01$

Table 2

ANALYSIS OF VARIANCE FOR NEGATIVE CONTACTS IN STUDENT-TEACHER SHAPING AS A FUNCTION OF WEEKS AND TEACHER REPLICATION

Source	df	ms	F
Subjects (S)	6	211.50	7.06**
Weeks (A)	8	562.75	18.80**
Teacher Rep. (B)	1	8.00	9.64*
A x B	8	1.25	.48
A x S	48	29.94	
B x S	6	.83	
A x B x S	48	2.60	

*$p < .05$, **$p < .01$

positive contacts has fallen below the base rates for Weeks 1 and 2, although this is not statistically significant.

The results on negative contacts are fairly analogous to those for positive contacts. Indeed, they appear to be mutually dependent, until we examine the extinction Weeks, 8 and 9. Here, although there is a significant increase in negative contact from the last week of treatment (Week 7) to the first week of extinction (Week 8), the frequency of negative contacts does not increase significantly between Weeks 8 and 9. Also, negative contacts during extinc-

Peer Use of Behavior Modification

Figure 1

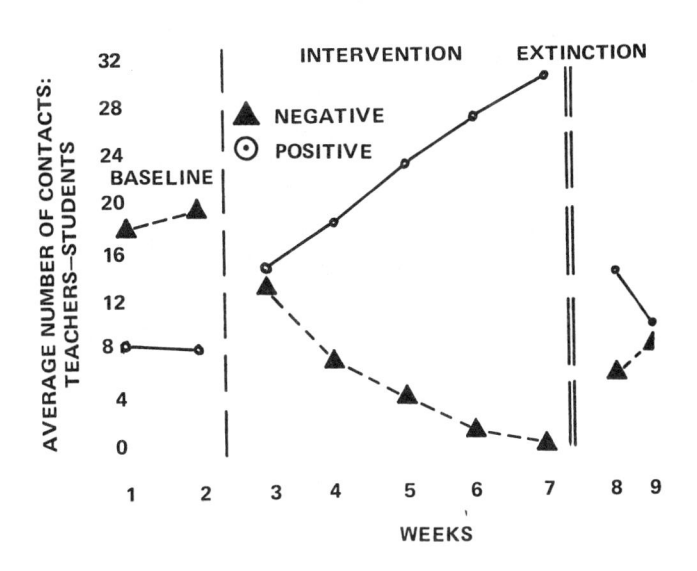

tion are still significantly fewer than for Weeks 1 and 2, the baseline weeks. It can clearly be seen that children can modify teacher behavior, at least temporarily. However, the teacher-clients appear to be quite dependent on a maintained reinforcement schedule for positive contacts; this is less the case for negative contacts, at least as far as these data can show us. Of course, the frequency of negative contacts might have increased to base-rate levels or even beyond in subsequent weeks, but these data are beyond the scope of the present analyses. Nevertheless, we might hazard a guess that teacher-clients did learn to be less punitive with training and that this training held to some extent even when the reinforcements were withdrawn. It does appear, however, that teachers, like most people, are backsliders and need a high level of reinforcement to maintain particular kinds of new behaviors.

A number of ethical questions are raised by this experiment, not the least of which is the surreptitious observation of teacher behavior by aides in order to establish a reliability coefficient. This was felt to be justified by the necessity for scientific validation of the procedure. The observations were in no way used as evaluation of teacher performance. These data will not affect teachers' retaining jobs, getting increments, or contribute to any of the rewards or punishments established by the school system. Data concerning teachers and children are confidential; our interest is in exploring the consequences of particular management techniques, not in specifying or evaluating individuals.

The procedures used seemed to be effective within a very short period of time. The children's labor contributing to effective changes was free; it is certainly less costly to employ pupils, using reinforcement readily available in the classroom, than it is to pay clinical personnel within the traditional medical model to change behavior.

DEVIANT CHILDREN CHANGE NORMALS

Another experiment consisted of training special education children (officially designated as emotionally handicapped) to modify the behavior of "normal" children. This was again done using the rationale of the social deviancy model and the need the experimenters felt to change the interface between children who were clashing. We observed that often the "normal" children scapegoated special education children, using derogatory terms such as "retards," "rejects from the funny farm," and "tardos." A popular game for normal children was "Saluggi": Bigger children throw one child's cap around while the unfortunate owner runs around vainly trying to reclaim his property. Being teased, ignored, and ridiculed are part of the social roles thrust upon special education children.

Method

The work with special education children consisted of individual counseling by two resource teachers. They explained and illustrated operant theory to the children. The counseling consisted of one 30-minute session per week for a nine-week period. Each special education child was asked to list those children who made school unpleasant for him. He specifically described the behavior of those children whose behavior he wanted to change and those children he wished to spend more time with.

Among the things recorded were the number of hostile physical contacts that took place on the playground with each child's arch enemy, if that was the problem, or the number of snubs or hostile remarks encountered. Positive contacts with particular children were recorded and quantified if the special education child's goal was to increase such interactions. The data collection was done by the special education children and handed in each day to their counselors.

This comprehensive effort to reintegrate special students into regular classrooms indicated that providing a student with academic skills is not sufficient. In most cases the student lacks the ability to make friends and deal with his peers effectively enough to avoid social ostracism. Teachers and administrators began working with small groups of students to develop a program in which the emphasis would shift from structuring a child's environment to giving a child the tools to manipulate and adjust the environment himself.

Organization of Peer Behavior Modification Project

The "Peer-to-Peer Behavior Modification Project" operated with children in learning opportunity classes and classes for the educationally handicapped. Learning opportunity classes are for "incorrigible" kids. Each includes students who have been on probation or who have been arrested. In most districts the school was completely segregated and separated from the regular campus. The students are usually sent to one of these schools for the duration of their education. The schools were on the regular campuses, and the goal was to quickly reintegrate the children into the regular program.

Atypical Children and Social Relationships

One teacher, Charles Wilson, described the students he deals with as suffering from the "sick chicken syndrome."

> In some ways these children are as atypical as sick chickens. I found that through our special education program we could take these atypical students, give them a highly prescriptive type of program, and return them to the regular classroom. I am not saying that we could return them on grade level or that they would be at the top of the class, but I could give them the academic skills to return to the regular classroom and not be the low man on the totem pole.
>
> However, I found constant failure in the area of social relationships. What could we do to keep the special education student from being a sick chicken, from being unhappy on the playground, from being picked on by his peer group, from being a loner, from being excluded from recreational situations? What skills could we give him so that he could join in and be part of the group, have a better feeling about himself, be once again included, and not only have his academic skills raised but also be able to do something about social situations as well?

Students Join Scientific Experiment

To begin the project, the staff selected several special education students who were either fully or partially integrated into the classroom. They told these students they wanted to conduct a scientific experiment and asked if they would be a part of it. They told the students they wanted to train them to change the behavior of other students. Most of the students responded very well to this suggestion. The staff also explained how important it was to collect scientific data accurately. Each special education student selected three students whose behavior he wanted to change, three students with whom he either wanted to reduce the amount of negative contact or to increase the amount of positive contact.

Each student was given a 3 x 5 card for each of his target students on which he kept a count of how many positive and negative contacts the two of them had. The program started with a trial period of five days to be sure the students had the right idea about collecting and turning in data. The counts turned in at the end of 10 days served as baseline data.

In order to check the reliability of the students' counts, trained observers were used. The observers were trained through viewing video-taped situations that could happen in the classroom or on the playground, so they could learn to differentiate between positive and negative contacts. The reliability checks were made at recess, lunch hour, and physical education time.

Students Learn Intervention Techniques

At the end of the 10 days, Charles Wilson began training the students to use certain intervention techniques, to act in certain ways in an effort to control or shape the behavior of their target students. The special education students realized that in order to do this they had to impart to the target students a certain amount of reinforcement theory. The students had to have within their grasp the idea that if one wants a behavior to recur, it must be positively reinforced, and if one wants a behavior to disappear it must not be reinforced, it must be ignored. The ignoring technique was very popular with the students, much more so than the praising. Apparently this technique gave them the feeling of really being a teacher's tool. Each made his intervention with target student #1 beginning the third week, with target student #2 the fourth week, and with the target student #3 the fifth week. Therefore, the baselines for target students #2 and #3 were longer than for #1. After the intervention stage, the students were asked to discontinue all forms of positive reinforcement to see if the negative behavior of their target students would again increase.

Carol Utilizes Praising and Ignoring Techniques

One of the students in the program was Carol, a 12-year-old girl in a regular classroom. This girl had previously been in a class for the educationally handicapped for two years. She was reintegrated into the regular classroom on a part-time basis.

Basically, Carol had difficulty establishing any kind of social relationship with other children. She always seemed to be on the outside looking in. This was the reason she was chosen for the project. She was referred to Charles Wilson, who asked her if she would like to take part in a scientific project whereby she might actually be able to increase her positive relationships with other children.

Since she was having difficulty on the playground, in the classroom, and with her teachers, Carol agreed to take part in the project. Mr. Wilson and Carol talked about what it was they were going to check and what type of behaviors really bothered her. She complained that the kids were picking on her and were laughing at her. So they isolated just one behavior that she would actually count.

One boy in her classroom was giving her a very bad time, especially picking on her on the playground. This boy was also in the special classroom part-time. Carol counted the number of times this boy made negative remarks to her on the playground. Each time one of these incidents occurred, she marked a 3 x 5 card containing 100 little circles. Every day after school Carol turned in her card to the school secretary.

This is the method by which the data were collected. Reliability checks were made to assure that the child was turning in accurate data. A trained observer went out onto the playground with the girl, remaining in the background, yet following the girl around under the pretense of being a needed playground supervisor. The observer turned in a card indicating the number of negative comments she had heard. The reliability was slightly above 90%. This percentage was achieved on all subjects, not just Carol. The actual observations continued for two weeks.

At the beginning of the third week, Mr. Wilson and Carol talked about specific techniques that could be used to change the boy's patterns of behavior. They decided on two techniques—the ignoring technique to extinguish the behavior and, once that was well established, the reinforcing technique of praising. Basically, these same two techniques were used with all subjects.

Along with this training session, Mr. Wilson used simulation and role playing techniques. He played the part of the boy who picked on Carol by making negative remarks, while she practiced ignoring his negative comments and offering praise when he exhibited positive behavior. This really gave her the feel of using behavior modification techniques. Then Carol went back out on the playground and continued to count the frequency of the boy's behavior. However, at the same time, she used the intervention skills of ignoring his negative behavior and praising his positive behavior as she had been taught in the training sessions. She continued to collect the data and turn it in daily. All this time the data were being plotted and graphed. The students often came in after school to look at the charts to see how they were doing and what progress they were making. The intervention phase of the project lasted approximately six weeks.

There was a considerable decrease in the incidence of negative verbal behavior. At the end of six weeks, all reinforcers were withdrawn. Carol was told, "We want to take away all the things you've done to see if the behavior will revert to the previous level." It did. It took awhile, but the negative behavior shot back up again. In Carol's case, it increased.

Instructional Planning for Exceptional Children

David Reinforces Positive Behavior

Mr. Wilson also worked with David, who constantly was referred to the principal's office for having difficulty with his teachers and other students. Mr. Wilson gave an example of how much trouble David had fitting in with the other kids.

> We had a seminar here last January involving Dr. William Glassar. David's class was selected to be a part of the demonstration. During the class meeting, in front of every teacher in the district, these kids began to pinpoint David's behavior. They were complaining about him right there in front of 600 teachers. This gives you some idea of the predicament he was in.

Later the principal referred David to Mr. Wilson. The experiment was explained to David. He was turned on by the idea. He said it really sounded crazy, but he was willing to give it a try. Mr. Wilson asked for the names of three students with whom he had a great deal of conflict and asked him to pinpoint that conflict. Exactly, what was it that took place? They pinpointed two single behaviors—the students either swore at David or hit him. They finally selected one student with whom David felt he had the greatest amount of conflict—a boy in class who cursed at David. David began counting and found that this behavior occurred anywhere from 5 to 10 times a day. He counted 41 incidents per week for the first two weeks.

At the end of the second week Mr. Wilson began teaching David reinforcement techniques. They talked about the kinds of behavior they wanted to occur. Mr. Wilson said, "If I praise you, you kind of like that and would like it to happen again, wouldn't you?" David agreed. "And," Mr. Wilson continued, "if someone says something nice to you after you've done something, chances are you will want to do that again." Mr. Wilson explained to David that if he positively reinforced a behavior, it would be more likely to recur, and that by ignoring negative behavior it would most likely decrease.

The staff had three training sessions with David during the first week of this intervention stage. As with Carol, role playing techniques were used to give David the feel of praising his target student each time he exhibited positive behavior and ignoring the student each time he exhibited negative behavior. David picked up these techniques very quickly. The number of times he was cursed at decreased to 21 at the end of the third week and was down to two by the end of the seventh week.

For the eighth and ninth weeks David was asked to stop reinforcing the target student's positive behavior. During this period the number of positive contacts decreased from 21 to 10, and the number of negative contacts increased from 2 to 10.

Mr. Wilson commented, "David did a great job during this study. In fact the principal who referred him to us just cannot say enough about what has gone on in this boy's life as a result. He says David is just not the same boy. He is adjusting to the regular class and is being accepted by his peers."

David, like the other students participating in this program, has learned how to "fit in."

Reliability. As with the student-to-teacher study, observers in the peer-to-peer experiment unobtrusively checked and recorded positive and negative comments by peer-clients. On positive contacts by peer-clients, correlation with the six student trainers and their observers ranged from .570 to .984. The average correlation across student-observer combinations is .824, rather low as reliability coefficients should go, but given the inherent difficulties in making surreptitious observations in playgrounds and classrooms, the best we could get.

The reliability for negative comments is about the same as for positive comments, ranging from .435 to .957, for an average of .876. In the peer-to-peer study each of the six students as behavior engineers had three client-peers who entered treatment on a staggered baseline, as schematized in Figure 2. Client A enters treatment after two baseline weeks, Client B after three weeks, Client C after four weeks. Reinforcements are subsequently withdrawn during two extinction weeks for all clients. Since there are six student-trainers, each line (A, B, and C) applies to six different client-peer combinations.

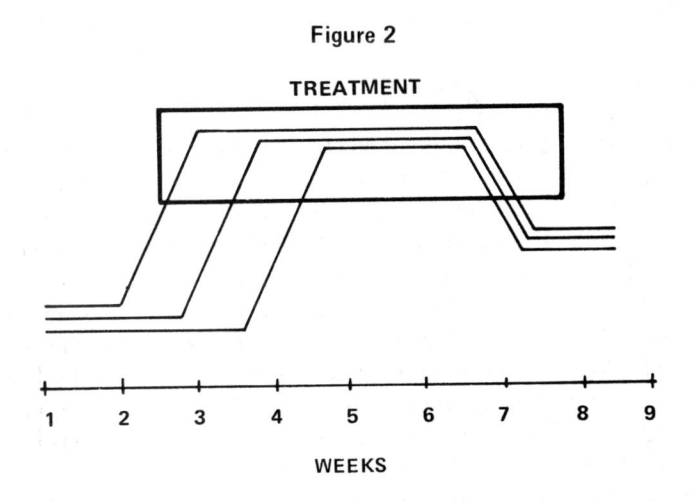

Figure 2

Results

Data were cast into separate analyses of variance, one for each frequency of positive and negative contacts by client-peers. Table 3 shows a summary of ANOVA for positive contacts.

Instructional Planning for Exceptional Children

Table 3

ANALYSIS OF VARIANCE FOR POSITIVE CONTACTS IN PEER-TO-PEER SHAPING AS A FUNCTION OF WEEKS AND TREATMENT-ENTRY CONDITIONS

Source	df	ms	F
Subjects (S)	5	81.00	5.08**
Weeks (A)	8	571.75	35.89***
Entry Cond. (B)	2	202.50	4.47**
A X B	16	15.44	1.73*
A X S	40	15.93	
B X S	10	45.30	
A X B X S	80	8.95	

*p = .064
**p < .05
***p < .01

If the staggered baseline has a reliable impact, we would expect significance for the interaction between Weeks and Treatment—Entry Conditions, the A X B interaction term. The interaction is significant with a probability of .06 (which we take seriously enough).

Figure 3 shows a plot of positive contact frequencies over the nine weeks of the experiment for client-peers in the three different entry conditions.

Figure 3

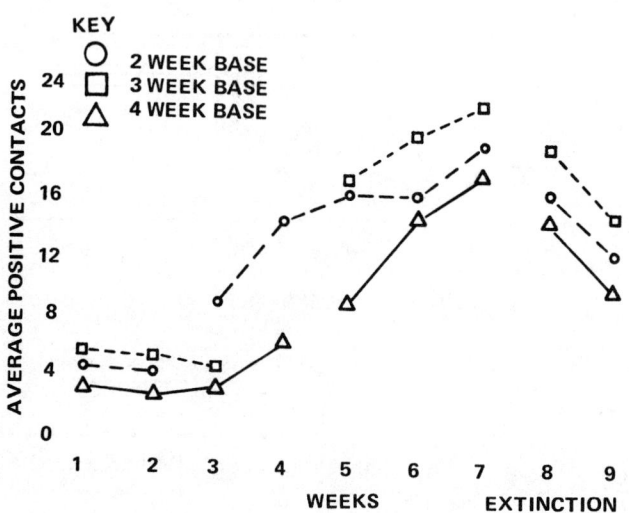

KEY
○ 2 WEEK BASE
□ 3 WEEK BASE
△ 4 WEEK BASE

(AVERAGE POSITIVE CONTACTS vs. WEEKS 1–7, EXTINCTION 8–9)

Things turned out pretty well according to plan with the exception that the difference between Week 2 (the last baseline week) and Week 3, the first treatment week for A type clients, is not significant. The corresponding differences between the last week of baseline and the first week of treatment for B and C type clients are significant drops in positive contact frequencies. These drops are still well above the baseline rates for all three client groups. This can be contrasted to what happened to the teacher-clients who fell back to their base rates during extinction of positive contacts.

Table 4 shows the ANOVA for negative contacts in the peer-to-peer shaping. Here, we must dismiss the Weeks by Entry Conditions interaction term as nonsignificant. There is, however, a clear effect for Weeks.

Table 4

ANALYSIS OF VARIANCE FOR NEGATIVE CONTACTS IN PEER-TO-PEER SHAPING AS FUNCTION OF WEEKS AND TREATMENT-ENTRY CONDITIONS

Source	df	ms	F
Subjects (S)	5	665.40	12.76*
Weeks (A)	8	1321.88	25.36*
Entry Cond. (B)	2	129.00	1.46
A X B	16	34.69	1.33
A X S	40	52.13	
B X S	10	88.50	
A X B X S	80	26.08	

*$p < .01$

Figure 4 shows average positive and negative contact frequencies contrasted for all eighteen client-peers combined, ignoring the staggered baseline conditions. Notice that negative contact rate shows a systematic drop with treatment beginning with Week 3, which actually reflects only a third of the client-peers in treatment. Extinction in Weeks 8 and 9 yields an increase in frequency of negative contacts, but once again these averages are still different from any of those for baseline weeks.

We note that, at least with reference to positive contacts, the students as behavior engineers are able to manage a fairly subtle posture, gradually bringing in a new client in successive weeks of treatment. They are doing about as well in exercising control over human behavior as many a graduate does in a Ph.D. thesis or as professionals who charge $50 an hour, for that matter.

Figure 4

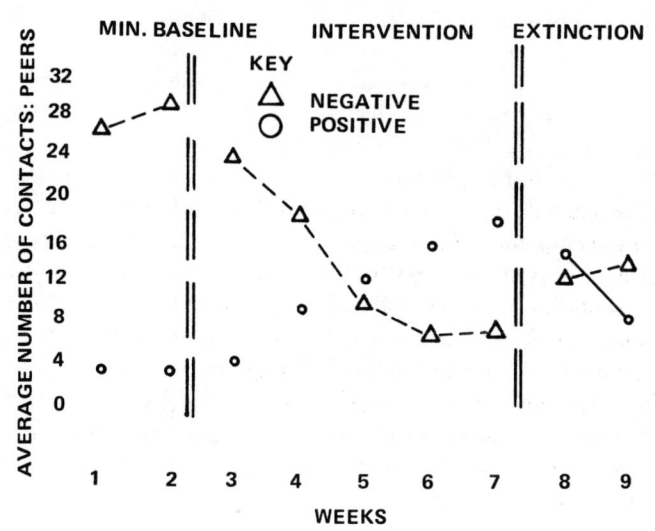

[Figure 4: Graph showing average number of contacts with peers across weeks 1-9, divided into MIN. BASELINE, INTERVENTION, and EXTINCTION phases. Key: △ NEGATIVE, ○ POSITIVE]

Our conclusions from this data are that deviant children can change the behavior of "normal" children and that hostile physical contacts (instances of teasing, etc.) were considerably reduced. Moreover, approach behaviors (such as invitations to parties and invitations to play in ball games, etc.) were considerably accelerated. At no time did any teacher intervene with the normal children and encourage or limit their behavior.

CONCLUSION

Behavior modification appears to be a powerful tool which can give "deviant" children the social skills and power to change the behavior of others toward them. While the "deviant" children undoubtedly changed their own behavior, the important thing remains that they did dramatically change the behavior of others toward them.

REFERENCES

Benedict, R. *Patterns of culture.* Boston & New York: Houghton Mifflin, 1934.
Chekhov, A. *Ward six and other short novels.* New York: Signet Books, 1965.
James, H. *Children in trouble: A national scandal.* New York: David McKay, 1969.
Rabkin, J. & Rabkin, R. Delinquency and the lateral boundary of the family. In P. Graubard (Ed.), *Children against schools.* Chicago: Follett, 1969.
Rhodes, W. C. The disturbing child: A problem of ecological management. In P. Graubard (Ed.), *Children against schools.* Chicago: Follett, 1969.
Szasz, T. S. *The manufacture of madness: The comparative study of the inquisition and the mental health movement.* New York: Harper & Row, 1970.

A major characteristic of severely handicapped children is the lack or insufficient development of language. In contrast to less handicapped children who have the ability to express themselves and are able to communicate with peers and teachers, severely handicapped children are extremely limited in communication skills. This presents significant problems to teachers and paraprofessionals. The authors provide directions for teachers in reviewing existing language programs, as well as a model for teachers to follow in teaching language. In addition to the meaningful discussion on language acquisition and the process of teaching language, they provide an excellent resource in terms of references.

Language Programming for the Severely Handicapped

Ken G. Jens, *University of North Carolina*
Ken and Jane Belmore, *Madison (Wisconsin) Public Schools*

Currently, one of the most popular but least adequately dealt with aspects of special education is that portion which deals with the education of the severely and profoundly handicapped. Pressure has been put upon educators to acknowledge and respond to litigations which have arisen on behalf of handicapped persons and to develop reasonable public school educational programs for them. Cases such as the *Pennsylvania Association for Retarded Children v. Commonwealth of Pennsylvania* (1972), *LeBanks v Spears* (1973), and *Mills v. Board of Education of the District of Columbia* (1972) have given clear indication that handicapped children of any kind should not be excluded from provision of an education suited to their individual needs. While some of these cases were clearly decided on behalf of *all* children excluded from public education because of handicapping conditions of any sort, there is even stronger support for providing services to the severely and profoundly handicapped. *Wyatt* v. *Stickney* (1972) and *New York Association for Retarded Children* v. *Rockefeller* (1973) demonstrated clearly that states are also expected to realize their obligation to provide educational services to institutionalized handicapped youngsters regardless whose wards they might be. Probably most important, however, is that set of decisions provided in *Wolf* v. *Legislature of the State of Utah* (1969), *Doe* v. *Board of Education of School Directors of Milwaukee* (1970), *McMillan* v. *Board of Education* (1970), *Reid* v. *Board of Education* (1971), etc., which reaffirmed the fact that our individual state constitutions and laws *guarantee an education to all children*.

One might ask, "Why all the sudden concern regarding the education of the severely and profoundly handicapped?" The answer should be obvious. Despite the fact that educators have been aware of their legal responsibilities regarding the education of all children, they have assumed the right to exclude those who are difficult to educate or whom they could show were extremely expensive to educate. In fact, there are still school systems that exclude children who do not have "adequate" language for communication, "adequate" self-help skills, or who have not yet reached a given mental age level, such as six years. The absurdity of this is very much apparent when one considers the basic function that schools can and should be assuming with regard to the development of language and communication skills as well as self-care skills for this population of children. In fact, development in these areas, among others, will certainly enhance the apparent mental functioning of even severely handicapped youngsters.

What does this mean for those of us working in the public schools? Obviously, it means that we can no longer rationalize our exclusion of any handicapped children from public school programs regardless of the severity of their handicap. It means that we can no longer exclude children because we "don't know how to teach them" or "do not have adequate facilities" for teaching them. Rather, it is implied that we should be using all of the information available to us to program for them in the most efficient manner possible.

This article was written explicitly for the classroom teacher who is faced with the responsibility of educating the severely mentally handicapped youngster or who is anticipating the imminent arrival of such youngsters in his or her classroom. We have attempted to provide information regarding specific but generalizable procedures which can be used in developing language skills as teachers identify problems of concern with severely handicapped youngsters.

There are numerous reasons why language programming is an essential curriculum area for severely handicapped students. The following statements are suggested as some of the more cogent arguments supporting language training.

Language Programming for the Severely Handicapped

1. The majority of severely handicapped students have been labeled deficient in speech, language, and overall communication skills. Jordan (1967) found these deficiencies in 40 to 79 percent of the population studied. The number of specific deficiencies was reported to increase with the degree of retardation.
2. Normal environmental conditions similar to those under which most children develop language skills do not lead to corresponding language growth in the severely handicapped. The effects of parent and/or peer modeling are minimal. There are numerous research articles suggesting that severely and profoundly handicapped students acquire language in developmental stages similar to nonhandicapped children but not under the same normal environmental conditions.
3. Much recent work has suggested that longitudinal, well-planned programs for teaching language skills to severely and profoundly handicapped students can be effective (Baer & Guess, 1971; Bricker & Bricker, 1970; Guess, Sailor, Rutherford & Baer, 1968; Lovaas, 1968).
4. In addition to the intrinsic value of improved or new language skills, language behaviors are essential prerequisites to the development of skills in most other curricular areas for severely and profoundly handicapped students (i.e., many self-help skills, vocational skills, and functional academic skills).
5. The potential for language development in severely handicapped children has not been determined to date. It is very likely that as our ability for language training improves, long-term gains in language development will be demonstrated in some severely handicapped students that exceed those currently thought possible.
6. Language, in addition to being a prerequisite to other essential skills, is one of the prominent factors separating severely handicapped persons from nonhandicapped persons. Appearances, motor skills, and academic abilities are of lesser import when integration of severely handicapped persons with nonhandicapped persons into some areas of normal societal living is seriously considered.

If some of the above arguments constitute justifiable reasons for teaching language skills to severely handicapped students, then it follows that teachers must have a frame of reference from which they can design and implement language training programs. Thus, the following outline is suggested as one scheme for organizing the components of language instruction for severely handicapped students.

1. *Specific skills essential for persons who teach language to severely handicapped students*

Instructional Planning for Exceptional Children

  a. What skills does the teacher need?

  b. Which of these skills does the teacher currently possess?

 2. *Strategies for the analysis of available language training programs*

  a. What language training programs are available?

  b. How can a teacher efficiently evaluate available programs?

  c. Which facets of a program are relevant to the current teacher/student situation?

 3. *Determination of a classroom model appropriate for meeting current student needs*

  a. Content

   (1) What skills should be taught?

   (2) Why should these skills be taught?

  b. Method

   (1) How can skills best be taught?

   (2) What materials will be needed?

  c. Evaluation

   (1) How is success determined?

   (2) What are the alternatives if success is not achieved?

   (3) What are the next steps if success is achieved?

The remainder of this article will attempt to provide functional information that may be used to facilitate the teaching of language by addressing each of these items. In addition, an exemplary segment of a language training program is provided.

SPECIFIC SKILLS ESSENTIAL FOR PERSONS WHO TEACH LANGUAGE TO SEVERELY HANDICAPPED STUDENTS

  Severely handicapped students are often dramatically different, if only in degree, from mildly handicapped or nonhandicapped students; teaching this population does require teachers equipped with unique competencies (Brown & York, 1974). The importance of these teacher competencies is directly related to the degree of disability presented in the student population. Thus, the more severely handicapped the student, the more well developed a teacher's competencies need to be. Competencies necessary for language instruction overlap considerably with the basic skills necessary to teach anything to severely handicapped students. Minimally, teachers must become competent and comfortable with the use of teaching techniques and strategies including modeling/imitation, reinforcement, shaping, prompting, fading, extinction, stimulus control, and generalization training. An operational definition of each of these techniques and examples of their use in language training are given in Figure 1. Further information regarding their use can be found in texts by Reese (1966), Whaley and Malott (1968), Bandura (1969), Sulzer and Mayer (1972), and Miller (1975) to mention just a few.

Teacher competencies necessary for language training obviously go beyond the basic behavioral techniques delineated in Figure 1. Skills which are necessary in designing the instructional situation prior to direct instruction include (1) the ability to task analyze segments of language, and (2) the ability to develop an instructional program in a sequence appropriate to the task analysis derived. These two skills are essential for teachers of severely handicapped students. It is the ability to specify what responses a student should make, and in what sequence the responses should be made, that determines the adequacy of the curriculum for language programming with this population. Hopefully, the example of one segment of a language program presented at the end of this article will suggest a means of task analyzing a set of language skills and a method of building an instructional program based on that analysis.

In addition to task analysis and instructional sequencing skills, further considerations vital to the instructional situation include the selection of appropriate materials and the arrangement of the classroom environment. The classroom arrangement should provide for control and presentation of antecedent stimuli as well as delivery of reinforcement for learning on a planned basis. Provisions should also be made for ongoing and end-product assessment.

The following also are appropriate for teacher consideration.

1. Importance of integrating language programming into other curricular areas
2. Necessity of communicating methods of instruction to parents, teachers, and other persons in the students' immediate environment
3. Availability of existing program and research information regarding language training for severely handicapped students.

What are the alternatives for teachers who do not have all of the skills delineated? It is unlikely that many teachers have mastered all of the aforementioned competencies. The important point is that teachers should thoroughly and objectively assess their competencies in terms of strengths

Instructional Planning for Exceptional Children

Figure 1
BEHAVIORAL PROCEDURES FOR USE IN TEACHING*

Procedure	Definition		Example/Use
1. Reinforcement (Positive)	1. The process of increasing or maintaining behavior through the presentation of a stimulus contingent upon the emission of the behavior	Use: 1.	Positive reinforcement may be used whenever the teacher desires to teach a new behavior, to increase a behavior already in the child's repertoire, or to maintain a behavior. To determine appropriate positive reinforcer, teacher may present an assortment and observe child in a free-choice situation.
a. Primary	2. Primary reinforcement has the effect of maintaining or perpetuating life	Use: 2.	Primary reinforcement should be used in the early stages of teaching and for children who do not respond to other forms of reinforcement.
		Ex: 2.	When child emits desired sound, teacher delivers food (candy, cereal, etc.).
b. Secondary	3. Secondary reinforcement has effectiveness because of prior systematic association with primary reinforcement	Use: 3.	Secondary reinforcement may be used with many children for whom primary reinforcement is not necessary. Praise, or physical approval (hug, pat), should always be given when primary reinforcement is used in order to establish these as secondary reinforcers.
		Ex: 3.	When child emits desired phoneme, teacher delivers pat on back and verbal praise.
2. Modeling/ Imitation	4. A procedure which occurs when the desired behavior is demonstrated, then copied by the student	Use: 4.	Imitation may be used when the child does not have the desired behavior in his repertoire but does have the skills necessary to perform the behavior, or some approximation of it.
		Ex: 4.	Teacher emits desired response and reinforces the child for repeating it.
3. Shaping	5. A procedure through which new behaviors are developed. The systematic reinforcement of successive approximations toward the behavioral goal.	Use: 5.	Shaping is used when the child does not have the skills to perform the desired terminal behavior.
		Ex: 5.	Teacher reinforces "b," "ba," "ball" in sequence when teaching the word "ball."

Language Programming for the Severely Handicapped

4. Prompting	6. A procedure through which extra discriminative stimuli are provided during the learning of a new behavior	Use: 6a. Ex: 6a. Use: 6b. Ex: 6b.	Prompting is used when a child needs additional cues. In the case of a child who has no language, physical prompts may be necessary. Teacher holds child's lips together to facilitate emission of "buh" sound. For a child who has language, verbal prompts may be used. Teacher shows ball and says, "It's a ball. Tell me what it is."
5. Fading	7. The gradual removal of discriminative stimuli such as cues and prompts	Use: 7. Ex: 7.	Fading is used when a teacher perceives that prompts are no longer necessary. Teacher puts fingers increasingly gently on child's lips while child emits "buh" sound or teacher shows ball and says, "Tell me what it is."
6. Stimulus Control	8. A procedure for discrimination training during which reinforcement is provided for responses to the presence of a certain stimulus and not for responses in the presence of other stimuli	Use: 8. Ex: 8.	Stimulus control is used when the teacher wishes to be sure that the child will apply his words only under appropriate circumstances. Teacher reinforces the word "ball" only when a ball is presented to the child.
7. Generalization	9. A process which occurs when the student responds to different stimuli in a similar manner.	Use: 9. Ex: 9.	The teacher programs for generalization when she wants to be sure that the word the child has learned will be used appropriately for all members of a class of stimuli. Child says "ball" when various balls or pictures of balls are presented.
8. Extinction	10. The reduction or elimination of a conditioned response by withholding reinforcement for that response	Use: 10. Ex: 10.	Extinction may be used when the child makes sounds other than those desired—for example, babbling, mumbling screaming. Teacher does not reinforce the emission of extraneous sounds.

*This is a minimal list of procedures which teachers should be able to use.

and weaknesses. In doing so, one is likely to find that he or she has competencies in most areas, but may need skill refinement in one area, such as planning language development programs for specific students. One reason for this is that there are so few commercially prepared packages designed for teaching language to severely handicapped students. Thus, the brunt of planning frequently falls on the classroom teacher. Detailed examples of task analyses and instructional program development appropriate for use with the severely handicapped are available (Brown, Scheuerman, Cartwright & York, 1973; Brown & Sontag, 1972; Brown, Williams & Crowner, 1974).

STRATEGIES FOR THE ANALYSIS OF AVAILABLE LANGUAGE TRAINING PROGRAMS

No attempt will be made to provide an analysis of language programs previously used with severely handicapped students within this article. A concise summary of information in this area has been provided by Snyder, Lovitt, and Smith (1975). Published studies and programs vary across several important dimensions beyond the skill areas taught. As previously mentioned, the ability to analyze studies and programs is highly desirable for teachers beginning language instruction with severely handicapped students. Figure 2 is offered to provide assistance in the analysis of programs along several dimensions related specifically to classroom situations.

The dimensions outlined in Figure 2 may be used as a guide in determining which aspects of a published language program are appropriate for particular students in a classroom setting. Different facets of one or more published programs may be combined, with modifications if they appear warranted, to form a basis for language training programs in these situations.

Reviewing several language programs prior to selecting elements of any for use is generally necessary since the range of language differences presented by students is frequently quite extreme and the content of various language programs varies considerably. Some language programs have focused on very early stages of development (Garcia, Baer, & Firestone, 1971; Jeffrey, 1972; MacAuley, 1968; Peine, Gregersen & Sloane, 1970; Schroder & Baer, 1972; Sloane, Johnston & Harris, 1968; Stewart, 1972) while others have emphasized the development of higher level expressive and receptive skills in severely handicapped populations (Baer & Guess, 1973; Barcia, Guess & Byrnes, 1972; Barton, 1970; Guess et al,; Schumaker & Sherman, 1970; Twardosz & Baer, 1973). It is extremely important that teachers avail themselves of opportunities to become familiar with language training programs available commercially and those suggested in the professional literature.

DETERMINATION OF A CLASSROOM MODEL APPROPRIATE FOR MEETING CURRENT STUDENT NEEDS

One of the most difficult questions for a teacher to answer is, "What did I teach Johnny, Susie, and Billy today?" In order to answer such a question it is imperative that teachers avail themselves of some form of feedback/decision making system. One of the most frequently mentioned systems for this purpose is the Test-Teach-Test model (Chalfant, Kirk & Jensen, 1968). In fact, teachers have been encouraged to use this and similar models with the implication that the use of such a model will surely bring success to their classroom. Unfortunately, the problems involved in providing success in teaching severely handicapped or, for that matter, any students are somewhat more complex. Certainly, such a model is basic when considering that teachers must have available a working model which allows them to make decisions about what they are doing on a day-to-day basis. The problem is, the aforementioned model is generally not discreet enough, as such, to be of much value in making decisions about *what* should be taught. Especially when one is concerned with the ultimate behavior to be attained by severely handicapped students, the need for logical sequencing of behaviors to be learned becomes critical. Immediately then, one is forced to expand his feedback/decision making system so that it includes at least the following questions.

1. What do I want to teach?
2. Why do I want to teach that skill or concept?
3. How can I teach it?
4. What materials will I need?
5. How can I know if I am succeeding?
6. If I am not succeeding, what do I do?
7. If I succeed, what do I do next?

What Do I Want to Teach?

When teachers ask the question, "What do I want to teach?" they are really asking, "What do I want the student to be able to do that he could not do in the past?" (Brown & York, 1974, p. 6). Teachers have become accustomed to looking for the "what" or content of instruction in curriculum guides or other written resources which they assume can be presented to them by someone who has overall responsibility for educational programming for the youngsters they teach. Unfortunately, this is not the case. While a few curriculum guides are available, most of them do not provide reasonable guidelines which classroom teachers can use in making curricular decisions regarding individual students for whom they must program. There are excep-

Figure 2
DIMENSIONS FOR CONSIDERATION IN REVIEWING EXISTING LANGUAGE PROGRAMS

1. What are relevant characteristics of the population receiving training?
   a. CA; MA; IQ scores; visible anomalies
   b. Institutionalized or noninstitutionalized population
   c. History of previous language training
   d. Entering language skills
      (1) Receptive skills
      (2) Expressive skills
      (3) Gestural skills

2. What specific language functions were taught?
   a. Expressive vs. receptive training
   b. Form of communication
      (1) Verbal
      (2) Gestural (hand signs)
      (3) Combined verbal and gestural
      (4) Other

3. What resulting language improvements occurred?
   a. Long- vs. short-term results
   b. Follow-up data after training

4. What methods were used for training language?
   a. Imitation training
      (1) Motor training, initially
      (2) Verbal training, initially
   b. Shaping; priming, fading, other operant techniques
   c. Principal technique employed

5. What was the teacher/student ratio?
   a. Individualized vs. group instruction
   b. Number of students taught within instructional setting
6. What specific materials were used?
   a. Classroom materials
   b. Special apparatus (reinforcement desk, etc.)
   c. Reinforcers
7. What skills did the language instructors possess?
   a. Psychologist or trained behavior analyst
   b. Classroom teacher
   c. Classroom aide
   d. Aides employed by institution
   e. Combination of personnel
8. Was there data supporting generalization of language skills?
   a. Generalization within instructional setting
   b. Generalization outside instructional setting
   c. Spontaneous generalization vs. elicited generalization
9. How long did the program take?
   a. Overall time period for program
   b. Length of teaching sessions
   c. Number of sessions per week
10. What modifications will be necessary to adapt this program for classroom use?
    a. Planning time required
    b. Professional assistance required
    c. Specific modifications necessary, i.e., material changes; group instruction feasibility

tions to this, of course, Bricker and Bricker (1970) and Sailor, Guess, and Baer (1973), for example, have provided language programs which are both well-developed and sequenced in a manner which contributes significantly to providing an answer to the question, "What do I want to teach?" The following guidelines may be of further assistance in selecting specific content for inclusion in a language training program.

1. *What objects does the child come in contact with most frequently during his daily activities?* Certain objects such as balls, spoons, cups, etc., may provide more naturally reinforcing interactions than other objects because they are functionally useful to the child. Initially, labels for objects that can be manipulated for some purpose should be considered when selecting vocabulary content for language training.
2. *Which people does the child interact with most frequently?* Names, as labels for people of importance to the child, should be considered as target vocabulary content. The ability to label people is reinforced by the natural response of the person hearing his name. The child's own name is always a primary target for receptive and expressive language training.
3. *What words and phrases does he hear most often in his instructional program?* Selection of key instructional words—such as *put, go, sit, stand*, etc.—that will become components of functional directions will facilitate functioning in both the educational and community environments. Other instructional terms—such as selected adjectives, adverbs, prepositions, and color words—should be taught as they become useful and meaningful to the child or as their use is occasioned in other instructional settings. Initially, stress may be placed on receptive language abilities, but expressive use of words and phrases should also be taught as soon as possible.
4. *What words or phrases are commonly used in the child's home?* Coordination with the parents is necessary to choose words and phrases for language training that can be used at home and at school. This provides the child with as many opportunities as possible for repeated practice and reinforcement of newly acquired language.
5. *What verbal responses will the child be asked to make most often in his environment?* Selection of words and phrases that will facilitate the child's interaction with his environment is essential. Words that enable him to express his needs—such as *play, eat, go, outside*—provide him with vehicles for self-initiated behavior and appropriate interaction with other people in his environment.
6. *What are the long-range goals for the individual student?* The long-range plans for a given child will be determined by teachers, parents, and concerned others. His ultimate station in life should be consi-

dered when selecting content for language training, focusing on words and phrases that will be useful given his probable life style and future environment.

To answer these questions, it becomes obvious that a teacher must assess not only a student's language abilities but also his language environment and what this language environment expects from the student.

The principle goals of student assessment should be to pinpoint that skill range within which language training should begin and to specify the direction in which instruction should proceed. There are numerous methods of accurately assessing student performance within a language program. The following sequence represents one possible method.

1. Select a developmental scale that is complete enough to yield a repertoire of language related behaviors of a severely handicapped student. Since there are several developmental scales in this area—Developmental Pinpoints (Cohen, Gross & Haring, 1975), the TARC Assessment System (Sailor & Mix, 1975)—a teacher could save time and effort by employing a published material rather than developing his/her own.
2. Utilize such a scale to assess developmental, expressive, and receptive language abilities of each student.
3. Combine developmental language information with an assessment of the student's language environment for the purpose of generating a complete picture of student's current language needs.

Why Do I Want to Teach That Skill or Concept?

The second question a teacher must ask herself as part of any teaching-learning program is "Why do I want to teach that skill or concept?" In the opinion of the authors, there are really only two legitimate answers to this question: (1) the skill or concept that one is about to teach is a prerequisite skill or concept for another useful behavior which it is intended to teach later; or (2) the skill or concept being taught has immediate usefulness for the student by either increasing his potential for meaningful interactions with others or providing him with increased ability to function independently. If, as we set about outlining what we will teach to given youngsters, we cannot fit our rationale for teaching given skills or concepts into either of these, we must indeed ask ourselves, "Why do I want to teach that skill or concept?"

How Can I Teach It?

Having decided what should be taught, the teacher must now answer the question, "How can I teach it?" This is probably the most difficult question a

Instructional Planning for Exceptional Children

teacher has to answer. Teachers look back forlornly to the methods' courses they took as part of their university programs for the answer—and, most frequently, they do not find it. The answer is not to be found solely in the selection of materials as is often implied via the suggestion that a teacher try yet another language program if he or she has not been successful with one or more already. Rather, we must learn to make use of empirical knowledge available to us regarding *how* children learn. Several teaching procedures which when mastered would provide a teacher with basic techniques and strategies for implementing of language programming have been delineated in Figure 1.

What Materials Will I Need?

Having settled on what you will teach and how you will go about the teaching function, it becomes necessary to ask oneself, "What materials will I need?" There are a good number of language development and/or training programs available for use with normal, culturally distinct and mildly handicapped populations. The Peabody Language Development Kits (Dunn, Horton & Smith, 1967) and the Distar Language Program (Englemann, 1969) are primary examples of such programs.

Fewer programs have been designed specifically for teaching language to severely handicapped populations—those youngsters who may enter an educational program with little or no functional language whatsoever. Among those which are available are *A Language Program for the Nonlanguage Child* (Gray & Ryan, 1973), *Language Acquisition Program for the Severely Retarded* (Kent, 1974), and the *Non-Speech Language Initiation Program* (Carrier & Peak, 1975). The development of materials for use in teaching this population is currently high priority, and a good deal is being produced. The American Association for the Education of the Severely and Profoundly Handicapped provides an information dissemination service to its members which is extremely invaluable and which teachers could readily use to stay abreast of the development of new materials in this area.

Given that materials for use with the severely handicapped are currently difficult to locate and obtain, it is extremely important that teachers of this population develop their ability to (1) use task analysis to delineate the responses their students should regularly be making, and then (2) determine what stimuli should occasion the occurrence of those reponses. These stimuli, the items in the environment to which students should respond, must then become the materials for our teaching programs.

How Can I Know If I'm Succeeding?

When each of the aforementioned questions has been dealt with and a teaching program is under way, the need for feedback becomes obvious. Critical decisions need to be made regarding the effectiveness of the strategies and materials which have been employed. Data must be obtained for the purpose of determining whether or not one is making progress toward the accomplishment of given objectives. The critical question confronting teachers now becomes, "What should I record?" The answer to this question is related directly to the objectives set forth when originally asking the question, "What do I want to teach?" Before we can measure any behavior we must have defined it operationally, i.e., in observable and quantifiable terms. Having done this, one has several options.

1. If trials are held constant from one teaching session to the next, "number correct" is an adequate measure. It constitutes one of the easiest ways to determine whether or not a student is making progress in a teaching/learning program. This method of assessment is problematical though in that, if data is to be compared from day to day on a meaningful basis, the number of trials occurring when teaching a given behavior must be held constant from day to day. For example, if one is working on the teaching of an object name such as *table*, a teacher might ask a student to "point to the *table*," "touch the *table*," or "put the ___ on the *table*," but the number of trials afforded students would have to be the same in all teaching situations, i.e., 10 trials per session. If this is not done, differences appearing from day to day may well be a function of the number of opportunities (trials) afforded a youngster while teaching a given concept of action. Examples of teaching programs for severely handicapped students which have utilized this type of measurement can be found in the papers compiled by Brown and Sontag (1972) and Brown, Scheuerman, Cartwright, and York (1973).

2. A second option available to teachers is to record the percentage of correct responses made by students per session. This type of measurement is preferrable to using number of correct and incorrect responses for each session. When using percentage of correct responses as a dependent teaching variable, the length of the teaching sessions or number of trials offered on a given day are not intrinsically important. There is a potential hazard inherent in recording the percentage of correct responses per session though. If the number of trials is not held constant from one session to the next, a student may be making more errors per session while showing higher percentages of correct responses, i.e., with 10 problems, 90% correct indicates 9 correct and 1 wrong response; with 30 problems, 90% correct indicates 27 correct and 3 wrong responses—an actual increase in both correct and incorrect responses. Examples of the use of percent of correct responses as a measure of learning are provided by Barton (1970) and Garcia, Guess, and Byrnes (1973).

3. Rate of correct responding can be recorded for each teaching session (number of correct responses divided by the time taken to emit them). Rate measures, while being somewhat more difficult for teachers to work with initially, provide the most meaningful kind of data for analyzing student learning. All responses are appropriate or inappropriate, despite their accuracy, in relation to a measure of time. A student may, for example, be able to respond verbally to simple questions; but if he does not do so within time limits which make his behavior socially acceptable, it will not be perceived as adequate. Once verbal responses are learned, they must be regulated in terms of rate so as to be acceptable in appropriate social circumstances. Examples of this type of recording have been provided by Freschi (1974) and numerous others.

If I Am Not Succeeding, What Do I Do?
If I Succeed, What Do I Do Next?

One of the obvious benefits resulting from the collection of data while teaching is that the data collected tells us immediately whether or not we are making progress toward the achievement of our objectives. The appropriate interpretation of data is often difficult though. When working with severely handicapped youngsters, we sometimes lose our objectivity and tend toward evaluation of our teaching programs on the basis of our own involvement or effort. This is reflected in statements such as "Gee, the ____ language program works great with these kids?" or "That imitation/modeling procedure sure seems to be working well!" which are frequently made without reference to student data. Freschi (1974) has provided examples of data reflecting several problems which frequently occur in the teaching/learning situation along with interpretive ideas and suggestions for solving them. In general, if a student is not making reasonable progress toward the criterion established for a given objective, teachers should consider the alternatives shown in Figure 3 as possible courses of action.

SEGMENT FROM A LANGUAGE TRAINING PROGRAM

In an effort to make the suggestions within this article concrete and of greater application in the classroom, the following example of one segment of a language training program is offered. This example is presented in the order of questions that were raised relative to the development of a classroom teaching model. Obviously, this set of language skills was selected, and a corresponding program was designed, for a particular group of students. The program's application to other severely handicapped students may or may not be appropriate. The segment represents one phase of receptive language

Language Programming for the Severely Handicapped

Figure 3
AN INSTRUCTIONAL FLOW CHART FOR USE WITH SEVERELY HANDICAPPED STUDENTS

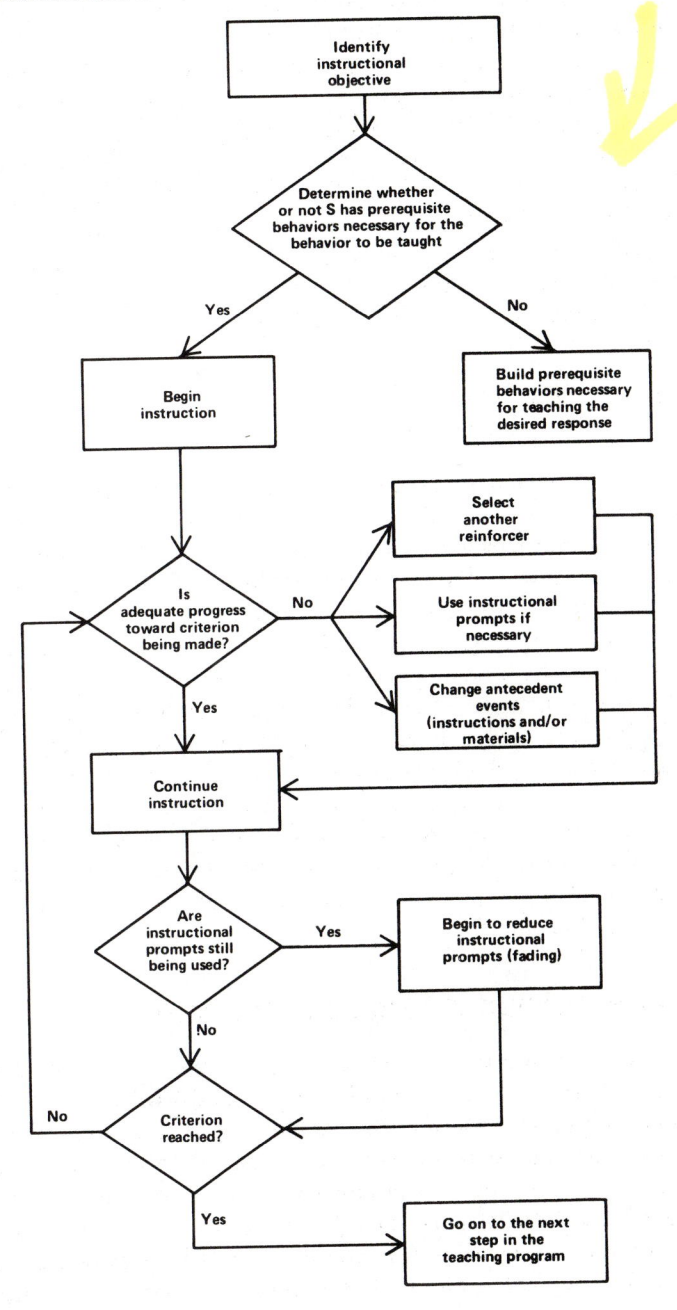

training which deals specifically with the understanding of words that denote a time and place sequence. It was developed for a group of five severely handicapped students in a public school classroom based on the following assessment procedures.

1. Developmental language skills were assessed using Developmental Pinpoints (Cohen, Gross & Haring, 1975). Specific areas assessed included students' responses to verbal requests. It was found that the students could respond to some one-component verbal directions but not to those involving *first, next,* and *last.*
2. An assessment of the language environments of the students showed that most would be in self-contained special education classes integrated in a regular elementary school for at least 3 or 4 more years. Thus the students would need to respond to the "language of school instruction" which includes the functional use of language concepts involving *first, next, last.*

1. What Skills Should Be Taught?

The instructional program outlined here is an attempt to provide direct and systematic instruction in a receptive language skill: understanding a selected word sequence denoting time and position in space. The word sequence chosen for instruction is *first/next/last.* The major or terminal objective of this program is stated as follows:

> Given a teacher direction or statement that includes the word sequence *first, next, last,* S will touch or label an object, person or pictured event that designates each position according to time (auditory cue) and/or position in space (visual cue).[1]

A task analysis approach such as that suggested by Batemen (1971) was used to delineate and sequence specific content objectives.

TASK ANALYSIS

Objective I: Teaching the word sequence *first, next, last* with time (auditory cue) and position in space (visual cue) presented concurrently. Given a set of objects, people or pictured events and an auditory cue (verbal explanation of position) containing the word sequence first, next, and last, S will touch or label the *first, next,* and *last* positions when the position in space (visual cue) is given concurrent with the auditory cue.

---

1. The objective here is not necessarily performance of each specific task (although that measurement across cues, tasks, and settings will be used for evaluation) but rather the ability to act appropriately upon word sequence cues. For example, in the bead stringing task the objective is not that the child string beads, but that he show comprehension of the language cues.

Part 1: Given a set of 3 beads of different colors and a verbal explanation, S will respond correctly to T cue, "Touch the one that is *first (next, last)."*

> Step 1: Given 1 bead on a string, S will touch *first* position after verbal explanation.
>
> Step 2: Given 3 beads on a string and a verbal explanation, S will touch the one in the *first* position.
>
> Step 3: Given 3 beads of different color on a string and a verbal explanation, S will touch the one in *next* position.
>
> Step 4: ... S will touch *first* and *next*.
>
> Step 5: ... S will touch *last*.
>
> Step 6: ... S will touch *first, next* and/or *last*.

Part 2: Given 3 objects and a verbal explanation, S will label or touch the one in each position *first, next,* and/or *last* when auditory and visual cues are concurrent.

> Step 1: S will respond to the cue, "Touch the one that is *first*."
>
> Step 2: S will touch the one that is *next*.
>
> Step 3: S will touch the one that is *last*.
>
> Step 4: S will touch the one that is *first, next,* and/or *last*.

Part 3: Given 3 people in a line one behind the other and a verbal explanation, S will touch or label the person in each position *first, next, last* when auditory and visual cues are concurrent.

> Step 1: S will touch the person in *first* position.
>
> Step 2: S will touch the person in *next* position.
>
> Step 3: S will touch the person in *last* position.
>
> Step 4: S will touch the person in *first, next,* and/or *last* position.

Part 4: Given 3 pictures each representing a daily event or activity and a verbal explanation, S will touch or label the event in each position *first, next,* and/or *last* when auditory cue is concurrent with visual cue.

> Step 1: S will touch the event that is *first*.
>
> Step 2: S will touch the event that is *next*.
>
> Step 3: S will touch the event that is *last*.
>
> Step 4: S will touch the event that is *first, next,* and/or *last*.

Instructional Planning for Exceptional Children

Part 5: Given 3 beads, objects, people, or pictured events *without* verbal explanation, S will touch or label the bead, object, person, or event in each position *first, next* or *last* upon T cue.

Step 1: Part 1, step 6 repeated without verbal explanation.

Step 2: Part 2, step 4 repeated without verbal explanation.

Step 3: Part 3, step 4 repeated without verbal explanation.

Step 4: Part 4, step 4 repeated without verbal explanation.

Objective II: Teaching *first, next,* and *last* when time (auditory cue) is not concurrent with spatial order (visual cue).

Given 3 objects, people, or pictured events presented in varied or ordered positions in space, S will respond correctly to teacher cue, "Touch the one that is *first (next* and/or *last)."*

Part 1: Given 3 objects and verbal explanation, S will touch or label the object presented *first, next,* and/or *last* in explanation upon T cue.

Step 1: S will touch object presented *first* in verbal explanation.

Step 2: S will touch object presented *next* in verbal explanation.

Step 3: S will touch object presented *last* in verbal explanation.

Step 4: S will touch object presented *first, next,* or *last* in verbal explanation.

Part 2: Given 3 people in a line and a verbal explanation, S will touch the person whose name was presented *first, next,* and/or *last* in the explanation upon T cue.

Step 1: S will touch person presented *first.*

Step 2: S will touch person presented *next.*

Step 3: S will touch person presented *last.*

Step 4: S will touch person presented *first, next,* and/or *last.*

Part 3: Given 3 pictured events or activities in varied order S will correctly touch the event that occurs *first, next,* and/or *last* upon T cue.

Step 1: S will touch the event that occurs *first.*

Step 2: S will touch the event that occurs *next.*

Step 3: S will touch the event that occurs *last.*

Step 4: S will touch the event that occurs *first, next,* and/or *last.*

Language Programming for the Severely Handicapped

2. Why Should These Skills Be Taught?

It is crucial that severely handicapped students be given as many methods as possible for ordering incoming verbal and nonverbal information. This specific word sequence was chosen because (1) it is frequently used in teacher directions, (2) it is useful in making directions clearer for students, (3) it can make instruction more efficient, and (4) it provides a framework for expanded instruction in time and/or position of objects in space. Severely handicapped students entering a regular public school building will need to be able to respond to many commands involving the terms *first, next, last*. For example, "Line up first." "You're next." "Who's next?" and "Raise your hand first." are frequently heard statements.

3. How Can Skills Best Be Taught? What Materials Will Be Needed?

The methodology for teaching these or any skills will vary somewhat according to individual teacher training and student differences. Nevertheless, the strategies presented are typical of those necessary when working with persons presenting severe language deficiencies. Specific methods are given for teaching each step of the task analysis.

Objective I: Teaching *first, next, last* with time (auditory cue) and position in space (visual cue) presented concurrently.

    Part 1: Beads

        Instructional Arrangement: Ss are seated across table from T

        Materials: Beads of various colors and a string

        Prerequisites: Color discrimination

        Teaching Procedure:

    Step 1: Teacher strings one bead as she says, "*First* is the (red) one. *S's name*, touch the one that is *first*." If S responds correctly, he is reinforced and T removes bead, picks a different colored bead, strings it and says, "*First* is the (green) one." T continues with each S until criterion is reached.

        Criterion: 5 correct responses out of 5 trials

        Correction Procedures

            1. Present cue again.
            2. Model, then present cue.
            3. Model, prime, present cue until response is correct, then reinforce.

Instructional Planning for Exceptional Children

Step 2: Teacher strings three beads of different colors. *T* says, "*First* is the (red) one." (*T* strings 2 more beads but does not give verbal explanation.) "*S's name*, touch the one that is *first*." Repeat for each *S* until criterion is met.

Criterion: Same as Step 1

Correction: Same as Step 1

Step 3: Teacher repeats stringing operation as in Step 2 saying, "*First* is the (red) one, *next* is the (green) one." (*T* strings last bead but does not give verbal explanation.) If *S* responds correctly, *T* removes beads and strings 3 beads of different colors repeating verbal explanation until criterion is met for each *S*. For incorrect responses, *T* begins correction procedure.

Criterion: Same as Step 1

Correction: Same as Step 1

Step 4: *T* strings beads as in Step 3 saying, "*First* is the (green) one, *next* is the (red) one." (*T* strings last bead but does not give verbal explanation.) "*S's name*, touch the one that is *first*." *T* waits for *S* response. If correct, *T* says, "Touch the one that is *next*." *S* is reinforced for correct responses. If response is incorrect after *first* cue, *T* repeats verbal explanation and presents cue again. If response is again incorrect, *T* begins correction procedure.

Criterion: 5/5 correct responses to both cues in one session

Correction: Same as Part 1

Step 5: Teacher strings beads as in Step 4 saying, "*First* is the (red) one, *next* is the (green) one, *last* is the (blue) one. *S's name*, touch the one that is *last*." *S* is reinforced for correct response. If incorrect, *T* repeats first two components of verbal explanation and says, "Touch the one that is *last*." If response is again incorrect, *T* begins correction procedure.

Criterion: Same as Step 1

Correction: Same as Step 1

Step 6: *T* strings beads as in Step 5 and gives verbal explanation, "*First* is the (red) one, *next* is the (blue) one, *last* is the (green) one. *S's name*, touch the one that is *first*." *T* waits for response. If correct, *T* repeats verbal explanation and says, "*S's name*, touch the one that is *last.*" Cues are then varied.

Criterion: Same as Step 1

Correction: Same as Step 1 or move back to previous step for repeated trials.

Steps 1 through 6 would now be repeated with the additional requirement that students actually place beads on a string in response to teacher verbal cues, i.e., "*First*, put the red one on the string. *Next*, put the green one on the string. Put the blue one on *last.*"

4. How Is Success Determined? What Alternatives Are Available If Success Is Not Achieved?

In this program success is determined by an ongoing evaluation of whether or not students achieve given criterion levels set for mastery of the steps necessary to reach each objective. Thus, when a student reaches the criterion set for one step, he progresses to the next step. However, if the student does not succeed in reaching criterion, the teacher institutes a correction procedure and continues teaching until criterion is met.

5. What Are the Next Steps If Success Is Achieved?

One major advantage of using a task analysis approach such as the one presented here is that it provides a method of predetermining the sequence in which content objectives will be taught. As the student masters each objective, the teacher moves to instruction on the next objective in the task analysis. In the example given in this article, when the student masters Step 6 of Objective I, Part 1, the teacher prepares to teach Step 1, Objective I, Part 2 (teaching the same skills with varying cues) which is the next step in the task analysis.

Ultimately, a student who is taught this entire segment of a language program should acquire functional understanding of the words *first, next,* and *last* across varying cues, events, objects and places. The teacher's next responsibility would be to see that this newly acquired skill is integrated into other curricular areas. Thus, the student should be using his understanding of *first, next,* and *last* in the development of math, self-help, and home-living skills to mention just a few. At the same time a reassessment of the student's language needs, considered in conjunction with available program information, will dictate new levels of language learning toward which one should strive.

CONCLUSION

Providing a meaningful educational program for severely handicapped students is an extremely complex process. Despite concerted efforts in this area, there are very few resources available to the classroom teachers who are responsible for educating these children at this time. This article presents an admittedly simplistic compilation of ideas and suggestions which it is hoped will be of some immediate usefulness to classroom teachers. Existing programs were not dealt with adequately, but it is hoped that teachers will avail themselves of the references provided for the purpose of pursuing more information regarding programs which seem appropriate to their use.

It seems obvious that we should be striving to establish a continuum of logical and functional language skills for the purpose of teaching them to severely handicapped students. It is imperative that our long- and short-term goals and objectives be specified and taught in a manner which does contribute to the maximum development of language skills over a period of time. As this is being done, we should also give consideration to the way in which given students will probably ultimately communicate. While the development of verbal language should be our goal for this population whenever feasible, we should not lost sight of the fact that gestural communication and the use of various types of communication boards can also facilitate the communicative abilities of this population significantly at times. Whatever the specific nature of the language program being used, we must constantly be reminded to ask ourselves, "Are measurable gains in language performance being observed?" and "Are new language behaviors being acquired within reasonable periods of time?" These questions are in effect the parameters which we must use to determine the effectiveness of our teaching programs.

It is also important that we integrate the results of our language training into the overall curriculum for the youngsters we teach. A critical question which we will consistently have to ask ourselves is, "Is the student using what he learns in the structured classroom situation in other places and situations and with other people? The overall worth of what we do with these youngsters will be determined by whether or not their interaction with their environment is improved immediately and, more importantly, for the future.

REFERENCES

Baer, D. M., & Guess, D. Receptive training of adjectival inflections in mental retardates. *Journal of Applied Behavior Analysis*, 1971, *4*, 129-139.

Baer, D. M., & Guess, D. Teaching productive noun suffixes to severely retarded children. *American Journal of Mental Deficiency*, 1973, *77*, 498-505.

Bandura, A. *Principles of behavior modification.* New York: Holt, Rinehart & Winston, 1969.

Barton, E. S. Inappropriate speech in a severely retarded child: A case study in language conditioning and generalization. *Journal of Applied Behavior Analysis*, 1970, *3*, 299-307.

Barton, E. S. Operant conditioning of social speech in the severely subnormal and the use of different reinforcers. *British Journal of Social & Clinical Psychology*, 1972, *11*, 387-396.

Bateman, B. *The essentials of teaching.* San Rafael, CA: Dimensions Publishing, 1971.

Bricker, W. A., & Bricker, D. D. A program of language training for the severely handicapped child. *Exceptional Children*, 1970, *37*, 101-111.

Bricker, W. A., & Bricker, D. D. Assessment and modification of verbal imitation with low-functioning retarded children. *Journal of Speech and Hearing Research*, 1972, *15*, 690-698.

Brown, L., Scheuerman, N., Cartwright, S., & York, R. *The design and implementation of an empirically based instructional program for severely handicapped students: Toward the rejection of the exclusion principle.* Part III. Madison, WI: Madison Public Schools, 1973.

Brown, L., & Sontag, E. *Toward the development and implementation of an empirically based public school program for trainable mentally retarded and severely emotionally disturbed students.* Part II. Madison, WI: Madison Public Schools, 1972.

Brown, L., Williams, W., & Crowner, T. A collection of papers and programs related to public school services for severely handicapped students. Volume 4. Madison, WI: Madison Public Schools, 1974.

Brown, L., & York, R. Developing programs for severely handicapped students: Teacher training and classroom instruction. *Focus on Exceptional Children*, 1974, *6*(2).

Carrier, J. K. & Peak, T. *Non-speech language initiation program.* Lawrence, KS: H & H Enterprises, 1975.

Chalfant, J., Kirk, G., & Jensen, K. Systematic language instruction: An approach for teaching receptive language to young trainable children. *Teaching Exceptional Children*, 1968, 1(1).

Cohen, M., Gross, P., & Haring, N. G. *Developmental pinpoints.* Seattle, WA: Experimental Education Unit, Child Development and Mental Retardation Center, University of Washington, 1975. (mimeo)

Doe v. Board of School Directors of Milwaukee, Milwaukee Circuit Court, Civilian #377770 (1970)

Dunn, L. M., Horton, K. B., & Smith, J. O. *Manual for the Peabody language development kit.* Minneapolis, MN: American Guidance Service, 1967.

Englemann, S. et al. *Distar® Instructional System.* Chicago: Science Research Associates, 1969.

Freschi, D. F. Where we are. Where we are going. How we're getting there. *Teaching Exceptional Children*, 1974, *6*, 89-97

Garcia, E., Baer, D. M., & Firestone, J. The development of generalized imitation within topographically determined boundaries. *Journal of Applied Behavior Analysis*, 1971, *4*, 101-112.

Garcia, E., Guess, D., & Byrnes, J. Development of syntax in a retarded girl by using procedures of imitation and modeling. *Journal of Applied Behavior Analysis*, 1973, *6*, 299-310.

Guess, D., Sailor, W., Rutherford, G., & Baer, D. M. An experimental analysis of linguistic development: The productive use of the plural morpheme. *Journal of Applied Behavior Analysis* 1968, *1*, 297-306.

Gray, B. & Ryan B. *A language program for the non-language child.* Champaign, IL: Research Press, 1973.

Jeffrey, D. B. Increase and maintenance of verbal behavior of a mentally retarded child. *Mental Retardation*, 1972, *10*(2), 35-39.

Jordan, T. E. Language and mental retardation: A review of the literature. In R. L. Schiefelbusch, R. H. Copeland, & J. O. Smith (Eds.), *Language and mental retardation.* New York: Holt, Rinehart & Winston, 1967.

Kent, L. R. *Language acquisition program for the severely retarded.* Champaign, IL: Research Press, 1974.
LeBanks v. Spears, Civil Action Number 71-2896, E. D. La. (1973).
Lovaas, O. I. A program for the establishment of speech in psychotic children. In H. Sloane & B. MacAulay (Eds.), *Operant procedures in remedial speech and language training.* Boston: Houghton Mifflin, 1968.
MacAuley, B. D. A program for teaching speech and beginning reading to non-verbal retardates. In H. N. Sloane Jr. & B. D. MacAuley (Eds.), *Operant procedures in remedial speech and language training.* Boston: Houghton-Mifflin, 1968.
McMillan v. Board of Education, 430 F. 2d 1145 (2nd Cir. 1970), on remand 331 F. Supp. 302 (1931).
Miller, L. K. *Principles of everyday behavior analysis.* Monterey, CA: Brooks-Cole Publishing, 1975.
Mills v. Board of Education of District of Columbia, 348 F. Suppl 866 (1972).
New York Association for Retarded Children, Inc. v. Rockefeller, 357 F. Supp. 752 (1973).
Peine, H. A., Gregerson, G. F., & Sloane, H., Jr., A program to increase vocabulary and spontaneous verbal behavior. *Mental Retardation,* 1970, *8*(2), 38-44.
Pennsylvania Association for Retarded Children (PARC) v. Commonwealth of Pennsylvania, 334 F. Supp. 1257, 343 F. Supp. 279 (1972).
Reese, E. P. *The analysis of human operant behavior.* Dubuque, IA: Wm. C. Brown Co. Publishers, 1966.
Reid v. Board of Education, 453 F. 2nd 238 (1971).
Sailor, W., Guess, D., & Baer, D. M. Functional language for verbally deficient children: An experimental program. *Mental Retardation,* 1973, *11*(3), 27-35.
Sailor, W., & Mix, B. J. *The TARC assessment system,* Lawrence, KS: H & H Enterprises, 1975.
Schroder, G. R., & Baer, D. M. Effects of concurrent and serial training on generalized vocal imitation in retarded children. *Developmental Psychology,* 1972, *6,* 293-301.
Schumaker, J., & Sherman, J. A. Training generative verb usage by imitation and reinforcement procedures. *Journal of Applied Behavior Analysis,* 1970, *3,* 273-278.
Sloane, H. N., Jr., Johnston, M. K., & Harris, F. R. Remedial procedures for teaching verbal behavior to speech deficient and defective young children. In H. N. Sloane, Jr. & B. MacAulay (Eds.), *Operant procedures in remedial speech and language training.* Boston: Houghton-Mifflin, 1968.
Snyder, L. K., Lovitt, T. C., & Smith, J. O. Language training for the severely retarded: Five years of behavior analysis research. *Exceptional Children,* 1975, *42,* 7-15.
Stewart, F. J. A vocal-motor program for teaching nonverbal children. *Education and Training of the Mentally Retarded,* 1972, *7,* 176-182.
Sulzer, B., & Mayer, G. R. *Behavior modification procedures for school personnel.* Hinsdale, IL: Dryden Press, 1972.
Twardosz, S., & Baer, D. M. Training two severely retarded adolescents to ask questions. *Journal of Applied Behavior Analysis,* 1973, *6,* 655-661.
Whaley, D., & Malott, R. *Elementary principles of behavior.* New York: Appleton-Century-Crofts, 1971.
Wolf v. Legislature of State of Utah, 3rd. District, Salt Lake County, Div. #182646 (1969).
Wyatt v. Stickney, 344 F. Supp. 373 and 344 F. Supp. 387 (1972).

One of the most common problems encountered by teachers of exceptional children involves the teaching of mathematical concepts. The authors give the reader an update on current methodologies and math programs, with specific attention to practical suggestions for remediating deficits in mathematics. The article is a good "refresher course" for the classroom teacher and provides direction for teachers in their efforts to improve math instruction for exceptional children and youth.

Mathematical Concepts and Skills: Diagnosis, Prescription, and Correction of Deficiencies

Lelon R. Capps and Mary M. Hatfield, *University of Kansas*

Current sentiment emphasizes the uniqueness of the individual in terms of his rights, particularly to equal educational opportunity. The fact that each child is special presents a challenge to all educators, and especially to educators of exceptional children. For each child, whether retarded, emotionally disturbed, physically handicapped, gifted or normal, the goal for all educators is to provide the best possible educational environment from which the child can gain the maximum benefit.

It is a mistake to think of any group of children, exceptional, ethnic or whatever, collectively and then instruct all members of the group in an identical fashion. Children classified as learning disabled or emotionally disturbed have unique variances in their deficiencies in mathematical skills and concepts. To impose a single fixed curriculum for students classified in either group does not allow adequately for their individual differences. A curriculum must have flexibility and latitude to allow for adjustments in the learner's style, time required for mastery, sequencing and instructional mode. The basic finding of Stodolsky and Lesser (1967) indicates that groups do differ in patterns of mathematical abilities as well as in verbal abilities.

However, the skills and concepts taught to individuals and groups of individuals are much more similar than different. The hierarchy of skills may differ with a given teacher's objectives, but the sequence of content is based upon a sequence of subordinate learnings prerequisite to attaining the terminal objective. To build this hierarchy requires repeated questioning concerning what subordinate skills are needed to attain a given objective. In order to accommodate the mathematically handicapped, one must carefully examine the existing hierarchy of skills and determine if further subdivisions of the skills in the sequence need to be made. Unless the curriculum was designed to be used with the mathematically handicapped, the steps or subordinate learnings probably need to be further subdivided. By translating the hierarchy into the smallest possible steps, there is a greater potential for a successful learning experience and a more positive attitude.

An example of a mathematical program that has attempted to decrease the difficulty level by expanding the number of steps in mastering mathematical concepts and skills is Project MATH. Project MATH, developed by Cawley and his associates (Cawley, Goodstein, Fitzmaurice, Lepore, Sedlak, & Althaus, 1975), has sequenced instructional objectives for mathematics instruction to the handicapped primarily by mathematical topics and has arranged all specifications within organizing matrices. While the sequence of content is not substantially different from that found in a mathematics program used in regular classroom settings, the nature of the hierarchy does differ.

Goodstein (1975) contends that the logical structure of mathematics is universal in nature. Thus, the term "mathematics for the handicapped" is misleading. It is not a case of a special mathematics for the handicapped but, rather, a case of how it is taught. The content does not differ substantially, but the time frame needed and instructional method do vary.

The use of concrete materials for introductory learning experiences is essential. Bruner's (1966) three levels of conceptual complexity (enactive-concrete; ikonic-pictorial; symbolic-abstract) particularly should be considered when dealing with mathematically handicapped children. Too often mathematics instruction centers on only the ikonic and symbolic response modes. Instructional materials must be modified to include all three response modes. Just as the rate of acquisition varies, there exists a variance in the modality used in the learning process for exceptional children. Armstrong (1970) proposed an intervention model which would emphasize an instructional environment that would be a function of the stage of cognitive development for the child (Piaget's component) and the level of mathematical concept

Mathematical Concepts and Skills

acquisition (Bruner's component). In two related studies on the mathematical learning of Trainable Mentally Retarded (TMR) and Educable Mentally Retarded (EMR), the TMR did significantly better under the manipulative, enactive representational mode. The EMR also learned better under the manipulative mode, but only on certain types of mathematical ideas.

The instructional triad of concrete-semiconcrete-abstract is critical to students with learning deficiencies in mathematical skills and/or concepts. *Many learning deficiencies might not occur in the first place if this instructional triad were the universal basis for all instruction in mathematical concepts.*

It is true that children can learn 8 × 7 = 56 by other procedures such as excessive repetition, but the question becomes, "Is this learning or training?" If one believes in the training premise, can it then be assumed that all hope for teaching exceptional children to reason or think is to be abandoned? For some students training may be adequate, but for most students learning is desired. All citizens, regardless of exceptionality, are entitled to reason to the best of their ability. Manipulative materials and experiences are an integral part of teaching such reasoning ability to students. Ultimately, mathematical skills and concepts must be applied in daily living. This requires judgment, reasoning, decision making and logic. Unfortunately, too many teachers of, and materials for, the mathematically handicapped rely on instruction that is abstract in nature and depends almost exclusively on repetition.

In discussing diagnosis, prescription, and instruction for the mathematically handicapped, the three major considerations are: (1) the content to be learned, (2) the learner, and (3) the materials of instruction.

THE CONTENT

In terms of content, it seems imperative that educators of exceptional children agree upon what mathematical skills and concepts the exceptional child can be expected to learn. There does not seem to be universal agreement among educators about the inclusion of reasoning skills for the exceptional child. Rather, there appears to be an abundance of emphasis placed on the mechanical, computational component of mathematics. In addition, much of this element comes through instruction at the abstract level rather than at the concrete, manipulative level. There seems to be disharmony between the practice and the philosophy of educating exceptional children in mathematics.

Current practice seems to indicate agreement in teaching EMR students the basic computational skills involved in using the four operations with whole numbers. However, the fact that agreement exists does not justify the correctness of a practice. If 40 minutes per day are spent on instruction in mathematics, the student will devote approximately one-sixth of his school-life for eight years to achieve about fourth grade proficiency. At this level there can be only limited confidence in the accuracy and, consequently, limited application to any decision that might be crucial.

Would it not be wiser to teach EMR students how to use a hand calculator to do the computations? Then, in turn, use the instructional time to teach the student how to use the calculator in solving everyday problems and how to estimate the reasonableness of the answer. Consider an EMR student as an adult faced with finding the total cost of his utilities. The person could add the several numbers using pencil and paper, but the time involved would be considerable and the accuracy questionable. Better, he would have available a hand calculator and would use it to make the computation. The time involved would be much less, with greater accuracy.

The hand calculator provides the opportunity to decrease the emphasis on the mechanics of computation and place increasing emphasis on a more functional mathematics curriculum involving the solution to everyday problems. Educators of exceptional children need to consider the implications of the hand calculator and reach agreement on revising the mathematics curricula accordingly. Traditional expectations of mathematical experiences for exceptional children need to be re-examined.

Another example involving mathematical content deals with decimals. Traditionally, a mildly mentally handicapped child would have had little experience with decimal notation or decimal fractions. Two trends make it imperative that this cannot continue if the student is to be a functional citizen. First, calculators do not accommodate common fractions such as one-third, one-half, etc., unless they are expressed in decimal equivalents. Second, conversion to metric measurement makes it mandatory that all citizens understand decimal notation as it is used in expressing equivalent measurements. For example, to change 38.97 meters to centimeters, the decimal point is moved two places to the right. Similarly, to change 3003 centimeters to meters, the decimal point is moved two places to the left. To learn the metric system requires an understanding of decimal notation, a topic not previously taught to students with an intellectual handicap.

In answer to the question, "What mathematical content should be taught to the learning disabled, mentally retarded, or slow learner?", the authors would suggest a simply-stated practice: A greater amount of the instructional time should be directed to diagnosing, prescribing, and instructing within those topics that are of the greatest relevance to the learner. This implies that not all content in the traditional curriculum is equally useful to all children, regardless of exceptionality. For some students, learning reasoning skills may be most helpful, while for others, learning reasoning skills may not be a practical or possible instructional goal. While reasoning skills would be useful and practical for the mildly retarded, such would not be the case for the TMR.

The teacher is the key to determining what content the child will experience and how it is presented. Unfortunately, most teachers have had little, if any, preparation in diagnostic and prescriptive teaching in the area of mathematics. Specific attention needs to be devoted to this aspect of teacher preparation. Also, with appropriate use of modern technology, considerable change can be effected in the mathematics curriculum for exceptional children. Finally, teacher expectations must be altered. It is questionable whether instruction limited to basic computational skills constitutes sufficient preparation for functional citizenship. Educators may accept low achievement as normal, thereby curtailing the child's growth in mathematical skills and concepts. Limiting the child's exposure to mathematical experiences because of low expectations leads to "underteaching" by the teacher and underachievement for the child.

THE LEARNER

Ideally, the teacher should implant in the learner a predisposition to learn but, unfortunately, when children already have some mathematical handicaps, this task becomes difficult. Understanding the child, how he learns, and the structure of mathematics are important pieces of information which allow the teacher to manipulate the learning environment. Instruction should parallel the child's mathematical conceptual development, which implies that a teacher should have ways to assess a child's mathematical foundation.

The work of Piaget and his developmental theory of logical processes suggest means by which a teacher may learn more about the child's mathematical foundation. First, the teacher must be aware of the main mathematics delivery system to which the child has been exposed. Did it consist of appropriate manipulatives upon which the child could act and experience, or was it primarily more verbal in character with a large amount of printed materials? As Callahan and Glennon (1975) warn, from the Piagetian perspective a child may "know" more than he can verbalize, whereas from the functional-verbally oriented perspective, the child may verbalize more than he meaningfully "knows."

In "The Wisconsin Studies" (Van Engen, 1971), first-grade children were tested on arithmetic tasks and Piagetian tasks. All 100 children were near mastery on basic addition facts $2 + 3$ and $4 + 5$ in a verbal format, but only 50 were capable of conserving the equivalence relationship through a physical transformation. Other researchers have tested the relationship between Piagetian class inclusion tasks and missing-addends tasks and between conservation and achievement in mathematics. These studies also indicate a disparity between the child's ability to verbalize a concept and the understanding of the concept.

Rather than being overly concerned about a child's lack of achievement in mathematics and at what grade level he is performing, the teacher should investigate ways to determine at what logico-mathematical level the child is operating and then provide concrete experiences to develop these structures.

The problem may be in maturation rather than a learning deficiency. Whenever a child develops the cognitive intellectual structures to deal with such concepts, the "deficiency" may disappear. A mathematically handicapped child may have been moved too rapidly through the levels of representation; i.e., from the concrete to the abstract. Appropriate manipulatives for the student to experience and act upon in the development of psychomathematical, deductive processes is an extremely important step for remediation. Teachers should plan for learning activities on each of the response mode levels to ensure that students will gain knowledge of the mathematics skills or concepts.

How does a teacher diagnose a child's ability to respond in each of the levels? Many tests are available for diagnosing the child's cognitive ability at an abstract level. These range from standardized mathematics achievement tests or diagnostic tests to teacher-made informal tests. All paper-pencil tests measure the symbolic-abstract level and, to some extent, the pictorial level of learning. Even the most popular diagnostic tests on the market are highly content-oriented instruments requiring performance in the learner's least proficient response mode—the graphic symbolic. Diagnosing at the concrete level of learning becomes more difficult, more time consuming, and requires more interpretative skill by the teacher. For these reasons, along with the scarcity of this type of test, little diagnosis of the concrete level of learning has been done. Piagetian interviews are an excellent source of such information. Copeland (1974) has described how these interviews can be conducted and the teaching implications for various responses.

Other researchers also have developed structured oral interview techniques to learn about the child's ability to deal with mathematical concepts and skills. Denmark (1976) has developed the Project for Mathematical Development of Children (PMDC) grade one and grade two. Cawley (1975) and his associates, as part of Project MATH, currently are field-testing the MATH Concept Inventory, a criterion reference instrument, and they also have developed a Clinical Mathematics Inventory.

Many researchers (Ashlock, 1972; Cawley, 1975; Glennon & Wilson, 1972) have praised the value of an oral interview with the child in which, through the child's verbalizations, one can discover the strategies the child uses to arrive at an answer. Once the flaws in the understanding are revealed, the teacher should use a variety of concrete materials and settings to see if the flaw persists.

If a child's weakest mode is visual, the ubiquitous ditto worksheets will not be the answer. The tactile and auditory modes are greatly under-used and should be considered in modifying the curriculum and materials to suit the learner. Research is being conducted by Uprichard at the University of South Florida to study a child's modality strengths and how this information can be applied to learning content in mathematics.

Cognitive style is another area which merits consideration. If the teacher complains that the child uses his fingers to compute, perhaps the child's cognitive tempo is reflective behavior, and anxiety over making a mistake produces such action. On the other hand, if the child makes many computational errors and does not seem to display a consistent error pattern, the child may be impulsive and needs encouragement to slow down and reflect about the quality and accuracy of answers.

Another characteristic of the learner needing attention is referred to by cognitive theorists as "discrimination performance." From the performance on a discrimination task, something can be determined about a child's level of readiness for language, mathematics skills, and reasoning ability. Young, immature children attend to one feature of a stimulus at a time (as Piaget calls "centration") and perhaps are not aware of other less salient features. For example, young children tend to be more color dominate than shape dominate. If given a color-form task, the child would center on the more salient color dimension rather than on the shape.

The strategies employed by Zeaman and Hause (1963) to study discrimination learning among mentally handicapped children rely heavily upon the inclusion of patterns. Project MATH (Cawley, et. al., 1975) has included patterns based on the premise that patterns will parallel the extended readiness period demanded of the mentally handicapped child and the extended non-reading period of the learning disabled child.

Sternberg (1975) has developed an instrument, Pattern Recognition Skills Inventory (PRSI), for use as a measuring and diagnostic tool to test a subject's ability to discriminate patterns. The clue to diagnosis in PRSI relates to a hierarchy in pattern recognition skills. Pattern discrimination appears to be a function of age and/or maturity in information processing.

It is imperative to know the learner before any corrective instructional process is begun. Too frequently, the teacher diagnoses the skill deficiencies and implements remedial instruction without assessing the learner's logico-mathematical development, response mode, cognitive style, or discriminatory learning abilities. The end result is failure to achieve any permanent change in the child's mathematical learning.

METHODS & MATERIALS

The synthesis of content and learner is the ultimate goal of mathematics instruction. Selection of appropriate methods and materials is critical to the successful outcome of this synthesis. Once the objectives have been determined in relation to our knowledge about the learner, selecting appropriate materials and instructional methods becomes critical to achieving the objectives. Many teachers minimize the importance of this aspect of the corrective process, evidenced by their over-reliance on drill sheets as a means of correcting the deficiency. For the mathematically learning disabled, paper-pencil tasks require the child to respond in one of his weakest response modes. This incompatibility between material and learner response mode results in limited retention on either a short- or long-term basis.

In selection materials it is important to know something about the sense mode of the learner and the materials. In the routine of daily living, approximately 80 percent of our sensory intake is visual, 11 percent is auditory and 2 percent is tactile. Materials for and methods of instruction can be classified as being oriented toward these three sense modes. Textbook materials rely heavily on visual skills to interpret. Manipulative materials may be visual if used for demonstration, but when used by children, they involve tactile as well as visual skills in learning. Since many children with a learning disability in mathematics may also suffer from some perceptual disability, it seems reasonable to conclude that the materials and methods employed in the corrective process should minimize reliance on the visual mode.

Corrective procedures must be based on a more auditory and/or tactile approach. Whenever possible, beginning instruction for any concept at any age level should be based on concrete experiences before proceeding to the symbolic, abstract level. When using concrete, manipulative devices in initial or corrective instruction, it is of utmost importance that the steps be verbalized and written in symbolic form *by the child* to help in the transition to more abstract levels.

The following example illustrates the manner in which a concept may be taught using each of the three senses independently. Assume you want a child to learn about "fourness." To teach the concept visually, a card with a pattern of four dots can be made as shows:

The card can be flashed and the student asked to identify the number. To teach the same concept auditorily, the teacher could, out of sight of the students, tap a specific note on the piano four times. Hopefully, the auditory approach also contributes to better listening skills on the part of the students. Finally, to teach the concept using a tactile approach, a card with four sandpaper discs could be placed in a closed container with an opening. The student is asked to reach through the opening and by "feel" determine the number of discs.

It is critical for the teacher to devise teaching strategies to utilize as many senses as possible in acquiring mathematical concepts. The two senses most neglected in teaching strategies and materials and, consequently, in most need of emphasis, are auditory and tactile. Teaching concepts via the auditory sense will require a bit of imagination on the part of the teacher, but it is possible to devise strategies for many of the mathematical skills and concepts. The University of Maryland's Arithmetic Center has been conducting research using exemplars which have been modified to enhance the tactile, kinesthetic, and auditory attributes. One example is the attachment of a bell to the mathematical balance to ring only when the instrument is in balance. Materials and methods may rely on various sensory modes for successful interpretation. One of the critical aspects of the corrective process centers on the selection of appropriate methods and materials in delivering the corrective instruction.

An example of the cruciality in selecting appropriate materials is apparent in working with regrouping in addition and subtraction. Suppose the child does not understand the regrouping procedure for addition and the teacher has many manipulative devices at her disposal. Which device is best to show how and when regrouping occurs in the example 53 + 29: Cuisenaire rods, Unifix cubes, Dienes blocks, multi-base abacus, closed abacus (9 or 10 beads per column), place value chart, bundling sticks, chip trading, or bean sticks? Not all of these materials are equally appropriate for teaching this given concept. Consideration must be given to any additional information known about the student. Does he tend to count on his fingers? Does he have any visual or perceptual problems? Are his fine motor skills adequately developed? Does the learner tend to perseverate? Is he easily distracted?

Attention also must be directed toward the attributes of the exemplars being considered. Are there any irrelevant features which may be a distractor or serve as a hindrance to concept formation? Does the material clearly represent the concept to be extracted? Does the material provide for easy individual manipulation by the child? Does the device exploit as many senses as possible? Does the device allow for abstraction?

The implications of this materials selection task can be illustrated in the skill of regrouping. In the exchangeability idea of how 10 of the column on the right can be exchanged or traded for 1 of the column on its left (10 ones for 1 ten) which exemplars show the child when the trade is necessary? The closed abacus meets this criteria, but the child must possess additional skills when given this device to work the problem 27 + 8. First the child shows the 27 in the proper columns (Figure 1). Then he begins to add 8 more in the ones column. Only 9 beads will fit in that column (to show the child when regrouping is necessary). He can fit only 2 more beads in the ones column (Figure 2). Then he must clear the ones column and add a bead to the tens column (Figure

Instructional Planning for Exceptional Children

3). Since the tenth bead does not fit in the ones column and is placed in the tens column, it may seem to the student that this is a trade of 9 for 1. The critical question is: Can the child remember how many of the 8 ones he added when the regrouping was necessary?

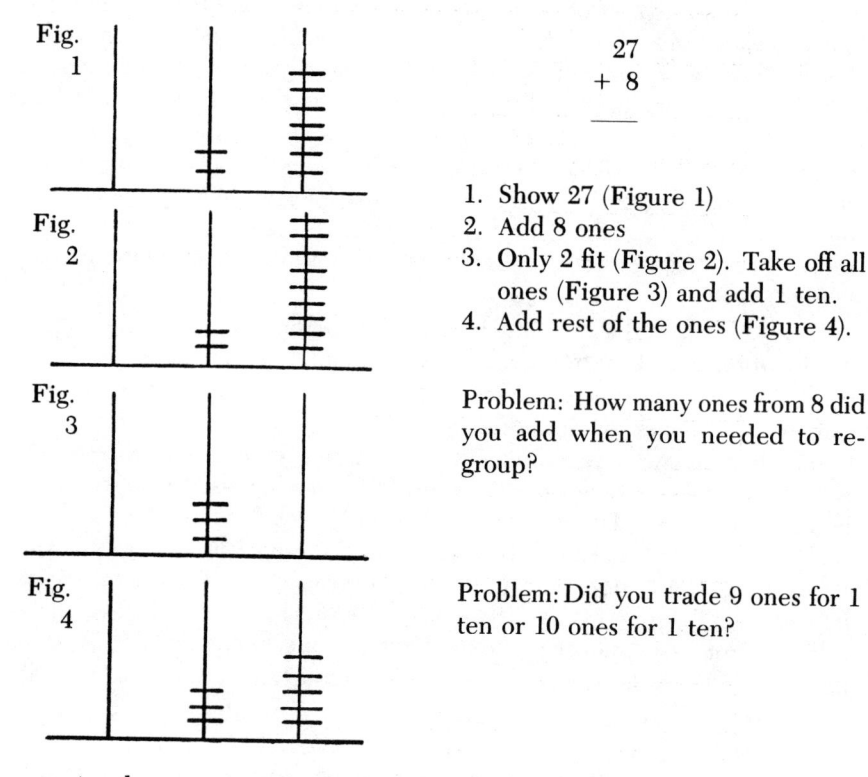

```
  27
+  8
-----
```

Fig. 1

Fig. 2

Fig. 3

Fig. 4

1. Show 27 (Figure 1)
2. Add 8 ones
3. Only 2 fit (Figure 2). Take off all ones (Figure 3) and add 1 ten.
4. Add rest of the ones (Figure 4).

Problem: How many ones from 8 did you add when you needed to regroup?

Problem: Did you trade 9 ones for 1 ten or 10 ones for 1 ten?

Another question is whether the same aid can be used to show the regrouping process in subtraction. If one believes that subtraction should be represented as the inverse operation of addition, it seems valuable to use the same aid, with the reverse sequence of steps. Is the closed abacus appropriate? No. The regrouped ten as 10 ones cannot be placed on the ones column.

Suppose the wooden Cuisenaire rods were selected instead of the closed abacus. The child clearly could see when regrouping is necessary and the exchangeability of groups of 10. In the example 27 + 8, the steps would be as follows:

1. Show 27 (Figure 5).
2. Add 8 ones (Figure 6). The combined length of 7 and 8 shows that there is more than 10.
3. Regroup the 7 and 8 into a 10 and a 5 (Figure 7).
4. Answer 3 tens and 5 ones (Figure 8).

Mathematical Concepts and Skills

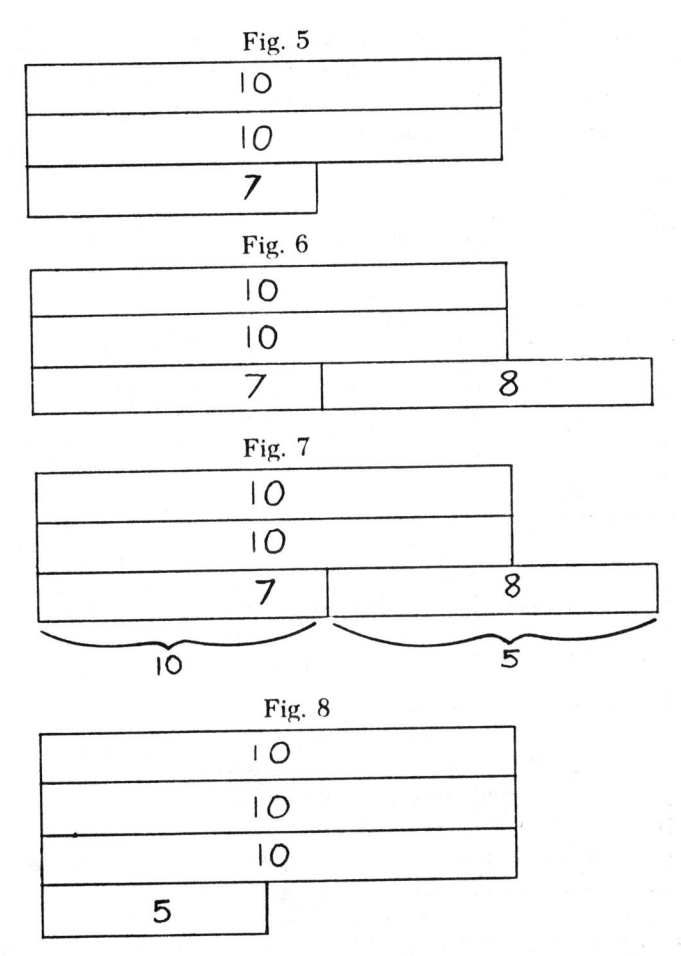

Fig. 5

10
10
7

Fig. 6

10
10
7	8

Fig. 7

10
10
7	8

⏟ 10   ⏟ 5

Fig. 8

10
10
10
5

Using the rods, the child readily can see at what point the regrouping is necessary and that the ones can be exchanged for one ten-rod, leaving 5 ones remaining. The rods can be manipulated easily and allow for abstraction of the concept. However, the teacher must be aware of two irrelevant attributes which are associated with the rods and which, if abstracted by the learner, might cause misconceptions—color and size. In our notational system, neither color nor size is an attribute associated with the system. We do not write a 7 in black ink and a 5 in yellow. Neither do we write a 7 as a larger numeral than the 5. The astute teacher must be alert to the possibility that when selecting the Cuisenaire rods, additional attributes are being introduced as a part of our notational system which may cause problems and erroneous concept formation in the child. It is important to the learning

Instructional Planning for Exceptional Children

process that the appropriate exemplar be chosen in relation to the skill being taught.

As another example, consider the disability of overreliance on rote counting. At the initial stages of learning an addition fact, counting is quite natural. However, the student who becomes over-reliant on counting is headed for almost certain difficulty when higher level addition skills are required in problems such as 368 + 249. For this reason, those involved in corrective teaching must be especially alert to students who exhibit an overreliance on counting. One appropriate corrective procedure is to prepare cards with standard configurations of dots as illustrated:

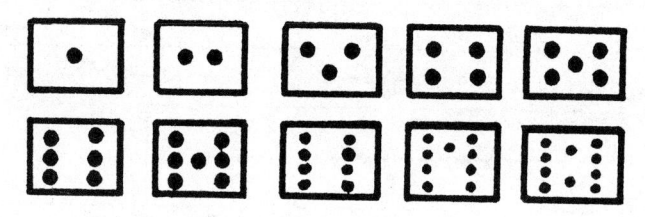

These cards can be flashed briefly, and students can be asked to display a numeral card to tell how many dots they saw. Once a student can do this with speed and accuracy, reliance on counting will begin to diminish.

Another manipulative aid that may be employed to diminish overreliance on counting is the wooden Cuisenaire rods, in which length and color assume a value. These rods have advantages over the cards for several reasons: The rods are not scored into individual units; thus, they would be useful with the rote counter because there is no opportunity to count to find the answer. The attributes of size and color that were irrelevant in teaching place value become beneficial in teaching numerosity. Other materials which frequently are used to teach addition and subtraction are chip trading, Unifix cubes, abaci, bundling sticks, and bean sticks. Each of these materials has discrete elements which encourage counting. Again the selection of the exemplar is critical to correcting the deficiency.

Wilson (1976) and his colleagues at the University of Maryland have devised a rating system to analyze the many exemplars available for teaching a given concept. The accompanying chart is a capsule analysis of several of the available materials, and lists some of the major features.

In materials selection, the importance of proper matching of the exemplar with the learner's style, the content to be taught, and the deficiency to be corrected must be emphasized. Also the teacher who is diagnosing and prescribing for a learning deficiency must give careful thought to the sequencing of instruction. No commercially prepared materials will do the job alone. The teacher must be knowledgeable and astute in her observations.

The role of preventive teaching merits attention. Summarizing the rela-

Mathematical Concepts and Skills

tionship of preventive teaching to remediation: The best remediation for learning problems in mathematics is quality teaching in the first place.

How many deficiencies are created by inadequate instruction when concepts are introduced for the first time? A child's initial experience with a concept is the time when it is most critical for the lesson to be well presented with concrete representation, as it is the most likely time for success. Presenting the initial lesson poorly spawns much "undoing" in terms of attitude and/or confusion.

Students often work this subtraction problem as follows:

$$\begin{array}{r} 63 \\ -25 \\ \hline 42 \end{array}$$

Note that the student failed to regroup and took the difference between the 3 and 5. This reveals a great deal about the manner in which the student was introduced to the regrouping necessary. Representation of the problem on the abacus is:

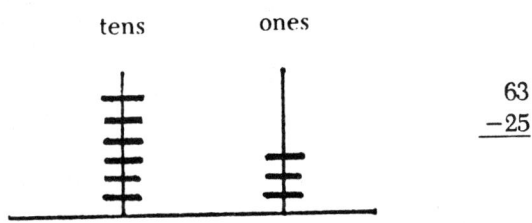

Pointing out the 63 shown and asking the student to remove 5 ones certainly could not result in taking the difference between 3 and 5. Students who make that error have been taught how to do the problem beginning at the symbolic level. Proper initial instruction utilizing an abacus or rods would have helped to avoid this error. Greater emphasis needs to be placed on the role of preventive teaching—in preservice teacher training programs, and (an even greater need) among teachers already in service. The availability of a learning disabilities teacher often allows regular classroom teachers an escape mechanism from dealing with a skill deficiency. By referring the student out of their realm of concern, classroom teachers fail to learn how to help the student and how to change their own instructional style to avoid or minimize the possibility of a similar learning problem occurring in the future.

The learning disabilities teacher has a moral obligation to aid the regular classroom teachers in changing their instructional style if it will result in better learning for the students. Correcting the 63-25 regrouping problem for the student, and then showing the regular classroom teacher how it might have been prevented initially, will improve the competence of the regular classroom teacher.

Instructional Planning for Exceptional Children

The role of learning disabilities teachers involves more than appearing on the scene, administering a battery of tests, diagnosing the difficulty, and submitting the results to the classroom teacher in a lengthy and sometimes incomprehensible written report. The resource teacher must be able to prescribe activities and materials to be used to correct the deficiency, and then must help the regular classroom teacher implement the prescription. The implementation process with the regular classroom teacher is the key to changing the instructional style of that teacher.

EVALUATION OF FOUR EXEMPLARS USED IN TEACHING PLACE VALUE

	Positive Attributes	Limitations
Cuisenaire Rods	Discourages counting Emphasizes 10 to 1 regrouping Adaptable to many grade levels Adaptable to many concepts Color cueing helps remember value of rod Easily manipulated	Color is irrelevant in terms of place value Size is irrelevant in terms of place value No fixed location to represent place value
Unifix Cubes	Easily manipulated Possible to structure various subsets using color Adaptable to many grade levels Adaptable to many concepts	May encourage counting Fixed location to represent place value is not apparent 10 to 1 regrouping may be obscured
Dienes Blocks	10 to 1 regrouping is obvious Adaptable to many grade levels Adaptable to many concepts Easily manipulated	No fixed location to represent place value May encourage counting
Closed Abacus (9 units)	Has fixed location to show place value Color cueing may help understand place value Easily manipulated	Cannot show more than 9 units Encourages counting Has limited application across concepts 10 to 1 regrouping may be obscured Limited application across grade levels Color is irrelevant in terms of place value

REFERENCES

Armstrong, J. R. An educational process model for use in research. *The Journal of Experimental Education*, 1970, 39(1).

Ashlock, R. B. *Error patterns in computations: A semi-programmed approach*. Columbus, OH: Charles E. Merrill Publishing Co., 1972.

Bruner, J. S. On cognitive growth. *Studies in Cognitive Growth*. New York: John Wiley & Sons, Inc., 1966.

Callahan, L. G. & Glennon, V. J. *Elementary School Mathematics: A Guide to Current Research*. Washington, DC: Association for Supervision and Curriculum Development, 1975.

Cawley, J. F. Proposal: Mathematical disabilities among handicapped children: Diagnosis and remediation: Unpublished manuscript, University of Connecticut, 1975.

Cawley, J. F., Goodstein, H. A., Fitzmaurice, A. M., Lepore, A., Sedlak, R., & Althaus, V. *Project MATH: A program of the mainstream series*. Wallingford, CT: Educational Sciences, Inc., 1975.

Copeland, R. W. *Diagnostic and learning activities in mathematics for children*. New York: Macmillan, 1974.

Denmark, Tom. *PMDC mathematics test*. Tallahassee, FL: Florida State University, 1976.

Glennon, V. J. & Wilson, J. W. Diagnostic-prescriptive teaching. *The slow learner in mathematics*. Washington, DC: National Council of Teachers of Mathematics, 1972.

Goodstein, H. A. Assessment and programming in mathematics for the handicapped. *Focus on Exceptional Children*, 1975, 1 (7).

Sternberg, L. *Pattern recognition skills inventory*. Northbrook, IL: Hubbard Scientific Co., 1974.

Stodolsky, S. & Lesser, G. Learning patterns in the disadvantaged. *Harvard Educational Review*, 1967, 37, 546-93.

Van Engen, H. Epistemology, research, and instruction. *Piagetian cognitive-development research and mathematical education*. Washington, DC: National Council of Teachers of Mathematics, 1971.

Zeamon, D. & Hause, B. J. The role of attention in retardate discrimination learning. *Handbook of mental deficiency*. New York: McGraw-Hill, 1963.

Accurate interpretation of observed behaviors, test results, and anecdotal information is critical to effective instructional planning. Moran's article provides a frame of reference for the interpretation of information; at the same time it argues for an affirmative role for the classroom teacher in the team process. She gives attention to the different types of information teachers receive in the overall evaluation process, as well as to the circumstances under which interpretation must occur.

The Teacher's Role in Interpretation of Reports

Mary Ross Moran, *University of Kansas*

After the decision has been made to refer a student for evaluation by a school psychologist, counselor, or clinical psychologist, the next problem to be faced by the teacher is how to interpret the subsequent report in ways that will help her implement the findings. The comprehensiveness and quality of reports vary so greatly among examiners that is is very difficult to state any generalizations about the document which the teacher will receive. With few exceptions, however, and regardless of the length of the report, it should contain three *types of statements*: Information, Inferences, Judgments. Although there is some overlap, these three types of statements are not to be confused with the three levels of assessment described above. All three statement types occur at each of the three levels of assessment.

INFORMATIONAL STATEMENTS

Statements which quantify behavior (such as "John earned a full-scale IQ of 95, a verbal IQ of 90, and a performance IQ of 102" or "Scores on all visual perception tasks were within normal limits for his age" or "John computed twelve two-digit addition facts in two minutes") or statements which report test behavior in observable terms (such as "John used his left hand for drawing and writing tasks") are statements which can be called Information. The chief characteristic of Information is that it is verifiable; that is, independent scorers and independent observers should reach a high level of agreement on statements if they are to be labeled Information statements.

If disputes about Information statements arise, it is possible to go to the test record forms or to a videotape of the testing session and resolve any dispute by reference to the observable facts. It is possible for Information to be inaccurate, as when an examiner applies the wrong table in translating raw scores to standard scores, but accurate Information cannot truly be disputable—it is subject to direct verification. Because Information is factual, it must be the basis upon which the other two types of statements are made.

INFERENTIAL STATEMENTS

The second type of statement always found in a report is an Inference, a statement made about the unknown on the basis of the known. Statements which would be classified as Inference are, for example: "Deficits in visual-motor integration skills are the basis for Jim's inability to complete written seatwork," or "Jim's test behavior is that of a dependent child who could be expected to function better in a one-to-one or small group setting than in a large group."

Inferences are not directly verifiable—that is, they are not factual. Instead they are interpretations of facts. There will not, therefore, be as high a degree of agreement among independent observers about Inferences as about Information. For example, two Inferences— "Jane demonstrated negative behavior throughout the test" and "Jane lacks self-confidence when faced with an unfamiliar task"—could both be based upon the same observation, that Jane did not attempt eight of ten subtest items in one test. Depending upon additional behaviors which Jane exhibited, either of these Inferences might be correct, and one would have to go to the test behavior to determine clusters of behavior which support negativism and those which support lack of self-confidence.

Inferences are thus documented by the massing of behavioral indicators to support alternative interpretations. The accuracy of Inferences depends upon the training and experience of the examiner. Inferences drawn by a conscientious, well-trained, and experienced examiner are likely to be accurate and useful; those drawn by a careless, poorly trained, or inexperienced examiner may be little more than conjecture.

Instructional Planning for Exceptional Children

JUDGMENTAL STATEMENTS

The third type of statement to be found in a report is a Judgment, which is a decision about what action should be taken. Typically, Judgments in a report are the recommendation—for example, "Jim's level of intellectual functioning, adaptive social behavior, and emotional status indicate that he is appropriate for placement in an EMR classroom" or "Joe would profit from a multisensory approach to reading instruction which would allow him to compensate for inadequate visual memory" or "Mary requires an intervention program in the classroom to motivate her to complete work without teacher aid."

Judgments are based upon Inferences, which are in turn based upon Information; therefore, Judgments are twice removed from fact, and error is subject to a compounding effect. Any Judgment can be only as sound as the Inferences and Information upon which it is based.

INTERACTION OF INFORMATION, INFERENCES, AND JUDGMENTS

An example of statements at each of these levels about the same child will clarify the relationships among the types of statements. The recommendation, *"Bob should be placed in a primary learning disabilities resource room for daily instruction in both reading and mathematics,"* is a Judgment. It is based upon the following Inferences:

> Bob demonstrates a language deficit which affects his ability to manipulate symbols; he lacks skills in revisualization, spatial relationships, directionality, and visual sequencing. He has average intellectual potential, but learning is limited by inadequate language and organization of visual information. Bob is also handicapped by overreliance on teacher aid, and he lacks the independent study and social skills to function effectively in a large group for instruction."

These Inferences are, in turn, based upon information such as the following:

> Bob earned a full-scale IQ of 93, a verbal scale of 80, and a performance scale of 111. Vocabulary and Similarities subtest scores were below the mean of other verbal scores. Bob did not carry out a sequence of two oral directions. Picture Completion and Coding subtests, as well as Bender reproductions, were below the norms for his chronological age and below his mean scores for other performance items. Bob stopped twice during pencil and paper tasks to ask for examiner aid; he also requested examiner aid on two out of three manual manipulation tasks. When a model was present, visual-motor tasks were completed with greater speed but rotations and inversions of direction still occurred. When the examiner demonstrated a visual-motor task, Bob asked for a repetition of the demonstration, then carried it out in an order the reverse of the model.

When a Judgment is supported by such detailed observations, it is possible for the teacher to determine easily if the Judgment is documented. But it often happens that only the recommendations are stated—Information and Inference statements are sometimes omitted from brief reports. This is only one of the possible problems which can be encountered by a teacher who is a critical reader of reports.

INTERPRETATION OF INFORMATIONAL STATEMENTS

Statements which can be termed Information represent factual material. Yet, Informational statements require some interpretation by the teacher who must be able to take into account error in measurement, differences in frame of reference for observations, and the distinction between observation and interpretation.

Error in Measurement

There is in any measurement, regardless of the factor to be quantified or the skill of the examiner. There are at least two reasons for such error. First, any sample of behavior at a specific time is subject to situational and environmental variables; second, any test is at best only a sample of the possible tasks which could measure a specific skill or process, and a different set of items could produce different results.

Therefore, the teacher should not interpret data reported in Information statements as absolute scores; instead, any score should be thought of as an estimate of the range of the student's ability on any given dimension rather than a discrete point. This range is best considered in terms of the standard error of measurement, which is a statistic supplied by the test publisher to describe the possible variations in the scores of a single individual if he took the test a number of times or took alternate forms of the test. Standard error is a band of probable inaccuracy on either side of the observed score. If the standard error of measurement for a given test is 3.6 for example, there is a probability of about two-thirds that a specific student's true score is within a range of 3.6 above or below the obtained score; for a score of 95, there is a high probability that the true score, if it could be determined, would lie between 91.4 and 98.6.

The fact that a child's true score can only be estimated is not justification to dismiss scores on standardized tests as useless because they are not precise. When an examiner uses a standardized test, at least he knows how much margin for error should be allowed, and he can draw his Inferences accordingly. We have no similar margin for error computed in regard to other possible bases for decisions—such as observation of daily work products, for example. Therefore, as long as test scores are considered to represent a band or range and as long as the examiner has used a valid and reliable instrument, criteria for which are beyond the scope of this article, test scores provide useful Information.

It is important for a teacher to make a distinction between recognizing the limitations of test scores and disregarding scores altogether. It sometimes happens that a teacher decides to dismiss test scores reported by another examiner because such scores do not agree with the teacher's own observations of the student. If the teacher has an impression, for example, that Bob's vocabulary is quite adequate in conversation, she may want to dismiss a test score which indicates that vocabulary is far below age norms.

Once a teacher has decided that she needs information about a student which could be answered by testing and once she decides to proceed by referring the child to a school psychologist, she is not then free to disregard the test results simply because she does not agree with them. In fairness to the student, all test results should be considered; if there are discrepancies between test scores and the teacher's observations, those discrepancies should be resolved rather than test scores dismissed.

Frame of Reference for Observations

Problems arise when a teacher who was not present for the evaluation reads the observations of the examiner and finds that the learner described in the report is different from the student known to the teacher. This can happen because teacher and examiner view the child under different conditions and from different points of view.

The teacher sees the student in a group, doing academic work, and in familiar surroundings. The teacher is usually concerned primarily with the way in which this individual fits into the classroom groupings, and she will note whether he is developmentally similar to other third graders she has taught. The examiner sees the student on a one-to-one basis, performing unfamiliar nonacademic tasks, under timing and stress, working with a comparative stranger. The examiner has been trained to observe subtle differences between individuals; use of standardized instructions and tasks elicits minor differences in response.

If a student is described differently from the way the teacher sees the learner, does this mean that the observations of the examiner are irrelevant to the classroom? On the contrary, problem-solving approaches of preplanning or trial and error, response sets of deliberation or impulsive guessing, initiative or dependence demonstrated in the testing situation can suggest intervention strategies in the classroom. The important thing is that the teacher consider the implications of different behavior in the testing situation. If the student performed better, the teacher should ask whether he might be more responsive to one-to-one tutoring by a peer or an aide in the classroom;

whether he requires more variety in tasks rather than limiting him to texts and workbooks; whether her own or the group's interaction with the child may be anxiety-provoking in the classroom. If the child performed less well in the testing situation, the teacher should ask what implications this has for the student's ability to cope with a different volunteer aide every day, with new instructional material, and with other changes in daily routine or personnel.

As long as the statements cover observable behavior, it is not reasonable for a teacher to take exception to the task behavior which is reported. The student may not appear that way to her, but she must accept the reality that the student behaved that way in the testing situation. Differences in the learner's behavior under the two conditions should then become the subject for discussion between examiner and teacher so that useful intervention approaches can emerge from insights about the student's task behavior.

Distinction Between Observation and Inference

Differences in frame of reference for observations can be identified by the thoughtful teacher, but problems which arise because an examiner has confused observations with interpretations of behavior are much less likely to be recognized even by the careful reader.

It is very difficult for many examiners to state Information rather than Inferences. A statement such as "Jim became angry when he could not assemble the fourth block design" is an Inference. The Information statement would read, "Jim worked on the fourth block design for 30 seconds without reproducing it; he then destroyed his attempt by overturning the blocks." It requires considerable skill and a great deal of self-discipline for an examiner to report observations as opposed to interpretations of what was observed. Statements of behavioral observations should be read critically to determine whether interpretation is included. A teacher should ask: Is that *observable*, or would the examiner have to go beyond observation to make that statement? Is that *behavior*, or has the statement gone beyond behavior to report feeling state or attitude of the student? Words which are likely to describe observable behavior are those which involve action, such as "Joe pointed to correct items rather than naming them" or "Joe kicked the chair leg repeatedly throughout the ten-minute subtest," as opposed to Inferences which might be stated as "Joe did not know the labels for common household items," or "Joe was tense throughout the ten-minute subtest."

INTERPRETATION OF INFERENTIAL STATEMENTS

When the examiner states Inferences, the teacher must check those Inferences against the weight of the supportive evidence and against previous experience with the same examiner. Since the accuracy of Inferences is dependent upon the training and experience of the examiner, which the teacher is in no position to judge, the teacher needs some method of attempting to validate Inferences. The teacher usually will wish to do so when the report lacks Information statements, when Inferences appear to go beyond the evidence of Information statements, or when Inferences appear to contradict test scores.

Lack of Information

If the teacher receives only the examiner's interpretations and recommendations without test scores or behavioral observations, she may question the accuracy of Inferences which do not agree with her own experience with the student. In such case, she should request the original test record sheets. If the examiner is willing to supply them, the test records considered with the report may answer the teacher's questions. If not, or if the examiner does not provide the record sheets, the teacher should request a conference with the examiner.

If the examiner's Inferences do not accord with the teacher's experience with a student, it is not enough for the teacher to say so and dismiss the report. Instead she should examine the responses to test items. She may find that the examiner's statement that Bill is far below average in verbal problem-solving is well documented despite her observation that Bill is highly verbal and always the first to raise his hand to answer a question. It is precisely this type of hidden deficit that may be revealed by standardized testing, and it is important that the teacher remain open to new data about a student.

There is a difference, however, between being open to new Information and being willing to accept Inferences without Information. The teacher is justified in requesting documentation for Inferential statements contained in reports.

Statements Beyond Information

If scores and test behavior are included in the report yet Inferential statements appear to be stronger than the evidence warrants, the teacher is also justified in requesting documentation. The usual explanation for such an occurrence is that the examiner had access to data which he did not compile himself. Sometimes, a student has had prior school district testing which the teacher has not seen. In other cases, a student has been evaluated at a community clinic without the teacher's knowledge.

If such reports are available to the examiner but not to the teacher, the result can be apparent discrepancies between the examiner's data and his Inferences. A good examiner will draw his Inferences from all available

The Teacher's Role in Interpretation of Reports

Information, and he would be wrong to disregard prior testing. But if such testing is not mentioned, the teacher cannot evaluate the Inferences. The teacher should request a conference with the examiner to discuss the basis for any statements which are not supported by the reported test data.

Statements Contradicting Scores

The Inferences which are usually most troublesome to teachers in reading reports are those which appear to contradict the reported scores. An examiner may report, for example, that verbal skills are strong, yet the teacher notes that three out of five verbal scores were far below the mean for other subtests. There are two possible explanations for such an occurrence.

The basis for inferring strengths might be the quality, as opposed to the quantity, of the responses. For example, it sometimes happens that because of test anxiety a student may miss easy items on the standardized test but respond correctly to much more difficult items. He will be penalized in scoring, but the level of his accurate responses will indicate his ability on the dimension being measured. The examiner bases his interpretation upon the individual responses, not just the overall score.

Another explanation may lie in the examiner's consideration of test behavior or situational problems during testing. The examiner may be able to say, for example, that visual-motor integration skills are well within normal limits, even though scores on three out of five performance items are significantly lowered. The student may have lost points because he did not look at the model, overdeliberated, or waited for examiner aid. If the examiner is satisfied that the items which were completed demonstrated adequate skills, the lowered score can be explained by the inappropriate test behavior.

In a comprehensive report, the examiner should include statements which reconcile test behavior with test scores so that the interpretation is clear. If this has not been done, a phone call or conference can clarify the Inference.

INTERPRETATION OF JUDGMENTAL STATEMENTS

Because recommendations which evolve from evaluation are the purpose of referral, Judgments about actions to be taken are the most important statements in the report. They are also the most difficult to interpret, since they are often far removed from fact. In a well-reasoned report, the Judgments flow from Inferences, which flow from Information; and there is a consistent, logical progression. In a less well-organized or overly brief report, Information or Inferences may be misplaced or omitted.

If Information is missing, it can be requested as suggested above. When

Inferences are not presented, however, it is more difficult for the teacher to isolate the source of discrepancy. But missing Inferences are not the only problem with interpretation of Judgments. The more common problem seems to be that recommendations are not stated in instructional terms.

Lack of Inferences

If a teacher receives only test data and recommendations, her problem is one of organization. She has the task of determining which test scores are related, and placing scores in groups on the basis of different kinds of relationships. Test behavior must also be organized to determine how the child's approach to tasks bears upon the recommendations.

The teacher will know that Inferences are missing if she does not find statements such as "Jack is functioning intellectually in the low-average range despite scattered scores in the borderline range" or "Pam is limited academically by fine-motor skills three years below her mental age." Such Inferences should support the action the examiner recommends. If they are missing, it is a formidable task to supply them.

The difficulty of the task is, though, only one reason to avoid leaving this responsibility to the reader of the report. Because Inferences must be drawn from the interaction of the demands of the task, the student's problem solving approaches and the situational conditions, it is essential that the person who states Inferences has observed the child throughout the testing session. For example, the same low score earned by two different students on a timed subtest such as the Coding section of the Wechsler Intelligence Scale for Children (Wechsler, 1974) must be interpreted differently if one student went right to work on the task, maintained attention, and worked continuously throughout the time limits, while the second child dropped his pencil once, looked around the room twice, and paused for several seconds within the time limits. The examiner is able to take such behaviors into account when drawing Inferences; one who was not present cannot evaluate the total test behavior even with extensive notes.

The burden or organizing Information in order to draw Inferences rests, then, upon the examiner so the teacher need not take that responsibility upon herself. If a report does not contain them, a teacher is justified in requesting summary statements about the student's strengths and weaknesses so that they can be considered in relation to the recommendation.

Omission of Procedures

A common complaint of teachers who refer students for testing is that the report merely identifies the problem areas but does not tell the teacher how to instruct the child. For example, the recommendation "Lisa's visual deficits and relative auditory strengths should be considered in designing reading instruction" leaves many questions for the teacher. Does this mean that she needs a strong phonics approach? If so, does she require a synthetics phonics method? Which series could she use? Which supplementary material? Should she receive instruction on tapes? Can she use worksheets?

A different type of recommendation—"Joe's motivational problems require a behavior intervention program which should be coordinated between his classroom and his home"—elicits just as many questions. Should he be placed on a contract? How about a daily report card with good work to be rewarded at home? What will he consider a reward? How can the parents best be involved? What are the priority behaviors to be targeted for change?

There may be a number of reasons why recommendations in reports are not stated in step-by-step procedural terms. One reason is that many training programs for school psychologists and counselors do not include intensive coursework in instructional methods and materials. Consequently, some examiners are not well enough acquainted with the possible options to be able to suggest specific instructional practices.

Even if the examiner is a former classroom teacher, suggestions for implementation may not be included for another reason—teachers do not always react favorably when examiners offer specific plans or programs. If the examiner makes recommendations so specific that they can be followed in cookbook fashion, many teachers react negatively to their limited involvement in the planning as they feel that their role is being usurped. If detailed procedures contain one or two suggestions which could not be implemented in a specific classroom because of space or materials limitations, a teacher may dismiss the entire package as "impractical." If the examiner suggests ways to individualize instruction in several academic areas, a teacher may protest that time pressures and 30 other students make implementation impossible. Such responses by teachers are understandable, but they lead to a dilemma on the part of the examiner who may be able to offer specific suggestions but has learned from experience that some teachers do not welcome instructional recommendations.

If a teacher prefers to design her own program for implementing recommendations involving classroom instruction, she will probably find that the general recommendations usually found in reports will suffice for her purposes. She may have access to curriculum specialists, a materials retrieval center, or special education teachers who could help her with modification of procedures or materials.

If a teacher genuinely welcomes specific suggestions for instruction or nonacademic intervention, she would be wise to ask for detailed recommendations when she forwards the referral questions. If detailed procedures are not then provided, she should request a conference with the examiner so that

Instructional Planning for Exceptional Children

she can ask questions about possible alternative ways to implement the recommendations. She will nearly always obtain useful ideas from such an exchange, and the examiner may be more willing to offer specific suggestions the next time one of her students is evaluated.

It is part of the teacher's role to communicate to an examiner what she hopes to gain from the referral. The examiner, the student, and the teacher will all profit from such a frank statement of expectations.

TEACHER'S ATTITUDE TOWARD INTERPRETATION OF REPORTS

A teacher is required to make many decisions about the instruction of each student assigned to her. In some cases, measurement of the student's behaviors will help her to make those decisions. If behaviors or conditions which are interfering with response to instruction can be identified by referral to diagnostic specialists, both the teacher and the student will benefit. The teacher's orientation toward the referral process and the inplementation of recommendations is crucial. To obtain the greatest benefit from the referral process, a teacher might consider adopting the following points of view.

1. Accept the Psychometric Orientation

When a teacher decides that she cannot answer her instructional questions about a student through classroom procedures and she refers the student for testing, she makes certain commitments to the psychometric approach. She must orient her thinking toward the comparison of that child with other children. This type of comparison in considered to be inappropriate by some teachers, who prefer to judge a student against absolute standards rather than norms. But the teacher cannot have it both ways. She cannot at the same time obtain the information she requires from standardized tests and choose to ignore the normative data.

Once the psychometric approach has been taken, test scores cannot be disregarded if the examiner considers them valid. Although it may be tempting for a teacher to do so, she is not justified in permitting her subjective appraisal of the student to supersede test data; instead, the two views of the student should be reconciled.

2. Consider Yourself a Member of a Team

When differing views of a student must be reconciled, it is important that the teacher feel free to confer with the examiner, the principal, and other professional personnel who work with the student. Only if members of the team view themselves as co-professionals—each with unique but equal skills to offer—can they disagree constructively or resolve apparent differences about courses of action.

Respect for the expertise of a fellow professional sometimes comes more readily to a teacher than does respect for her own expertise. Some teachers may defer to the decisions of a psychologist, for example, out of awe at the mystique of specialized knowledge which teachers do not have, without recognizing the value of their own understanding of the learning process and their access to unlimited samples of the student's behavior. Women teachers may defer to fellow professionals who are men, because acculturation has led them to consider the male voice as the voice of authority. Such orientations are not compatible with a team concept.

At the other extreme, some teachers may consider that they are the only ones who can make decisions about students assigned to them. Too many examiners have had the experience of accepting a referral from a teacher, testing, writing a report and recommendations, only to learn that the teacher has not implemented any of the examiner's suggestions nor requested a conference with the examiner to discuss any areas of disagreement. This type of passive rejection of the work of a fellow professional is seriously damaging to the referral process and unfair to the student who deserves to have all available information considered before decisions are made about him.

3. Respect Confidentiality of Reports

When a teacher considers herself a professional team member, she recognizes that test scores, task behaviors, summaries of functioning levels, and statements about the student's needs are appropriately discussed only with members of the team or with the student's parents. Statements drawn from reports are not shared casually in the teacher's lounge.

In addition to the responsibility to avoid verbal publication of test findings, a teacher is expected to exercise care over the disposition of the written report. Placing a report among the student's graphs or charts may permit a volunteer parent aide to gain access to it. Leaving a report exposed upon a desk may mean that another student will see test scores or summary statements. Inadvertent exposure to aides, peers, or nonprofessional school staff may mean that a student's status will be inappropriately discussed.

4. Maintain Realistic Expectations.

Even though a teacher constructs sound referral questions and the examiner conducts a comprehensive assessment, it is too much to expect that instructional problems can always be solved by referral. For stubborn instructional dilemmas, testing will prove less useful than systematic trial teaching over time; for daily programming, the teacher's own assessment is essential to answer questions of materials selection, sequencing, and pace. The availability of diagnostic specialists does not limit the teacher's responsibility for instructional decisions. Referral to specialists is merely one possible recourse available to the classroom teacher who recognizes her final responsibility for establishing instructional objectives and implementing individualized programs to meet those objectives.

REFERENCES

Adamson, G., Shrago, M., & Van Etten, G. *Basic educational skills inventory.* Olathe, KS: Select-Ed, 1972.

Arthur, G. *The Arthur adaptation of the Leiter International Performance Scale.* Washington, DC: Psychological Service Center Press, 1952.

Ayres, J. *Southern California perceptual-motor tests.* Los Angeles: Western Psychological Services, 1968.

Beery, K., & Buktenica, N. *Developmental test of visual-motor integration.* Chicago, IL: Follett, 1967.

Bender, L. *Bender visual-motor Gestalt test for children.* New York: American Orthopsychiatric Association, 1938.

Colarusso, R., & Hammill, D. *Motor-free visual perception test.* San Rafael, CA: Academic Therapy, 1972.

Connolly, A., Nachtman, W., & Pritchett, E. *Keymath diagnostic arithmetic test.* Circle Pines, MN: American Guidance Service, 1971.

Dunn, L., & Markwardt, F. *Peabody individual achievement test.* Circle Pines, MN: American Gudiance Service, 1970.

Durrell, D. D. *Durrell analysis of reading difficulty.* New York: Harcourt, Brace & World, 1955.

Gates, A., & McKillop, A. *Reading diagnostic tests.* New York: Teachers College Press, 1962.

Goldman, R., Fristoe, M., & Woodcock, R. *Diagnostic auditory discrimination test.* Circle Pines, MN: American Guidance Service, 1974.

Harris, D. B. *Goodenough-Harris drawing test.* New York: Harcourt Brace Jovanovich, 1963.

Hiskey, M. S. *Nebraska test of learning aptitude.* Lincoln, NE: Marshall S. Hiskey, 1966.

Jastak, J. F., & Jastak, S. R., *Wide range achievement test.* Wilmington, DE: Guidance Associates, 1965.

Kirk, S., McCarthy, J., & Kirk, W. *Illinois test of psycholinguistic abilities.* Urbana, IL: University of Illinois Press, 1968.

Leiter, R. G. *Leiter international performance scale.* Santa Barbara, CA: Santa Barbara State College Press, 1940.

McCracken, R. A. *Standard reading inventory.* Klamath Falls, OR: Klamath Printing Company, 1966.

Moran, M. R. Nine steps to the diagnostic-prescriptive process in the classroom. *Focus on Exceptional Children,* 1975, 6, 1-14.

Murray, H. A. *Thematic apperception test.* Cambridge, MA: Harvard University Press, 1943.

Roach, E. G., & Kephart, N. C. *Purdue perceptual survey rating scale.* Columbus, OH: Charles E. Merrill, 1966.

Rorschach, L. G. *Rorschach psychodiagnostic plates.* New York: Grune & Stratton, 1954.

Silvaroli, N. *Classroom reading inventory.* Dubuque, IA: W. C. Brown Company, 1973.

Sloan, W. *Lincoln-Oseretsky motor development scale.* Chicago, IL: Stoelting, 1954.

Spache, G. *Diagnostic reading scales.* Monterey, CA: McGraw-Hill, 1963.

Templin, M., & Darley, F. *The Templin-Darley tests of articulation.* Iowa City, IA: Bureau of Educational Research and Service, State University of Iowa, 1960.

Terman, L. M., & Merrill, M. A. *Stanford-Binet intelligence scale.* Boston, MA: Houghton-Mifflin, 1973.

Wechsler, D. *Wechsler intelligence scale for children*—revised. New York: Psychological Corporation, 1974.

Morse's description of the helping teacher's role focuses on an approach to solving problems with children. Although the article does not present techniques on instructional planning, it is highly relevant to the instructional mission of special education teachers in that a prerequisite of effective instructional planning is to establish a climate conducive to learning, for the student, and to teaching, for the teacher. Morse's "crisis teacher" concept has been demonstrated over the years as an effective approach. The suggestions in the article, moreover, are not limited to teachers who have been assigned to "crisis teacher" roles; the techniques are applicable to all teachers and to all exceptional children.

The Helping Teacher/Crisis Teacher Concept

William C. Morse, *University of Michigan*

To understand the fundamental purpose of any special education program, it is necessary to examine the nature of its origin. Who stimulated its development? What problems was it designed to solve? Typical new programs come from state department offices or designated committees.

The crisis teacher idea was conceived by a staff of elementary teachers in a high problem incidence school during a series of case conferences being held with a consultant. The purpose was simple: to provide a more adequate educational program for pupils with socioemotional problems through adding conjoint assistance to the regular classroom.

DEVELOPMENT

As the group examined the classroom dilemma, they came to the following conclusions: While case conferences and consultation had a function, something more was needed to produce change. Individualized, external therapy helped some but often left the classroom behavior virtually untouched. The morale and productivity of a teacher depended upon finding more effective ways to cope with the most difficult children. The impact of a few pupils on the learning climate and the experiences of peers could be devastating. The typical "discipline" route, whether administrated by teacher or administrator, was seldom a corrective influence. Somehow the problem behavior had to be case in a new format to encourage social learning rather than punishment.

At this point in time, the system proposed a first special class for the emotionally disturbed to deal with the situation. This group of teachers resisted nominating candidates based upon three considerations. First, they could not imagine how a teacher could conduct a class of "ten of these." It would be utter chaos. Second, most of the children they were concerned about and felt responsible for were not a problem one hundred percent of the time. Third, given one class of ten for a large population, these teachers were too realistic to see this as any relief. At best, their whole school might have two places in such a class. Parenthetically, it is interesting that periodic examination of current statistics by the Michigan Association for Emotionally Disturbed Children indicates that less than a third of the disturbed children are getting help. The national overall figure for special education at best is about 50%. Thus, these teachers were realistic about the promise of special education through classes.

This led to an examination of the myth of the grade level classroom where children were supposed to fit. There is a fantasy that one teaches the "fourth grade" or "fifth grade," and teachers will sometimes protest inability to move to a new level which they cannot possibly teach. After a cursory psychological examination of the variance in ability, achievement, motivation, and social development in the various classes, it became only too evident that we never did away with one-room schools. The fact is, as any teacher knows, there are 26 classrooms if there are 26 children; but to make 26 highly appropriate and productive classrooms coalesce in one room reminds one of the trials of Job. The marvelous adaptability of most of the 26 growing, immature human organisms and one mature one usually keeps the classroom operation from disintegrating.

Perhaps the real reason the classroom can survive at all lies in the affinity of most children and adults as social beings. Associating with one's kind seems to gratify a certain social hunger. The teachers delineated three aspects to the group as a setting for learning.

1. Much of the learning which takes place is really individual but perforce takes place in the presence of classroom peers. This generates a great deal of comparison with how others are doing and injects a whole

Instructional Planning for Exceptional Children

    substrata of emotional life even when not cultivated by the teacher.
 2. One can learn from peers who, in various ways, help one understand. In the classroom of 26, each pupil has the potential of one/twenty-sixth of the adult and assistance from 25 peers, though help from the latter sometimes gets categorized as cheating.
 3. There are some things one cannot learn without social intercourse; these include social skills and the proper practice of much affective life. Adults are basically suspicious of the power of group life since the adult, as a minority, finds it difficult to coerce, dominate, or even lead the group. But there is always contagion, imitation, formulation of group roles, and the emergence of group codes on the overt or covert level.

For the most part, teachers are group workers who unfortunately have had little help in the utilization of groups in learning. The solution implied by the new class for disturbed children was simple—regroup the deviant ones in smaller arrangements called special classes. If we take the percentage of special children at 10%, we would remove 2.4 children and leave the rest called "normals" for the regular teacher.

In their seminars, the teachers sought another solution. As long as we teach children in large groups with a minimum of teacher input per child, there will be some children who cannot function effectively at certain times. The teacher of the large group cannot be expected to handle everything put into a given classroom. The particular pupil has a right to a greater time and expertise investment at times of crisis. The other class members have a right to their fair share of the regular teacher's investment. The teacher has a right to respite care and conjoint efforts for the child in distress. And all of this should take place as a natural education assistance process without labels, punishment, or implications of failure.

The Plan

These realizations began a phase of more creative discussion. What really would help the regular classroom to become a more adequate learning environment? The term "mainstreaming" had not been invented in 1960, but these teachers focused on the essence of that process by listing their observations concerning the disturbed-disturbing child. Several propositions were advanced.

 1. Even the very disturbed child is not "all disturbed all the time," meaning there are only certain periods when the disturbed pupil cannot function in the larger group setting. These periods may be at certain regular times or in the press of a crisis. But most of the time

The Helping Teacher/Crisis Teacher Concept

the disturbed child can benefit and fit into the regular class.
2. What is needed is direct assistance. Consultation is one thing, but real help is another. Psychologists and the like might offer advice, but they did not know what it was like to try to administer a classroom with these kids in the room.
3. In the "olden days" the principal took over these children, talking to them and tutoring them. The role of the contemporary administrator as middle management leaves very little time for more than a quick once over. The help these teachers wanted should be always available, yet the principal is often otherwise occupied or at meetings.
4. A repressive "disciplinary" approach does not work. Sending a child to the office, or some other exclusion, seldom helped the youngster.
5. The direct service helping person should be omnipresent, not itinerant, and be trained as a teacher, but a special teacher. The helping person should be able to respond to the disturbed child in crisis but be able to help with both academic and emotional problems for all children. Many of the disturbed youngsters needed direct counseling help with their self-concept, but just as many could find growth through therapeutic (as contrasted to academic) tutoring.
6. There were times when the "helping teacher" could assist best by coming in and taking over the classroom while the regular teacher worked through a phase of a problem with a youngster.
7. Help should be based upon the reality of how the child was able to cope with the classroom, and not on categories, labels, or diagnostic criterion. It was pointed out that many normal children need help during a crisis in the classroom or in their lives, just as the chronic and severely variant youngster does.

What these teachers asked for in essence was an **overgroup** person who would deal with di_ urbance regardless of the manifestation. These teachers requested an educator, not a clinician, to give the emergency help when needed. There was even a willingness by each teacher to take an extra pupil or two in order to save the cost of the new type of special teacher. To have help available when it was needed was seen as the best total assistance. In 1961, the crisis/helping teacher became one method of delivery of special education services recognized by the state code.

MIDDLE PHASE

Soon after the program got underway, "crisis teacher" became "helping teacher." No school felt comfortable having a crisis environment, although one way of getting this resource in the early days was to compete with other schools in documenting the highest problem index! As it happened, the first helping teachers were not certified special educators for the disturbed. They were "naturals" with an unusual combination of common sense and green thumb empathy which enabled them to become exemplary disseminators of service and innovators in practice. While the design had merit, more credit was due to the skill of the first helping teachers than to the format. The classroom where they worked contained resources for pupils and teachers. A divided glassed-in corner enabled private individual conversations to take place while the other children were working on self-sustaining activities in the larger section. The unusual talent of the early crisis teachers masked the difficulties inherent in the new role. As the function became institutionalized and legitimized as special education, it became evident that no formal program design is a substitute for individual capability. Nor is there any substitute for cultivating faculty interest in any school starting such a program. Unless the added teacher role is seen as essential, it will remain isolated in the school milieu.

As the idea of the helping teacher matured and spread, a wide range of individual practice emerged. Some of this variation would be under the heading of "best use of unique self-attributes and style," while other variations represented escape into single functions such as academic tutoring or play therapy. The service concentration was on the social and emotional disturbance based on behavior in the school setting. Studies indicated that the range of those who became "regulars" for sustained help ranged from 2 in one school to 24 in another, out of some 350 pupils. The crisis ranged from 4 to 600 per year in various schools.

First Referrals

An eclectic core makes up the role of the helping teacher. Like all mental health services, the task is never ending. The more help available, the higher the goals. Needs outstrip resources. The basic training required by the state was certification as a teacher for the emotionally disturbed. At first children were referred by teachers or administrators on the basis that the pupil could not cope with the classroom situation (acting out or academic tasks) or appeared to be in need of encouragement and support (the low self-esteem and depressed types). The diagnostic services of the school psychologists and school social worker were employed to provide diagnostic information, family involvement, and individual counseling as the need became evident. Parents were informed of the availability of the service and were invited to seek consultation or particular help for their child. In rare instances, children came on their own. For example, a group of girls petitioned for some meetings like the "bad boys" were having. They wanted sessions to talk over their problems, too.

Basic Approach

The basic approach is psychoeducational, with an interest in the whole of the child's life in and out of school. The diagnostic "can of worms" has been discussed at length elsewhere (Morse, 1974); it can be said here that, in place of a categorical emphasis, a grid of dimensions concentrated on the present functioning in the various aspects of the affective, cognitive, and motor domains. Explanatory etiological materials were put to the service of understanding the child's current status. The assets and resources of the individual and his life space were compiled. These in turn led to the formulation of immediate and long-term goals with appropriate educational interventions. The evaluation and replanning phase constituted the final aspect. The focus was on resolving the child's problem in whatever way was most feasible. In addition to traditional efforts, the use of "big brothers" for identification, peer tutoring, group activities, and family support are illustrative.

The psychodynamic and behavior modification approaches were entertained since the system was not theory bound. Intervention choice is a consequence of diagnosing the problem and available resources, with an emphasis on eclectic thinking (Cheney & Morse, 1972). The resolution might include a detailed tutorial sequence or psychotherapy or both, but in every case alleviating the classroom situation received primary attention. Stiver (1974) studied the manifold ways of helping teachers, based upon a modification of Catterall's taxonomy (1970). He found the teachers dealt with all types of problems: socioemotional, academic, classroom behavior, academic motivation, peer problems, learning disabled, and pre-delinquent. It was clear that most helping teachers used techniques which were an extension of regular educational procedures, with an emphasis on support and encouragement. Some employed play therapy while others emphasized the academic approach, one hopes on the basis of differential diagnosis. However, the match between the intervention and the indicated problem was not always clear. Gabriel and Sarnecki (1969) found the clientele mostly disruptive and the attention to parent involvement high.

Basic Orientation

The basic orientation was the contemporary life space of the child rather than a case history-historical emphasis. The point of beginning focused on what is going on in school—"You look sad," "You got upset, and we should see what we can figure out about it." For most children adequate diagnostic information to start work was available from observation and data in the life space, the child's reality. The everyday things which happened or conditions which were evident served as the point of departure. Often there was already more information than one knew how to utilize. A Rorschach to attest the anger, a children's apperception test to discover depression, a self-esteem inventory to reveal despair—these are not necessary. The problems were known, but solutions were elusive. Show and tell, stories and pictures, crumbled assignments, social role evidence, authority hostility—do we always need tests? On the other hand, there were always certain children whose natures no one could fathom. Sometimes what appeared to be a clear and simple situation turned complex. More complete diagnosis then became essential to provide reasonable intervention plans. The diagnostician was asked first to observe, to talk to the regular and helping teacher, and then to be selective in formal assessment to answer particular questions. Social workers had the function of more intensive work with the family situation. On the basis of both diagnostic and pragmatic experience, referrals to more specialized aid such as the special class, group activity, intensive individual or family therapy, tutoring, or Big Brothers might be discussed with the parents. If the evidence indicated that outpatient, day school, or inpatient care was an option, this too would be brought into the picture.

LIFE SPACE INTERVIEWING

The basic mediating tool for dealing with affective problems was Life Space Interviewing (Long, Morse & Newman, 1976), which differs from most techniques in flexibility and is designed to fit work in an action setting. Life Space Interviewing also provides "diagnosis on the hoof," because it leads to continual reevaluation of strategies. The interview was used as a functional way to deal with crises or the sustained problems. While considerable time would be devoted to individual pupils, group interviews would be the mode chosen when the problem involved two or several youngsters. When it came to interventions appropriate for the school environment, how a medium was used—rather than what the medium was—formed the basis of differential help to children. Reading therapy is more than remedial reading, and both are school appropriate. Children have art class, but noninterpreted self, family, and free drawing might assist in externalization of a problem. Recess equals play, and play therapy is a normal extension. Teachers talk a lot to children, with counseling an extension. Children form groups for their activities, and the school can design more specialized types of groups.

Interventions

The first question was always how to use a school medium as an intervention. The substance of this point of view has been described at length (Cheney & Morse, 1972). The way to improve a child's self-esteem might be to concentrate on tutoring in a skill, to assist in finding a friend, to unwind some paraprofessional's involvement during this phase is vital. He/she must understand what the objectives are for a certain child, as well as the activities proposed to meet those objectives.

At this time, persons responsible for the student begin to employ the means to reach the goals and objectives stipulated in the IEP. The professional and paraprofessional work together closely in planning the instructional program for the services they will be providing in the special education program. The paraprofessional should at this time ask any unanswered questions regarding the child's program, and should offer suggestions.

Carrying Out the Instructional Program. In carrying out the total instructional program for the exceptional child as specified on the IEP, the paraprofessional's role is that of a team member who works with the special education teacher. Instructional responsibilities for the paraprofessional center on follow-up or reinforcement activities, while initial concept instruction involving the presentation of new lessons or tasks is the responsibility of the teacher. The teacher should plan cooperatively with the paraprofessional in assigning responsibilities to this person. The teacher may wish to work with individual pupils or small groups on particular learning problems while the paraprofessional helps other class members, listens to reading, or the like. In turn, paraprofessionals might tutor individual children or work with groups, using materials and techniques chosen or designed by the teacher.

Implementation of the full service mandate could be difficult for some small, rural areas/districts. In such areas, where a professional serves a large geographic area, the paraprofessional can provide continuous instruction to the exceptional child under the supervision/consultation of the professional, who would work with him/her and the child at least twice a week. The paraprofessional could be assigned to a teacher or the principal in a small elementary or secondary school and follow through with the program arranged by the itinerant staff. Thus, a child who may require such ancillary services as speech, physical therapy, or occupational therapy can receive the benefits of consistent training sessions.

Certain specialized situations are apparent in which the use of a paraprofessional can greatly enhance the program for the exceptional child. For example, a paraprofessional could assist in transportation of a severely multiply handicapped child, in which an adult in addition to the driver is recommended to ride along to supervise and give needed attention to the child, who may have serious behavioral and physical problems. The paraprofessional also could begin some of the programming for the child during the bus ride, by working on such skills as behavior management, communication, or socialization. The ride to and from school for some children often takes an hour or more, and facilitating the educational program in this manner may enable provision of the six-hour school day requirements for certain school districts.

Another specialized setting in which paraprofessionals can be effectively used is in mainstreaming exceptional children into regular education programs. PL 94-142 mandates the least restrictive environment for handicapped children, and the percent of time to be spent in a regular education program must be stated on the IEP. Utilization of the special education paraprofessional in mainstreaming aids this process. He/she can provide tutorial assistance to the exceptional child who is served part-time in the regular education program, or by freeing regular class teachers to spend more time with the mainstreamed students.

Evaluation of the Instructional Program. A significant component of the IEP process is evaluating the child's individual plan. PL 94-142 requires that the IEP be reviewed and updated periodically. The teacher and the paraprofessional can work together in monitoring the day-to-day progress of student growth toward the short-term objectives of the IEP. Paraprofessionals can provide input to the teacher on tasks in which they have been involved in implementing, and can recommend program change. Reassessment of the total instructional program thus can be carried out in less time and with fewer problems.

SUMMARY

The IEP process involves more than a written plan for a child. The written aspect is just one phase of the total programming for exceptional students. The entire program, if it is to be workable, requires team effort. The trained special education paraprofessional, as a member of the educational team for an exceptional child, can be involved appropriately in all phases of the IEP process.

If the goal of an individualized plan for each exceptional child is to be realized, a differentiated plan must be operationalized. The trained paraprofessional can be the link between quality educational programming and individualization of services.

Part 3
Evaluation

Richard J. Whelan, *University of Kansas Medical Center*

Evaluation is a set of observable, sequential procedures which are used to determine if a planned program is functioning below, at, or above expectations. Proper application of evaluation procedures enables detection of gaps between what is and what should be. These gaps may not be negative, in that a program can exceed planned objectives—a positive gap. The word *program* can be used to refer to an administrative group, an entire classroom, or a piece of instructional material used with only one child. Program evaluation is a varying and critical responsibility for all educators who arrange means to ends. The classroom teacher, the supervisor, and the administrator cannot avoid evaluation. They can only determine to do it well or poorly. Doing it poorly victimizes children; doing it well benefits children.

In a sense, this book is paradoxical in devoting a separate, distinct portion to evaluation. After all, assessment is an integral part of evaluation. And instructional planning should not be done without concurrent planning for evaluating the impact of instruction. Why then have a separate section on evaluation? The reason becomes obvious: It is far easier to write about evaluation than to do it. It is far easier to point to the need for program evaluation than to conduct the evaluation. The doing requires learning an identifiable set of skills associated with evaluation planning and implementation. These skills must be mastered before they can be applied appropriately. The individuals contributing to this part of the book have mastered evaluation skills. More importantly, they have applied them in the real world of children, teaching, and learning. Their contributions to this book contain enough information to enable acquisition of evaluation skills. These skills will not be learned by one, two, or even more readings of the content. Rather, their acquisition will require intensive analysis and synthesis of the written material and opportunities for application to programs. Acquisition takes time and

Instructional Planning for Exceptional Children

hard work, but the payoff for children far outweighs the difficulty in learning and applying new knowledge.

Educators are responsible for arranging means to attain desirable ends. Evaluation assists in identifying the extent to which the ends are met, not met, or exceeded. Used properly, evaluation also assists educators in evaluating if ends are desirable and realistic. Little good is derived if a child achieves an end (objective or goal) that is not desirable and realistic, and it may even be debilitating in that it represents time lost in helping the child acquire important skills.

Evaluation permeates all aspects of instructional planning. "How do I evaluate this?" is a question that must be asked during goal formulation, during instructional activities, and during the application of what is learned in other situations. The selections in the following section enable educators to help find the critical answers to evaluation questions.

The selection by Brinkerhoff is especially timely in that the requirements of PL 94-142 are considered as essential to the foundation of a program evaluation strategy. The Discrepancy Evaluation Model (DEM) has been found to be useful in evaluating personnel preparation programs, as well as service programs for exceptional children. The DEM is a flexible strategy for evaluation. It can be applied to a wide variety of activities including administrative arrangements, workshops, and classrooms.

Brinkerhoff is a practitioner of program evaluation. He has brought together those experiences and a logical approach to evaluation design, so the reader, through careful study, can begin the important task of evaluating programs.

Evaluating Full Service Special Education Programs

Robert O. Brinkerhoff, *University of Virginia*

The past decade has seen a dramatic increase in the demand for public accountability of public programs and, hence, a demand for program evaluation. The new program mandate of PL 94-142 represents a call for even greater attention to program evaluation requirements, perhaps more stringent than those of other educational or social service programs.

These requirements stem both from law and from customary social expectations. In general, the public demands to know how its tax dollars are spent, and with what effect; and public schools often are foremost in the public's vision. PL 94-142, in its requirement that all handicapped individuals must be provided publicly funded education and related services, creates additional demands for program evaluation, to the extent that the evaluation will document legal compliance, in addition to assessing the effectiveness of educational efforts.

As many professional educators are aware—sometimes painfully—there is an historical trend toward increasing expectations for the institution of public education. Simply put, the schools are expected to fulfill an increasing range of services. The public school is unique, too, in that it often is the setting in which the symptoms of social ills and problems erupt into public awareness, and at the same time is the institution to which the public turns for a cure to these ills. The emergence of legally mandated full service special education programs seems to fit this pattern, and the program evaluations attached to these programs will have to be sensitive to the public's rising expectations.

PL 94-142 represents a promise to the public that all handicapped persons shall be educated. Despite its stature as statute, however, the promise is vague and, therefore, may be hard to keep. The programs developed to make good this promise will, necessarily, further define the meaning, limitations, and expectations of that promise, and therein lies the rub. Detractors of the new public law contend, among other things, that the law is premature in that it outstrips our technology and, therefore, our ability to comply. They may be right in their contention but probably are wrong in their conclusion. Most likely, it is right to move ahead and wrong not to do so. In any case, the law is fact and we *will* move ahead.

That the definition of these legally mandated programs will change and develop over time is a mixed blessing for program evaluation. Because the programs are new, or will represent new programmatic requirements for existing services, evaluation efforts can be planned and considered from the inception of these programs. This is the ideal condition for program evaluation, but such timing rarely has been available. Too often, evaluation has been a hastily constructed, partially planned activity tacked on at the end of a program. We now have an opportunity to do it right, and thereby make the effort dramatically easier and more productive, subsuming it into the normal program development, implementation, and operation processes.

Admittedly, these new programs are full of ambiguity and are based on partially defined and potentially controversial principles and guidelines. Required operating principles such as "least restrictive environment" or "appropriate" education are difficult to define. Qualifications for identifying and prioritizing clientele are elusive; treatment options may be marginal; and many options are theoretically arguable. Costs are unsure. None of these problems translates to a good reason why programs should not be set in motion, but all represent elements which must be considered carefully in program evaluation.

Evaluation must expect to define initial—perhaps tentative, perhaps arbitrary—standards for many areas of program operation and outcomes. It must expect to present these standards in readily understandable language and format and must provide for their change and revision. It must expect to document the reasons underlying these changing expectations. It must recognize and help others recognize that education is a world of tentative technology and ambiguous expectations, and that the new full service programs are part of that entity, probably even more nebulous, particularly early in their history. Educational changes are hard to come by, and harder still to document.

TENTATIVE DEFINITION AND SCOPE OF PROGRAM EVALUATION

Figure 1 graphically represents a systematic definition of the rationale and function of any educational program and provides the basis for defining the purpose and scope of program evaluation.

The program pictured in Figure 1 shows that a certain process (called the "treatment program") is to be instituted to select and provide treatment to the subpopulation that, in the eyes of the program's initiators, needs that treatment. Further, if the subpopulation receives that treatment, takes part in the program, some changes will occur in treated members of the subpopulation. The basis for the need and the reason for thereby desiring the treatment derives from the existence of some social problem (such as, "Handicapped persons don't share equally in the nation's prosperity").

The entire range of the figure—A through E—represents the program at the national level, or the program as mandated by PL 94-142. Portions B, C, and D represent the particular program to be initiated by a school district or consortium of districts. That is, the district will identify and select those persons to be treated and organize the needed staff resources (B) to implement the program (C) in order to bring about the program's objectives (D). The local program's evaluation is seen as being concerned with portions B-D and is not concerned with evaluation activities relating to portion A or E in the figure. Thus, the scope of the evaluation is defined so as *not* to require that it demonstrate or validate a need for the program, nor that it demonstrate that the program have some social utility. This author doesn't mean to contend that these issues are irrelevant, but only that they do not belong within the scope of the local program's evaluation responsibilities.

Figure 2 delineates in more detail the responsibilities within the scope of local evaluation. The particular program operations are listed with their concomitant evaluation activities.

The above definition of evaluation does not include functions such as determining program need, nor of diagnosing the particular needs of any given program participant. These, of course, are critical functions and they

Instructional Planning for Exceptional Children

**FIGURE 1
PL 94-142 PROGRAM STRUCTURE**

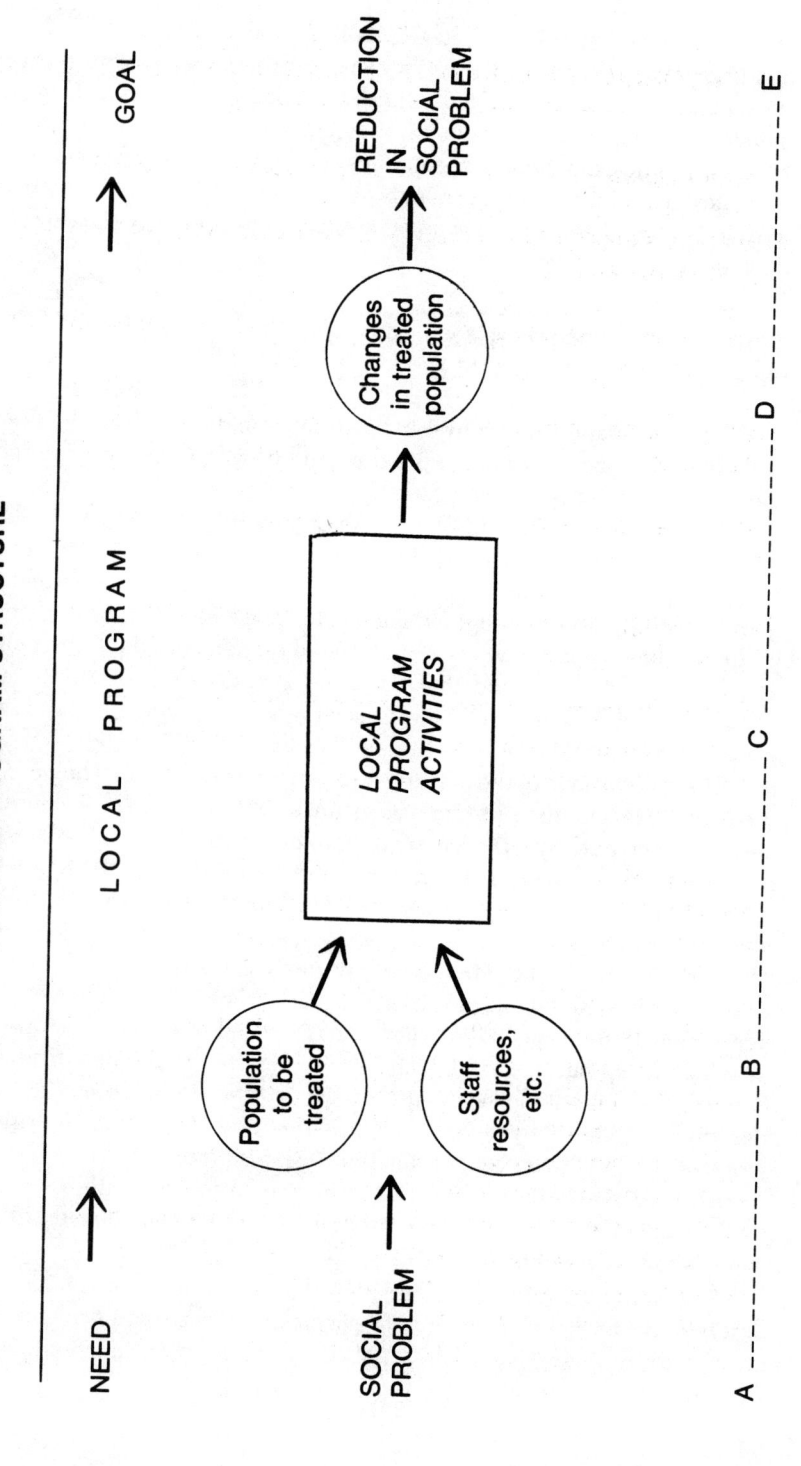

NEED → | LOCAL PROGRAM | GOAL →

SOCIAL PROBLEM → (Population to be treated) → [LOCAL PROGRAM ACTIVITIES] → (Changes in treated population) → REDUCTION IN SOCIAL PROBLEM

(Staff resources, etc.) →

A -------- B -------- C -------- D -------- E

354

FIGURE 2
PROGRAM OPERATIONS/EVALUATION RESPONSIBILITIES

Program Operation	Evaluation Responsibility
↓	↓
Determine standards for operating procedures and goals	Explicate program standards
Organize staff and resources	Document resources actually allocated
Identify and select the treatment population	Document and verify characteristics of treatment population selected
Deliver the treatment program	Document program activities actually delivered
Effect changes in the treated population	Assess changes in the treated population

sometimes are deemed a part of evaluation, but they are not considered to be within the scope of program evaluation as defined and discussed here. Design of the program, determination of its content and structure, and the program's implementation and operation are all a part of program function, and should be distinguished from the evaluation function. Evaluation will be applied *to* these program functions, for the purpose of their documentation, assessment, and improvement.

This basic, if somewhat arbitrary, distinction between *program* and *evaluation* function is critical to a definition of evaluation. Most simply put, evaluation is seen as a function that determines the extent to which the program's standards have become manifest in reality.[1] By this definition, evaluation compares the actual performance of the program to the standards set for the program's operation. This definition is portrayed in Figure 3.

The reader should be careful not to confuse this definition's distinction between program management/operation and evaluation with the fact that in application, the program's management is responsible for carrying out the evaluation. The distinction refers to the function of evaluation as opposed to the function of the program, not to the person who carries out these functions. In many cases—in fact, in the desirable case—the persons (i.e., program

---
[1]This is, essentially, the original definition of the Discrepancy Evaluation Model (Provus, 1971).

FIGURE 3
DEFINITION OF EVALUATION

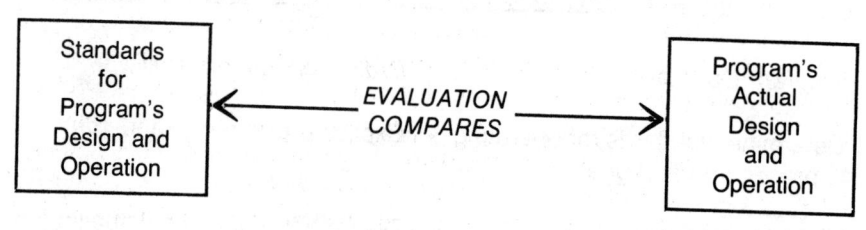

```
┌─────────────┐                              ┌─────────────┐
│  Standards  │                              │  Program's  │
│     for     │      EVALUATION              │   Actual    │
│  Program's  │ ←────COMPARES────→           │   Design    │
│  Design and │                              │     and     │
│  Operation  │                              │  Operation  │
└─────────────┘                              └─────────────┘
```

managers) responsible for implementing the program also are responsible for carrying out the program's evaluation.

Evaluation, then, is an activity that clarifies and explicates the standards for a program, then determines the extent to which the program's actual performance meets these expected standards. Given this definition, evaluation's first task is to document the standards for all phases of the program's operation, making explicit those criteria from within and outside the program against which its performance ought to be compared. The second task of evaluation is to collect information on the program's actual performance in order to document that performance and determine the extent to which it meets the standards set for it.

PURPOSES

Four major purposes for evaluation are proposed:

1. To clarify and communicate the expectations, or standards, for the program;
2. To document operation of the program, particularly those phases of operation requiring legal compliance;
3. To assess impact of the program on its intended recipients; and
4. To provide information to revise and improve the program.

Although all of these purposes are critical, they overlap and are complementary. In the author's view, however, any evaluation of a special education program should be designed so as to serve each; thus, each will be discussed separately.

Purpose 1—Explicate the Standards for the Program

Evaluation is necessarily a comparative act. When one evaluates anything, or makes judgments about something's worth, he or she compares what exists to some standard for that thing.

Suppose, for example, that we wish to determine whether or not the movie *Deep Esophagus* is suitable for viewing by our children. We might determine the extent to which it meets established code ratings, deciding that we will accept only a "G" or "PG" designation. Another alternative available is to be guided by the opinions of other groups, perhaps professional critics, or parents in our neighborhood. Or we might simply go to the movie ourselves, then base a judgment on our own experience. In any case, we hold the particular movie against some standard, or set of standards, and render a judgment (an evaluation). Often, such as is the case when one proclaims a preference or judgment, the standards underlying that judgment are implicit and are brought into focus only at the time the judgment, or evaluation, is made.

In evaluating an educational program, we must have a standard against which to compare the program. Ambiguity and value conflicts, however, may surround definition of standards for educational programs, particularly those springing from response to PL 94-142. These programs will be controversial, as they involve differing social groups, additional costs, educational treatments of marginal effect and debatable theoretical origin, important social goals and vaguely defined guidelines. Adding additional spice to this brew is the observation that our society traditionally holds high expectations for its educational enterprise, yet is increasingly sensitive to education's rising costs.

We cannot fairly evaluate these programs without some reasonable consensus as to their expectations. To this extent, the first purpose of the evaluation takes on a sort of educative mission; it must not only explicate the standards, but communicate them to the public and program staff and participants in an understandable form. All parties need to be informed as to whom the program will serve, what resources and staff will be required, what particular activities will be conducted, and what educational outcomes can reasonably be expected to result. Without these standards, evaluative judgments can and will be made throughout the life of the program based on arbitrary and changing values. Clarification of the program's expectations prior to its operation allows for those expectations themselves to be judged and evaluated without jeopardizing the program's operation.

Evaluation of programs can take two forms, and discriminating one from the other is critical to the integrity of a program, even though both are legitimate. In the one instance, a program may be judged not on what it actually does, but what it sets out to do—its intent, not its actual operation. In the other instance—given that intent has been accepted—a program can be judged on the extent to which it lives up to that intent in its actual operation. Both kinds of evaluation are crucial. Often in practice, however, the distinction between these two kinds of evaluation becomes blurred; and the resulting evaluation is often dysfunctional. An example of this practice may occur when a program is visited by third-party professionals and these evaluators may render negative judgments seemingly on a program's operation—often with devastating results to the staff—when they are in fact judging the program's intent, instead of the faithfulness with which it is carrying out that intent.

Careful and explicit delineation of standards for a program's operation allows for their fair evaluation in the arena of professional and other value judgment prior to judgments about operation of the program. This explication also provides a set of referent and agreed upon standards for actual operation of the program, against which its performance may be compared.

Purpose 2—Document Program Operation

Evaluation must document actual program operation for many reasons. In general, program evaluation attempts to determine whether or not a particular program works. Based on estimates of its effect, one can decide if the program responsible for those effects is worth further support. To do this, a fairly accurate picture of what program in fact took place is needed. Thus, a good deal of an evaluation's effort needs to be directed toward simply documenting the details of the program's actual operation. Because of the inevitable "Murphy's Law"[2] and other maxims pertaining to the best laid plans of mice and men, we can be fairly certain that no educational program will take place exactly as it was planned. The program that takes place—not necessarily the program in the plan, or proposal—is responsible for whatever changes occur. We need to know what that real program was.

Program documentation also must be sensitive to reporting the actual costs of a program. Any benefits accruing to a publicly supported program must be weighed against what it cost to attain those benefits. A dollar spent here is a dollar that cannot be spent there. Thus, a part of the documentation of the program's operation must be dedicated to recording the costs of that operation, both in dollar and other costs, such as staff time and facilities usage.

PL 94-142 programs carry with them an additional documentation need: Localities mounting these programs are required to demonstrate compliance with the law, and in most cases, this law is procedural. That is, the new law requires that these programs plan and carry out certain processes (due process, individual educational planning, etc.); any evaluation of these programs should be expected to document these critical activities, providing data that can demonstrate the extent of compliance.

A final argument for careful process evaluation derives from the developmental nature of all educational programs and, in particular, the ambiguous nature of some aspects of PL 94-142 programs. Much of education is still a sort of "black box"—what really works, and why, is unknown. The more

[2]This "law" states that what can go wrong, will.

knowledge we can gain about what was tried, and with what effects, the more light we shed in that box's murky interior.

A more immediate need for careful process documentation arises from the vague definitions of some aspects of the new law's provisions. The "least restrictive environment," for instance, is difficult to define, and will actually differ from case to case. If and when more specific and generalizable definitions are available, they will stem from actual practice. For this and many other operating characteristics of 94-142 programs, there is no alternative other than trying something in good faith and testing several strategies, both within and among programs. Each of these strategies should be carefully and faithfully documented so none of this valuable experience is lost. The evaluations should tell who was treated, in what environment, by whom, and in what way.

Purpose 3—Assess Program Impact

Several reasons substantiate why the impact of these new programs must be assessed. And, as in the foregoing purpose, these derive from technical, legal, and professional bases. Knowledge of results is, in a sense, the critical end point of program evaluation. Without such knowledge, accountability is incomplete, and systematic revision and improvement of program operations impossible.

Program impact must be defined and assessed at several levels. Impact outcomes can be defined generally in two ways: individual changes and institutional changes. At the total program level, the evaluation should seek definitions for, and assess the impact on, changes in groups of individuals receiving services from the program and changes in the availability of services as a result of program implementation. The evaluation should seek further to determine the differential effect of differing program services and activities. The program may provide successful service to one type of handicap but less successful service to another, for instance; some parent orientation activities may prove more effective than others, and so on.

At the individual level, the evaluation must provide information on the extent to which individual educational goals are achieved. These data should derive directly from individual educational plans and should be collected on a regular interim and final basis. Data deriving from individual goal achievement can, of course, be used in aggregate form to assess impact at more general program levels, as well as for particular program components.

Purpose 4—Facilitate Program Revision

This purpose for program evaluation is discussed last because it overlaps with all the previous purposes. Information collected by the evaluation for the other reasons can and should be used for this fourth major purpose—that of revising the program during and after its operation in order to improve it. This kind of evaluation usually is referred to as *formative* evaluation, and is one of evaluation's most valuable benefits.

In essence, formative evaluation mimics a kind of learning theory, common in all purposeful human behavior. An initial behavior is conceptualized, then tried. On the basis of the results of that effort, another, more refined behavior is attempted; feedback occurs again, and the ensuing behavior is further refined, and so on. Although this cycle of attempt-feedback-knowledge of results-reattempt occurs naturally in individual human behavior, it is not so readily come by in large scale educational programs.

Formative program evaluation must be planned beforehand to optimally benefit revision of the program, and must be amenable to constant revision. Evaluation of this sort determines areas or events in the program's expected sequence of operation at which trouble is likely to occur or critical decisions will be needed, then projects the kind of information that will best resolve that situation, planning to collect and report that information in a timely fashion. Thus, if parents' reaction to a particular orientation procedure in a program is unknown, one might decide to elicit some parent feedback in the early stages of that program component's operation.

Information on individual goal attainment, of course, provides a formative benefit in that it can provide, over time, an estimate of the efficacy of various educational strategies. Other program impact data serve this same function, as these data can be collected both during and at the end of program operation cycles.

Other Criteria

Three additional major criteria relating to implementation should be met by these evaluations:

1. The evaluation should be "staged" to follow growth and development of the program;
2. The evaluation should be designed to be conducted by regular program personnel, with a minimum of outside technical assistance;
3. The program description, standards, evaluation questions, and data collection procedures should be made public.

Staging the Evaluation

Any educational program can be seen to have a sort of "life-cycle."

Evaluating Full Service Programs

Roughly speaking, a program begins with a planning stage, during which intended operating procedures and objectives are considered, revised, then adopted. That plan then is installed; staff are hired, facilities equipped, pupils selected, resources acquired and allocated, and start-up processes begun. In many instances the installation stage requires recycling back to the planning stage. Once installed, a program begins to operate its planned activities; staff are trained, pupils begin receiving instruction, administrative meetings are conducted, etc. Recycling is characteristic, as it is discovered that some activities won't work as planned, additional resources are needed, and so on. Finally, a program stabilizes; it concentrates its efforts on its revised activities, and its procedures become more coherent. From these activities, revised and modified as they are, will come the program's final results. It will produce its "terminal" objectives—often and necessarily different from those of its original plan.

The primary purpose of formative evaluation is to facilitate and enhance orderly growth of the program, to help it stabilize. Feedback on discrepancies between performance and plan in the installation and early operation stages allows for more informed decisions on modifications and revisions, in addition to identifying areas in which such decisions are needed.

A past history of evaluation failures probably results, in large part, from inattention to the natural developmental phases of a program. In many cases, experimental or quasi-experimental designs were cast at the inception of a program, with the noble intent of accurately assessing the program's goal achievement. Most often, the program itself was changed enough, or never installed as called for in the plan, so that the experimental design was rendered invalid. The point is that accurate measuring of the program's final outcomes is crucial, but should not be attempted prematurely. Early evaluation efforts should be aimed at assessing the extent of the program's installation and the integrity of its processes and activities. This not only enhances growth of the program, but allows for concomitant changes in its evaluation procedures to better gauge its impact.

The evaluation should be designed to shift its focus through the four stages described below. None of these stages is particularly discrete. They overlap, and recycling among them can and should occur throughout the life of the program. Evaluation staging is not limited to "new" programs; it may be followed even in a program currently underway. In an ongoing program, a program design still would be constructed, though it would represent the program's intended operation at whatever point in the program it is begun. The following stages might then be differentially applied to differing parts of the program. Activities just finishing would be ready for the fourth stage; beginning activities would benefit more from second or third stage evaluation.

Evaluation in the first stage should be directed at the program's plan

Instructional Planning for Exceptional Children

itself. Its design can be explicitly documented, showing what resources it intends to consume, what activities it will engage in, and what objectives it will achieve. This document then can be subjected to evaluation, using criteria of comprehensiveness, logical consistency, theoretical soundness and, importantly, compliance with laws and regulations. Evaluation at this stage relies on professional judgment and appeals to professional, theoretical, and legal standards.

Second stage evaluation determines the extent to which the program's intended resources have been allocated and its planned preconditions met. As discrepancies between the plan (now the *standard*) and performance are discovered, the program may be altered to function with the diminished or altered resource, or additional efforts made to procure the resource as planned.

Process evaluation characterizes the third stage. This evaluation focuses on actual performance of the program's intended activities and the extent to which the program is producing its interim, or enabling, objectives as planned. For example, such questions as: "Are team diagnoses being completed as planned? Are IEPs being produced on schedule? What role are parents playing in the placement process?" should be pursued. As in the previous stage, the program plan serves as the referent standard. Again, discrepancies between plan and performance call for management action and, likely, program revision.

Over time, and as the second and third evaluation stages are conducted, the program stabilizes and moves toward production of its terminal objectives. Assessment questions—the fourth evaluation stage—now are appropriate. Measures need to be planned and developed regarding the extent to which these terminal objectives are achieved. Evaluation here focuses on educational changes in pupils, or other expected outcomes of the program.

Providing for Self-Implementation

Evaluation should be considered a regular part of program activities and designed into the program's total plan as such. Likewise, all program personnel should expect to engage in evaluation activities as a routine part of their job. Evaluation measures, particularly in the second and third stages, can be simple without jeopardizing their utility. Data collected in these stages often consist of counts of persons, time, activities, or objects and, thus, monitoring is similar to routine record-keeping. Many of the measures of educational need and achievement used routinely in a special education program can be used, in individual and aggregate form, as an index of program effect.

Outside consultation may be needed and appropriate in the first and fourth stages. Evaluation of the program design itself requires professional judgment, and the brief use of consultants for this stage may be indicated. Fourth stage evaluation may require some outside consultation, particularly in the selection or development of instrumentation, and also in the analysis of data. In general, however, the bulk of the evaluation can and should be carried out by regular program staff. The general approach described in the following section is intended for self-implementation.

Making the Evaluation Public

The term "public" as used here has two meanings: It applies to the program staff itself, and to the general community in which the program is located. Evaluation is often not a particularly warmly received or regarded activity. It may have been responsible for some past pain and is likely to stimulate anxious, even fearful feelings. Much of this reputation of evaluation may be attributed to its prior usage in a non-public manner. Evaluation criteria often are not explicit or available to those to whom they are applied. Evaluation procedures often have been developed independently of program staff and operating concerns and thus may be seen, at best, as obscure and, at worst, secretive. This unfortunate history and reputation are sadly true but, fortunately, avoidable for the future.

Evaluation can be far less threatening and considerably more useful to program revision if people involved in and by the program are parties to development of the comparative standards and procedures of evaluation. Discrepancies between performance and standards that have been publicly determined and agreed upon provide powerful stimulus for change. Program personnel who have helped set standards and design evaluation procedures are far more likely to accept those standards and cooperate with those procedures.

In the general community, the public should be informed of program intentions—planned resources, activities, and expected results. Transmission of such information is trust-building and, if the public is invited to respond to and comment on program intentions, realistic expectations are more likely to develop. Many problems emerge when the public receives negative evaluation findings at the conclusion of a program about which they've received little previous information. Then, schools are caught in the situation of trying to explain reasons for problems after those problems have received public exposure and aroused anger. After anger is aroused, any explanation, regardless of its validity, garners little support. Given prior information on the background and likelihood of operating problems (inevitable in the conduct of educational programs) and given interim information on a problem's development and efforts to correct it, the public is certain to be more supportive.

Instructional Planning for Exceptional Children

A part of the evaluation effort should plan to provide the public with program design information (the standards for the program) in an easily understood language and format. The public also should be informed as to what evaluation questions and procedures will be pursued. As the program develops and its evaluation collects information, the public should receive regular progress reports based on the evaluation's findings. The general evaluation approach discussed next can be adapted readily for such public dissemination.

AN EVALUATION APPROACH

The evaluation procedures suggested in this section derive directly from the Discrepancy Evaluation Model that has been applied successfully in several public school and higher education settings. The reader should find this approach usable in designing or adapting an existing design for evaluation of a local full service special education program.

The three major parts consist of:

1. Developing the program's design—a functional analysis of the program's expected operation and the standards to which it intends to adhere;
2. Delineating the set of questions or concerns the evaluation intends to address; these represent questions the evaluation will answer and parts of the program it will investigate and monitor; and
3. Determining the data collection system the evaluation will pursue; this will outline the performance information the evaluation will collect in order to "answer" the evaluation questions.

This evaluation approach aims at and intends to address the scope and purposes outlined in the first section of this article; an approach that intends to gauge the efficacy of whatever program the school system mounts and provide a systematic information system that allows modification and improvement of the program. The model, content, and guidelines for conducting an actual full service program must come from those who conduct the program; its standards will be theirs, definitive of their values and the authorities they recognize. This discussion, however, will help a program explicate these standards and determine how implementable they are in a programmatic effort.

Program Design

Documentation of program design provides an operational definition of the program's intent. As such, it can serve two major purposes: (1) To provide a means by which the program's plan can be comprehensively defined and thereby reviewed by its staff and consumers or evaluated as a plan by professionals; and (2) To provide a basis for identifying critical aspects of program operation that should be monitored and evaluated. A potential third use for program design documentation, or an adaptation of it, is as a device for orienting interested parties (such as parents) to the program's intended operation and objectives.

The program analysis begins with a definition of the program's major components and subcomponents. This should be based on a functional analysis of the program; it should provide a picture of the major activities that the program intends to operate. It also should show how these activities are interrelated and what operating dependencies among the components are expected to exist.

Figure 4 shows one possible component analysis for a special education program. The arrows connecting components indicate functional dependencies, showing how one component is intended to provide another with an enabling objective. In this example analysis, component 5 represents the function where educational activities take place and, thus, is the component responsible for producing the program's terminal objectives—its intended learning outcomes or other changes in pupils. The other components in the program exist to support this component or provide its critical enabling objectives. From this graphic analysis, some components—by the program's definition—obviously cannot operate successfully without the successful operation of prior components. Operation of the educational component (5), for instance, requires input from component 4 in the form of individualized education plans, or relevant diagnostic and prescriptive information. These and other such critical dependencies in the program's design may indicate areas for particular evaluation emphasis.

After a workable set of components and subcomponents has been charted, the program design should give a detailed description of the operating plan for each. For a complex component (such as 5), further analysis of subcomponents probably is necessary. The detailed plan for each component should define the following information:

Input: staff needed; clients/receptors to be served or affected; materials necessary; facilities required; equipment, etc.; administrative preconditions needed.

Process: specific activities to be conducted; who will do what, where, with whom, how. In component 4, for example, the process description should include how the interdisciplinary teams will be formed and dispatched, where and when diagnoses will be conducted, how par-

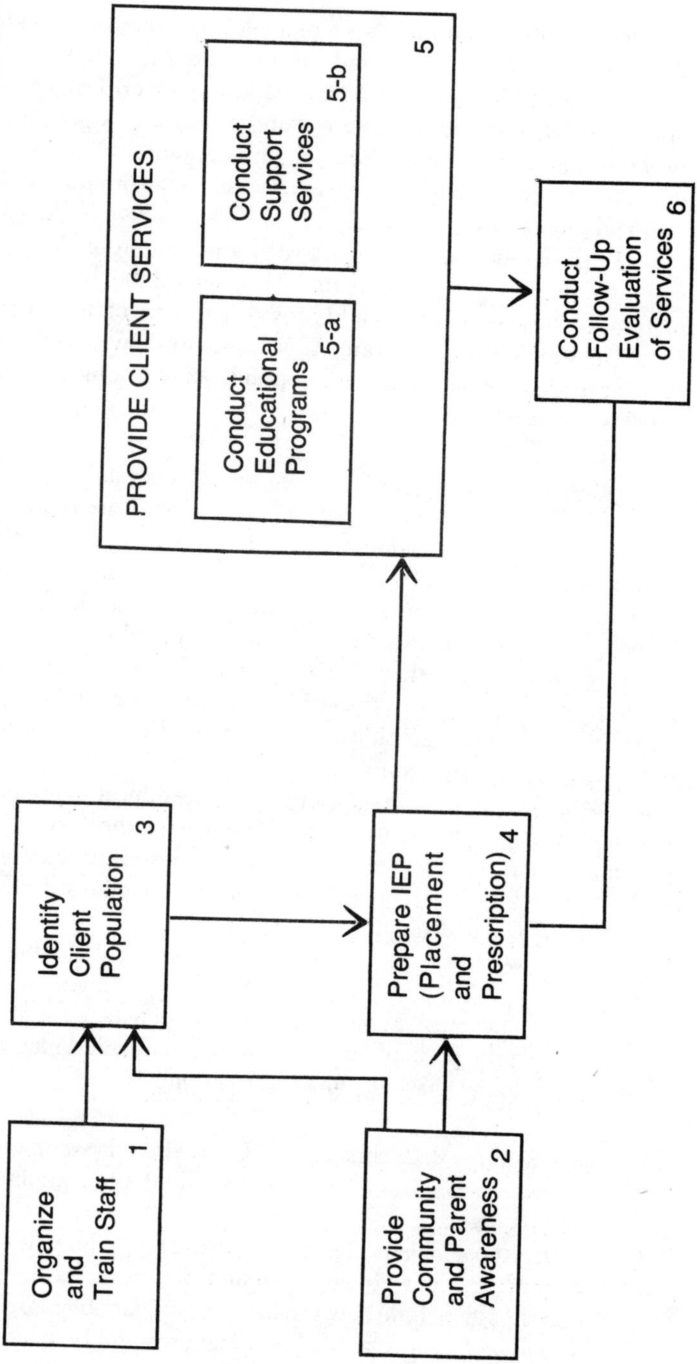

Instructional Planning for Exceptional Children

FIGURE 4
SCHEMATIC ANALYSIS OF A 94-142 PROGRAM'S DESIGN

ents will be notified and involved, how children will be transported, and so on.

Output (the component's intended objectives): what products will be produced; what changes in the client will occur; what learning outcomes will be effected; etc.

The process descriptions contained in the program design are especially critical. They provide an operational definition of exactly how the program will take place and, as such, enable an accurate process evaluation and monitoring procedure. PL 94-142 programs have to pay particular attention to monitoring and documenting activities and procedures. A careful delineation of the plan for those procedures and activities facilitates the design of an efficient monitoring process.

Evaluation Questions

Evaluation questions are the particular hypotheses that an evaluation intends to address. The evaluation collects information on performance of a program that will be used to answer the evaluation questions. An evaluation question applicable to a special education program might be, for instance, "What educational gains did pupils make?" The answer derives from information collected pertaining to the actual educational performance of pupils in the program.

The evaluation questions a program should pursue derive from two major sources. First, particular areas of concern must be addressed according to federal, state, or local guidelines. Second, an analysis of program design and the critical dependencies and activities it portrays will highlight evaluation needs crucial to testing and improving the program.

PL 94-142 is explicit in its requirements for evaluation, stating that programs should assess the effectiveness of efforts to educate handicapped children—yet it does not delineate more specifically the aspects of a program that must be evaluated. An analysis of program requirements, however, makes evident these areas and aspects of the program in which evaluation is appropriate. Many of the program requirements are procedural; the astute evaluation seeks to document the extent and nature of these procedures. Some such evaluation questions gleaned from the guidelines are:

1. Relative to preparation of IEPs:
   —How many IEPs are produced? When?
   —For whom and for what reasons are these IEPs produced?
   —To what extent do the IEPs meet state and local content criteria?
   —How much time, money, etc., is expected to produce IEPs?

2. Relative to diagnostic teams:
   —Who actually prepares the IEPs?
   —What teams are formed? When? Who is on the teams? What are their credentials?
   —What roles did the various team members play?
   —How do team members spend their time? In what activities?
3. Relative to parent involvement:
   —What notification did parents receive? When?
   —In what orientation activities did parents participate?
   —What roles did parents play? In what activities?
   —How many independent evaluations were requested? Conducted?
4. Relative to staff training:
   —Who received training? How much?
   —What training activities were delivered? Who attended?
   —What was the effectiveness of this training?
5. Relative to identification:
   —Who was identified and selected?
   —What identification procedures were used?
   —How many clients, of what categories, were identified?
6. Relative to treatment and education:
   —Who received what services?
   —How much time, of what nature, did categories and numbers of clients spend in educational treatment?
   —What educational gains were made?

The evaluation questions above do not represent a comprehensive list—nor a "required" one. They are intended as a guide, and perhaps will stimulate other questions. They relate directly to some of the program guidelines, and could also very easily be made a part of routine record keeping procedures.

Further additions to a list such as the one presented should come from an analysis of *each* of the component descriptions in the program design. Because costs of program services are crucial both to budgeting and federal funds acquisition, evaluation questions relating to key resource consumption also should be formulated for *each* component in the design.

Evaluation questions relative to the instructional component of the program should derive from and be responsive to the particular instructional strategies to be used. In any case, evaluation should be directed at documenting the actual instructional procedures conducted, monitoring pupil progress and determining resources expended.

A mainstream definition by Kaufman, Gottlieb, Agard and Kukic (1975) provides a good generic model for defining areas in which evaluation questions for the instructional component could be developed. In this definition, they stress the importance of considering the clarification of individual responsibilities, planning and programming factors, and integration of the pupil into the mainstream. Integration of the pupil must be considered not only in temporal (i.e., time in the regular classroom) but also instructional and social interaction terms. Thus, the evaluation should seek to determine the amount of "regular" and other instructional activities received by special education pupils in the program, and should make an effort to determine the nature of these instructional activities. The extent and nature of social activities (interaction of special education pupils with regular education pupils) also could be monitored and documented.

The evaluation, too, should pay considerable attention to generating evaluation questions relating to expected—or unexpected—program outcomes. A useful procedure, for each component in the program design is to develop a list of expected outcomes, objectives, or areas of impact. From this list, one can generate a relevant set of evaluation questions, such as:

—To what extent have regular education teachers' attitudes toward exceptional children improved?
—Are parents more knowledgeable than before about techniques for participating in their child's education?
—What educational gains are achieved by pupils?
—To what extent are pupils in special education programs accepted by their peers?
—What proportion of previously self-contained classroom pupils now receive services in the mainstream?

Again, the list is partial and would, of course, vary according to particular program goals.

A program also should generate a set of evaluation questions particular to its own developmental needs. These formative evaluation questions should be pursued in areas of the program in which information will be required to test the efficacy or feasibility of certain procedures, or where critical management decisions are anticipated. The primary source for determining such questions is the program design. Areas of the design in which specific formative evaluation questions might be useful are:

—Points of heavy functional dependence. The design can reveal dependencies in which the expected outcome of a particular component is especially critical to successful operation of the rest of the program. The production of accurate and adequate IEPs may be such a point.
—Areas in which design adequacy questions are unresolved.
—Areas undergoing development or experimentation.
—Activities with a history of problems.

Instructional Planning for Exceptional Children

—Areas marked by or likely to be subject to disagreement.
—Procedures based on unresolved or questionable theory.

Once compiled, the total set of evaluation questions should be reviewed and prioritized. Attention to the staging of evaluation should help in determining the priority of evaluation questions and the sequence in which they should be addressed.

Constructing the Data Collection Plan

After the final set of evaluation questions has been determined, the final step in the evaluation planning process is to develop a plan that will collect program performance information addressing these questions. Each evaluation question poses a query about the extent to which the program is operating as planned or achieving its desired outcomes. These questions are to be answered with data about actual operation of the program. For instance, an evaluation question might be, "To what extent were parents involved in the placement process?"; data to answer this question would derive from records of actual parent involvement or might be collected from the parents themselves, perhaps by questionnaire. Each question in the evaluation plan should have attached to it some procedure for gathering program performance data sufficient to yield an answer to that question.

In general, two methods are to be pursued in developing this data collection plan. The first involves using all potential existing data collection procedures, and the second involves developing new ones. The school milieu in which the program will function already is full of record keeping and other data collection procedures. Pupils are tested regularly, attendance records are kept, appointments are recorded, logs kept, and so on. A list of these extant procedures can be arrayed next to the set of evaluation questions the program wishes to pursue, noting the extant procedures that can be used as is, or slightly adapted, to provide data for given evaluation questions. Many evaluation questions can be covered by existing data collection procedures.

For evaluation questions not provided for by extant procedures, other data collection methods will have to be employed. Already developed instruments from commercial sources may provide suitable data in some instances, but inevitably the program will need to develop some new data collection procedures of its own. For these evaluation questions, some possible *indicants* must be identified.[3]

Often, several indicants may be desirable for one evaluation question. If, for example, the question is, "To what extent are special education children accepted by regular education pupils?" some possible indicants might be:

---
[3] An indicant is some observable or recordable event that, if measured, might "indicate" an answer to an evaluation question.

amount of time the pupils spend in play together; teachers' perceptions of social acceptance; other pupils' perceptions of or attitudes toward the special pupils. Measures for these indicants then need to be designed along with a system for their administration. A second reference to the extant data collection procedures list may provide coverage for some of the indicants generated.

Whenever possible, overlap among measures to be used and data collection procedures to be employed should be utilized to best advantage; any particular data collection procedure should be used to provide data for as many evaluation questions as possible. The major costs of evaluation derive not from the number of evaluation questions one seeks to answer, but from the extent of data collection procedures employed. Collecting information costs time and money, as do aggregation and analysis of this information.

Many program impact evaluation questions can be answered with aggregated data. Data deriving from the routine diagnosis, instruction, and evaluation of individual pupils in the program can and should be regularly aggregated as a measure of the effectiveness and progress of program components. In this instance, new measurement techniques are not required, but forms and procedures for aggregating these data will need to be designed.

The goal attainment scaling procedures recommended by Howe and Fitzgerald (1977) could be effective measures for individual pupil growth; the numerical data they offer could be aggregated easily within and across program instructional components to provide overall indicators of the progress and impact of these components.

In considering a self-implementable evaluation design for a local special education program, *simplicity* should be a goal. Relatively simple measurement procedures can work; "fancy" evaluations (control groups, factor analysis, multivariate designs) are not necessarily best. Such procedures can be powerful, but they may be inappropriate and impractical for many programs. An elegantly designed evaluation that doesn't get applied is of far less value than the simpler, cruder one that does.

Many simple, inexpensive data collection procedures are appropriate for the bulk of evaluation questions relevant to special education programs, and they can produce accurate, useful data. Behavioral record logs maintained by teachers and their program staffs provide useful process data. Simple checklists and usage records likewise are useful, accurate, and inexpensive. Self-report questionnaires, appropriately designed and applied, can be used for many evaluation questions dealing with parent and other involvement in program activities. Again, measurement needn't be elaborate to be useful; often, the opposite is true. Similarly, data analysis can be simple; in many cases, basic frequency distributions are adequate. Most data collected will be nominal—ordinal at most—and, therefore, obviate more elaborate analyses and transformations.

Two important documents should be produced to represent the program's evaluation procedures. The first should give each evaluation question the program intends to pursue, then show for each the specific indicators and measures that will be employed to determine an answer to that question. If the principle of economy of measures is followed, this notation will repeat certain measures and data collection procedures. It will provide, however, a comprehensive list of the program's evaluation questions, and will be a ready reference for showing how any of those questions will be answered.

A second document should list each data collection measure to be employed, noting for each the instrument administration schedule, analysis technique to be used, respondents, administrators, and any other pertinent logistic information pertaining to that procedure. This document represents a workplan for the evaluation and details collection and analysis responsibilities.

These two documents, combined with the program design, provide a thorough explanation of the program's intended evaluation efforts and show how and where they relate to the program's intended operation and objectives.

SUMMARY

Public Law 94-142 entails many new program requirements for states and local school service programs. In many instances, new services and procedures are necessary, accompanied by new personnel in new roles. Publicity and controversy attending the advent of these new programmatic requirements has heightened public awareness; new public expectations will be formed. These events point out and focus on the importance of comprehensive, careful program evaluation.

Evaluation of full service special education programs not only must demonstrate their effectiveness, but also is called upon to clarify program standards and document program operations to demonstrate compliance with law and program guidelines. Because many aspects of these programs are developmental, program evaluation should be further expected to facilitate the systematic growth, revision, and improvement of special education services.

To fulfill those purposes, evaluation efforts should be designed to complement developmental stages of the program itself. Although evaluation's ultimate aim is to assess program impact—its goal achievement—it cannot practically or validly do so unless it also has investigated critical program installation and implementation variables. Evaluation should begin by carefully explicating the program design; i.e., a detailed outline of its intended operation and the standards which it is expected to meet. This design can itself be subjected to scrutiny and evaluation, and also serves as a standard against which to gauge the program's installation and operation.

The standards, procedures, and findings of the evaluation should be made available to all program participants and to the public in general. The evaluation will realize its maximum power as a force for change to the extent that program participants are involved in its design and operation.

Finally, the evaluation needs to be as simple as possible. Special education programs have their hands full delivering and maintaining their services. Evaluation is a necessary program component but will work best when carried out by regular program staff as a part of routine program operation. Evaluation must be implemented in order to work; it must be workable in order to be implemented.

REFERENCES

Howe, C., & Fitzgerald, M. Evaluating special education programs. *Focus on Exceptional Children*, Feb. 1977, 8(9), 1-11.

Kaufman, M., Gottlieb, J., Agard, J., & Kukic, M. Mainstreaming: Toward an explication of the construct. *Focus on Exceptional Children*, May 1975, 7(3), 1-12.

Provus, M. M. *Discrepancy evaluation*. Berkeley: McCutchan, 1971.

One of the many important issues associated with evaluation is the readiness of people to accept the need for it—and the willingness to act upon that need. This selection describes procedures for reducing reluctance to engage in what admittedly is a complex and arduous task, that of program evaluation.

A second issue relates to the tactics of implementing an evaluation plan. The authors have described a model, actually in use, which is applicable at several levels, from the individual child through program administration. A unique feature of the model is a provision for scaling results as to attainment of expectations, being below them or being above them.

Evaluating Special Education Programs

Clifford E. Howe and Marigail E. Fitzgerald,
University of Iowa

Material for this article has been summarized from work prepared for the Iowa Department of Public Instruction (Howe & Fitzgerald, 1976). It is not intended as the final word in program evaluation, nor as a cookbook set of procedures. It does outline a model which has been field tested, with the most useful aspects retained.

Iowa has recently reorganized into 15 intermediate units called Area Education Agencies (AEAs) to provide special education, media, and other services to areas with school populations ranging from a low of approximately 15,000 to one with almost 130,000 pupils. It seems certain that recent legislation will require more accountability and evaluation procedures for individual children than has historically been the case. Iowa's legislation essentially mandates special education for all handicapped students, and requires annual reevaluation of the appropriateness of the program and student placement (State of Iowa, 1974). It is further indicated that school districts, in conjunction with the Area Education Agency, must develop procedures designed to evaluate and improve special education programs and services.

At the federal level, the Education for All Handicapped Children Act (P.L. 94-142, 1975) mandates that each state obtaining funds under this act must provide for evaluation procedures to ensure the effectiveness of programs designed to meet the educational needs of handicapped children (including evaluation of individualized education programs). Evaluation must be carried out at least annually.

Several models have been proposed in the past decade which focus on evaluation in education. One of the most extensive was that developed by Phi Delta Kappa's Research Advisory Committee under the authorship of Stufflebeam and others (1971). Recognizing that evaluation of educational programs was long overdue, they developed a model which combined knowledge of the process as well as product evaluation. Their model views the roles of evaluation as being made up of context, input, process, and product (CIPP). The outcome of evaluation is seen principally as providing useful information for making decisions about program alternatives.

Stufflebeam deals with the reasons educational evaluation has either been done poorly or not at all in the past. Included are symptoms such as avoidance (the process is viewed as painful), anxiety (evaluation is viewed as a judgment, often of personal competency), immobilization or lethargy and lack of interest, skepticism regarding whether evaluation can really be done or whether the results are of any use, and a lack of significant differences as the result of much educational research (leading to frustration on the part of the practitioner). Stufflebeam suggests ways in which these difficulties could be overcome and proposes models which will be useful to practitioners (1971).

Popham (1972) proposes a more restricted view of evaluation, and ties it to instructional objectives and criterion-referenced measurement. This handbook provides practical application in the process of constructing and measuring objectives. Emphasis is placed on learner performance data. Evaluation is viewed as a process of determining the desired ends or goals of the educational system, and judging the worth of educational means through both formative (process) and summative (product) assessment. Although his model is not limited to measures of individual student change data, this is the major emphasis.

A third model for educational evaluation is the technique long used by various accrediting associations (NCA, etc.). Stufflebeam (1971) categorizes this as evaluation based on professional judgment. Evaluative criteria are provided, but the major work is done by the schools themselves through a self-study procedure which usually takes about a year. After it is completed, a visiting team of experts and peers comes to the school to observe for a few days, studies the data provided by the school, and renders judgments and recommendations regarding the quality of the program. The major strength of this technique is usually seen in the self-study aspect, where a school and community critically evaluate themselves, thus investing enough of themselves in the evaluation effort to be willing to make and implement decisions for improvement.

An extension of the models above, and one which seems to be very relevant to special education programs, is that of Goal Attainment Scaling (GAS), proposed by Kiresuk and Sherman (1968). These techniques were originally developed from grants by the National Institute of Mental Health, and focused on ways of determining the effectiveness of different treatment approaches for patients in community mental health centers in the Minneapolis area.

In summary, it would appear that successful program evaluation is concerned with two major issues. The first is that of determining the technical approach which appears to have the highest likelihood of yielding useful data to use in making decisions regarding future directions for the program. For the individually-tailored program in special education, it would seem that the use of Goal Attainment Scaling provides promising possibilities.

The second issue which seems critical is that of developing a readiness in the organization to undertake program evaluation. Time should be spent with those involved to reduce defensiveness, develop trust, and reach a consensus regarding both the purpose of evaluation and the process to be used. If educational evaluation can be seen, as Stufflebeam (1971) states, "as the process of delineating, obtaining, and providing useful information for judging decision alternatives," then the effort can be viewed in light of its real purpose.

Figure 1 shows that program evaluation must occur throughout the organization and may take different forms at different levels. While evaluation of individual children is specific to each pupil at Level III, it becomes much more general at Level I. Middle management in Level II uses techniques from both Levels I and III and helps tie the entire process together.

SETTING THE STAGE

For change to occur in an organization, some significant member needs to be the instigator and begin the dialogue with key staff members. Most AEAs in Iowa do not now have an organized program evaluation system, and the director of special education would seem to be the logical person to initiate such an effort. The director must first be convinced of the importance of evaluation efforts. Once this commitment is made by the director, time is needed for informal discussion with the leadership staff.

Our experience suggests that an initial session of not less than two hours

Evaluating Special Education Programs

Figure 1
PROPOSED MODEL FOR EVALUATION OF SPECIAL EDUCATION AEAs

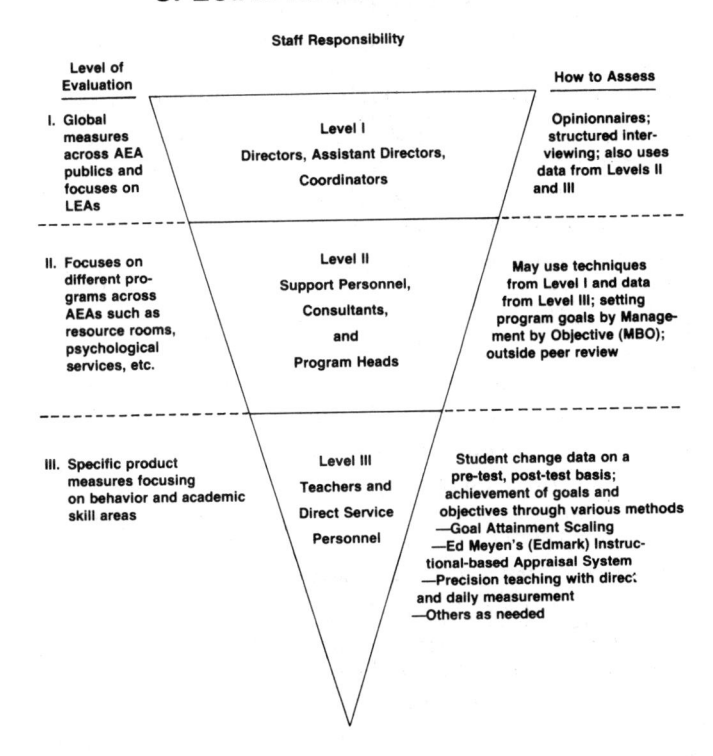

Staff Responsibility

Level of Evaluation		How to Assess
I. Global measures across AEA publics and focuses on LEAs	**Level I** Directors, Assistant Directors, Coordinators	Opinionnaires; structured interviewing; also uses data from Levels II and III
II. Focuses on different programs across AEAs such as resource rooms, psychological services, etc.	**Level II** Support Personnel, Consultants, and Program Heads	May use techniques from Level I and data from Level III; setting program goals by Management by Objective (MBO); outside peer review
III. Specific product measures focusing on behavior and academic skill areas	**Level III** Teachers and Direct Service Personnel	Student change data on a pre-test, post-test basis; achievement of goals and objectives through various methods —Goal Attainment Scaling —Ed Meyen's (Edmark) Instructional-based Appraisal System —Precision teaching with direct and daily measurement —Others as needed

is necessary, and that several followup sessions of similar length may be required. During these preliminary discussions, the desired outcome is to overcome resistance to the idea of evaluation and to begin to formulate a plan of positive action. The following topics usually come up in these initial sessions, and need to be resolved:

Q: Are we really going to have to do this sometime in the future in order to get funds, or is this just another passing fad?

A: All signs seem to point in the direction of increasing accountability for appropriateness of programs and to accumulate some evidence showing that the approach used is beneficial. Legislation and Rules in Iowa now require systematic evaluation and will probably become more stringent as the AEAs mature. P.L. 94-142 will become operational in the near future, and includes strong statements regarding evaluation plans in order to qualify for these federal funds for the handicapped. It would appear that token evaluation systems won't suffice for the future.

Q: We already have too much to do, and if this becomes another requirement, who is going to do it and where are we going to get the time? How about hiring someone who is a specialist in evaluation?

Instructional Planning for Exceptional Children

A: One way to manage an evaluation system is to use "third party" or outside evaluators. This supposedly has the advantage of not adding to the work load of the present staff, and of guaranteeing an objective approach. Many federal projects, such as Title III grants, use this technique. However, there are disadvantages and one of the major ones is that the existing staffs in an AEA may not invest themselves in the operation and instead see it as a one-time effort conducted by outside paid professionals. Another way to view program evaluation is to think of it as a long-term management technique where the evaluation data become a part of the decision-making process on an ongoing basis. Outside specialists can be used for specific tasks occasionally, but the evaluation effort is really a part of the long-term management of the AEA and all leadership staff should contribute to it.

Q: Aren't we really talking about evaluation of staff, and judgments being made about the personal competence of individuals?

A: It would be dishonest to say that program and staff evaluation are completely separate from each other. Both are important, and need to be done. However, the emphasis on program evaluation is broader than an individual teacher, psychologist, or speech clinician. The purpose is to gain information that is program-wide, such as determining the impact of the total program of speech services in an AEA, for example, rather than focusing on the competency of one speech clinician. Obviously, the success of the total program evaluation aggregates the results for the total program, and the individual remains anonymous. Evaluation of an individual serves another purpose and should not be confused with program evaluation.

Q: Many evaluation studies gather dust in the files and much research ends up with conclusions of "no significant differences." How do we know we won't be embarking on a similar enterprise?

A: You don't, really, but that is a strong argument for planning it ourselves as a management tool on a long-term basis, of asking evaluation questions that make sense for our AEA, and of using the results for planning for the next year or several years. We have to make these decisions anyway, and evaluation results should be viewed as just another piece of information which will help us when we must set priorities and make hard decisions.

Q: Okay, I'm convinced. How do I begin with my staff of ten consultants, for whom I am responsible?

A: You need to remember that they will have the same, or perhaps even more, misgivings or questions about evaluation that we've struggled with in the past few hours and sessions. Start slowly, allow at least two hours in a beginning session with all of them, and let them voice all their concerns as well as ideas as to what form the evaluation should take. Expect them to feel avoidance, anxiety, and skepticism, and deal honestly with these feelings. Try to develop credibility of the evaluation process and outline the risks involved. One sure way to encounter difficulty, or perhaps even failure, is to present the evaluation scheme in terms of a dictate from the top. An honest approach might be to say that we will be committed to a continuing evaluation effort, but that the form and methods used are matters to be decided by the group.

The following sections are intended to give ideas and examples of how evaluation might be used by an AEA throughout the various levels of the organization. Evaluation moves from specific child change data as a major component in Level III, to much more general attitudinal data for the total program at Level I.

LEVEL I EVALUATION PROCEDURES

Level I evaluation is concerned with general views held by consumers throughout the AEA regarding programs and services for the handicapped. The procedure could be likened to a "Gallup Poll" approach, and samples attitudes from a variety of publics. Stratified random sampling procedures are used so that numbers of respondents are manageable in terms of costs, yet yield a reliable and valid picture of the present status of the organization.

Figure 2 shows an example of an opinionnaire which was field-tested in AEA 16 in the spring of 1976 (Johnson, 1976). Questions included were selected as being of high priority by the leadership staff, including the director and assistant director of special education, supervisors, and consultants.

The staff decided there were eight different subgroups that should be canvassed, including:

Local education agency superintendents
Local education agency building administrators
Special education support staff
Special education instructional staff
Regular education instructional staff
Parent groups for the handicapped
Outside agencies (mental health centers, private schools, etc.)
Secretarial staff in the area education agency

Different subgroups could be chosen by another AEA if, in their judgment, the opinions of such groups were important to the success of the AEA. A minimum sample of 40 was selected from each subgroup with populations which were larger than 40. For those groups whose entire population in the AEA approximated 40 or fewer, all were included in the sample. Where sampling was done, a table of random numbers was used.

A total of 217 opinionnaires was mailed, with 168 returned, for an overall response rate of 77%. This level of response is quite high, considering the diversity of populations sampled and the fact that no additional followup mailings were made. The rate of return varied among groups from 100% for superintendents, 85% for building administrators and special education instructional staff, to a low of about 50% for regular teachers and parent groups.

Opinionnaires were returned to a neutral agency outside of the AEA to protect anonymity and encourage more honest responses. Data from the opinionnaire were then tabulated, using a standard computer program which yielded results for each question in the form of means and standard deviations for each of the eight groups. In addition, percentages of each group responding from 5 (agree strongly) to the other extreme of 1 (disagree strongly) were provided on the computer printout for each item.

Figure 2
OPINIONNAIRE
PERCEPTIONS OF SPECIAL EDUCATION SERVICES IN AREA EDUCATION AGENCY 16

This form is an attempt to get feedback from various groups on selected aspects of special education services provided by AEA 16. The purpose is to learn from you those things which you feel the AEA is doing well, and those which should be improved or discontinued. The results will be used to evaluate our present position and to plan for the future.

Below is a series of statements with which you may agree, disagree, or have not had any basis for answering. Please blacken the appropriate box for each statement and return in the enclosed envelope. It takes only 5 or 10 minutes and will be a great help to us.

	Agree strongly	Agree somewhat	Neutral	Disagree somewhat	Disagree strongly	No basis on which to answer
1. More services are being provided for handicapped children as compared to last year	☐	☐	☐	☐	☐	☐
2. Better services are being provided for handicapped children as compared to last year	☐	☐	☐	☐	☐	☐
3. Staff of the AEA are available when I need them:						
psychologists	☐	☐	☐	☐	☐	☐
consultants	☐	☐	☐	☐	☐	☐
speech clinicians	☐	☐	☐	☐	☐	☐
social workers	☐	☐	☐	☐	☐	☐
special education administrators	☐	☐	☐	☐	☐	☐
hearing services	☐	☐	☐	☐	☐	☐
4. The AEA Division of Special Education should reduce the number of programs it administers directly and turn these over to local school districts	☐	☐	☐	☐	☐	☐
5. Too much money is currently being spent for special education, often at the expense of regular education	☐	☐	☐	☐	☐	☐
6. Decisions made regarding special education at the AEA central office include about the right amount of consultation with those involved at the local level	☐	☐	☐	☐	☐	☐
7. Sufficient supplies and materials are provided for each handicapped child	☐	☐	☐	☐	☐	☐

	Agree strongly	Agree somewhat	Neutral	Disagree somewhat	Disagree stongly	No basis on which to answer
8. The quality of consultation provided by the special education AEA staff is high	☐	☐	☐	☐	☐	☐
9. There is a sufficient quantity of consultation and support staff available from the AEA to adequately support instructional programs for the handicapped	☐	☐	☐	☐	☐	☐
10. The time it takes for a handicapped child to be processed, from original referral to placement, is a good investment of effort	☐	☐	☐	☐	☐	☐
11. Staffing children with various professionals meeting as a group is a good idea	☐	☐	☐	☐	☐	☐
12. The system of referral for a child is working well	☐	☐	☐	☐	☐	☐
13. A major reason for AEA providing some services is the lack of program offerings by local school districts	☐	☐	☐	☐	☐	☐

ADD ANY STATEMENTS THAT YOU THINK SHOULD HAVE BEEN INCLUDED:

14.   ☐ ☐ ☐ ☐ ☐ ☐

15.   ☐ ☐ ☐ ☐ ☐ ☐

16.   ☐ ☐ ☐ ☐ ☐ ☐

OTHER COMMENTS YOU MAY WISH TO MAKE:

Instructional Planning for Exceptional Children

From this summary, the 18 questions asked were rank-ordered from high to low in terms of degree of agreement. Inspection of the data also pointed up specific subgroups whose responses varied significantly from the overall group.

This information gave the leadership group in AEA 16 a good indication of the general reaction to various aspects of special education services. It is common practice to stop at this point in the procedure and to use these data as input for planning and decision making. However, it is our feeling that another step should be taken to validate results, probe in more depth the indicated problem areas, and solicit suggested changes for improvement. For this followup, we used the technique of structured interviews.

The leadership staff used the opinionnaire data to derive the questions to be asked during the structured interviews, focusing on those areas where there was disagreement among groups or where responses were most negative by the majority of the groups. The advantage of this particular approach is the ability to narrow the range of questions asked and avoid the "shotgun" effect of including many broad questions or of guessing as to what the critical issues are.

Summarizing Structured Interview Data

The interview team should meet with the special education director after interviewing has been completed, to share the major themes which emerged. This should be done while the team is intact and before leaving the AEA. Nothing is more devastating to the process than to have the AEA director wait for several weeks before getting any feedback on results.

After the verbal exit interview with the AEA director and whatever additional staff he or she wishes to include, a short written report is usually prepared within the next week, summarizing strengths and weaknesses observed and indicating possible recommendations. As a final step, and if the special education director so wishes, the chairman of the interview team meets with the director and his or her leadership staff to further discuss the results of the opinionnaire and structured interviewing, and to help plan intervention strategies for future change. At this point, all original data have been returned to the AEA for its use.

Evaluation procedures for Level I are AEA-wide, sample opinions of the various publics served by special education, and combine opinionnaire data with followup structured interviewing. Trust and anonymity are important ingredients for the data to be accurate and useful, and for the process to proceed without undue defensiveness. All original data and results are given to the AEA for its use in assessing the current situation and in planning for the future. If done correctly, the entire process takes a minimum of time and yields useful data.

LEVEL II EVALUATION PROCEDURES

Level II comprises middle management AEA personnel, including supervisors, consultants, and program heads. They are responsible for an area of support services or type of instructional program. Level II personnel also provide a link between instructional programs in the schools and the overall management of special education programs at the director level.

Program evaluation for Level II can utilize the opinionnaire and structured interview techniques outlined earlier under Level I. Questions asked and opinions sought are more narrowly-focused, and related to a specific program such as psychological services, audiology, resource rooms, etc. Because the focus is more delineated, it is possible to go into more depth, as well as to make comparisons of various approaches to delivery of services. Interviewers can be selected from peers in other AEAs throughout the state.

Management by Objective (MBO)

Much has been written about MBO, and the general procedures are common knowledge. We encountered some resistance to the technique and made modifications which retained the major concepts but reduced the amount of detail which is usually associated with the technique. Using an MBO approach can add a major component to program evaluation. It makes planned work efforts explicit, establishes timelines, and pinpoints responsibility. Program development can be planned in a more orderly fashion, reducing the likelihood of decision-making occurring as a defensive posture. A staff person's time can be better utilized and focused on those objectives which have higher priority. The technique also provides a concrete basis for staff supervision and for coordination among staff at the middle management level.

Another variant, which we believe has considerable potential, combines elements of MBO and Goal Attainment Scaling. Goal Attainment Scaling techniques are outlined in detail in the next section, but a sample of one Goal Scale is included in Figure 3 to show how major work priorities can be scaled (Howe, 1976).

Note that only major activities are scaled and that the form is not filled with a great amount of detail. All management and supervisory positions involve some maintenance activities which are routine and must be done. However, they should not be the most important activities of a manager, and need not be included in a Goal Scale. Some type of monitoring of a clerical nature will usually suffice to ensure that routine chores are completed on time.

Middle management is a critical part of any organization, and program evaluation is particularly important at Level II positions in AEAs. The master plan has been developed by the state and the AEA director and his or her staff.

Figure 3
GOAL ATTAINMENT SCALE

August 1976 Start Date	June 1977 Score Date			Student Name
	Howe Teacher			School
Score	Percentile *Entry Level		× Exit Level	Town

SCALE HEADINGS:	SCALE 1: MONITORING AEA 16	SCALE 2: NEW PROGRAM DEVELOPMENT	SCALE 3: TRAINING STATE CONSULTANTS	SCALE 4: STATE PLAN
LEVELS:	(weight 1 =)	(weight 2 =)	(weight 3 =)	(weight 4 =)
Most unfavorable outcome thought likely	AEA 16 will abandon current plan and will not invest further in program evaluation efforts.	No new AEAs will participate in program evaluation efforts beyond token involvement.	DPI staff fails to become involved and does not attend any inservice training sessions.	AEAs request more staff and money with no evidence as to effectiveness of current operation.
Less than expected success	No further refinement of current evaluation plan.	One or two new AEAs will develop segments of an evaluation system.	Minimum of two DPI staff will participate in one or more inservice training sessions.	Majority of requests for staff and funds based on subjective opinion and emotion.
Expected level of success	AEA 16 will continue evaluation effort and operationalize pilot plans for collecting child change data with monitoring by me.	Minimum of three new AEAs will develop a program evaluation system with me in 1976-77.	Frank Vance, John Lanhan and two consultants will participate with me in inservice training of AEA staff for evaluation.	Evidence of some "outcome data" in state plan and of use of such data in future planning decisions.
More than expected success	Complete AEA-wide evaluation system will be operational with monitoring by me.	Four or five AEAs will participate in developing an evaluation system.	Several DPI staff will assume leadership in developing and monitoring AEA evaluation systems.	Annual plan and fiscal requests tied to evaluation evidence of current operation.
Most favorable outcome thought likely	Complete AEA-wide evaluation system will be operational and function without my help or monitoring.	More than five AEAs will develop a system.	State Division of Special Education will require an evaluation system of AEAs and will monitor progress.	Additional positions authorized to AEAs by State Superintendent based on outcome data showing success of program.

It is the job of the supervisors, consultants, and program heads to see that the plan is translated into action and to measure the results.

We see middle management as the key to successful program evaluation. It is the supervisor and the consultant who must deal with the problems of efficient application of technical skills to the teaching process, systematic ordering of the process so that teaching can take place with measurable results, and the maintenance of teamwork among the principal participants in the process.

LEVEL III EVALUATION PROCEDURES

Evaluation at Level III focuses specifically on child change data. The two most frequent approaches to documenting change in students are the use of pre- and post-test batteries and the recording of progress on specific behavioral objectives. Other useful systems are available commercially, such as the *Instructional Based Appraisal System* (Meyen, 1976) and various remedial curricular programs. Specific behavior recording, precision teaching, and classroom observation approaches may also provide excellent evaluative data on changes in students.

We view evaluation of student progress as primarily a teacher function, since it is most important to the child. The choice of evaluation approach used at Level III depends in part upon the intended use of the results of the evaluation. To meet the intent of recent state and federal legislation for the handicapped, evaluation should provide an annual review of student progress, assist in determining where to go with each child, and should directly relate to the planning and improvement of the instructional program.

An extension of the models cited above, and one which seems to provide promising possibilities to special education programs, is Goal Attainment Scaling as proposed by Kiresuk and Sherman (1968). Goal Attainment Scaling can be viewed as a logical evaluation approach for individualized programs using instructional objectives, prescriptive teaching, and behavior charting methods. It asks the teacher to predict the results for a specified future time and then provides a simple way of scoring the actual outcomes. The method concentrates on the major priorities thought important for each child, and can handle different priorities for different children.

We have piloted Goal Attainment Scaling in a number of communities and with many different types of special education programs. Teachers and support staff have been largely enthusiastic in learning the technique, and have found it a satisfying approach to individualizing program efforts and in evaluating their outcomes. Mastery of the technique comes from actually sitting down and writing scales for individual children. The first ones will be laborious and time-consuming. A complete Goal Attainment Scale can be written in about one-half hour after having done the first five or ten.

Goal Attainment Scaling Procedures

Scale Development. A number of priority areas should be selected for the student. These priorities will not necessarily include all the important work to be done with each child, but should be representative of the major goal areas to be concentrated upon in the special education program during the time covered by the Goal Attainment Scale. Typically, these major problem areas will have been identified in the child's staffing. Goals can then be determined by the teacher and support staff charged with responsibility for planning the child's program.

Once the priority areas for scaling have been identified, each should be given a title. The title may be abstract, theoretical, or vague. It is designed to focus the attention of someone inspecting the scale on the major goal areas being evaluated. The title may also be thought of as the place where the teacher constructing the scale has an opportunity to indicate the general problem area to which the specific variables described in the body of the scale correspond.

When priority areas have been selected and titles identified for the scale, a numerical weight (numbers 1, 2, 3, 4, or 5) can be added to each scale below the title. The weighting system indicates the relative importance of the scale. The scales can also be used without weighting if all goals are judged to be equally important. The higher the number used, the more significant the scale is relative to other scales. The title box can also be used to indicate any special sources of information for the scale, such as normative test data like KeyMath or Durrell Reading Tests. Figure 4 shows a complete Goal Attainment Scale example where the specific priority areas are not equally important. The scales have been weighted 5, 4, 3, and 4 respectively (Leone, 1975).

The key level for predictive purposes is the expected level, or middle box, on each five-point scale. The expected level presents the best, most realistic prediction possible of the outcome which will have been attained by the student at the score date. The statements ought to be realistic, so that the expected level of each scale reflects what outcome realistically could be attained by the score data, not necessarily what should be attained. The estimate of the expected outcome ought to be independent of the student's current level of functioning. It may be that the expected level outcome would reflect no change or even regression; in spite of the undesirableness of this situation, it belongs in the middle box if this outcome is thought most likely.

The expected level is usually developed first and should be the most likely outcome. The other outcome levels should be constructed after the expected level and should be thought less likely to occur. It is not required that all levels be written in on the scale, but at least one box on each side of the middle box must be specified. Thus, at least three of the five boxes or levels must be completed for each scale.

The "more than expected success" and "most favorable outcome thought likely" levels offer teaching objectives and guide program efforts and planning in the future. Although humanitarian instincts would lead us to hope we could accomplish these higher outcomes, the accurate use of the Goal Attainment Scaling technique would not allow these levels to be reached very frequently. Similarly, the "less than expected success" and the "most unfavorable outcome thought likely" should not occur as frequently as the middle box out-

Evaluating Special Education Programs

Figure 4

GOAL ATTAINMENT SCALE

9-1-75	6-1-75		Student Name
Start Date	Score Date		
	P. Leone		School
	Teacher		
Score	Percentile		Town
	*Entry Level		× Exit Level

SCALE HEADINGS:	COURSE CREDITS	TASK BEHAVIOR	USE OF LEISURE TIME	REGULAR CLASS INTEGRATION
LEVELS:	(weight 1 = 5)	(weight 2 = 4)	(weight 3 = 3)	(weight 4 = 4)
Most unfavorable outcome thought likely	Will fail all 7th grade classes and/or be excluded from continuing attendance in regular classes.	Almost no work accomplished in spite of continual teacher intervention.	Continual pattern of starting and soon thereafter quitting.	More than 20 hours per week of special class contact.
Less than expected success	Will fail two regular 7th grade classes.	Completes a quarter to a half of assignments with continual prodding and ultimatums.	Completes most of requirements with frequent adult supervision (3 or more per week).	12-20 hours of special class contact.
Expected level of success	Will fail one regular 7th grade class, but will pass on to 8th grade.	Completes half of expected assignments in resource room with frequent prodding.	Joins sports team, league, or club and completes season with periodic adult supervision (once per week).	Maintains appropriate behavior to the extent that he will have only 11 special class contact hours each week during last quarter.
More than expected success	Will successfully pass all 7th grade classes with D or C average.	Completes most assignments with 1 or 2 reminders.	Continues in 2 or more after-school groups with periodic supervision.	1-10 hours of special class contact.
Most favorable outcome thought likely	Will successfully pass all 7th grade classes with a B average.	Completes most assignments with no reminders.	Completes requirements of one team, club, league, or group with no special supervision.	Maintained completely as regular 7th grade student with no direct special class service.

come. Nevertheless, these less favorable outcomes are important to balance the picture of possible outcomes to pinpoint children and priority areas needing closer evaluation, and to help judge when special needs go beyond the program's capacity to meet them.

We recommend that more than one person be involved in writing the child's Goal Attainment Scale. In Iowa, the child's teacher, the Area Education Agency special education consultant, and the program's supervisor may share this responsibility and periodically meet and confer on the child's progress and the program's usefulness. The team may use this format to clarify and differentiate responsibilities in accomplishing the predicted outcomes.

Having a team of professionals involved in the Goal Attainment Scaling process provides a check and balance mechanism to avoid setting expected level statements unrealistically high or low. If the outcome statements must be agreed to by the program supervisor and the special education consultant, the likelihood of setting expected levels too low to "look good" or too high is minimized. With the use of pre/post normative test data as an additional element in the total evaluation process, the concern and/or likelihood of such an event occurring is reduced.

Learning to write Goal Scales is a developmental process. You learn primarily by experience, and gradually improve in being able to specify level outcomes within priority areas. Although an individual program is written for each student, there is some overlap of scales among students. After having written a number of scales, you will find that you can often draw from the bank of earlier scales for some items.

Scoring and Interpretation. The student's level of functioning at the time the scale is developed can be noted on the Goal Scale form by placing an asterisk in each box for entry level. At the followup score date, the scales are marked with an "X" for outcome. Two possible kinds of effectiveness measures can be collected from the Goal Attainment Scaling system: Whether or not the "expected" levels of outcome are reached, and whether or not change occurred. The degree of change can also be documented on the basis of the post-test data or records gathered at the predetermined date. To score the Goal Attainment Scale, scores of -2 (most unfavorable), -1 (less than expected), 0 (expected level,) $+1$ (more than expected), and $+2$ (most favorable) are given for each final outcome. A formula or calculation table is then used to convert these scores to standard scores with a mean of 50 and a standard deviation of 10.

In order to add composite Goal Attainment Scores of various children or to compare one child longitudinally, some cautions of a statistical nature should be kept in mind. The various goal scales should be done realistically, so that the expected mean value for the group is near zero (standard score = 50) and with a standard deviation approximating one (converted standard score = 10). Stated another way, about two-thirds of the composite scores of the total group should fall within the "expected level of success" on the Goal Attainment Scale; about 10% to 15% should obtain scores of "less than expected success"; 10% to 15% should receive "more than expected success"; and very few (2% to 5%) should achieve scores at the extremes of "most favorable" or "most unfavorable outcome thought likely." If there is considerable variance from this as a group, the effect is that some composite goal scores will have heavier weights than others and make the comparisons less valid. The cautions just noted should not discourage use of the technique, but should be kept in mind.

Applications for Use. As indicated earlier, results from individual evaluation scales are potentially useful in a variety of applications. First, scored scales provide information on individual child changes upon which decisions regarding the student's continuation or change in placement can be initiated and resolved. Secondly, the scored scale in and of itself is a data base on the child's placement that can be inserted into the student's cumulative folder for documentation of placement and subsequent instruction. Thirdly, the scale provides the teacher, the Area Education Agency special education consultant, and the program's supervisor a systematic means to review the achievements of the students served in the program.

The potential for comparing program models as well as types of instructional designs (behavior modifications, use of paraprofessionals and/or associates in instruction, teaching methods, etc.) over the years is an aspect yet to be explored as the implementation of the process proceeds to its conclusion. Indeed, the use of Goal Attainment Scaling as described in the proposed model appears to be most promising.

REFERENCES

Howe, C. E. *Goal scaling used to evaluate major work priorities.* Unpublished manuscript. College of Education, Division of Special Education, University of Iowa, Iowa City, IA, 1976.

Howe, C. E., & Fitzgerald, M. E. *A model for evaluating special education programs in Iowa Area Education Agencies.* Des Moines, IA: Iowa State Department of Public Instruction, Division of Special Education, 1976.

Johnson, W. *An example of an opinionnaire field tested in AEA 16 in the spring of 1976.* Unpublished manuscript, Director of Special Education, Area Education Agency 16, Mount Pleasant, IA, 1976.

Kiresuk, T., & Sherman, R. Goal attainment scaling: A general method for evaluating comprehensive mental health programs. *Community Mental Health Journal,* 1968, 4(6), 443-453.

Leone, P. *Sample of complete goal attainment scale example where specific priority areas are not equally important.* Unpublished manuscript, Child Psychiatry Service, University of Iowa Hospitals and Clinics, Iowa City, IA, 1975.

Meyen, E. *Instructional based appraisal system.* Bellevue, WA: Edmark Associates, 1976.

Popham, W. J. *An evaluation guidebook: A set of practical guidelines for the educational evaluator.* Los Angeles: The Instructional Objectives Exchange, 1972.

State of Iowa. *Rules of special education.* Des Moines: Department of Public Instruction, 1974.

Stufflebeam, D. L., et al. *Educational evaluation and decision making.* Itasca, IL: Peacock Publishers, 1971.

Use of the word assessment *in the title of this article is not antithetical to evaluation activities. Rather, evaluation includes before instruction (assessment) and during instruction (planning) elements as well as after instruction (results). Heiss selected two components of the evaluation process that often are neglected in implementing evaluation procedures. He describes in considerable detail ways in which input (child variables) and processes (instructional variables) can be matched precisely to ensure that the outputs (results) approximate, meet, or exceed objectives of instruction. In essence, Heiss has described a set of tools that a teacher or instructional team can use to help ensure child progress.*

Relating Educational Assessment to Instructional Planning

Warren Heiss, *Montclair State College*

One of the positive effects of the learning disabilities movement has been the focus on "diagnostic/prescriptive teaching," a synergistic relationship between the assessment of learning and treatment procedures. While this relationship is desirable, there is often a gap between the assessment of learning and the delivery of appropriate learning activities.

Several explanations can be offered for the distance between psychoeducational assessment and instructional planning. These include:

1. The diagnostic effort is often removed in its context from the treatment effort.
2. In many instances, the diagnostician is not the same person who delivers the instruction.
3. It is often assumed that the evidence uncovered in a diagnostic procedure "causes" the dysfunction in academic performance, when in fact the diagnostic evidence is simply a correlate of the dysfunction.

Of importance here is the recognition that the typical model for diagnosis is reductionistic, and that this reduction overlooks the context for the learning and assigns inappropriate causes to the presumed disorders. This reductionistic approach is illustrated in Figure 1.

Figure 1 shows that referrals of children with learning problems flow from a recognition of poor performance in academic areas (I). To verify this, norm-referenced tests are used (II) to estimate the degree to which the child is falling behind his or her peers. When this degree of "behindness" is established, a search is begun to locate causes. This search more often than not results in "correlate" testing (IV). It can be seen, then, that the direction of reduction is a movement from an academic context which the referral was made to an analysis of the correlates of the problem. Missing from that reduction, and of importance for this article, is a qualitative analysis (III). The premise of this paper is that the more nearly the assessment of learning approximates the context in which the learning problem was found, the greater the degree of success in matching instructional planning to instructional assessment.

FIGURE 1
Reductionistic Factors in the Evaluation of Learning

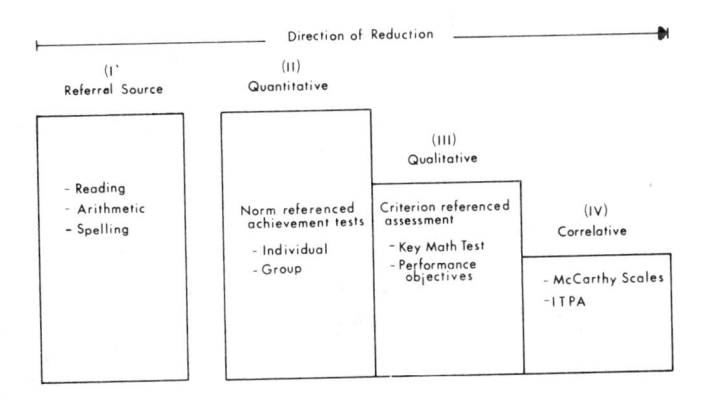

```
|─────────── Direction of Reduction ───────────▶|

     (I')              (II)
Referral Source    Quantitative

                                   (III)
                                Qualitative

  - Reading
  - Arithmetic    Norm referenced   Criterion referenced      (IV)
  - Spelling      achievement tests assessment             Correlative
                    - Individual    - Key Math Test
                    - Group         - Performance
                                      objectives         - McCarthy Scales
                                                         - ITPA
```

The search through this qualitative realm is of particular use by both diagnosticians and instructors, because it forms the interface between the two. At some point, the interpretation of diagnostic data must be related to instructional planning. Correlate measures may hold clues as to *how* to teach a given child, but rarely do such measures provide information about *what* to teach a child. This article offers techniques for developing ways of qualitatively assessing learning behavior as it relates to classroom performance.

TASK ANALYSIS

Instructional planning and the evaluation of the outcomes of that planning are directly related to the degree to which learners and learning activities are appropriately matched. Task analysis provides a way of displaying and evaluating diagnostic data for the purposes of making this a sound match. Lerner (1976) explains the meaning of task analysis properly:

> ... task analysis is a method that is used to provide further diagnostic information; it is an approach to evaluation designed to lead to appropriate teaching. Two ways to think about task analysis are . . . (1) the *modality-processing* approach . . . (2) the *skills-sequence* approach . . . . The first analyzes the child, while the second analyzes the content to be learned (p. 108).

Lerner's definition recognizes that instruction and the evaluation of instruction are based on both processes and products. From the perspective of task analysis, "processes" refer to those correlates of learning which reside with the child. "Products" are those content elements of the learning situation which are related to academic skill areas, curriculum, and instructional materials. Essential, then, for instructional planning and evaluation is a matching of processes (correlates) with products (content). From the standpoint of the practitioner, decisions regarding instructional planning and evaluation depend upon an ability to develop hypotheses within the realm of process and product analysis. In effect, the instructional planner must have a repertory of questions available for continuous use throughout the course of the instruction. The next two sections of this article offer schedules of such questions which attend to the correlates and content of instructional planning and evaluation.

Developing Correlate Questions

To provide for task analysis using correlates of learning, a grid is provided in Figure 2. The Task Analysis Grid contains a series of items in three general areas: decoding, processing, and encoding. Each of these areas is further divided into major components, with each component subdivided into specific qualities.

The *decoding* area contains haptic, auditory, visual, and sensory integration (SI) components. These represent the modality systems available in the learner for application to the perception of a task. Each of the modality systems has been subdivided into task demands which may require discrimination, closure, memory, or sequencing. The decoding component of sensory integration (using two senses simultaneously) has been separated into auditory-visual (Aud.-Vis.) and visual-haptic (Vis.-Hap.).

The *processing* area is described by features taken from Guilford's (1967)

FIGURE 2
Task Analysis Grid Showing Correlate Behaviors

© W. E. Heiss, 1974

TASK ANALYSIS GRID

DECODING				PROCESSING					ENCODING	
Haptic	Auditory	Vision	SI	Cognition	Memory	Convergent	Divergent	Evaluation	Motor	Vocal
Discrim. / Closure / Memory / Sequen.	Discrim. / Closure / Memory / Sequen.	Discrim. / Closure / Memory / Sequen.	Aud.-Vis. / Vis.-Hap.	Figural / Symbolic / Semantic / Behavioral	Figural / Symbolic / Semantic / Behavioral	Figural / Symbolic / Semantic / Behavioral	Figural / Symbolic / Semantic / Behavioral	Figural / Symbolic / Semantic / Behavioral	Tracing / Copying / Drawing / Pointing / Gesturing / Pattern Bld. / Writing	Single Word / Phrases / Sentences / Extended Sp.

TASK

Instructional Planning for Exceptional Children

work and Meeker's (1969) analysis of Guilford. Guilford suggests that there are intellectual processes known as "operations" and defined as:

1. *Cognition*—referring to recognition or discovery of information.
2. *Memory*—referring to the retention and reproduction of information.
3. *Convergent production*—referring to the process of arriving at the single conventional solution to a problem.
4. *Divergent production*—referring to the process of developing novel solutions; creativity.
5. *Evaluation*—referring to the development judgments.

In addition, Guilford postulates that these operations act on various forms of content, of which four types have been defined:

1. *Figural*—referring to information that is concrete (that can be seen, heard, or felt).
2. *Symbolic*—referring to data in the form of abstract symbols (letters, numerals).
3. *Semantic*—referring to the attachment of meanings to symbolic information.
4. *Behavioral*—referring to information of an affective nature regarding the self or others.

The *encoding* area is divided into the major components of "motor" and "vocal." Each of these components is subcategorized into empirically determined behaviors, as required by various tasks. Motor behaviors include tracing, copying, drawing, pointing, gesturing, pattern building, and writing. Vocal behaviors are described along a sliding scale defined by single word utterances, phrases, sentences, and extended speaking (telling a story), as demanded by various tasks.

Overall, then, the Task Analysis Grid provides 45 correlate behaviors which may be implicated in the learning process in varying patterns, depending on the task at hand. In essence, these correlates act as question sources which aid in deciding how a child is processing information in a given task setting. The correlates may be observed informally, or tested by formal procedures.

To illustrate how the Task Analysis Grid might be used, Figure 3 presents an analysis of the 12 subtests from the Illinois Test of Psycholinguistic Abilities (Kirk, McCarthy & Kirk, 1968). It shows the distribution of the 12 ITPA subtests across the 45 possible correlates on the Task Analysis Grid. (Note: The analysis of the ITPA across the grid correlates is based on "best fit judgments." Only the major correlates deemed to be required for solving ITPA subtest questions are indicated.)

If we wish to show the relative strengths and weaknesses of these correlates in a given case, this can be done by rating the ITPA subtest performances as "good" (+), more than six scale score points above the child's mean; "average" (0), within six scale score points of the child's mean; or "poor" (−), more than six scale score points below the child's mean. Figure 4 illustrates the conversion of ITPA scale scores into the three rating categories, and the distribution of those rating patterns on the Task Analysis Grid.

FIGURE 3
Distribution of the Twelve ITPA Subtests Across Correlates on Task Analysis Grid

TASK ANALYSIS GRID

DECODING

TASK	Haptic: Discrim.	Haptic: Closure	Haptic: Memory	Haptic: Sequen.	Auditory: Discrim.	Auditory: Closure	Auditory: Memory	Auditory: Sequen.	Vision: Discrim.	Vision: Closure	Vision: Memory	Vision: Sequen.	SI: Aud.-Vis.	SI: Vis.-Hap.
AUD REC.					•									
VIS REC.									•		•			
VIS. SEQ MEM											•	•		
AUD. ASSOC.					•	•	•	•						
AUD. SEQ. MEM.					•		•	•						
VIS. ASSOC.									•					
VIS. CLOS.									•	•				
VERB. EXP.	•								•					•
GRAM. CLOS.					•	•			•					
MAN. EXP.									•					
AUD. CLOS.					•	•								
SOUND BL					•									

PROCESSING

TASK	Cognition: Figural	Cognition: Symbolic	Cognition: Semantic	Cognition: Behavioral	Memory: Figural	Memory: Symbolic	Memory: Semantic	Memory: Behavioral	Convergent: Figural	Convergent: Symbolic	Convergent: Semantic	Convergent: Behavioral	Divergent: Figural	Divergent: Symbolic	Divergent: Semantic	Divergent: Behavioral	Evaluation: Figural	Evaluation: Symbolic	Evaluation: Semantic	Evaluation: Behavioral
AUD REC.			•				•				•									
VIS REC.		•				•				•										
VIS. SEQ MEM		•				•				•										
AUD. ASSOC.			•				•				•									
AUD. SEQ. MEM.		•				•				•										
VIS. ASSOC.		•				•				•										
VIS. CLOS.		•								•										
VERB. EXP.	•				•				•				•							
GRAM. CLOS.			•				•				•									
MAN. EXP.		•				•				•										
AUD. CLOS.		•								•										
SOUND BL		•								•										

ENCODING

TASK	Motor: Tracing	Motor: Copying	Motor: Drawing	Motor: Pointing	Motor: Gesturing	Motor: Pattern Bld.	Motor: Writing	Vocal: Single Word	Vocal: Phrases	Vocal: Sentences	Vocal: Extended Sp.
AUD REC.								•			
VIS REC.				•							
VIS. SEQ MEM						•					
AUD. ASSOC.								•			
AUD. SEQ. MEM.									•		
VIS. ASSOC.				•							
VIS. CLOS.				•							
VERB. EXP.								•	•	•	
GRAM. CLOS.								•			
MAN. EXP.					•						
AUD. CLOS.								•			
SOUND BL								•			

FIGURE 4
Rated ITPA Subtest Scale Scores Distributed Across Correlates on Task Analysis Grid

TASK ANALYSIS GRID

DECODING

		Haptic				Auditory				Vision				SI	
	TASK	Discrim.	Closure	Memory	Sequen.	Discrim.	Closure	Memory	Sequen.	Discrim.	Closure	Memory	Sequen.	Aud.-Vis.	Vis.-Hap.
–	AUD. REC.					–									
o	VIS. REC.									o		o			
+	VIS. SEQ. MEM.											+	+		
–	AUD. ASSOC.					–	–	–	–						
o	AUD. SEQ. MEM.					o		o	o						
–	VIS ASSOC.									–					
+	VIS CLOS.									+	+				
o	VERB. EXP.	o								o					o
–	GR. CLOS.					–	–			–					
o	MAN. EXP.									o					

PROCESSING

		Cognition				Memory				Convergent				Divergent				Evaluation			
	TASK	Figural	Symbolic	Semantic	Behavioral	Figural	Symbolic	Semantic	Behavioral	Figural	Symbolic	Semantic	Behavioral	Figural	Symbolic	Semantic	Behavioral	Figural	Symbolic	Semantic	Behavioral
–	AUD. REC.			–				–				–									
o	VIS. REC.		o				o				o										
+	VIS. SEQ. MEM.		+				+				+										
–	AUD. ASSOC.			–				–				–									
o	AUD. SEQ. MEM.		o				o				o										
–	VIS ASSOC.		–				–				–										
+	VIS CLOS.		+								+										
o	VERB. EXP.	o				o				o				o							
–	GR. CLOS.			–				–				–									
o	MAN. EXP.		o				o				o										

ENCODING

		Motor							Vocal			
	TASK	Tracing	Copying	Drawing	Pointing	Gesturing	Pattern Bld.	Writing	Single Word	Phrases	Sentences	Extended Sp.
–	AUD. REC.								–			
o	VIS. REC.				o							
+	VIS. SEQ. MEM.						+					
–	AUD. ASSOC.								–			
o	AUD. SEQ. MEM.									o		
–	VIS ASSOC.				–							
+	VIS CLOS.				+							
o	VERB. EXP.								o	o	o	
–	GR. CLOS.								–			
o	MAN. EXP.					o						

ITPA scale scores and ratings for a child-

Aud. Rec.	17 –	Aud. Seq. Mem.	31 o
Vis. Rec.	30 o	Vis. Assoc.	10 –
Vis. Seq. Mem.	43 +	Vis. Clos.	34 +
Aud. Assoc.	9 –	Verb. Exp.	28 o
Gram. Clos.	17 –	Man. Exp.	27 o

Relating Assessment to Instructional Planning

By inspecting the pattern of "+," "o," and "−" symbols on the grid, statements about the relative strengths and weaknesses of the various correlates may be made for this case. It can be seen in this instance that, on a comparative basis, the rated ITPA scores show strengths in visual decoding correlates and weaknesses in auditory ones. Beyond this, an analysis of the processing correlates indicates that the child exhibits difficulty in manipulating tasks containing semantic content, while tasks containing figural and symbolic content are processed relatively easily. An inspection of the rating patterns for the encoding correlates supports the picture of a child who can express himself better motorically than vocally. (You should explore other rating patterns and develop hypotheses regarding the relative strengths and weaknesses displayed by this child.)

It is important to recognize that this type of analysis requires the evaluator to view the interaction among decoding, processing, and encoding correlates. For the pattern of rated scores given in Figure 4, there is a relationship between the depression in certain auditory decoding correlates and processing correlates. Negative ratings have been applied to those correlates of the ITPA subtests which require the auditory processing of semantic content. When the content of the auditory subtests is symbolic in nature, the child shows relatively good performance. An analysis of this sort reminds the evaluator that the descriptive statement, "The child presents evidence of auditory decoding problems," is insufficient unless it is coupled with the modifier, "when the task requires the processing of semantic content."

The existing patterns of correlate behaviors as described by the Task Analysis Grid are valuable only as they explain academic problems. Knowing that a child exhibits a visual sequencing deficit has meaning only to the extent that it helps to shed light on the child's spelling or reading problem.

Developing Content Questions

The task analysis of academic skill areas is best accomplished through the use of sets of instructional objectives. Many sources exist for lists of such objectives. To illustrate the use of instructional objectives, the materials provided by the Instructional Based Appraisal System (IBAS) will be used (Meyen, 1976).

Table 1 is a partial listing of instructional objectives from IBAS for reading and mathematics. (Note: For reading, the complete list from IBAS includes 73 objectives categorized under the headings of reading readiness, word attack skills, comprehension, study skills, and reading extension. For mathematics, 100 objectives are categorized by numeration, symbols and geometry, addition and subtraction, multiplication and division, fractions, word problems, measurement, money, and time.)

TABLE 1

EXAMPLES OF INSTRUCTIONAL OBJECTIVES TAKEN FROM THE INSTRUCTIONAL BASED APPRAISAL SYSTEM

Index to Reading Objectives

A. **Reading**

Reading Readiness
- A-2   To assist the student in the recognition of shapes.
- A-3   To assist the student in matching objects by categories.
- A-9   To assist the student in indicating words which sound alike and words which sound different.

Word Attack Skills
- A-14   To assist the student in identifying the initial consonant.
- A-15   To assist the student in identifying the final consonant.
- A-18   To assist the student in identifying the short vowels.
- A-19   To assist the student in identifying the long vowels

Comprehension
- A-42   To assist the student in the use of picture clues.
- A-45   To assist the student in finding the main idea of a story.
- A-51   To assist the student in predicting outcomes.

Index to Mathematics Objectives

B. **Mathematics**

Numeration
- B-1   To assist the student in identifying sets of actual or pictured objects.
- B-2   To assist the student in matching equal sets.
- B-4   To assist the student in matching unequal sets.
- B-5   To assist the student in correctly using the terms "more than," "less than," and "the same as."
- B-7   To assist the student in correctly using the ordinals: first, second, last.

Symbols and Geometry
- B-17   To assist the student in identifying geometric shapes: circle, square, triangle, rectangle.
- B-19   To assist the student in drawing the following geometric shapes: circle, square, triangle, rectangle.

One feature of the IBAS objectives is the fact that they address the instructor and/or evaluator. By using the verb phrase "to assist," allowances are made for reaching the objective by capitalizing on the pattern of correlate behaviors defined by the Task Analysis Grid. Essentially, these lists of instructional objectives represent a question pool for evaluating learning.

If the objectives as listed in IBAS are appropriately descriptive of the instructional program in a given classroom, the objectives can serve several purposes.

1. The lists may be used as an evaluative checklist for each child.

Notations may be made indicating when a child shows evidence of having mastered an objective.
2. The lists may be used as criterion-referenced schedules for evaluating measurement devices. For example, items from the Peabody Individual Achievement Test (Dunn & Markwardt, 1970) can be matched to lists of objectives to determine the variety of skills and behaviors measured.
3. The lists may be used as a framework for the design of instructional activities. In this regard, the instructional objectives define *what* should be taught, while the pattern of the correlates from the Task Analysis Grid defines *how* the activity is to be presented.
4. The lists may be used to evaluate features of instructional materials. Knowing that certain instructional materials are aimed at the acquisition of specific objectives allows for a more cogent match between the materials and the learner.
5. The lists may be used as a communication device between diagnostician and instructor. If instructors can develop their referral questions in terms of the objective statements, diagnosticians can focus on areas of inquiry related to these referrals.
6. The lists may be used as reporting devices to parents and teachers for communicating the instructional progress of a child.

In general, then, lists of instructional objectives become referents for making qualitative judgments to bridge the gap between quantitative and correlate measurement. Instructional objectives can be applied directly to the planning and evaluation of educational activities. If the planning is appropriately designed, teaching/learning activities become both diagnostic and prescriptive in nature.

BLENDING QUALITATIVE AND CORRELATE ANALYSES

To illustrate the relationship between qualitative analysis (the use of instructional objectives) and correlate analysis (Task Analysis Grid), the sample inquiries which follow were developed. The inquiries employ instructional materials in the form of transparent overlays as shown in Figure 5 (Weiss, et al., 1966). (Note: Each overlay is projected in sequence. As an overlay is added, more information is added. Following the addition of each overlay, questions are asked and responses are recorded.)

The nature of questions to be asked and the tolerance limits for responses must be adjusted by the instructor/evaluator as a function of the purpose of the exercise. In earlier sections of this paper, two sources of questions were made available. One set of questions may be developed from instructional objec-

Instructional Planning for Exceptional Children

tives (Table 1). Another set of questions evolves from the Task Analysis Grid (Figure 2). To provide a framework for these question sources, Goldstein's (1975) inductive teaching procedure is helpful. The inductive teaching procedure is a way of eliciting responses from children in a systematic way.

What follows, then, are three areas of inquiry—inductive, instructional objective, and correlative—useful for framing diagnostic/prescriptive teaching activities. For each area of inquiry, a brief explanation is provided, followed by suggested questions.

Inductive Inquiry

Goldstein (1975) suggests the use of inductive questioning when presenting instructional activities. This approach is in the form of a five-stage paradigm. The stages are as follows:

1. *Labeling.* Questions which elicit the identities of the major components of what is to be explored (e.g., names of objects or actions).
2. *Detailing.* Questions which elicit the attachment of specific characteristics to major components (e.g., size, color, position, quantity).
3. *Inferring.* Questions which elicit the conclusion of what the function or condition of a major component is, based on appropriate labeling and detailing.
4. *Predicting.* Questions which elicit responses about the inference when additional data are made available. These questions often take the form of "What if?" questions.
5. *Generalizing.* Following a series of prediction questions, the elicitation of a response of conceptual nature that provides the child with a category or classification for the major component(s) under consideration.

The inductive questioning procedure is a reductionistic method. If a generalization cannot be reached, more opportunities for prediction must be given. If inappropriate responses to prediction questions are given, the inference must be reestablished. If the inference is incorrect, details must be reviewed or expanded. If details are not perceived, the major component (label) to be explored must be redefined.

Table 2 is an inductive inquiry related to the instructional materials shown in Figure 5. Because Table 2 is only a sample of an inductive inquiry, not all possible questions or responses can be presented. The issue is one of moving from label and detail questions through to inference, prediction, and generalization questions. As responses are elicited, begin to consider those questions to be used in the instructional objective inquiry.

Relating Assessment to Instructional Planning

TABLE 2

INDUCTIVE INQUIRY

Overlay 1

Questions	**Anticipated Responses**
"What do you see?"	"An elephant."
"What else is there?"	"Clouds."
"What can you tell me about the elephant?"	"It has legs, tusks (teeth), tail, eyes, ears."
"How many clouds are there?"	"Two."
"How many elephants are there?"	"One."
"Where is the elephant?"	"Up there in the clouds, in the sky"
"How did the elephant get there?"	"It flew" (accept any response)

Overlay 2

Questions	**Anticipated Responses**
"What do you see now?"	"Elephant, houses, trees, a boy, a street, buildings, bushes."
"What can you tell me about the buildings?"	"They are big (tall); they have windows."
"How many trees are there?"	"Four."
"How many windows are there?"	"A lot." (any reasonable count)
"Where is the elephant?"	"On top of the building, on the roof."
"Where is the boy?"	"Next to the building, near the tree, under the tree."
"What is the boy doing?"	"Running, looking at the elephant."
"How did the elephant get there?"	"In the elevator," "It was dropped by a helicopter." (accept any response)

Overlay 3

Questions	**Anticipated Responses**
"What do you see now?"	"A parade, more people, another building."
(Continue asking questions to elicit all pertinent details.)	
"How did the elephant get there?"	"It's a balloon."

Instructional Objective Inquiry

The instructional objectives shown in Table 1 may be converted to questions for the purpose of assessing student performance, or for developing diagnostic/prescriptive activities. In the inquiry that follows, (Table 3), the instructional objective code is listed and an illustrative question(s) is provided related to the content of each overlay of the transparency material shown in Figure 5. In addition, each question will be based on the responses elicited in the inductive inquiry.

The choice of instructional objectives for use in an inquiry such as this is a function of what needs to be known by the instructor/evaluator. While this inquiry is being developed, begin to think of those correlate behaviors (Task Analysis Grid) that warrant investigation.

Instructional Planning for Exceptional Children

TABLE 3
INSTRUCTIONAL OBJECTIVE INQUIRY

Overlay 1

Objectives	Questions
A-14	"Listen to these words: tail, tusks, teeth. What sound do these words begin with?"
A-15	"Listen to these words: tusks, legs, eyes, ears, clouds. What sound do these words end with?"
A-9	"Do these words sound the same or different? elephant-clouds; teeth-legs, trunk-ears."
A-51	"How did the elephant get there?"
B-1, B-4, B-5	"How many clouds are there? How many elephants are there? Are there more clouds than elephants?"

Overlay 2

Objectives	Questions
A-9, A-14, A-15	Repeat as in Overlay 1 with added words: house, boy, street, buildings, bushes, windows.
A-42	"Can someone tell me a story about this picture?"
A-51	"How did the elephant get there?"
B-1, B-2, B-4, B-5	"How many trees are there? How many buildings are there? How many people are there? How many elephants are there? How many clouds are there?"
	"Are there more trees than clouds? Are there more trees than buildings? Are there the same number of people as elephants?"

Overlay 3

Objectives	Questions
A-9, A-14, A-15	Repeat as in Overlays 1 and 2, using added words.
A-42, A-45	"What happened in this story?"
A-51	"How did the elephant get there?"
B-1, B-2, B-4, B-5	Repeat as in Overlays 1 and 2, using added sets of marchers and crowds.
B-7	"Find the first person in the parade."
	"Where is the last person in the parade?"

Correlate Inquiry

Inquiries regarding the correlates of learning may be made within the context of both inductive inquiries and instructional objective inquiries. Using the Task Analysis Grid (Figure 2) as a question source, situations may be created to establish the degree to which the behaviors listed on the grid are intact. Table 4 integrates the instructional objectives inquiry (which is already based on the inductive inquiry) with the correlate inquiry.

Relating Assessment to Instructional Planning

FIGURE 5
Transparency Overlay Sequence

Overlay 1

Overlay 2

Overlay 3

TABLE 4
CORRELATE INQUIRY

Overlay 1

Correlate Behaviors	Instructional Objectives	Situations
Visual Disc.	A-2	Provide children with cutouts of both cloud formations. Have children match them to projected images.
Auditory Disc.	A-9, A-14, A-15	Using elicited words from inductive inquiry, develop word pairs and question children as to their likenesses and differences as the words are repeated aloud. Vary questions to elicit sameness or difference based on initial and final sounds.
Divergence	A-51	Provide the children with an opportunity to express as many ideas as possible for "how the elephant got there."

Overlay 2

Correlate Behaviors	Instructional Objectives	Situations
Visual Memory	A-42	After showing Overlay 2, remove it and ask children to tell what is missing.
Tracing	A-42	Project Overlay 2 on the chalkboard, and have different children trace around objects with chalk.
Visual Disc. Symbolic-Conv. Pattern Building	A-3, B-1, B-2 B-4, B-5	Provide children with cutouts of objects projected in Overlay 2 (two buildings, elephant, boy, four trees, two clouds). Have children match them to the projection. Ask children to sort objects by type. Count the number of objects in each group. Question children about which group has "more," "the same," and/or "fewer" objects.
Drawing	A-51	Project Overlay 2 on chalkboard. Have children draw responses as to how the elephant "got there."

Overlay 3

Correlate Behaviors	Instructional Objectives	Situations
Visual Disc. Visual Seq. Visual Memory Memory/Conv. Extended Sp.	A-42, A-45	Project each overlay in sequence. Allow enough exposure time for each child to view the image. Remove the transparency and ask children to tell the story.
Visual Clos.	B-2	Project Overlay 3 on chalkboard. Have children draw windows on building at top-left until there are equal sets of windows on each face of building.

SUMMARY

Adequate assessment for appropriate instructional planning requires bridging the gap between the diagnostic event and the development of instructional plans. Instructional assessment and planning must take into account the relationship between *what* is to be learned and *how* it is to be presented.

Task analysis is one technique for creating a closer match between assessment and instruction. This paper reviewed procedures for developing task analysis of measures of correlates of learning by presenting a Task Analysis Grid. In addition, it is shown that instructional objectives can be used to analyze the subject matter structures of reading and mathematics.

Finally, the relationship between correlate analysis and instructional objective analysis was demonstrated, through the use of inductive questioning procedures as they applied to a given piece of instructional material. This resulted in the formulation of a series of inquiries useful for assessing and planning instruction. Overall, the more nearly assessment approximates instructional events, the more effective that assessment will be as an aid to planning those events.

REFERENCES

Dunn, L. & Markwardt, F. *Peabody individual achievement test*. Circle Pines, MN: American Guidance Service, 1970.
Goldstein, H. G. *The social learning curriculum*. Columbus: Merrill, 1975.
Guilford, J. P. *The nature of human intelligence*. New York: McGraw-Hill, 1967.
Kirk, S. A., McCarthy, J. J., & Kirk, W. D. *Illinois test of psycholinguistic abilities* (Rev. ed.). Urbana, IL: University of Illinois Press, 1968.
Lerner, J. W. *Children with learning disabilities* (2nd ed.). Boston: Houghton Mifflin, 1976.
Meeker, M. N. *The structure of the intellect: Its interpretation and uses*. Columbus: Merrill, 1969.
Meyen, E. L. *Instructional based appraisal system*. Bellevue, WA: Edmark Associates, 1976.
Weiss, M. J., et al. *Tweedy transparencies visual lingual reading program*. Florham Park, NJ: Bessler, 1966.

The movement to educate children who exhibit a wide range of behavior variance in the same learning environment is labeled as mainstreaming or placement in the least restrictive environment. As Keogh and Levitt emphasize, professionals too often have advocated for the concept of mainstreaming rather than the "how to" of it. The outcome of this paradox is that children become the victims rather than the beneficiaries of good intentions.

This selection provides descriptions of mainstream evaluation studies, but its most important contribution is in the realm of future program development needs and the continued evaluation of results obtained from actual program changes. As the authors state, educators must be child advocates in word and *deed, thus making programs the servant rather than the master of this advocacy.*

Special Education in the Mainstream: A Confrontation of Limitations?

Barbara K. Keogh and Marc L. Levitt
University of California–Los Angeles

Reflecting on the course of American education, historians of the future may well refer to the period of the 1960s and 1970s as the "Years of the Law." Litigation and legislation have addressed abuses in traditional public educational systems; the results have been dramatic, abrupt, and emotionally charged. Major Federal direction to change was contained in the Elementary and Secondary Education Act of 1965 (P. L. 89-10) which recognized that "millions of children did not perform adequately in their schools and that many schools and teachers were ill equipped to help them" (Halpern, 1975). Included in those groups of pupils in need of additional or compensatory help were handicapped children. Special education, that frequently neglected and overlooked part of the educational system, became a major target for change.

In addition to legislative action on the Federal level, state and local educational establishments were challenged and attacked by parents and other consumer groups. The right to education, more specifically the right to *appropriate* education, was at issue. Detailed review of the relevant litigation has been provided by other authors (see Cohen & De Young, 1973; Kirp, 1973; Kirp, Buss & Kuriloff, 1974). Of particular importance is the point that legal decisions provided the basis and impetus for change in educational programs and procedures, influencing both the nature of services and the pupil populations to be served. Although possible inequities and inadequacies in educational programs were known to educators for some time, it was legal and legislative mandates which forced a notably reluctant educational establishment to change (Weintraub, 1972).

As important as it is to emphasize the effects of litigation and legislation on changes in educational practice, it would be naive and inaccurate to report that all of the mandates have been translated into successful programs. The courts have spelled out the respective rights and responsibilities of pupils and educational systems and have mandated change. But as noted by attorney Bancroft in a recent address in San Francisco (1975), courts have limitations. Legal decisions and legislative action do not necessarily ensure development of optimal or even appropriate programs. Funding support is frequently lacking or, at best, minimal. There are inadequate numbers of trained personnel and limited substantive information about teaching-learning conditions for exceptional pupils. Although in most cases sympathetic with the court and legislative mandates, educators, too, have limitations. In a number of programs for exceptional children, we may be approaching a "confrontation of limitations." Many current mainstream educational efforts may well be dramatic examples.

MAINSTREAMING IN THE CONTEXT OF SOCIAL CHANGE

In the broadest sense, mainstreaming refers to instruction of pupils within the regular educational setting. Said simply, the regular educational program is viewed as bearing primary responsibility for educating all pupils, including those with handicapping conditions. In a field frequently characterized by vested interests and provincialism, the enthusiastic and almost unanimous acceptance of "mainstreaming" as the optimal plan for educating most exceptional children is truly remarkable. Few educational innovations have so caught the fancy of special educators and parents alike, and a broad variety of mainstream educational programs for widely diverse exceptional pupils have sprung up throughout the country. On the national level, the National Advisory Committee on the Handicapped in 1974 endorsed the goal of placement in the "least restrictive" educational environment; Federal support for development of mainstream efforts is apparent at both operational and research levels—for example, major BEH funding for Project Prime (Kaufman, Semmel & Agard, 1974). Training institutions have rewritten preservice curricula for the preparation of teachers and traditional categories of classification and grouping are disappearing. Self-contained special education is "out"; resource rooms, integrated placement, and consultant teachers are "in."

Ethnic and Minority Status

Mainstream education is congruent with other social changes involving handicapped individuals: decentralization of institutional programs to local communities; removal of physical barriers to access for physically handicapped individuals; mandated "set-asides" in Federally supported Head Start and vocational education programs. Certainly mainstreaming is consistent with broad issues involving rights to education, due process guarantees, and the like, and must be viewed within the social-political context of the 1960s and 1970s. The massive Coleman report (Coleman, 1968) provided documentation for the confounding of ethnic minority status and poor achievement in school. Recognition of inequities in opportunities and rights associated with ethnic and/or socioeconomic status were delineated, and the powerful influences of these conditions on educational decisions became apparent. It was argued that traditional self-contained special education programs inadvertently served to maintain the status quo by providing educational programs based on limited and often inaccurate assumptions about pupils' abilities and competencies—i.e., programs reinforced the very characteristics on which the pupils had been placed, so that selection and instructional systems were in a sense mutually self-supporting or self-perpetuating. Many of the practices in both selection and placement and in instructional services came under attack in the courts. As noted by Ross, DeYoung, and Cohen (1971), despite the diversity of individual cases considered in the courts, there have been common issues and complaints having to do with inappropriate selection and administration of screening and placement tests, abridgement of individual child and parental rights in screening and placement decisions, inadequacy of educational programming following placement, and negative effects of labelling. Although these criticisms were directed primarily at practices within self-contained special education programs, they were clearly related to the confounding of ethnic or sociocultural differences with special education status.

Labelling

Legal legislative decisions have for the most been directed at the large number of pupils removed from the general or regular educational program and placed in special self-contained programs or classes for the educable mentally retarded. Early work by Mercer (1970) demonstrated clearly that there was overrepresentation of ethnic minority pupils in EMR programs, and that identification and placement practices have resulted in less than optimal programming. Of particular concern was the possible negative, even insidious, effects of labelling which might be derived from placement in EMR programs. The extensive literature on expectancy effect (see Brophy & Good, 1974, for a comprehensive review) as well as common sense provide support for the notion that labels may have serious negative social and educational consequences for children. Labelling has become a major and often emotional concern where special education services are considered; and as noted by MacMillan, Jones, and Aloia (1974), in the minds of many the labelling effect "explained" the problems of children in school. The fervor with which the labelling effect was taken up suggests that some believe that children's educational problems are primarily due to their being labeled; thus, to remove the label is to ameliorate the problem. Mainstream placement was seen as a way of ensuring educational opportunity and success as well as providing educational services consistent with legal and legislative mandates, and at the same time removing possible effects of pejorative labels. It is not surprising that the mainstream idea has appeal and that it has received such enthusiastic endorsement. It reflects the social and philosophical zeitgeist of the times. There is, unfortunately, a "giant step" between concept and practice.

EVIDENCE OF EDUCATIONAL EFFECTS

Despite the popularity of the concept and the legal, philosophical, and social support for mainstreaming, review of available information on the topic yields more rhetoric than evidence. As noted by Chaffin (1974) and Kaufman, Gottlieb, Agard, and Kukic (1975), emphasis to date has been on administrative arrangements more than on instructional or curricular matters. A variety of administrative options for delivery of services to exceptional pupils within the regular classroom or school have been described by Beery (1972), Birch (1974), Chaffin (1974), and Guerin and Szatlocky (1974). Various mainstream models emphasize somewhat different options—e.g., a contract model (Gallagher, 1972), a "zero-reject" model emphasizing responsibility of the regular class teacher for the mainstreamed pupil (Lilly, 1971), and a multi-alternative model (Adamson & Van Etten, 1972). Mainstreaming plans in other parts of the country are consistent with the six models proposed by the California State Department of Education in guidelines for return of former EMR placed pupils into regular programs, these programs referred to as "transition programs."

It should be noted that most of the mainstream models provide effective techniques for the placement of the exceptional child in the regular program and identify the kinds of special support services needed. Few guarantee, let alone evaluate, what happens to the child once placed. Administratively, the trend has been to move rapidly away from the self-contained classroom and to place pupils within the regular class setting. Guerin and Szatlocky (1974) found that former EMR placed pupils benefitted most from full day placement in regular classes. But as noted by Kaufman et al. (1975), mainstreaming and integration are not synonymous. In their view, three important components of mainstreaming are temporal, instructional, and social integration. These are likely independent but interactive. Kaufman et al. stress that mere physical time in the classroom is not enough, arguing instead that mainstreaming must involve services which lead to integration on the other dimensions. Unfortunately, support services for children and teachers in mainstream placements have frequently been variable, often limited, and sometimes missing entirely. Lacking is delineation of a possible pupil by program interaction, getting at the question of *which* kind of administrative and instructional arrangement in the regular program is appropriate for children with *which* kinds of educational characteristics. As noted by Gickling and Theobald (1975), "the philosophical commitment to mainstreaming seems to have outraced its research support" (p. 312).

Inconclusive Program Effects

Importantly, evidence which allows evaluation or program effects is for the most part lacking and, where available, is inconsistent and inconclusive. Since Dunn's (1968) challenge to special educators to develop alternative models for providing services to mildly retarded pupils, a number of researchers have attempted to test various integrative plans. There are some trends which seem to support Dunn's contention that EMR pupils are better off in integrated educational programs; yet, overall, there are few clear-cut outcomes which allow definitive interpretation. Consistent with findings of Richmond and Dalton (1973), Guerin and Szatlocky (1974) found the EMR pupils' behavior in the classroom and the ways they were perceived by their teachers were a function of the program model used and the degree of integration which existed within each type or model. These researchers found that the greater the degree of integration within a program, the more "normal" the behavior of EMR pupils. In contrast, Monroe and Howe (1971) found that the amount of time junior high school EMR pupils were integrated was negatively correlated with their acceptance by regular class peers. To confound the question further, Iano, Ayers, Heller, McGettigan, and Walker (1974) report that EMRs were no better accepted by their peers in an integrated resource room than in a special class. Yet, using sociometric techniques, Goodman, Gottlieb, and Harrison (1972) found the EMR pupils who were in an integrated program were rejected significantly less often than EMRs in a self-contained special class, findings consistent with those of Gampel, Gottlieb, and Harrison (1974). Still more recently, Gottlieb, Gampel, and Budoff (1975) confirmed the high incidence of "prosocial behavior" and "positive attitudes toward school" of integrated EMR pupils when compared to those EMR pupils in self-contained classes, although these investigators noted the persistent finding of lack of acceptance by regular class peers. Using still different outcome criteria, Haring and Krug (1975) reported that lower socioeconomic status EMR pupils, given an individual experimental one year "transition" program, acquired basic academic and social skills at a rate which allowed placement in a regular class, and that they maintained academic and behavioral adjustments after one year of being in regular classes. It appears, thus, that the type of administrative arrangement and the amount of integration within a given model may differentially affect academic, behavioral, and social outcome measures for EMR pupils. Despite inconsistencies and confusion, overall there is some continuing, albeit tentative, evidence of mainstream placement. Still at issue is determination of the important, even critical, parameters of mainstream programming, so that in this possible "confrontation of limitations" individual children are provided appropriate education.

UCLA RESEARCH ON MAINSTREAMING

As part of the Special Education Research Program conducted through the University of California at Los Angeles and the California State University at Los Angeles (Keogh, Kukic & Sbordone, 1975), researchers have been involved for several years in study of various aspects of mainstreaming in California. Of particular relevance and interest is work directed at the so-called "transition" program in California, as these programs represent a kind of pilot mainstream effort. Our data are limited but are among the few systematic and objective sets of evidence which allow other than intuitive, speculative generalizations about mainstreaming. Examination of transition programs may be useful, given the importance of mainstreaming nationally.

In 1970 the California State Legislature began a series of legislative actions which have had direct and far-reaching effects on exceptional children and the California public schools which serve them. Legislative decisions brought about changes in procedures and practices in identifying and planning for exceptional children, dealt with the confounding of educational exceptionality and ethnic minority status, and emphasized the rights of exceptional individuals to appropriate and adequate education, as well as spelled

Instructional Planning for Exceptional Children

out procedures to due process. The 1970 California legislation also required that all then EMR-placed pupils be reevaluated in light of more stringent identification criteria, so that inappropriately identified or misplaced pupils could be placed in regular programs. Permissive legislation also provided financial support to local school districts for implementation of "transition" programs to facilitate pupils' return to regular classes. Estimated numbers of transition pupils range from 14,000 to 22,000. Almost 250 districts in the state had formally approved transition programs between 1970 and 1974. A comprehensive review of the legal and legislative background of transition programs may be found in the report by Keogh, Levitt, and Robson (1974). The effect of the legislation was to require review and/or reevaluation of pupils in EMR programs, to require explanations of variance in EMR placement when number of minority pupils exceeded their representation in the district as a whole, and to provide additional support for districts to develop effective ways of integrating these pupils into the general education program. This, indeed, was a pilot mainstream program. It seems reasonable to ask what we have learned from it that might facilitate broader mainstream efforts.

District Program Modifications

Several studies conducted through the UCLA Special Education Research Program provide evidence pertinent to the question. In one major project the focus was on delineation of the kinds of programmatic modifications developed by districts to provide supplemental transition services, the kinds of staff development utilized, the techniques for evaluation of program effectiveness, and the recommendations and suggestions of district professionals as to ways to improve services for pupils in transition status (Keogh, Levitt, Robson & Chan, 1974). Our intent was not to determine if programs had or had not been effective, but rather to find out what, in fact, happened in districts implementing transition programs. Administrators in 10 selected school districts were interviewed personally, and they provided detailed descriptions of their programs; administrators in 156 other districts with transition programs supplied information through a mailed questionnaire. Interview respondents tended to be somewhat less optimistic as to program effects than were questionnaire respondents. Several findings have direct relevance to larger mainstream questions. Whereas all districts in our study sample reclassified pupils formerly in EMR status, some districts reclassified pupils formerly in EMR status, some districts reclassified all eligible pupils from EMR to Educationally Handicapped (EH) or to some other special education category; others placed pupils in full day, self-contained transition classes (a "new" special education category?); still others integrated former special class pupils totally into regular classes. The single most popular transition model was regular class placement with paraprofessional aides in the classroom. Almost all transition options utilized some kind of tutorial arrangement in an effort to provide individualized help in subject matter areas. Inservice training for staff serving transition pupils was conducted by approximately half the sample districts. Direct instructional personnel, e.g., teachers, aides and tutors, were the major target groups for such specialized training; few districts provided staff development for principals, school psychologists, counselors, or others working with transition pupils and those who teach them. For the most part effectiveness of inservice programming was unknown, and administrators expressed need for help in development of comprehensive inservice planning and programming (Boyd, 1975).

Administrators reported generally positive but mixed perceptions of outcomes or effects of transition programs on pupils and school personnel. For the most part findings were consistent across district parameters of size and ethnic representation. Administrators were in agreement that the review and reclassification process had corrected some previous inequities in placement, but there was less confidence that transition programming *per se* had been consistently beneficial to transition or regular class pupils. Placement in regular programs was viewed as having positive effects on transition pupils' social adjustment, self-concepts, and the like; there was less support for the beneficial effects of placement on pupils' educational achievement. Overall, there was a high degree of uncertainty about program effects due, in large part, to inadequate systems for evaluation. In the few districts evaluating their transition programs, findings were generally positive but lacked comprehensiveness. It was not possible to determine with confidence the kinds or extent of program outcomes although, subjectively, perceptions of the administrators tended to be positive. Unfortunately, data on which to evaluate program effects on transition and regular pupils were frequently not kept. Comprehensive descriptions of operational aspects of programs are lacking. In a sense, we are left to assess unknown programs in terms of unknown outcomes. The point is critical given the importance of the mainstream movement.

Transition Pupil Performance

The major purpose in a second project was to follow up formerly EMR placed pupils to determine how effectively they were performing in regular programs (Levitt, Keogh & Hall, 1975). Said directly and simply: How successful are transition pupils in regular classes? Despite the simplicity and directness of the question, operational criteria for determination of success and failure are complex; review of relevant research demonstrates that they vary according to investigator and study. In the present project the two major areas or general criteria were academic achievement and social-behavioral adjustment. Three sources of information provided evidence relevant to these two criteria—systems information having to do with demographic findings, e.g., school attendance, referrals for special help, and the like; classroom teachers' current perceptions of pupils' characteristics as measured by a series of academic and social-behavioral rating scales; results of district-wide achievement tests.

The study was conducted in a large California school district serving a major metropolitan area. Socioeconomic status of residents ranged from high income to welfare levels, and the district is generally consistent with the total state in pupil ethnic representation. The subject population was drawn from all 18 junior high schools serving grades 7, 8, and 9. This grade range was selected because transition funding existed for a four year period (1970-74) and the majority of EMR pupils could be expected to have been in the upper elementary grades at the time of reclassification (Keogh, Becker, Kukic & Kukic, 1972). An additional reason for limiting the sample to the junior high school range was that high dropout rates may be expected as transition pupils enter senior high school (Watkins, 1975; Yoshida, 1975). In this district a total of 399 pupils were reclassified from EMR to regular status between 1970 and 1972. Of these 399 pupils, 267 or 67% were identified as junior high school pupils in grades 7, 8, or 9 in the spring, 1975. Current school placement (location), administrative status (regular of special class), and demographic characteristics (sex, ethnicity, etc.) were determined for these 267 target pupils. Overall, 57% of the original junior high target sample was located at local schools within the district. This group constituted the primary target sample.

Each of the 153 transition pupils was matched with four regular class pupils drawn from his/her required English class. These regular class peers, matched to the target pupils for similarity of sex and ethnicity, were selected randomly within each English class, comprising a comparison group of 497 pupils; 530 additional regular class controls were also added as a comparison sample. Use of large numbers of peers not only provided reasonable comparison groups, but also protected the confidentiality of former EMR placement of the transition pupils. Regular class teachers (N = 145) were asked to summarize their impressions of each sample pupil in their classes, using a series of simple rating scales and a semantic differential scale. Teachers were not told that any pupils had ever been in special education programs. Teachers were asked to rate each pupil relative to other pupils in the class. In addition to teachers' perceptions of pupils' current educational and social-behavioral performance, current standardized achievement test scores were used. Six of the 18 junior high schools were Title I schools and served over 70% of the transition sample. The Comprehensive Test of Basic Skills had been administered by district personnel to all pupils in these schools; thus, it was possible to compare transition and matched and control pupils on this index as well as on demographic records and teachers' perceptions of pupils' performance.

Demographics

The three data sources yielded interesting if sometimes discouraging findings as to the current performance of transition pupils. While 57% (153) of the former EMR placed pupils were being served in regular classes, a significant proportion of the original 267 pupils were, again, clearly outside of mainstream education. Eighteen (7%) pupils had been reassigned to special classes for EMR, and 26 (10%) had been classes for Educationally Handicapped. Twelve (5%) were "lost" from the transition sample because of court placements to residential or correctional schools; sixteen (6%) had been transferred to other schools or were in suspended status due to some kind of guidance action; fourteen (5%) transferred to other schools outside the district; twenty-eight (11%) pupils were unknown to local schools. Thus, fifth-six (22%) of the pupils in the original sample had been reassigned to special education status within regular schools or were assigned to court, correctional, or district continuation schools. The 22% figure appears consistent with data offered by Watkins (1975) who found 25% of her transition pupil sample required continued special education services.

Teacher Perceptions

In terms of performance of former EMR placed pupils who were being educated in regular programs, it was found that transition pupils were consistently rated by their teachers as doing less well academically than were their matches in the same classrooms. Watkins (1975) also found that teachers gave lower grades to transition pupils than to their peers. While not as clear as academic performance measures, transition pupils in our sample were rated by teachers as having significantly more social-behavioral difficulties and adjustment problems than their classmates. It should be emphasized that pupils were not being rated in terms of national norms or standardized scores, but were rated relative to pupils in regular classes where they were placed. Thus, findings of consistent and significant differences between transition and nontransition pupils are especially powerful.

Achievement Tests

In addition to teacher/pupil referenced data, transition and matched pupils' performances were compared on norm referenced, standardized

Instructional Planning for Exceptional Children

achievement tests. Analysis of achievement data was confined to six schools receiving Federal support monies. Although there were 18 junior high schools in the district, these six schools contained 70% of the transition pupil sample. In terms of academic performance as measured by standardized achievement tests, transition pupils did significantly poorer than their matched peers. Differences held for both reading and arithmetic measures. The six sample schools generated achievement scores below grade level expectations compared to other junior high schools in the district and to the normative group to which this test is referenced. The point to be emphasized is that transition pupils performed significantly below their nontransition peers even when the performance of peers was not up to the average in the district and/or in the normative sample. This significant and consistent difference in achievement was particularly discouraging when coupled with the results of the analyses of teachers' assessments of their pupils' performance.

Teachers perceived significant differences between transition and nontransition pupils even when nontransition peers scored "below average" on standardized achievement tests. This point becomes especially important given the fervor with which special educators eschew pupil labels. It is often argued that traditional special education disability labels are prime variables influencing, even causing, low pupil achievement and social and behavioral disturbance. In the present study, the vast majority (over 95%) of teachers did not know that any of the sample pupils had formerly been in special education classes. Thus, it seems unlikely that performance levels can be explained primarily in terms of labelling or teachers' expectancy effects. Rather, it seems more likely that poor achievement levels may be related to inadequate preparation for regular programs, to specific deficits in subject matter skills, and/or to needs for more powerful supplemental instruction. Drawing on an earlier study of EH and EMR pupils (Keogh et al., 1972) in which characteristics of over 1300 special education pupils were reviewed, it was found that EMR pupils as a group were approximately 3-4 years behind their chronological age grade placement expectancy and that specific skill deficits continued to be large as the child moved into the upper grades. In the case of transition pupils in our current sample, it is likely that they were behind in skill levels while still in special education classes. Apparently earlier special education experience or later placement in a regular program for as many as four years was not sufficient to bring them to the performance levels of their classmates.

Teacher Attitudes

Finally, results of several studies of teachers' attitudes and knowledge about exceptional pupils and how to teach them are of direct relevance to mainstreaming. Hewett and Watson (1975) presented elementary school teachers (N > 1000) with a series of six vignettes describing behavioral and learning characteristics of children previously placed in self-contained special education classes. Teachers were asked to indicate how these pupils should be taught in a regular classroom, what was the probability of their success, if their presence in the regular program would work to the benefit of other children, and the like. In essence, these investigators found that teachers were able to distinguish among the various patterns of pupils' characteristics described in the vignettes but that teachers had little knowledge of how to provide differential instruction for them. Although the majority of teachers felt that the exceptional children described would be better off in a regular program than in a self-contained one, they were also concerned that there would be negative effects on regular class peers and, importantly, that the demands on teachers would be increased greatly. Few felt confident in meeting these demands.

Hewett and Watson's findings were consistent with those of McGinty and Keogh (1975) who developed a questionnaire aimed at determining what teachers think they need to know in order to teach exceptional children in the mainstream, and to determine how competent they feel in these areas. Replies from almost 400 teachers demonstrated that there was considerable agreement as to what teachers thought they needed to know; unfortunately, there was almost unanimous agreement that they did not know it. As example, 88% of the respondents indicated that knowledge of the characteristics of exceptional children was important, yet only 27% felt qualified in this area. Taken as a whole, the findings indicated that, despite their willingness to work with exception children, few teachers feel competent to do so.

There was compelling evidence as to the need for comprehensive inservice training to prepare regular class teachers for mainstreaming. Several major topics in addition to knowledge about exceptional children stood out. Few teachers felt knowledgeable in planning and implementing specialized remedial educational programs; few were comfortable in teaching exceptional children in a broad spectrum of subject matter areas, viz. physical education, science; few were aware of resource or support services within or outside the school. Interestingly, a large number of teachers in the sample expressed awareness of the importance of the social and affective aspects of mainstream classrooms; the majority of sample teachers, however, reported that they were not knowledgeable or comfortable in how to help pupils in this regard. As noted earlier in this paper, there is evidence that the nature of the interaction between mainstream pupils and their peers is a critical ingredient for success, yet few regular class teachers feel that they can help children on these important social and affective dimensions.

Results of the studies of teachers' attitudes and competencies are particularly interesting given the results of an earlier project assessing the role of school psychologists in special education programs (Keogh, Kukic, Becker,

McLoughlin & Kukic, 1975). Review of school psychologists' training and actual on-the-job activities suggested that, whereas the majority are well qualified to test and, in fact, spend most of their time in various aspects of testing, almost none is expert in classroom management, remedial curriculum planning, and the like, and few are experienced in facilitating affective, social aspects of the educational program.

Taken as a whole, findings from this series of studies identifies forcefully the need for inservice training for all regular program personnel in order that they may deal effectively with mainstreamed pupils. The point is particularly important, as mainstreaming by definition requires accommodation of both regular pupils and staff as well as the exceptional pupils who are being mainstreamed. Whereas the direction and mandates for mainstreaming of exceptional pupils have come from forces external to the regular education system, it seems inescapable that it is the regular system which must respond and change. A major question concerns the ability and willingness of those in the regular educational program to make these changes.

SOME CONCLUSIONS AND INTERPRETATIONS

Our review of the work of others as well as the findings from studies conducted through the UCLA research program leads us to some conclusions or generalizations which, although equivocal, are nonetheless worthy of consideration. As an idea or concept, mainstreaming has received considerable attention and widespread support. As an operational program it has received limited attention and lacks evidence or data upon which to make evaluation or even analysis. Mainstreaming as an educational plan came about because of externally imposed pressures on the system and because educators recognized the need to provide more effectively for pupils viewed as mildly retarded. The concept has been generalized and broadened to include pupils with other handicapping conditions—indeed, in the minds of some, to include all pupils alike. The difficulties come when the idea is translated into programs, as the parameters of programs relative to characteristics of handicapped children are uncertain, even unknown. What kinds of instructional modifications ensure academic and social success for a visually or hearing impaired child in the regular classroom? How can we structure a teaching program to provide for the full range of individual differences in skill level within the mainstream classroom? The full continuum of services as an ideal receives enthusiastic endorsement; but how to deliver these services remains uncertain. It is of some interest to note that, from our ongoing contacts with public school personnel, it is apparent that the closer one is to the actual operation of programs, the less certainty there is about mainstreaming. Legislators and state or district administrators are enthusiastic advocates, building principals are for the most part positive, and classroom teachers are frequently ambivalent.

Despite good intentions of regular and special educators alike, it is apparent that formal educational programs have had only limited success in providing for exceptional pupils. Examination of educational histories of many of our "transition" pupils yields a kind of *deja vu* feeling. Early on in the elementary school classroom teachers identified particular pupils as being different from or less adequate than their peers on academic, social, or behavioral dimensions. These pupils were referred to school psychologists who, in the main, painstakingly elaborated the obvious to teachers; the referred pupils, indeed, evidenced deviant scores of one type or another. As some special education program was viewed as necessary, many of these pupils were placed in special classes for the educable mentally retarded, thus removed from the mainstream. A combination of external legal and legislative pressures coupled with questions as to the efficacy of special classes and the confounding effects of socioeconomic background on school achievement lead to enthusiastic support for return to regular classrooms. Many pupils with varying educational competencies and skills were placed in regular programs and expected to perform *as if* they had had the same experiences and skills as their regular class peers. We seem to have come full circle. Teachers now identify many of the same pupils as underachievers and as having problems, and these pupils continue to score below their classmates or normative groups on standardized achievement measures.

It seems clear that neither regular nor special programs have adequately prepared these pupils for academic, social and/or behavioral success. It might be argued that, if special education placement had a viable impact on pupils' performance, our transition data would reflect higher outcome indices. Additionally, it might also be argued that placement in a regular education program had only limited effects, as the majority of mainstreamed pupils are still behind their classmates in performance levels. The process began with teachers identifying pupils' academic and social-behavioral problems. Many years later teachers continue to identify the same pupils as having academic and social-behavioral problems, in spite of interventions of both special and regular education. We, indeed, may be approaching a confrontation of limitations.

Several specific points derived from the research literature deserve attention, as they may help point the direction for more effective mainstream programs in the future.

- Mere physical placement in the regular classroom is not enough to ensure either academic achievement or social acceptance. Many exceptional pupils have specific needs which require accommodation and attention. Exceptional pupils are frequently behind their classmates in actual skills levels, requiring specialized and continuing remedial help. Exceptional children and their classmates may also need help in the social-affective aspects of life in the classroom. As noted by Kaufman et al. (1975), mainstreaming has temporal, physical, and social dimensions. We propose an additional "educational" dimension such as relevance. Mainstreaming is not just a function of time and proximity. It seems more likely that successful mainstreaming occurs when there is congruence in educational competence.

- The impact of labelling as an explanation for educational failure or behavioral deviance is seemingly overestimated. Removal of a pejorative label does not necessarily lead to changes in pupils' behaviors or competencies. Teachers respond in part at least to how pupils behave and how they achieve, not just to what they are called. As there is considerable evidence to suggest that labels provide little insight into remediation of children's problems, labels are undoubtedly best forgotten wherever possible. It is naive, however, to suggest that pupils' problems are in fact "caused" by labels and thus can be "cured" simply by removal of those labels. To suggest that we can ensure successful mainstreaming of exceptional pupils by removing labels is to overlook real and important individual differences which must be taken into account in educational planning.

- Despite recognition that mainstream education places major, perhaps prime, responsibility for education of exceptional pupils on regular educators, it is clear that few regular class teachers feel competent to take on this task. Preservice training and credential requirements for teachers must include study of exceptional children. Implementation of inservice training for teachers already in the classroom is critical. Given the consistent evidence as to regular educators' lack of understanding of educational characteristics of exceptional children, the inservice aspect of mainstreaming is of the highest priority.

- Effective individual instructional programs require appropriate analysis of pupils' educational abilities and styles. Traditional psychometrics, the stock-in-trade of many school psychologists, are limited in educational power and relevance. More sensitive and educationally oriented analytic techniques are needed to provide the basis for educational programming for exceptional pupils in regular programs. Closely related, school psychologists and counselors, key people in decisions about individual pupils, often lack background and experience in dealing with exceptional pupils. As with regular class teachers, pre- and inservice training of school psychologists must be part of a total mainstream effort.

A POINT OF VIEW

In an address on mainstreaming pupils into regular education programs presented at the American Association on Mental Deficiency meeting in 1974, Jane Mercer suggested that the *why* of mainstreaming is to be understood in the perspective of history, that the *who* of mainstreaming is in large part a decision of the courts, but that the *how* of mainstreaming "is the current challenge of public education" (Mercer, 1974). We agree with Professor Mercer's analysis and suggest further that the *how* of mainstreaming is plagued by inadequate research, poor record keeping, and confusion of political, social, and economic influences on education. Despite the intuitive appeal of many approaches to mainstreaming, we have seen little data which argue persuasively for any particular program. We strongly endorse the point of view that, unless there is clear evidence to the contrary, pupils should be educated in the mainstream. We argue vigorously, however, that optimal education requires more than categorical placement, even if the category is the regular class.

In order to achieve success in school many exceptional pupils need specialized, ongoing help as a supplement to regular instruction. Where the primary educational program for exceptional pupils is carried out within the mainstream, these specialized services must be available and functional in regular classes. In our opinion it is both reasonable and possible that these important supplemental services can be provided within the context of regular class instruction. It should be emphasized, however, that such services are often expensive and require coordination and cooperation of a number of professionals and paraprofessionals within the educational system. The point to be made is that successful mainstreaming may well require more, not less, attention and effort than did traditional special educational programs.

Finally, and most importantly, we emphasize that the real value of any educational program must be established in terms of effects on the pupils who are the participants. Educators in general, and special educators in specific, seem prone to confuse their own good intentions and enthusiasms with program outcomes. In the case first of segregated programs and now of mainstreamed programs there are few firm data on which to determine program effects. In our generalized enthusiasm for one kind of program or another, we seemingly have overlooked the most important ingredient—the pupils who require educational accommodations. It seems likely that no single program is "best" for all pupils. We must, therefore, focus our efforts on identification of the pupil and program characteristics of relevance. We must be willing to put our philosophies and our motives to the test. We must be pupil advocates, not program advocates.

REFERENCES

Adamson, G., & Van Etten, G. Zero reject model revisited: A workable alternative. *Exceptional Children*, 1972, *38*, 735-738.

Bancroft, K. J. Presentation at the Conference on Mainstreaming: Controversy and Consensus. San Francisco State University, May, 1975.

Beery, K. *Models for mainstreaming*. Sioux Falls, SD: Dimensions Publishing Company, 1972.

Birch, J. *Mainstreaming: Educable mentally retarded children in regular classes*. Minneapolis: Leadership Training Institute/Special Education, University of Minnesota, 1974.

Boyd, R. M. *School administrators' views of inservice training for transition program personnel.* Los Angeles: University of California, 1975. (Technical Report SERP 1975-A1)

Brophy, J. E., & Good, T. L. *Teacher-student relationships: Causes and consequences*. New York: Holt, Rinehart & Winston, 1974.

Chaffin, J. D. Will the real "mainstreaming" program please stand up! (or. . . should Dunn have done it?). *Focus on Exceptional Children*, 1974, *6*(5), 1-18.

Cohen, J. S., & DeYoung, H. The role of litigation in the improvement of programming for the handicapped. *The First Review of Special Education*, Volume 2. Philadelphia: Journal of Special Education Press, 1973, 261-286.

Coleman, J. S. The concept of equality of educational opportunity. *Harvard Educational Review*, 1968, *38*(1), 7-22.

Dunn, L. M. Special education for the mildly retarded—Is much of it justifiable? *Exceptional Children*, 1968, *35*, 5-22.

Gallagher, J. J. The special education contract for mildly handicapped children. *Exceptional Children*, 1972, *38*, 527-535.

Gickling, E. E., & Theobald, J. T. Mainstreaming: Affect or effect. *Journal of Special Education*, 1975, *9*(3), 314-328.

Gampel, D. H., Gottlieb, J., & Harrison, R. H. Comparison of classroom behavior of special-class EMR, integrated EMR, low IQ, and nonretarded children. *American Journal of Mental Deficiency*, 1974, *79*(1), 16-21.

Goodman, H., Gottlieb, J., & Harrison, R. H. Social acceptance of EMRs integrated into a nongraded elementary school. *American Journal of Mental Deficiency*, 1972, *76*, 412-417.

Gottlieb, J., Gampel, D. H., & Budoff, M. Classroom behavior of retarded children before and after integration into regular classes. *Journal of Special Education*, 1975, *9*(3), 307-315.

Guerin, G. R., & Szatlocky, K. Integration programs for the mildly retarded. *Exceptional Children*, 1974, *41*(3), 173-179.

Halpern, S. ESEA ten years later. *Educational Researcher*, 1975, *4*(8), 5-9.

Haring, N. G., & Krug, D. A. Placement in regular programs: Procedures and results. *Exceptional Children*, 1975, *41*(6), 413-417.

Hewett, F. M., & Watson, P. C. *Teacher attitudes toward mainstreaming: A preliminary report*. Los Angeles: University of California, 1975.

Iano, R. P., Ayers, D., Heller, H. B., McGettigan, J. G., & Walker, V. S. Sociometric status of retarded children in an integrative program. *Exceptional Children*, 1974, *40*(4), 267-271.

Kaufman, M. J., Gottlieb, J., Agard, J. A., & Kukic, M. B. *Mainstreaming: Toward an explication of the construct*. Washington, DC: Bureau of Education for the Handicapped Intramural Research Program, 1975.

Kaufman, M., Semmel, M., & Agard, J. Project PRIME—An overview. *Education and Training of the Mentally Retarded*, 1974, *9*, 107-112.

Keogh, B. K., Becker, L. D., Kukic, M. B., & Kukic, S. J. *Programs for EH and EMR pupils: Review and recommendations*. Los Angeles: University of California, 1972.

Keogh, B. K., Kukic, S. J., Becker, L. D., McLoughlin, R. J., & Kukic, M. B. School psychologists' services in special education programs. *Journal of School Psychology*, 1975, *13*(2), 142-148.

Keogh, B. K., Kukic, S. J., & Sbordone, M. W. *Five years of research in special education: A summary report*. Los Angeles: University of California, 1975. (Technical Report SERP 1975-A-19)

Keogh, B. K., Levitt, M. L., & Robson, G. *Historical and legislative antecedents of decertification and transition programs in California public schools.* Los Angeles: University of California, 1974. (Technical Report SERP 1974-A3)

Keogh, B. K., Levitt, M. L., Robson, G., & Chan, K. S. *A review of transition programs in California public schools.* Los Angeles: University of California, 1974. (Technical Report SERP 1974-A2)

Kirp, D. L. Schools as sorters: The constitutional and policy implications of student classification. *University of Pennsylvania Law Review*, 1973, *121*(4).

Kirp, D. L., Buss, W., & Kuriloff, P. Legal reform of special education: Empirical studies and procedural proposals. *California Law Review*, 1974, *62*(1), 40-155.

Levitt, M. L., Keogh, B. K., & Hall, R. J. *Follow-up study of transition pupils in regular education programs.* Los Angeles: University of California, 1975. (Technical report SERP 1975-A-11)

Lilly, M. S. A training based model for special education. *Exceptional Children*, 1971, *37*, 745-479.

MacMillan, D. L., Jones, R. L., & Aloia, G. F. The mentally retarded label: A theoretical analysis and review of research. *American Journal of Mental Deficiency*, 1974, *79*(3), 241-261.

McGinty, A. M., & Keogh, B. K. *Needs assessment for inservice training: A first step for mainstreaming exceptional children into regular education.* Los Angeles: University of California, 1975.

Mercer, J. R. Sociological perspectives on mild retardation. In H. C. Haywood (Ed.), *Socialcultural aspects of mental retardation.* New York: Appleton-Century-Crofts, 1970.

Mercer, J. R. *The who, why, and how of mainstreaming.* Paper presented at the Annual Meeting of the American Association on Mental Deficiency, Toronto, June, 1974.

Monroe, J. D., & Howe, C. E. The effects of integration and social class on the acceptance of retarded individuals. *Education and Training of the Mentally Retarded*, 1971, *6*, 20-24.

National Advisory Committee on the Handicapped. *Annual Report: Full Educational Opportunity Under Law.* Washington, DC: Government Printing Office, 1974.

Richmond, B. O., & Dalton, J. L. Teacher ratings and self-concept reports of retarded pupils. *Exceptional Children*, 1973, *40*(3), 178-183.

Ross, S. L., Jr., DeYoung, H., & Cohen, J. S. Confrontation: Special education placement and the law. *Exceptional Children*, 1971, *38*, 5-12.

Watkins, A. V. *An assessment of the status of special education students who have returned to regular classrooms for intellectually normal pupils.* Unpublished doctoral dissertation, Claremont Graduate School, Claremont, California, 1975.

Weintraub, F. J. Recent influences and law regarding the identification and educational placement of children. *Focus on Exceptional Children*, 1972, *4*(2).

Yoshida, R. K. Personal communication, February, 1975.

The following selection is a major contribution in the area of program evaluation. Borich has taken the educator out of the restrictive box of product measurer. As important as that function is, the evaluator also is needed as a participant in program planning and development. As can be discerned by reading Borich's model and examples, program evaluation is not a simple task if it is done correctly. However, if Borich's model is followed, not only will evaluation be done correctly, but the outcomes will far outweigh the energy expended to do it.

The probability of achieving desirable and realistic child progress is increased through use of the model. If educators truly support the concept of accountability, they must apply stringent quality controls to program evaluation procedures.

Program Evaluation: New Concepts, New Methods

Gary D. Borich, *University of Texas*

The failure of many efforts to evaluate educational programs stems from a lack of understanding of the programs themselves. An *educational program* is a set of hierarchically arranged instructional experiences that interrelate to generate several well-defined terminal outcomes. The purpose of *program evaluation* is to revise, delete, modify, add to, or confirm the efficacy of these experiences.

The key to understanding how and why a program brings about the outcomes it does lies in that program's hierarchical structure, or the way in which its components build upon one another to achieve outcomes greater than those that can be expected from any single part. It is the program evaluator's understanding (or misunderstanding) of this systematic interrelationship of components that often determines the utility and relevance of the evaluation to program developers and implementers. When evaluators fail to base their evaluation designs on a thorough understanding of program purpose and organization, their results and conclusions seldom address the needs which prompted the evaluation. Since their results and conclusions fail to integrate existing conceptions of the program, they cannot provide direction for program revision or modification.

Need and Purpose of Decomposition

A "components" view of an educational program assumes that behavior is generated or changed by specific, discrete instructional activities, and that the interrelationships among these activities build to more general behaviors at program completion. In any large-scale program that encompasses an almost endless array of instructional experiences, some activities can be expected to benefit program participants, some to hinder program participants, and still others to have no measurable effect upon them. The purpose of program evaluation is to assess the instructional activities that comprise the global program in a manner that makes possible the rendering of a judgment as to whether these activities should be revised, deleted, modified, unchanged, or supplemented with additional instructional components.

The role of program evaluation, then, is not only to decompose the program and, hence, understand the nature of its parts, but also to collect evaluative data from which to judge the adequacy of each component. Should a program component fail to engender the intended outcome or to relate with other program components to produce more comprehensive program outcomes, the effectiveness of that program component can be questioned.

Generally, program evaluation has placed little emphasis on the hierarchical nature of the program and, thus, has often failed to address the program's generic purpose—to gradually build more complex outcomes through hierarchically arranged instructional experiences.

Underlying the concepts presented in this article is the belief that program evaluation cannot be divorced from program definition, that evaluation functions not only after but also *during* program development, and that the evaluator cannot judge a program's parts without considering the composition of the whole. In the concepts that follow, the evaluator will be seen not only as an analyzer of data and reporter of program effects, but also as a logician and systems analyst. This perspective differs from typical notions of the role and function of the evaluator. While traditional representations of the evaluator are not entirely invalid, they often portray the relationship between the evaluator and program planners, designers, and developers as limited and distant. Such a relationship allows the evaluator minimal exposure to the program in its earliest stages and affords him little opportunity to assist planners, designers, and developers in fostering a common conceptualization of program components and their interrelations.

The traditional view of program evaluation is best illustrated by arranging the role functions of those involved in program planning, development, and evaluation on a single continuum, as shown in the top half of Figure 1. Traditionally, *program planning* has included two roles: the planner and the designer. *Program development* has involved the roles of developer and formative evaluator. And *program evaluation* has included both the formative and summative evaluator, the latter being primarily responsible for comparing the program with a control or alternative program.

Unfortunately, such a continuum of activities and role functions separates planning and development activities from what are seen as legitimate evaluation activities. This distinction between developer and formative evaluator has prompted many to view the two as opposing forces, some arguing that the formative evaluator must guard against the influence of the developer who is likely to be favorably biased toward the program, and others arguing that the developer and formative evaluator must work in close relationship in order to achieve the best mix of evaluation and development.

In practice, this conception of role functions often encourages the emergence of formal boundaries between program planning, program development, and program evaluation. Where one activity ends, the next begins with a different set of tools and techniques. Thus, it is not uncommon to find planners, designers, developers, and evaluators each beginning their work with a different "picture" of what the program is supposed to accomplish. While the professional boundaries generated by these roles may be inevitable with a compartmentalized view of planning, development, and evaluation, we need not persist in maintaining this conceptualization with the emergence of a methodology that allows us to link these role functions. While some insights have been gained into the evaluative process by these highly specialized roles, any further division of the evaluator from the developer and planner may not be in the best interest of program planning, development, *or* evaluation.

The bottom portion of Figure 1 presents a second continuum, on which the evaluator is shown contributing to initial planning and development. Here the evaluator, rather than entering the scenario late in the development process, plays an integral role in program planning and development *alongside* planners and developers. What are the evaluator's functions in this new role?

The revised role of the evaluator as depicted in the figure demands a technique that can be applied throughout the planning, design, development, and evaluation process to define and describe the program, to clarify its purposes and intents, and to foster a common conceptualization of it among

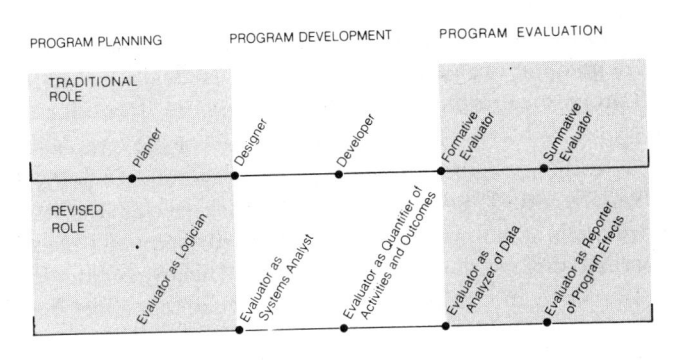

FIGURE 1

Some Old and New Conceptions of the Evaluator

project personnel. Ideally, such a technique would provide a basic language to use in articulating the program during all stages of planning, design, development, and evaluation. It also would allow the evaluator to serve as *logician* and *systems analyst* in order to clarify and focus the work of the planner and designer, as *quantifier of program activities and outcomes* to provide data for analysis, as *analyzer of data* to determine program effects, and as *reporter of program effects* to communicate results and conclusions.

Traditionally, program development and evaluation have been viewed as two distinct roles or functions, related in sequence but not substance. Formal training in instructional design and development rarely includes evaluation concepts and vice versa. While the notion of formative evaluation may link development and evaluation in theory, it has in practice failed to achieve significant symbiosis between these two activities. Given the nature of program development, it seems strange that it has taken evaluators so long to pose a closer relationship among evaluation, development, and planning under the aegis of formative evaluation. It is equally strange that in the 10-year period since the concept of formative evaluation has been articulated, the concept has produced so few tools by which evaluator can relate to, understand, and communicate the nature of a developing program.

THE NATURE OF DECOMPOSITION

Structured hierarchical decomposition is a technique that can be used to interrelate the role function of planner, designer, developer, and evaluator. It is a simple and straightforward concept, best explained in terms of Bloom's (1972) *Taxonomy of Objectives in the Cognitive Domain:* Knowledge, Comprehension, Application, Analysis, Synthesis, and Evaluation. Decomposition, the *sine qua non* of analysis and synthesis, is ideally suited to complex educational programs in which it is difficult to see the "forest for the trees."

Decomposition has six distinct characteristics. First, structured hierarchical decomposition graphically shows the components of a program (called transactions or activities). Second, it charts the flow of activities from beginning to end of the program, revealing the nature and sequence of experiences to which participants will be exposed. Third, it uncovers constraints upon program activities by indicating sources of influence that affect implementation of particular activities. Fourth, structured decomposition forces the integration of program parts by simultaneously detailing both the activities to be provided and the behavioral outcomes to be expected. Fifth, it fosters a common conception of the program by providing planners, designers, and evaluators the opportunity to work in team-like fashion on the decomposition and modeling task. And, sixth, structured decomposition builds for planners, designers, and evaluators a working vocabulary with which to describe key concepts in concise semantic and graphic terms for use across the planning, design, development, and evaluation phases of the program.

Structured decomposition achieves the above objectives by depicting the program hierarchically, in topdown fashion. Program detail is introduced gradually so that substantive detail is integrated into the whole without obscuring the overall intent or "big picture."

Figure 2 presents the decomposition process by showing program activities as boxes and the outcomes or "data" expected from these activities as lines connecting the boxes. When a program activity is decomposed into subactivities, interfaces among subactivities are shown as arrows. The title of each subactivity along with its interface arrows circumscribes a context in which program planners, designers, developers, and evaluators can work in detailing the precise nature of that subactivity.

A typical procedure is to evaluate a program by focusing on its sequence, beginning with activities on day 1 and following through to day n. This practice can unnecessarily confine the evaluator's understanding of the program to lateral flow. Hierarchically organized transactions and results can evade the myopic view of the development team, no matter how thorough their efforts to uncover all program activities and planned outcomes. In such a case, the problem is often not with the specialists who are attempting to define and describe the program but with the one-dimensional model they are using to evaluate it. Structured decomposition keeps the hierarchical intent of the program in full view while gradually introducing substantive detail, using input, output and control arrows to relate activities at a given level to those at any other level.

Program transactions are brought to life via inputs, controls, and outputs

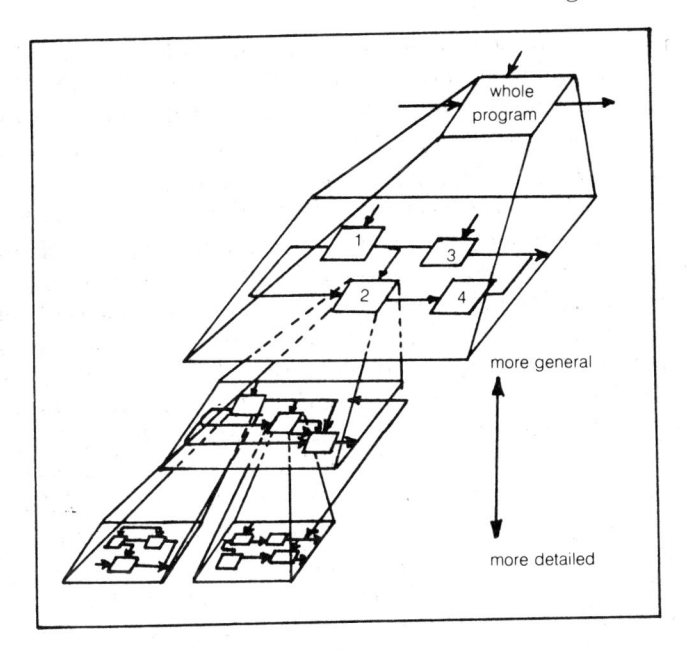

Each module in a model is shown in precise relationship to other modules by means of interconnecting arrows. When a module is decomposed into submodules, all interfaces between the submodules are shown as arrows. The title of each submodule plus its interfaces define a well-constrained context for the detailing of that submodule.

FIGURE 2

Decomposition Process

which lead to or emanate from each activity box. Inputs, always positioned on the left side of an activity box, represent raw data (e.g., participants, materials, processes) which stimulate the transaction and are eventually converted to output, or "changed" participants, materials, or processes. Control data, always indicated by arrows at the top of the activity box, indicate how the input may be constrained (e.g., by $), regulated (e.g., by policies), or modified (e.g. by knowledge of the quality of output) to produce the output. And, output data, shown by arrows emanating from the left side of the activity box, indicate the behavioral effect or finished "product" expected as a result of the program activity represented by the box.

Application of structured decomposition starts with the most general or abstract description of the program to be planned, developed, and evaluated. If we confine this description to a single "transaction," represented by a single box, we can then decompose or break down that box into a number of more detailed boxes, each of which symbolizes successively more detailed program activities. Each of these more detailed boxes can be further decomposed to amplify information contained in the parent boxes. This top-down approach thus avoids the complication of considering too many details too soon by introducing substantive detail gradually, and in meaningful steps, to form an overall picture of the interrelationships among program transactions.

Today, most organizations and agencies communicate planning and design decisions to program developers with a program proposal which describes the planned activities and their intended effects. The proposal is often the most formal expression of program intent. Not coincidentally, it is usually the only document available to aid program evaluators in selecting and guiding their own activities. Because the proposal must often respond to political as well as substantive considerations of the funding agency, it frequently provides only a broad, global description of program components, unified by loose scaffolding upon which global program objectives must often be supported. Thus, the proposal rarely serves program developers and evaluators as a definitive guide to intended transactions and expected outcomes. Hence, not only are evaluators uninvolved in the development process, but developers themselves are often unsure of program intents since planning and design decisions are poorly communicated from program designer to program developer. Clearly, there is a need for a systematic methodology by which to transmit planning and design decisions to developers and to systematically define, focus, and refine program transactions and intended outcomes *prior to* formative evaluation. It seems only natural that the evaluator should assist in the early articulation of program concepts by serving as logician and systems analyst during the planning and design phases. A systematic methodology for accomplishing this purpose is structured hierarchical decomposition.

STRUCTURED DECOMPOSITION DEFINED

The idea that the human mind can understand any amount of complexity, as long as it is presented in small, accessible chunks that are linked together to make the whole, is the basic assumption of structured decomposition. For the past several years computer software development specialists have been developing, applying and improving general but practical approaches to handling complex system problems. The approach taken in this article borrows heavily from the work of Douglas T. Ross (1977), which has become known as the Structured Analysis and Design Technique (SADT)®, one of a family of structured decomposition techniques. The basic ideas of these computer software specialists, however, are applicable to any field in which there is a need to effectively communicate the interrelationships among activities and outcomes occurring in complex systems or programs.

In the area of software computer technology, the application of decomposition methodology to real-life environments has significantly increased the productivity and effectiveness of teams of specialists involved in a development project (Ross & Schoman, 1977). The structured decomposition approach provides methods for thinking in an organized way about large and complex programs, for working as a team with effective division and coordination of effort and roles, and for communicating planning, development, and evaluation decisions in clear and precise notation.

The following fundamental assumptions underlie the application of structured decomposition to program evaluation:

1. Programs are best studied by building a model which expresses an in-depth understanding of the program, sufficiently precise to serve as the basis for program development.
2. Analysis of any program should be top-down, modular, hierarchic, and structured.
3. Program activities should be represented by a diagram which shows components, their interfaces, and their place in the hierarchic structure.
4. The model-building technique must represent behaviors to be produced, transactions to be provided, and relationships among these behaviors and transactions.
5. All planning, design, development, and evaluation decisions must be in writing and available for open review by all team specialists.

Structured decomposition uses a model to define the program. As indicated, this modeling process may be applied to a variety of programs, whether or not they are highly structured.

Structured decomposition systematically breaks down a complex program into its parts, henceforth called instructional transactions. Structured decomposition starts with a general or abstract description of the program, which serves as a working model from which successively more detailed portions of the program are conceived. Graphically, this process involves division of a cell representing the overall program into a number of more detailed cells, each symbolizing a major transaction within the parent cell. The extent of analysis within any step of structured decomposition is limited to a small number of transactions, each of which is further broken down in succeeding steps of the process. This approach ensures uniform, systematic exposition of successive levels of detail.

Because the complex interrelationships among program activities do not lend themselves to clear and concise expression in prose, structured decomposition utilizes a graphic language designed to expose detail gradually in a controlled manner, to encourage conciseness and precision, to focus attention on module interfaces, and to provide an analysis and design vocabulary for use by program planners, developers, and evaluators.

In summary, structured decomposition is a methodology which can be used by planners, developers, and evaluators for:

—thinking in a structured way about large and complex programs;
—communicating planning and design concepts to developers and evaluators in clear and precise notation;
—insuring the accuracy, completeness, and quality of an evolving program description with procedures for review and approval;
—documenting program evolution, planning and design history, and related decisions;
—working as a team with effective division and coordination of effort;
—managing and guiding the development of a project; and
—providing strategic concepts for assessing the results of the planning, designing and development process.

From an adequately constructed decomposition of the program, it should be apparent why the program was created and the technical, operational, and economic considerations that provide criteria for the various component parts of the program; what the program is to be in terms of its specific components and activities; and how the planned program is to be constructed and implemented.

BEGINNING THE EVALUATIVE PROCESS: USING THE DECOMPOSITION

From an examination of the decomposition of program activities and outcomes, evaluators often can suggest program modifications on logical grounds. Planners, designers, developers, and evaluators all use the decomposition model to interpret the program's meaning and to bring all parties who have a stake in the program into agreement about its intents and purposes. The heart of the decomposition is program transactions. The evaluator, in particular, uses decomposition to identify incongruencies between transactions and outcomes. Many times these incongruencies, unnoticed with lateral flow decomposition techniques such as PERT diagrams, appear so obvious with hierarchical decomposition that program development is halted until logical relationships between transactions and outcomes can be achieved either by redefining behavioral expectations or revising the nature of program transactions. In addition, program evaluation efforts may be temporarily shifted to redefinition of ambiguous parts of the program and construction of better, more effective transactions and more realistic outcomes.

Program Evaluation

Several concepts can help the evaluator affirm the logic of the relationships mapped by hierarchical decomposition. These concepts serve as primary links in the process of uncovering mismatches between program intents and program transactions and between program transactions and expected outcomes. To affirm that logical relationships among these are in evidence from the decomposition diagrams, the evaluator identifies the level of inference of each program transaction and classifies each output as a terminal or enabling behavior. Here is how the process works.

Transactions that are directly related to the behavioral outcomes expected of participants at program completion (let's call them terminal outcomes) are considered low-inference: We can infer that completion of the transaction will improve performance on the terminal outcome. The transaction may even require the participant to perform a portion of the behaviors that are expected at program completion. In such a case we say the fidelity of the transaction is high. The judgment that successful completion of the transaction by program participants will lead to improvement in their terminal behavior is small (low inference).

Figure 3 illustrates three conditions of fidelity between program transaction and terminal outcome. In the first instance, the overlap between the behavior produced by the transaction and the type of performance expected at program completion is almost complete. Here, fidelity is high: One need make only a small inference that if the transaction is successfully completed, terminal performance will improve. In the second instance, some fidelity is apparent, but the overlap is not nearly as great as in the first case. This transaction would be called medium-inference. In the third example, only a small portion of the behavior expected as a result of the transaction matches that which is expected at program completion and, thus, the transaction is one of high-inference and accordingly has low fidelity with the terminal behavior.

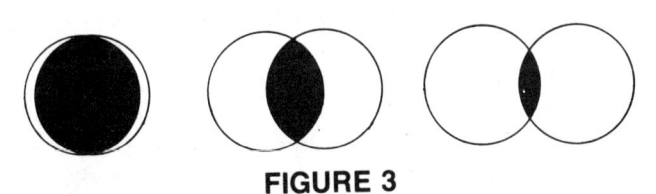

FIGURE 3

Degrees of Fidelity between Instructional Transaction and Terminal Outcome

Not surprisingly, low-inference transactions are linked to terminal outcomes by relatively few enabling behaviors. Their relationship to the behaviors expected of participants at program completion is direct and uncluttered by many mediating processes.

Instructional Planning for Exceptional Children

On the other side of the coin are high-inference transactions which, due to their low fidelity to terminal behaviors, must be connected to the latter via many mediating processes and clustered with other transactions before their impact on the terminal performance of program participants can be measured. This relationship is illustrated in Figure 4.

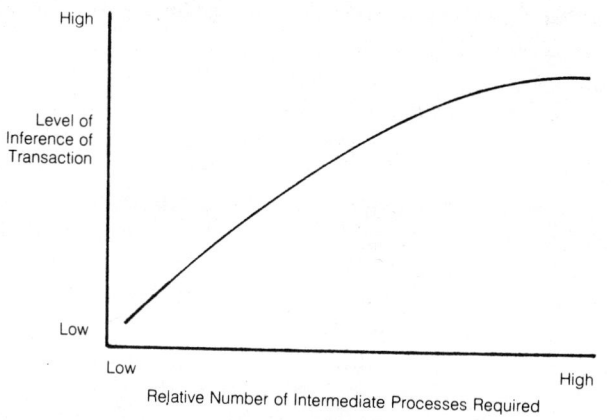

FIGURE 4

Generalized Curve: Relative Number of Intermediate Processes required for Transactions at Different Levels of Inferences

Note that at some point along the curve in Figure 4, the curve flattens and the number of mediating processes required to link the transaction to the terminal behavior may exceed available resources. Transactions at higher levels of inference may not be cost-effective. Both low- *and* high-inference transactions are important ingredients in program composition, and developers must not favor one over the other. Typically, high-inference transactions comprise orienting or introductory activities, such as reading a chapter in a book, listening to the teacher lecture, playing a recording, etc. Each by itself is likely to improve a terminal outcome (e.g., reading at grade level) only slightly, if at all. While the fidelity of these transactions to terminal program outcomes may be low, they nevertheless may be prerequisite to a long sequence of transactions and enabling behaviors which together comprise a significant and necessary portion of the program. Low-inference transactions, on the other hand, are directly related to terminal outcomes and may actually require program participants to perform all or a significant portion of the behaviors expected at program completion.

Figure 5 depicts the structured hierarchical decomposition of a program

Program Evaluation

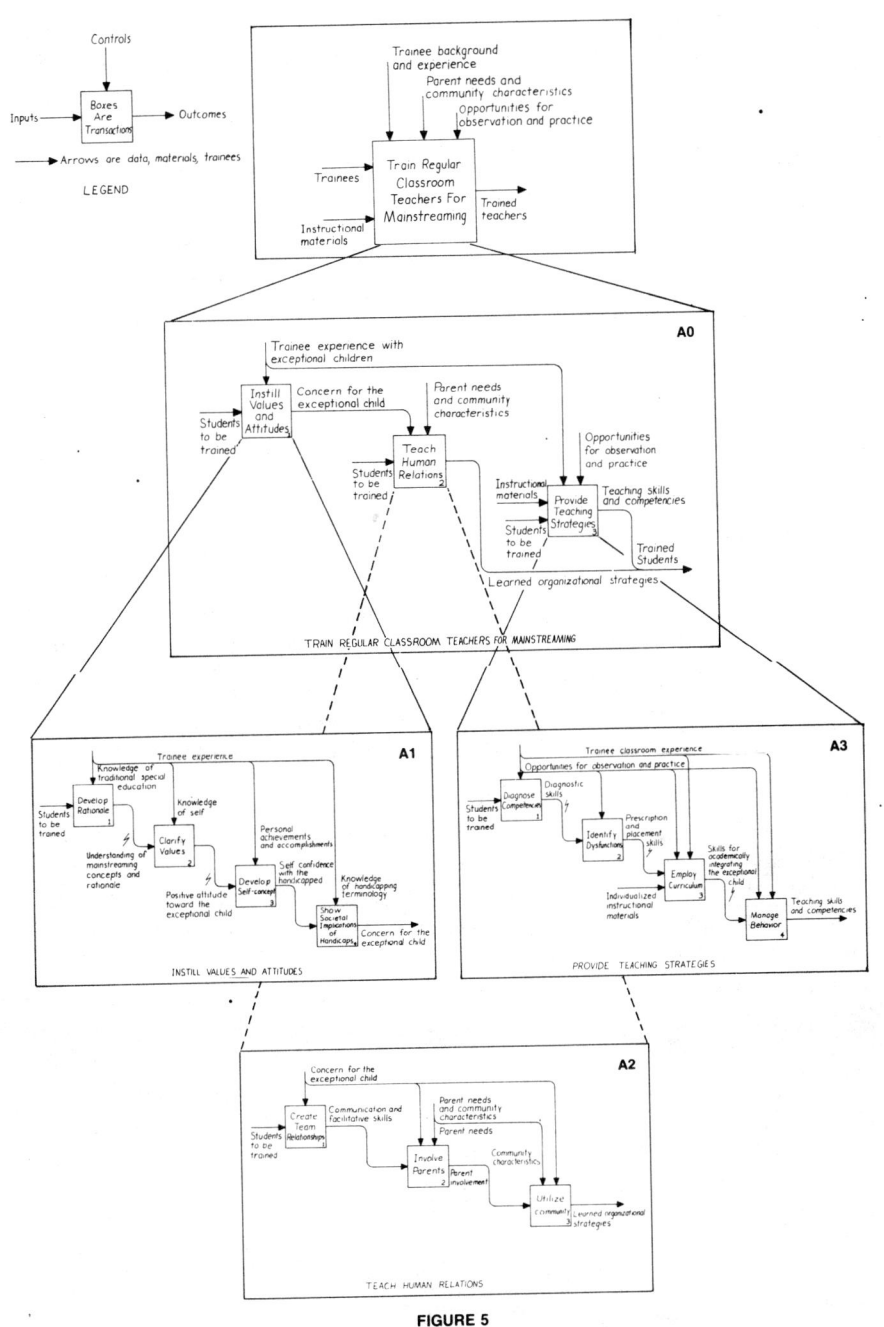

FIGURE 5
**Hierarchical Decomposition of a Program
to Train Regular Classroom Teachers for Mainstreaming**

(Using Structured Analysis and Design Technique)
(SADT).* SofTech, Inc.)

435

designed to prepare regular preservice teachers for mainstreaming. Try to identify its low-inference and high-inference transactions by noting the relative proximity of the instructional activities shown in the boxes to the activities the trainees are expected to perform at program completion. Remember higher-inference transactions commonly comprise more global, orienting or introductory experiences that are prerequisite to lower-inference transactions which approximate the real-life tasks for which training is being provided.

The concepts of high- and low-inference help the evaluator to determine gaps or mismatches between program intents and program transactions and between program transactions and program outcomes. Often program planners and developers make what evaluators call "inferential leaps" by espousing certain objectives for a program, but failing to provide the resources of specifications by which to incorporate the required transactions into the program at the appropriate level of inference. Or, transactions can be mismatched to outcomes in a similar manner.

For example, (1) high-inference transactions are sometimes expected to produce behaviors which approximate terminal outcomes, or (2) low-inference transactions are sometimes expected to produce enabling behaviors which may have little or no relation to terminal outcomes. Just the opposite should be noted on the decomposition model. In the second type of mismatch noted above, the cost-effectiveness of the match-up might be questioned. Low-inference transactions usually are costly to develop because their purpose is to produce *performance* as well as to instill *knowledge;* thus, the desired enabling behavior could be attained in a more efficient and less expensive manner. Such mismatches are exposed by decomposition diagrams since transactions (shown as boxes) and expected behaviors (shown as output arrows) are contiguous.

Table 1 provides readers with an opportunity to practice matching transactions and outcomes. The answers to this exercise can be found at the end of this article.

BEHAVIORS, VARIABLES AND COMPETENCIES

Many of the ambiguous findings produced by evaluation studies can be traced to poorly defined outputs. Outputs can be expressed not only as enabling the terminal behaviors but also as behaviors, variables, and competencies. It is important for evaluators as well as designers and developers to note the distinction among these concepts.

The term *behavior* involves the most general level of description. The meaning of a behavior often is conveyed by relating it to other constructs with which we are already familiar. For example, the behavior inherent in the phrase "teacher warmth toward children" may be conveyed by describing the

TABLE 1

Matching Transactions to Outcomes

Choose the most appropriate outcome on the right for each transaction on the left.

TRANSACTION	OUTCOME
____ reading about a concept	1. evaluation; i.e., decision-making, appropriately judging or selecting the concept in an ongoing setting
____ writing or completing exercises about the concept	2. application; i.e., using the concept in a situation different from the one in which it was learned
____ practicing the concept in a simulated environment	3. comprehension; i.e., translating the concept into different terms, summarizing it, organizing it differently
____ using the concept in a real-life (performance) setting	4. knowledge; i.e. recognition and recall of facts, defining terms, recalling names

teachers as friendly, intimate, or affectionate with her children. At this level, the behavior may be described without being observed or measured but simply in terms of related or associated concepts. A teacher's clarity of presentation, variety of style, enthusiasm of manner, and organization of content are typical of behaviors described at this most general level. Because behaviors like these are described in such general terms, they must be tied to specific variables and competencies in order to be useful to the evaluation process. Variables and competencies, then, are derived from behaviors.

The word *variable* refers to the terms in which a particular behavior is to be observed and recorded. A variable specifies behavior by stating explicitly the way in which the behavior is to be measured. Variables redefine behaviors in terms of the operations that are necessary to observe and to measure them. These operations express the behavioral concept in the form of a measurement, which represents the level of differentiation at which the particular behavior can be reliably observed and distinguished from other behaviors.

Just as general behavioral concepts are used to derive variables, variables are used to determine the next level of behavioral description. *Competencies*, like variables, are characterized by a metric or scale. However, unlike variables, competencies include the specification of a desired quantity of behavior, which is referenced in the metric. Competencies identify a single level of proficiency, or a range of levels, determined through theoretical or empirical processes, at which a program participant should perform. Unlike variables, competencies are either attainable or not attainable. Hence, it is the level of proficiency which is critical, not—as in the case of variables—

Instructional Planning for Exceptional Children

simply the separation and differentiation of various degrees of behavior. The process of deriving competencies from behaviors and variables is depicted in Figure 6.

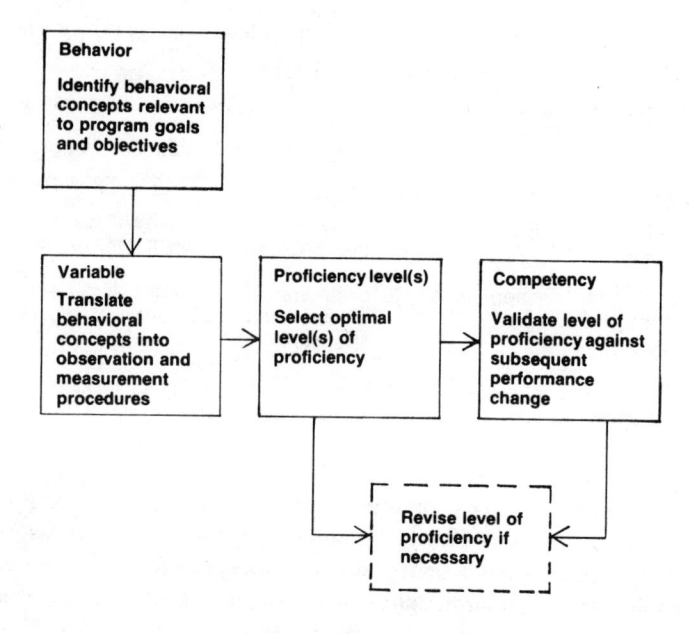

FIGURE 6

The Developmental Task of Deriving Competencies

In examining the decomposed model of a program, it is important to note whether the outputs are expressed in terms of behaviors, variables, or competencies, and whether or not they can be quantified at the competency level.

In the hierarchical decomposition of a program, the evaluator notes not only the conceptual precision with which outputs can be translated into competencies, but also changes in output descriptions across levels of the decomposition—from knowledge competencies, which specify cognitive understandings, to performance competencies, which specify skills and processes. As implied earlier, high-inference transactions are commonly linked with knowledge outputs and low-inference transactions with performance outputs. Knowledge competencies often are the legitimate goals of high-inference transactions consisting of early program experiences; performance competencies, on the other hand, are the legitimate goals of low-inference transactions involving real-life tasks that will be encountered at program completion. It is performance competencies, therefore, that become the basis for summative judgments about the program's effectiveness.

Outputs identified on the decomposition model are examined for their "quantifiability," preferably at the competency level. In addition, the progression of outcomes from general to detailed levels of decomposition is examined for an increasing frequency of outputs that are expressed in terms of the participant's competence on tasks expected at program completion.

DECOMPOSITION AND EVALUATION AS A TEAM EFFORT

The decomposition becomes a working document for project personnel to use in discussing the program. It by no means is intended to be impervious to change and critical assessment but, on the contrary, is meant to serve as an initial definition of the program and a vehicle by which to reconcile differing viewpoints held by members of the staff. Upon completion of the design phase, members of the team meet and each works through details of the decomposed model, usually prepared by the evaluator but reviewed by team members during development.

It is commonplace to learn at such meetings that each member of the team has a slightly different interpretation of the program. These differences often persist through the entire development phase and into program evaluation, complicating implementation and evaluation decisions. One purpose of the decomposed model is to identify and correct misconceptions among team members *before* development begins and to resolve inconsistencies and clarify ambiguities which may remain after planning and design are completed. The decomposition at this stage has four distinct effects:

1. Because its development is a team effort, it forces staff to use a common vocabulary and mode of expression in describing the program.
2. It exposes differing and sometimes extraordinary viewpoints of the program. It is not uncommon—and is in fact, healthy—at this stage to have various team members develop competing decomposition models from which to select a final version.
3. The decomposed model of the program serves as a framework in which to identify mismatches between transactions and intended outcomes (i.e., inferential leaps overlooked in the planning and design phase). Here, logical contingencies between transactions and enabling outcomes, and between enabling outcomes and terminal outcomes are a prime consideration.
4. The decomposed model serves as a framework for examining the nature of the outcomes intended. Outcomes that are stated as unoperationalizable behavior are replaced by more conceptually concise and quantifiable

outcomes and, if possible, expressed as competencies to be exhibited by program participants. Also, the sequence of outcomes is closely examined to assure that those stated as knowledge competencies at general levels of the decomposed model are ultimately transformed into performance competencies at detailed levels of the decomposition.

AN EVALUATION MODEL

After revisions in the program structure are made from the initial decomposition, the empirical work of the evaluator begins. This work entails the election of transactions and groups of transactions to be evaluated and rests heavily on the structured decomposition of the program done during the planning and design phases. A model of the evaluator's task is presented in Figure 7.

The evaluator's work can be represented in six stages. The first stage involves reviewing program proposals and related documents and interviewing planners, designers, and developers about the program's objectives and purposes. From these data the evaluator, in cooperation with planners, designers, and developers, creates a structured decomposition model of the intended program—a model which is continually revised to increase the clarity of program concepts, to eliminate "inferential leaps," and to resolve differences in viewpoint which may exist among members of the development team.

The second stage is the decomposition itself. This stage becomes the foundation for all subsequent activities of the evaluator. Until the structured decomposition model of the program is completed, the evaluator's work is mostly qualitative and nonempirical in nature. However, completion of the decomposition model is a cue to the evaluator to begin the quantitative, empirical process of assessing the intended impact of the program and its components. The decomposition serves as a reference for the evaluator as he or she begins synthesizing "evaluative dimensions" which are gleaned from the individual diagrams (modules) of the decomposition model.

The evaluator arrives at these evaluative dimensions by working through three distinct entities that characterize the decomposed model. The first and most general of these is referred to as a subsystem. Subsystems are referenced on the decomposition model as the first diagram after the initial single-box description of the program has been written. Subsystems represent the initial breakdown of the global program into its components. The subsystems of our training program in Figure 5, for example, are shown in diagram AO.

The second entity of a decomposed model is the "module," which represents all subsequent transaction groups and further analyses within each of the subsystems. Modules are easily discernible because they always represent

Program Evaluation

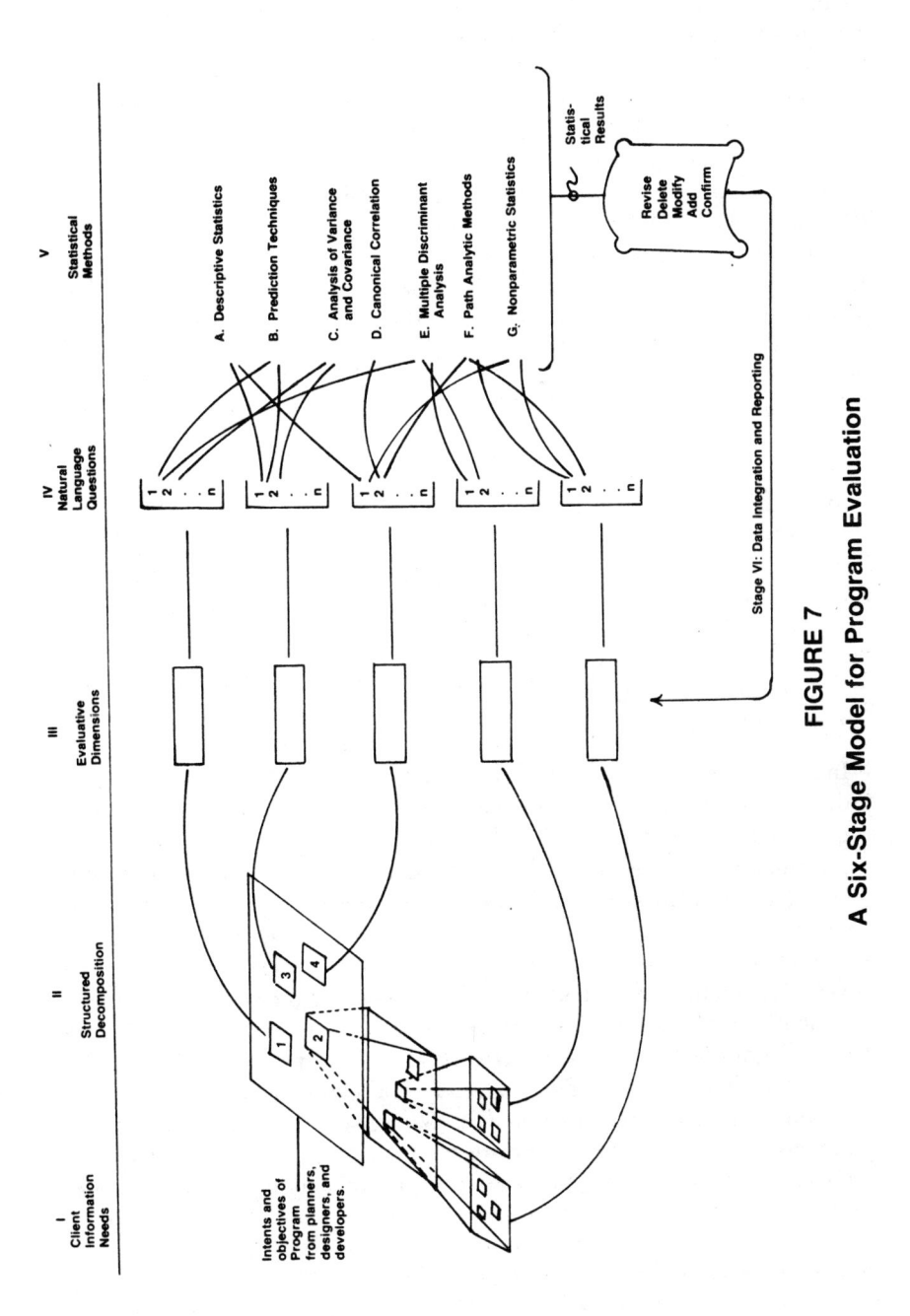

FIGURE 7

A Six-Stage Model for Program Evaluation

further division of subsystems. Modules are simply successive levels of detail within a particular subsystem and are depicted as homogeneous groups of transactions. They always appear as a single diagram, or page, in the overall decomposition model.

The third entity within structured decomposition models is the transaction. Transactions involve a further level of detail and are represented as activities, or boxes, within modules. They are always interrelated by inputs, controls, and outputs both within and between modules at successive levels of detail. Since a module contains a set of homogeneous transactions at a single level of detail, the purposes of these transactions can be easily grouped under a single generic classification. This generic purpose, or *dimension*, may be defined with the title that defines the module itself. For example, in diagram AO, Figure 5, there are three modules and, therefore, three evaluative dimensions: "instill values and attitudes," "teach human relations," and "provide teaching strategies." They are represented by diagrams A1, A2, and A3, respectively. Evaluative dimensions help the evaluator to reduce the important concepts in a large and complex program to a manageable number that capture the full flavor of the program. Thus, nothing is lost in the formation of evaluative dimensions since smaller, more detailed portions of the program are neatly tucked within more general modules which become the subject of evaluation.

A *priori* formulation of evaluative dimensions is critical to meaningful program evaluation. The conceptualization of these dimensions provides the following advantages:

—In projects containing voluminous data of varying importance, evaluative dimensions can focus activities and identify data that are most relevant to questions being asked. Evaluative dimensions provide criteria for setting priorities among the data and ensure that evaluation activities will not get "bogged-down" in irrelevant detail. By guiding the evaluation effort, these dimensions bring a conceptual handle and framework to program intents and objectives.

—The construction of evaluative dimensions also ensures that subsequent evaluation activities will be congruent with the informational needs of the client organization. To be effective, evaluative dimensions must reflect what the client wants to know. Therefore, the development of evaluative dimensions is a critical component of the overall evaluation, because such dimensions link the client's priorities to the available data in a meaningful manner. In short, these dimensions ensure that the most relevant questions will be answered.

To be sure that these dimensions reflect appropriate informational needs and to obtain critical comments about his or her conceptualization of the evaluation effort, the evaluator submits the evaluative dimensions to the development team for perusal before collecting and analyzing data. This interaction can and often does yield conceptual insights about what sponsoring agencies want to know about the program, thus allowing the evaluator to become more "in tune" with sponsor intents and objectives for applying the evaluation findings.

Since evaluative dimensions necessarily group transactions into a single, more parsimonious configuration, evaluative dimensions often contain slices of the program structure which can be meaningfully evaluated. Thus, in Stage IV (Figure 7), the evaluator uses the evaluative dimensions to compose natural-language questions (expressed in everyday, common-sense terms) which can provide practical information to those who will use the evaluation results. Natural-language questions, therefore, are user-oriented, geared to those who must act on the results of the evaluation. They should have strong intuitive appeal to those who will implement and revise the program and a direct bearing on decisions that will be made in subsequent applications of the program.

After constructing and ordering natural-language questions from evaluative dimensions, the evaluator chooses in Stage V one or more statistical methods to answer these questions. The methods available range from descriptive statistics, which might identify trends using simple graphs, to more sophisticated techniques, which might pinpoint causal relationships between specific transactions and intended outcomes or differences between alternative versions of the same transaction. The evaluator need not have a thorough understanding of the internal workings of many of the statistical tools he uses, but simply a knowledge of the types of questions to which they apply and the computer programs by which to execute them. Many supposedly sophisticated techniques employing advanced mathematics inaccessible to the evaluator a decade ago can now be easily implemented with computer programs available to virtually every computer installation in the country.

The seven statistical methods indicated in Stage V are groupings or sets of procedures—as opposed to individual procedures—which can be applied to a wide variety of natural-language questions. As the connections between Stages IV and V indicate, more than one statistical technique can, and wherever possible should, be applied to each natural-language question to cross-validate the findings relevant to that question. This procedure guarantees convergent validation of any conclusions drawn and enhances the credibility of the evaluator's report.

A. *Descriptive statistics.* This grouping includes measures of central tendency and variability (mean, standard deviation, estimates of variance, and various graphing techniques) which can reveal trends in the behavior of program participants. A question that might be addressed by this group of

Instructional Planning for Exceptional Children

statistics is: Does the implementation of program materials vary by teachers?

B. *Prediction techniques.* This grouping consists of single and multiple variable regression techniques. These are used to show the relationship between variables. For example, does a teacher's use of program materials in the classroom vary as a function of the amount of experience she has had in using similar materials (i.e., is degree of implementation predictable on the basis of length of experience with similar materials)?

C. *Analysis of variance and covariance.* This grouping consists of single and multiple classification comparisons. These techniques permit statistical analyses of the interactions between any two or more variables. For example, is degree of implementation of program materials highest when the teacher is familiar with similar materials (first variable) and is teaching a small number of students (second variable), and lowest when these conditions are reversed?

D. *Canonical correlation.* This technique is the generalization of multiple regression to any number of dependent and independent variables. It identifies common variance in any two sets of variables and is used to study the underlying relations between these variables. Its most common applications have been to input-output analysis and cost-benefit analysis. For example, input variables might be (1) the number of hours teachers are trained in using program materials, (2) the number of staff and support personnel required, and (3) the number of instructional materials used; and output variables might include various measures of trainee performance, such as attitudes and cognitive understandings. Canonical correlations can identify various relationships between the two sets of variables and specify the contribution to each to the overall relationship.

E. *Multiple discriminant analysis.* This technique is similar to regression analysis. It can be used to identify those variables that are most critical to participant performance. The technique allows maximum discrimination between groups of participants within the program. It can be effectively used to determine what variables best discriminate two groups of trainees on variables such as attitudes toward, knowledge of, and ability to execute specific teaching strategies. Statistical solutions might indicate, for example, that personality, prior training, attitude, and experience account for group differences.

F. *Path analytic methods.* These techniques are used to hypothesize and test relationships among selected variables. They are applied primarily to determine causal relationships among variables. For example, it might be hypothesized that the extent to which a trainee implements specific teaching strategies is dictated by previous experience in the classroom, and to a lesser degree by attitudes and cognitive understandings. Path analysis indicates whether relationships between variables and outcomes are causal or spurious.

G. *Nonparametric statistics.* This grouping includes techniques such as chi square (χ^2) and the sign test, which are employed when the data base fails to meet the assumptions required by the parametric methods described above.

The five foregoing stages tie available data to informational needs in a logically consistent manner. This model maximizes the information yield of an evaluative study, since each stage is built upon the preceding stage and all partners in the development process participate in formulating the evaluative dimensions and natural-language questions from which the data collection is planned. Involvement of the development team at various stages of program implementation ensures that evaluation activities will address relevant issues and provide additional data that may have been overlooked in earlier formulations of the program.

In Stage VI, the evaluator reports conclusions about each evaluative dimension based on results of the statistical procedures. As noted in Figure 7, conclusions are posed in terms of the original evaluative dimensions, thereby giving statistical results continuity and an intuitive, common-sense appeal. The report is organized according to the evaluative dimensions (major headings) and the natural-language questions (side headings).

The evaluator's final task is to make recommendations to the program development team concerning the efficiency of various program modules. The answers to natural-language questions often have implications for specific transactions within modules. Consequently, evaluator recommendations are made at the transaction level whenever data permit. These recommendations, which are directed to the development team, reference specific aspects of the program for which data have been collected from evaluative dimensions and natural-language questions. They generally advise program developers to *revise, delete, modify, add,* and *confirm* given modules and transactions. Developers then proceed with the program changes for which personnel and fiscal resources are available. Finally, the structured decomposition model is revised to reflect the changes that are made and to accurately communicate the program in final form to all those who have a stake in it.

REFERENCES

Bloom, B. S. (Ed.). *Taxonomy of educational objectives: The classification of educational goals*, Handbook 1, Cognitive domain. New York: David McKay & Co., 1972.

Ross, D. T. Structured analysis (SA). A language for communicating ideas. *IEEE Transactions on Software Engineering*, January 1977, SE-3 (1), 16-34.

Ross, D. T., & Schoman, K. E. Structured analysis for requirements definition. *IEEE Transactions on Software Engineering*, January 1977, SE-3 (1), 6-15.

Answers to Table 1: 4, 3, 2, 1.

The following article is a succinct yet comprehensive analysis of the mainstreaming thrust in education. It describes historical forces that influenced the push for integration of handicapped with nonhandicapped children and differences in meaning attributed to mainstreaming as a function of individual perceptions; e.g., administrator as contrasted to teacher.

Further, and of more critical importance, MacMillan and Semmel have stated clearly what needs to be done now and in the future to serve the handicapped within public schools, be they mainstreamed or not. They also describe a model by which mainstreaming programs can be evaluated, a process for actually determining if the handicapped are indeed served in a manner that elicits rather than extinguishes individual competence and satisfaction.

Evaluation of Mainstreaming Programs

Donald L. MacMillan, *University of California–Riverside*
Melvyn I. Semmel, *Indiana University*

Beginning in the 1960s a sequence of events resulted in the increasing trend away from educating handicapped learners in special classes and toward integrating handicapped learners into regular classes for the majority of their school day. In the 1970s momentum for integration increased as a result of court decisions (e.g., *Diana v. State Board of Education*) mandating the return of certain handicapped learners to general education. These court decisions were followed by legislative enactments in certain states which frequently provided for the return of handicapped learners to regular classrooms.

Recently, PL 94-142 was enacted at the national level and marks the culmination of efforts to promote regular class placement for handicapped learners. Today the battle cry in special education is for *mainstreaming*, and although there may be some serious impediments (see MacMillan, Jones, &

Meyers, 1976), the question clearly is no longer *whether* to mainstream but rather *how* most effectively to mainstream.

One encounters in the literature a host of terms—some slogans without precise meaning, and others that are used loosely to mean various things. The term "mainstreaming" has come to be applied to any number of programs that only vaguely resemble one another—ranging from mere delabeling, to educational integration, to deinstitutionalization (Dailey, 1974). Mercer (1974) described mainstreaming as the educational equivalent of *normalization*, the Scandinavian principle advocating life conditions for handicapped persons which approximate "normal" as closely as possible in light of the individual's limitations. Applied to education, this principle has meant to many the placement of handicapped learners into regular classes unless the individual's limitations are so compelling that a more protective or restricted placement is necessitated.

Court cases and PL 94-142 include the term "least restrictive environment" (LRE) in lieu of mainstreaming, probably feeling it has a more explicit meaning (Semmel & Heinmiller, 1977). Beyond the clear belief that the regular class is preferred to any other educational alternative, an operational definition of the least restrictive environment has yet to be provided. However, what is clear now is that evidence must be provided to justify placement of a handicapped learner in any alternative other than the regular class.

THE IMPETUS: POLITICAL OR EVIDENTIARY?

The trend away from special classes and the move toward integration parallels closely the civil rights cases pertaining to racial desegregation. Court cases have highlighted what special educators knew for some time—that the identification process for mildly retarded (EMR) children resulted in disproportionately high numbers of ethnic minority children in special classes and that the EMR level was objectionable to the children so labeled. Further, special classes did not result in the achievement gains originally anticipated. Special education (at least that associated with the education of mildly retarded children) was cast in an extremely unfavorable light, and those implicated in the process of identifying children as EMR (e.g., school psychologists) were similarly condemned for their role in the labeling process.

Special educators' sentiment against the special class was supported by the publication of Dunn's (1968) influential paper. Yet, it was unlikely that change could be brought about rapidly from within the educational system, and in extreme cases the educators actually prompted organizations to bring suit against them (see Burt's analysis of the P.A.R.C. case, 1975). In virtually every case brought to court charging violations of due process, the educators did not defend themselves, but instead were silent in their defense.

Briefly, consider the points raised by Cohen and DeYoung (1973) as major arguments in special education cases: (a) tests used to measure intelligence are inappropriate as they do not accurately measure learning abilities of the plaintiffs; (b) unless the tester is familiar with the cultural background and language of the child, he functions incompetently; (c) parents have not been informed and involved in the placement process; (d) the special class is inadequate and fails to develop adequate educational and vocational skills; and (e) placement and labeling do irreparable personal harm.

These five allegations have been made repeatedly in court cases while the existing evidence on four of these points fails to support the allegations. Reviews by Cleary, Humphreys, Kendrick, and Wesman (1975) regarding appropriateness of tests; the reviews by Sattler (1973) and Meyers, Sundstrom, and Yoshida (1974) regarding "incompetent" test administration; those of Guskin and Spicker (1968) and MacMillan (1971) on the adequacy of the special class; and the review of MacMillan, Jones, and Aloia (1974) pertaining to the effects of labeling and placement consider the research evidence on the various allegations and serve to challenge the plaintiff's charges.

From a research perspective, the allegations made in these court cases, with the exception of that pertaining to parental involvement, have simply not been answered. Unless those defending themselves were unaware of the evidence, one is led to believe that defendants did not want to defend themselves—that they wanted the charges that would result from court decisions supporting the plaintiffs, since the evidentiary basis for the benefits that would accrue to the mainstreamed child is lacking. Another way of viewing this issue is that while mainstreaming may not prove better than segregated EMR programs, it would in all likelihood prove to be no worse!

The disenchantment with self-contained special classes culminated as a result of several lines of reasoning that coalesced at about the same time and in a social climate that was receptive to the rights of the handicapped. Minority group children were overrepresented in special EMR programs, following legal fights over racial segregation slightly over a decade earlier. Research evidence, while often inconclusive, was interpreted as failing to substantiate the validity of special educational programming. One question, however, is not easily answered when reviewing the move away from special classes and toward mainstreaming—specifically, was the impetus behind mainstreaming political rather than evidentiary? In other words, were the court decisions that led to mainstreaming decided on the basis of law rather than evidence? If so, it is perplexing that so much "evidence" was introduced into those cases by the attorneys for the plaintiffs, albeit evidence that supported the allegations.

If the impetus behind mainstreaming is political or legal, then one might raise the question regarding the need for evaluation of mainstreaming in the sense of collecting evidence on outcomes of interest regarding the progress of handicapped children who are in the regular class. After all, if the violations of due process, segregation in special classes, and violations of dignity resulting from labeling are morally or legally wrong, then the abolition of those practices is an end in and of itself. Further evidence on the state of these children is unnecessary.

We do not present these two conflicting positions to suggest wrongdoing, but rather to question (1) the basis for the court decisions that led to mainstreaming and (2) the need for sophisticated evaluation data pertaining to the educational state of children. Even if the courts used law as the basis for the decisions, we will assume here that there is, nevertheless, the professional concern for how children are affected by mainstreaming—hence, evaluation is necessary. Accordingly, we turn our attention to the definitional problem related to the mainstreaming movement in an attempt toward achieving a clarity and utility of the educational facets subsumed under the mainstreaming construct.

DEFINITION OF MAINSTREAMING

Apparently no consensus definition of mainstreaming is held among educators. Therefore, it is impossible to establish what defining elements are necessary for a program to qualify as mainstreaming. In general terms, definitions offered to date fit one of two categories: (1) those which merely state something about desegregation and/or delabeling; and (2) those which feature some steps in which a child is assisted while in the regular education program. Probably the most widely cited definition is that offered by Kaufman, Gottlieb, Agard, and Kukic (1975):

> Mainstreaming refers to the temporal, instructional, and social integration of eligible exceptional children with normal peers. It is based on an ongoing individually determined educational needs assessment, requiring clarification of responsibility for coordinated planning and programming by regular and special education administrative, instructional, and support personnel (pp. 40-41).

This definition contains three major components—integration, educational planning and programming, and clarification of responsibility. If all three elements must be present (particularly to the degree specified in the article) in order for a program to qualify as mainstreaming, then no program to date constitutes mainstreaming.

The Kaufman et al. definition presents the field with a number of problems. While these authors achieve a degree of clarity in their definition, they imply that the three facets are necessary defining features of mainstreaming programs. We are led to ask: How much and of what quality must a program reveal relative to these variables in order to qualify as "mainstreaming"? Further, the definition implies that all three characteristics must be present to qualify. The utility of such a stringent set of criteria appears limited inasmuch as most existing so-called mainstreaming efforts are limited to 50% or more time integrated in regular grades. In other words, from an evaluation point of view, it is not feasible to exclude programs which do not emphasize educational planning and programming and clarification of responsibility.

It may well turn out that levels of quality in all three components are necessary for effective mainstreaming programs. But, in the absence of such data, it appears in the best interest of definitional utility and clarity to focus on temporal integration as the necessary, albeit not sufficient, criterion and to indicate that temporal integration is simply a proxy for a wide variation in quality and quantity of educational variables.

In 1970 a series of legislative enactments resulted in programs to "transition" former EMR students into regular programs in the State of California. At that time, mainstreaming was heard as the descriptor for such transitional programs; yet, when a follow-up of the success of these children who had returned to regular classes (Meyers, MacMillan, & Yoshida, 1975) revealed some negative findings, it has been said that this was not mainstreaming. The point is that until a workable definition is constructed of the elements which must be present in order for a program to constitute mainstreaming, there is no way to begin to evaluate mainstreaming.

EVALUATION OF SPECIAL CLASSES: AN ILLUSTRATION
Problems With Between-Groups Designs

Efforts to evaluate the special class as an administrative arrangement for educating EMR children took the form of comparing children in an EMR special class with children of comparable IQ enrolled in a regular class (see Guskin & Spicker, 1968; Kirk, 1964; MacMillan, 1971, for reviews of this research). Typically, the mean achievement scores are compared and one administrative arrangement judged *superior* if the children in that program achieve at a level reliably higher than those of children enrolled in the alternative. Similar comparisons were made between the two groups on some aspect of adjustment.

Consideration of these efforts at determining the efficacy of the special class is instructive, and problems encountered can be avoided in evaluation of mainstreaming. Despite a host of methodological problems that render the results uninterpretable, these studies can serve to exemplify problems inherent in comparing one program (e.g., the self-contained class) to another (e.g., mainstreaming program). First, between-groups designs assume homogeneity within a given program (e.g., self-contained classes), which we know not to be

Evaluation of Mainstreaming Programs

the case (Kirk, 1964; Bruininks & Rynders, 1971). A variety of factors differentiate one special class from another or one mainstreaming program from another. For example, the curriculum may emphasize basic tool subjects to a greater or lesser degree; the ability of the teacher varies; the instructional materials and strategies differ. All these factors and others (e.g., class size, classroom climate) are capable of influencing the outcomes (such as academic achievement and some measure of social adjustment) commonly used to evaluate such programs.

In the efficacy studies, the self-contained special class differed from regular class placement in several global ways:

1. Class size was smaller.
2. The teacher of the EMR class received special training.
3. The curriculum emphasized social and vocational development to a greater degree.
4. The children were formally labeled EMR and physically segregated.
5. The modal ability level of class peers is lower than is the case in a regular class.

A gross comparison of mean scores of achievement or adjustment masks the elements of the special class which are related to the superior or inferior performance on one of the outcomes evaluated. For example, if the mean score on a standardized test of achievement is lower for special class EMR students, is it because of the lower pupil/teacher ratio, or is it due to the lack of emphasis in the curriculum on basic subjects tapped on the test of achievement? The between-groups design only allows you to say that the combination of factors which collectively constitute a regular class results in superior or inferior achievement when compared to the combination that constitutes a special class. Moreover, the subtle factors (e.g., how good a given special class teacher is) are probably more important than all the factors listed previously, and the effectiveness of the teacher varies considerably from one EMR class to another.

Implications for Evaluating Mainstreaming Programs

The efficacy studies have been subject to close scrutiny and generally have been found wanting. Nevertheless, some of the problems that plagued these earlier efforts at evaluation continue to pose problems for those undertaking to evaluate mainstreaming programs.

First, in his critique of the efficacy studies, Kirk (1964) observed that from study to study the meaning of "the special class" differed dramatically, making comparisons of results hazardous. Similarly, in mainstreaming programs the precise curricular and instructional components of what is called

Instructional Planning for Exceptional Children

"mainstreaming" vary widely. In short, program diversity is the rule, not the exception, in mainstreaming (Guerin & Szatlocky, 1974; Jones, 1976a). Major differences were reported in terms of who was integrated, the amount of time they spent in the regular class, teaching strategies used, and support services made available (Guerin & Szatlocky, 1974).

In addition to differences in program characteristics, one must take into consideration the various types of children affected by any mainstreaming program (MacMillan et al., 1976). This suggests that different models be adopted by different schools; however, PL 94-142 goes beyond that and provides for individualized educational plans (IEPs) for each child without a given model, thereby creating even greater diversity in program specifics.

In response to court mandates and the like, an obvious group of handicapped learners consists of those children who have been enrolled in educational program for handicapped children who the courts have ruled must be returned to regular classes. These children had been in most cases segregated in special programs and as a result of the courts' decisions required to return to a regular class. The mainstreaming "program" will have to facilitate their return in terms of:

1. Remediating achievement lags, since the EMR curriculum delayed instruction in reading and math, thereby compounding the achievement gap that initially led to classification as EMR or LD.
2. Modifying behavior problems in some cases that were manageable in a class with a low teacher/pupil ratio and/or assisting the regular class teacher so that he or she can manage the behavior.
3. Enabling regular class teachers to accommodate a wider range of individual differences in their classes by providing them with needed instructional strategies and curricular goals appropriate for the formerly handicapped children.

Another population of children who are a focal point of mainstreaming programs consists for the most part of a younger group of children who were not identified as handicapped learners prior to the wave of court actions and legislation, but had they been in school during the earlier time frame would have been segregated (MacMillan et al., 1976). This population can probably be subdivided into two distinct subgroups:

1. Children who are identified as handicapped learners but, in keeping with provision for these needs in the least restrictive environment, will stay in the regular class. Presumably these children will avoid the stigmatization associated with the special class; however, the academic and/or behavior problems are no less a problem and must be provided for.

2. Children who before the changes in state guidelines and definitions (e.g., Grossman, 1973) would have been classified as handicapped learners but no longer qualify to receive special education services. These children are "normal" but exhibit learning and/or behavior problems in both nature and to the extent that in the past were considered beyond what could be tolerated in a regular classroom.

These more recent cohorts will not pose the same problems as those of the first group described. They have not been exposed to a "special" curriculum that delayed instruction on basic tool subjects. Instead, whatever achievement lags exist occurred despite exposure to the regular curriculum. Consideration probably should be given to the appropriateness of educational goals commonly available via the regular education curriculum.

Another group of children affected by mainstreaming are the regular class students into whose classes the handicapped learner is enrolled via one of the avenues discussed above. It is reasonable to assume that some impact will be felt—some benefits may accrue to these children, and some adverse consequences may result. Additional resources in the class, improved quality of instruction, and greater individualization of instruction might result in improvement in the quality of education for all children, and certainly exposure to handicapped learners provides an opportunity for learning about differences and toleration. On the other hand, the introduction of handicapped learners could result in undue teacher time being devoted to these few students at some cost to classmates whose instructional program could suffer.

In short, all children in the schools are going to be affected by mainstreaming. To be comprehensive, evaluation will have to consider these distinct populations separately. Also, mainstreaming is bound to affect school personnel as their roles are expanded with the introduction of handicapped learners into the regular programs. Teachers are the most directly affected since they will be held accountable for the child's progress. However, school psychologists will also feel the impact of PL 94-142 in terms of procedural guidelines for identification, and to the degree that they become involved in designing the IEPs called for by this legislation.

Both formative and summative evaluations should include the various groups affected by mainstreaming *separately* and not focus exclusively on one of the populations.

TYPES OF EVALUATION IN THE CONTEXT OF MAINSTREAMING

In light of the variations in programs of mainstreaming and the variations in the groups of children that are affected by any mainstreaming, between-groups designs appear of questionable validity for evaluating mainstreaming programs. Moreover, it is apparent that far more sophisticated approaches to evaluation must be employed if we are to truly understand those elements of programs that work as opposed to those of little or no value. Given the newness of mainstreaming programs, it is advisable to study the process of mainstreaming in the early stages and direct evaluation efforts at understanding those components that are working well—in other words, emphasizing *formative* evaluation as opposed to *summative* evaluation.

Efforts to evaluate special classes and, more currently, mainstreaming programs have focused on summative evaluation; that is, the purpose of the evaluation is to determine the overall effectiveness of one program (e.g., special EMR classes; a specific mainstreaming program). Certainly, there is a need for summative evaluation, but given the lack of preliminary work on various models of mainstreaming, it seems equally important in the early stages to evaluate the relationships among educational processes. Formative evaluation attends to evaluation of specific components.

One approach to formative evaluation, as outlined by Stufflebeam, Foley, Gephart, Guba, Hammond, Merriman, and Provus (1971), will be used as a basis for the following discussion. These authors differentiated several types of evaluation: context evaluation, input evaluation, process evaluation, and product evaluation.

Context Evaluation

The purpose of context evaluation is to provide a rationale for determination of objectives. The intent is to generate objectives that, when met, will result in improvement of the program. In the context of mainstreaming, some of these determinations have been made for the school system by the courts and legislatures; nevertheless, the diagnosis of problems that must be overcome to achieve the objectives is clearly a need when mainstreaming is to be implemented.

Objectives. One of the first steps in evaluation is the specification of significant outcomes that will be measured to see if they have been achieved. In other words, what does one anticipate to be affected by the mainstreaming program? At this point in time, the outcomes hypothesized to be affected can only be inferred as they have not been stated explicitly.

For example, is it thought that the academic achievement of mainstreamed EMRs will be positively affected by enrollment in the regular classroom and being exposed to the stimulation of more capable classmates? Or will the mainstreamed EMR be intimidated rather than stimulated by their more able classmates and, as a consequence, achievement affected adversely? Moreover, how does academic achievement rank in terms of importance among alternative outcomes such as self-concept, acceptance by peers, attitudes towards school or post-school adjustment? Unless the specific outcomes of importance are specified, one cannot proceed to select instruments and procedures with which to measure those outcomes in any reasonable fashion.

In the broad sense, the overarching goal of all treatment programs for the retarded is to assist them in a fashion that enables them to function in settings in a way that their behavior is acceptable and avoids evaluation as inappropriate or maladaptive. In the classroom context, mildly handicapped learners (e.g., ED, EMR, LD) initially came to the attention of teachers because they failed to adapt to the academic and/or deportment standards. That is, these students were exhibiting maladaptive behavior in the classroom; moreover, they deviated to the extent that it was felt they could not be maintained in the regular classroom. The goal then seems to be to achieve adaptation. Three ways of achieving adaptation have been specified by Nihira and Shellhaas (1970):

1. Some effort is made to alter existing behaviors of the individual to develop new behaviors, in order that the individual can satisfy existing environmental demands.
2. Place the individual into an environment which tolerates the existing behaviors of the individual.
3. Some effort is made to alter the environment in which the individual resides in order that its requirements are more congenial to the individual as he is.

In the past, the second option was primarily used—the handicapped learner was removed from general education and placed into a special class where demands and expectations were adapted to accommodate the behavioral limitations of the children. Note that the demands in the regular class remained unchanged, and children who failed to meet them were removed. In addition, the mildly handicapped learner was immediately adaptive in the special class because this environment tolerated the behavior that led to his removal from the regular class.

Mainstreaming seems to fit best the third option of Nihira and Shellhaas (1970), in which the regular class is asked to either: (a) tolerate a wider range of behaviors as adaptive, or (b) provide services that alter the maladaptive behaviors in the regular class so that the individual is adaptive to the regular class. To date, discussions of mainstreaming have failed to consider directly whether regular education is willing or able to accommodate the wider range of individual differences that will result from mainstreaming in terms of instructional objectives or instructional strategies.

For example, in the EMR curriculum an objective of rather high priority was the development of vocational skills and social skills that would enhance the individual's ability to get along in an occupational setting. Are we now going to include that as an objective available under the rubric of general education? Or do we implicitly decide that the goals of general education are appropriate for mildly handicapped learners, and that all that will be tolerated is lower level performance in pursuit of these goals without labeling it as deviant or substandard?

In other words, to the extent that mainstreaming requires tolerance on the part of general education it is essential that we explicate what will be tolerated (more varied educational goals or the degree of mastery of existing educational goals). MacMillan et al. (1976) considered this problem by distinguishing between a *program* and *services* as they wrote:

> When children were placed in a special EMR class they were placed into a program that had goals and objectives quite different from general education. The activities were geared towards vocational competence and social adjustment to a far greater extent than was true for regular education. This raises several issues in the context of mainstreaming.
>
> First, when a given EMR child is mainstreamed, those making the recommendation should know that this move represents a shift in some important educational goals for the child. Are the goals of general education more appropriate for that child than those of the EMR program?
>
> Second, providing a resource teacher to support the regular class teacher does not necessarily alter the state of affairs. Resource teachers do not have educational goals and they do not represent a program; rather they deliver services—assessment, prescription, remedial instruction, etc. Hence, they supplement the regular class teacher but the programmatic goals are those of the regular education program.
>
> The third issue goes back to the readiness of regular education and pertains to the willingness and ability of general educators to provide programs with vocational an social adjustment objectives more closely resembling the EMR program. This would entail major accommodative changes on the part of general education, something unlikely to take place (pp. 7-8).

Until the objectives of mainstreaming are explicit, it is impossible to specify the outcomes to be considered and select instruments and procedures with which to assess those outcomes.

In the majority of cases of mildly handicapped learners who are mainstreamed, some direct services will have to be provided in order for them to function adequately. Throne (1975) made this observation, albeit in a context different from mainstreaming:

> ... the normalization principle ignores the fact that by definition the retarded do not develop normally in response to normative procedures. For individuals to be correctly designated retarded means retarded only after normative procedures have been tried and found wanting. Referring to someone as retarded except in response to failure of normative procedures is *non sequitur*. While specialized procedures may or may not succeed in helping the retarded to become more normal, they always are the prescription of choice over normative procedures if more normal lives for the retarded are indeed the ends sought (p. 23).

In educational terms, mildly handicapped learners already have been approached with normative (or regular education) instructional procedures and were not benefitting. That is what first brought attention to them prior to certification as EMR, ED, or LD (see Mercer, 1973; Meyers, Sundstrom, & Yoshida, 1974). Now as these children are mainstreamed, extreme caution is called for lest it be assumed that ordinary instructional strategies are adequate—which would seem to be the case only if some experience intervening since certification has remedied the problem that initially led to the child being designated as a mildly handicapped learner. Specialized techniques are called for and will hopefully serve to assist the handicapped learner to his fullest educational attainment and as a result be able to perform in the mainstream of education and life.

Various Reasons for Mainstreaming. If the question is asked, "What are you trying to accomplish with mainstreaming?" we believe the answer would vary considerably among those asked. This takes us back to the impetus for mainstreaming. Some (e.g., Dunn, 1968) appear to advocate mainstreaming in the belief that certain benefits will accrue to mildly handicapped learners that have not been forthcoming in previous educational alternatives (i.e., self-contained classes).

In earlier papers, MacMillan (1976; MacMillan et al., 1976) noted the concerns of administrators —the civil rights courts cases directed against special classes and the overrepresentation of ethnic minority children in those classes; the cost of running programs for handicapped learners. As a result, when an administrator of a program is asked whether a program is "good," he will assess:

1. How cost effective the program is;
2. How many children are served in the program;
3. Does the program, at least, avoid adverse publicity?

In California, after a massive decertification of EMR children in response to court cases, reports issued by the State included data on the reduction in minority percentages in EMR programs (Simmons & Brinegar, 1973) and the number of children removed from EMR programs. The assumptions here are that if a lot of children are served, fewer dollars are spent, the percent of minority children is reduced, and the program avoids court cases, then mainstreaming is good.

In order to complete the picture of mainstreaming, it is necessary to assess the effects on children. This second perspective (i.e., the *child-oriented perspective*) tends to be that taken by the researcher; however, it is important that different perspectives for evaluating mainstreaming may lead to quite different conclusions. A program may be inexpensive, serve a great number of children, and avoid obvious problems, yet the children enrolled in the program may fail to make progress academically or socially.

MacMillan et al. (1976) noted that when one asks persons occupying different roles how to evaluate mainstreaming, the answers received will differ systemically. For example, a district administrator may consider a mainstreaming program "good" if it is cost effective and results in very few lawsuits, but a classroom teacher may judge the same program as "poor" because inclusion of handicapped learners both increases the behavior problems in his class and makes instruction more difficult. Neither has touched upon the changes in child behavior. Keogh and Levitt (1976) noted a similar phenomenon:

> It is of some interest to note that, from our ongoing contacts with public school personnel, it is apparent that the closer one is to the actual operation of programs, the less certainty there is about mainstreaming. Legislators and state or district administrators are enthusiastic advocates, building principals are for the most part positive, and classroom teachers are frequently ambivalent (p. 8).

In order to accommodate these perspectives, MacMillan et al. (1976) distinguished between the *administrative perspective* and the *child-oriented perspective*. One can easily add to the list, possibly the most obvious addition being a *legal perspective*.

Administrators speak about cost, the number of children served, favorable or unfavorable publicity, and the trouble caused by programs (e.g., lawsuits, opposition from minorities) when discussing programs. For example, in California when thousands of EMR children were certified, one index published by the California State Department of Education pertained to the change in the proportion of children from various ethnic groups that resulted from this action (Simmons & Brinegar, 1973). A drop in the proportion of minority children is "good," a program increasing excess costs per pupil is "bad" and so on.

Data bearing on the administrative pespective often fail to provide insight into whether a particular program is beneficial or detrimental to children. In order to evaluate the effects on children, it is necessary to go into the collection of child data which, while desirable, is not without a series of problems (discussed later). Nevertheless, it is important to consider the varied perspectives, as mainstreaming is of interest to many persons and groups—administrators, teachers, parents, school boards, legislators, child advocate groups, researchers, and others—each of whom may be interested in different kinds of information.

In context evaluation school personnel must be aware of precisely what is hoped to be achieved for their handicapped children by mainstreaming. Once this is achieved, one must consider the distinction between perspectives that suggest differing evaluative data to be collected: Administrators, parents, teachers, and children may define "good" programs in terms of quite different outcomes. Once these objectives are specified, they should be prioritized to facilitate policy decisions in light of evaluative data that will be forthcoming, as the evidence is likely to be mixed with regard to outcomes evaluated.

Input Evaluation

The object of input evaluation is to determine how resources can be most efficiently deployed to achieve the goals of the educational program. First, we must determine the capabilities of the school district to provide the resources necessary to accomplish the program goals. Next, decisions must be made regarding the strategies that will be used to achieve the goals of the program. Third, we must assess designs for implementing a particular strategy. Through these steps, we are able to establish specific designs to achieve program goals. Moreover, district personnel can evaluate whether they possess the needed services to implement the program and, if not, can identify what resources will be necessary to obtain from sources outside the district. Efficiency of various designs can be compared in terms of costs, procedural barriers and staff employment. In one sense, input evaluation predates actual program implementation and calls for logical evaluation; where data exist, they can be empirical.

Mainstreaming Models. Any number of "models" have been proposed for mainstreaming. Some involve the use of paraprofessionals; others use resource teachers; others the use of consulting teachers. In addition, there are considerations regarding the deployment of psychologists, curriculum specialists, and other school personnel who serve handicapped children in the schools (e.g., speech therapists). Various alternatives may be most appropriate for a given school district given the characteristics of that system and the characteristics of the handicapped children being mainstreamed. Therefore, one of the first aspects of input evaluation is considering and weighing the advantages and disadvantages of the various models that could be used in mainstreaming children.

Cost. In considering which model to use, cost can be roughly estimated for the alternatives. How many resource teachers will you employ? What qualifications will be required (which may dictate the salaries the individuals might command)? Or is it less expensive to hire paraprofessionals for each class into which children would be integrated? Other factors might suggest which of these alternatives is viable.

For example, do your regular class teachers possess the skills necessary to promote the academic and adjustment growth desired, or will the school have to hire teachers (resource or consulting) to assist regular class teachers? If it is necessary to hire resource teachers, a district then may not be able to afford to hire paraprofessionals. Some districts seem enthused about mainstreaming in the belief that this will be less costly than running self-contained classes. One could question this belief, since resource teachers spend a lot of time waiting for children to come out of their regular class and, after working with these children, must wait for a convenient time to return the children to their regular class so as not to interrupt instruction.

Instructional Planning for Exceptional Children

What special materials, self-contained instructional packages, expertise in behavior controlling approaches, or specific instructional strategies must be made available to the regular class teacher, the resource teacher, or must be possessed by the regular class teacher in order that the program objectives can be achieved? Anticipation of these needs should be clarified during input evaluation, and provisions made to obtain these materials and skills prior to implementation of the program.

Another dimension to be considered is the barriers that might be encountered and alternative approaches to minimize their impact on the program. One obvious impediment is the opposition that can come from the regular class teachers (see MacMillan, et al., 1976). In fact, some preliminary results of a mainstreaming program (Shotel, Iano, & McGettigan, 1972) revealed the negative attitudes of regular class teachers toward EMR children, which were not modified as a result of exposure to these children in a mainstreaming context. Another potential problem pertains to acceptance of handicapped children by their nonhandicapped classmates; the literature does not warrant optimism regarding the social plight of the handicapped when they are integrated (see Gottlieb, 1975).

Nevertheless, as barriers to the successful achievement of program objectives are noted, specific designs will be planned to break down the barriers. Certainly, involvement of regular class teachers prior to implementation is essential given the ambivalence expressed by teachers toward mainstreaming (Keogh & Levitt, 1976; MacMillan et al., 1976; Meyers et al., 1974).

Process Evaluation

Following the input evaluation, a course of action is initiated which is the most efficient and beneficial means by which program goals can be achieved. Process evaluation can be initiated once the design is implemented, providing periodic feedback to those who must implement the program. Stufflebeam et al. (1971) specify three major objectives of process evaluation: (a) to identify defects in the implementation, (b) to provide needed information to decision-makers, and (c) to provide an ongoing record of the procedure as it occurs. Process evaluation enables modifications in procedures when existing approaches fail to yield anticipated results. In addition, at a later point in time it enables us to determine retrospectively why certain objectives were not achieved.

Defects in implementation. Monitoring of the project in terms of overall objectives enables us to specify anticipated costs of the project at some point in time, degree of progress made by students in achievement areas, the extent of interaction anticipated between handicapped and nonhandicapped learners, and the like. By collecting progress data, trouble areas can be identified. If the students are failing to make the progress anticipated in reading, for example, the project staff is directed to examine the program elements intended to promote reading achievement. Modifications in the program can be made in light of data and input from project personnel in terms of what alternative approaches (possibly rejected during the input evaluation stage) seem warranted.

Information for decision-makers. A major problem with summative evaluation is that once it is completed it is too late to do anything about areas of failure; when you find at the end of the project that reading achievement suffered, it is too late to modify the project to promote reading achievement for that cohort of children for that year. However, process evaluation entails collection of ongoing data pertaining to the outcomes of importance. Program evaluators will monitor the progress of the program and the children enrolled in the program, and can obtain the kinds of information needed by decision-makers in order to make the necessary policy decisions.

In many instances where summative evaluation alone is employed, decisions are made during the implementation stage on an intuitive basis and often in the absence of any evidence. However, if evaluators work closely with those responsible for decision making, the decision-makers are able to request data that can assist in making the necessary decisions.

Description of activities. A third function of process evaluation is the ongoing description of activities as they occur, in descriptive terms. These kinds of information are particularly useful in a retrospective sense. When the program results in the achievement of objectives or the failure to achieve these objectives, one can go back to the process evaluation data to find reasons for the success or failure in the achievement of these objectives.

In one sense, these data provide a description of what actually took place as contrasted to what was planned to take place in the design of the program. On the other hand, if the implementation resulted in significant variations from what was planned, the evaluator can avoid attributing changes in child behavior to program elements that were never really implemented in the classroom.

Product Evaluation

The fourth type of evaluation concerns the assessment and interpretation of outcomes both *during* and at the end of the project cycle. In the context of formative evaluation, the concern is primarily with the measurement of objectives during the program, and is frequently done by means of establishing criteria and determining whether the program is achieving these objectives as it proceeds. In other words, if objectives of a mainstreaming program include some anticipated degree of peer acceptance and some degree of improvement in reading comprehension, one can devise operational objectives that are reasonable to expect halfway through the academic year and then measure the criteria associated with these objectives. One is able to determine whether reasonable progress is being made toward the achievement of objectives by comparing these measurements to the standards established.

SUMMATIVE EVALUATION

Programs for the education of handicapped learners traditionally have been evaluated in terms of outcomes which can be categorized under one of two major rubrics: (a) achievement and (b) adjustment. Each of these can be broken down further in terms of achievement in specific content areas (e.g., reading, math) and perspectives on adjustment (e.g., self-perceptions, peer perceptions, etc.). A cursory examination of the efficacy studies reveals that the outcomes against which the regular and special class students were evaluated were some aspect of achievement and adjustment. Similarly, critics of the special class point to the failure of special classes to promote significantly superior achievement or adjustment. Therefore, an implicit case has made for these facets as legitimate outcomes for evaluating mainstreaming programs.

As indicated earlier, the summative evaluation of mainstream programs should consider not only the handicapped learner who is mainstreamed but also the nonhandicapped learner into whose class the handicapped learner is integrated. Moreover, those charged with policy decisions are likely to be confronted with a contradictory set of results, making decisions even more difficult (MacMillan, 1976). For example, assume that the data reveal that handicapped learners benefit from a mainstreaming program in terms of adjustment but are adversely affected in terms of achievement. Or, consider the possibility that the handicapped learners are benefitted by the mainstreaming program while the regular class peers into whose class they are integrated are adversely affected. Anticipation of possible conflicting results suggests that during the context evaluation stage, not only should objectives be established but in addition they should be prioritized. Having done this, policy decisions can be made more readily despite results that are contradictory.

In terms of perspectives, one must consider the child perspective in evaluating any mainstreaming program. While cost, number of children served, proportion of ethnic minority children enrolled, and similar kinds of information are interesting, they provide no insight whatsoever regarding effectiveness of the program on children. Mainstreaming is aimed at being beneficial for children, and the only way that outcome can be evaluated is by securing information about the children. When mainstreaming children exhibit problems in language functioning, the use of instruments which require that the child understand instructions, follow directions, understand vocabulary, and respond to written alternatives present obvious problems in obtaining reliable and valid data.

INSTRUMENTATION AND INTERPRETATION

One impetus that led to mainstreaming was the concern that segregation of handicapped learners in special classes had either an adverse effect, or at least no beneficial effect on: (a) peer acceptance, (b) self-acceptance, (c) student attitudes, and (d) academic achievement. The efficacy studies on which these concerns were based have been criticized in terms of the procedures and instruments used to measure these outcomes. Yet these same kinds of children (e.g., with language problems) will serve as a source of data in mainstreaming evaluations, and little progress has been made in the development of procedures and instruments for tapping the outcomes mentioned above. These problems have been discussed by Jones (1976). Space limitations preclude an extended discussion here, but some of the concerns, in brief, involve:

Peer Acceptance

Traditionally, when attempting to ascertain the degree to which one child is "accepted" by another, one relies on sociometric methods. Jones (1976b) questioned the validity and stability of results derived from sociometric methods used with atypical populations. Possibly a more serious challenge to this approach evolves from answers to the following questions:

1. How vulnerable are sociometric ratings to events that immediately precede administration of the scale? (For example, a teacher praises one child and reprimands another just before the scale is administered.)
2. What is the relationship between sociometric ratings and actual behavioral interactions among class members? This refers to the attitude-behavior relationship discussed in the sociological and social-psychological literature (e.g., Schuman & Johnson, 1976).
3. How class-specific are the results of sociometric results or under what conditions is a child accepted or rejected? In other words, to what degree can one compare a child's sociometric status in one class to another child's status in a different class or from reading groups to the playground?

While sociometric procedures are useful for a teacher to gain some insight into the social patterns in his or her class, we are questioning its usefulness as a dependent measure in an evaluation design.

Another problem arises in the interpretation of sociometric data. When a child is found to be given a low sociometric rating by his peers, the following problems exist in interpretation:

1. Race and mainstreaming are often confounded, since the mainstreamed population is disproportionately drawn from minority groups.
2. Is the child rejected or ignored because of the stigma associated with his status as a mainstreamed student (if classmates know his status), or because he exhibits behaviors to which the classmates object? This can be confused further by race and/or sex of the target child.

In short, sociometrics (and probably any other paper-and-pencil measure) should be supported by other data (e.g., behavior observation) in order to provide convergent data on the same outcome. In addition, we need critical evaluation of sociometric devices with handicapped learners.

Self-Acceptance and Adjustment

If mainstreaming exerts an influence on the child, one might anticipate that the child will feel better about himself ("I'm a normal student") or that he will devalue himself as a result of being confronted constantly by peers who are more able than he is—in either case, the child's feelings of self-worth or the extent to which he is "well-adjusted" personally.

Gardner (1966) discussed the problem of reliance on self-concept scales and tests of personality developed for use with and standardized on, nonhandicapped populations when these instruments are used with mildly retarded subjects; however, the concerns are equally applicable to the mainstreamed child. For example, on the California Test of personality, realistic answers to questions (e.g., "Do most of your classmates think you are bright?") will be scored as wrong, or lead to the conclusion that the child is maladjusted.

A review of literature on self-concept (Shavelson, Hubner, & Stanton, 1976) contains an analysis of the major scales available for measuring self-concept. Again these scales are of unknown validity for handicapped populations. The language and vocabulary demands introduce bias or error into the data. Moreover, the retarded are known to give more socially desirable answers than do children of average intelligence (Crandall, Crandall, & Katkovsky, 1965; Jones, 1976b), which contributes additional error to the data when children (assuming they comprehend what the question asks) give an answer they think they should give instead of the answer that reflects their actual feelings.

Other problems in interpreting self-concept measures arise when, in the case of a handicapped learner, a low self-concept is found. Does one attribute that to an adverse effect of mainstreaming or—to put it bluntly—is this a realistic self-image? The use of pre- and post-test data would enable one to consider changes in self-concept related to a particular educational program instead of employing a post-test only and encountering the interpretive problems mentioned above.

Student Attitudes

Jones (1976b) noted the desirability of obtaining measures of the attitudes of both mainstreamed children and regular class peers. It is crucial, however, to recognize the complexity of attitudes and their measurement, and not to assess superficially how the child feels about school. Jones contended that to get a meaningful picture of child attitudes, one would want to tap the following:

1. General attitudes toward school.
2. Attitudes regarding the teacher-student relationship.
3. Attitudes toward peers.
4. Feelings about attending school.

To which one might add:

5. Attitudes toward specific program elements, such as being taken out of the classroom to be taken to a resource room.

The literature now reflects the importance of the "referent" in any studies of attitudes toward the handicapped (Gottlieb, 1975). The attitudes expressed will vary as a result of referent differences, as they will as a function of the method and/or instrument used to measure attitudes, such as rating scales, semantic differential, or adjective check lists (see Gottlieb & Siperstein, 1976).

Interpretation of data on attitudes must be interpreted with extreme caution (Gottlieb, 1975; Schuman & Johnson, 1976), since an assumption underlying research on this topic is that one's expressed attitudes (usually on a paper-and-pencil test) are an index of one's actual behavior. Moreover, in order to draw any causal inferences between mainstreaming and attitudes, it would be necessary to obtain attitude measures prior to initiation of the program and again at points later during the implementation phase of the project.

Academic Achievement

Any evaluation of mainstreaming is likely to entail the measurement of achievement, and standardized tests of achievement have a number of significant advantages over tests made by teachers (Gordon, 1975); the uniform procedures for administering and scoring and the established norms add to the validity of the results. However, test makers have not typically included the types of children likely to be mainstreamed (i.e., handicapped learners) in the standardization sample. Jones (1976b) expressed concern over the use of such tests with mainstreamed children:

1. Questions may be phrased in a manner that does not lend itself to comprehension by children with language problems (EMR, some LD).
2. Most tests are sensitive to performances at the middle range, but may not be valid for children at the extremes.
3. Reliability is questionable at the extreme ends of the distribution.

Some of these problems can be accommodated by using an "out-of-level testing procedure" (see Yoshida, MacMillan, & Meyers, 1976; Yoshida, 1976), where the student's teacher selects the level of the test most appropriate for the student; this procedure yielded excellent psychometric properties. In addition, one must be sensitive to changes that may be necessary in administration procedures due to problems in attention, frustration, and disruption that can affect all children being tested in the group. One investigation (Nystrom, Yoshida, Meyers & MacMillan, 1977) revealed that in cases where educationally handicapped learners were untestable in a *large* class, it was possible to obtain optimal assessment in groups of eight.

Given that many of the children who will be mainstreamed are minority children, Jones (1976b) pointed out that evaluators must be sensitive to "assumptions" made by test constructors:

> Those relevant to present concerns include the following: (a) each child understands the question being asked in the same way, (b) a child's cognitive function is observable only through the Anglo language and the Anglo value framework based upon Anglo experiences, (c) a people have the same experiences; therefore, the same questions can be asked of everyone. A corollary assumption is that a question means the same thing in all environments, and (d) a label or name for a cognitive component is a precise description of the whole component (p. 242).

This concern boils down to one of the degree which tests of achievement are "culture bound," an issue explored in detail by Cleary, Humphreys, Kendrick, and Wesman (1975).

Therefore, while standardized tests of achievement will be used extensively in efforts to evaluate achievement, these are not problem-free.

The interpretation is further confused by the fact that grade equivalents of the various tests may not be comparable among the tests (i.e., they are unknown) at the lower levels. One study (Loret, Seder, Bianchini, & Vale, 1974) has equated reading scores of various achievement tests for grades 4, 5, and 6.

CONCLUSIONS

In this article we traced the forces that ultimately led to the current trend to provide needed special services for handicapped learners in the least restrictive environment. Establishing the basis for court decisions that mandated such provisions is difficult (evidence was presented, yet current values clearly influenced these decisions). Nevertheless, we conclude that regardless of the basis for such decisions, evaluation of mainstream programs is essential so that we can provide the best education possible for handicapped learners—an impossibility without information regarding the effect of program elements on child-related outcomes.

The lack of agreement on a definition of mainstreaming continues to be problematic and represents an impediment to evaluation efforts. Until agreement is reached, it is essential that evaluators describe in detail the elements of the programs they are evaluating so that others can ascertain the similarity between that program and ones in which they are involved.

A major theme is the inadequacy of between-groups designs for evaluation of mainstream programs and the need for procedures that relate program elements to significant outcomes in order to isolate program components that promote or inhibit behavior changes. Toward that end, we have applied a model for evaluation described by Stufflebeam et al. (1971) to mainstream evaluation in an effort to show the various types of evaluation (context evaluation, input evaluation, process evaluation, and product evaluation) needed for a comprehensive evaluation.

Finally, we discussed the problems involved in the use of existing instruments for measuring the outcomes for handicapped learners; namely, peer acceptance, self-acceptance, attitudes, and academic achievement. The uncritical use and interpretation of existing instruments will yield invalid data which can lead to policy recommendations with deleterious effects on the children involved. We have attempted to delineate complexities involved in the measurement of outcomes that are hypothesized to be affected by mainstreaming.

The use of achievement data as an outcome is of greatest interest in terms of the amount of gain in achievement observed in children undergoing mainstreaming. Yet, a recent paper (Linn & Slinde, 1977) discusses the problems inherent in using gain scores to draw inferences, which are in fact unjustified whether one uses difference scores, residual scores, or estimates of true change. None of the procedures discussed can make up for the lack of random assignment, which is unfeasible in many situations.

While evaluation of mainstreaming is necessary to insure that handicapped learners will be exposed to the best education possible, a comprehensive evaluation will require hard work and cannot be undertaken in a cavalier fashion. Moreover, considerable basic work was yet to be done in developing instruments and procedures appropriate for use with the handicapped learners under consideration. Advocates for these children must not allow evaluations consisting of superficial and invalid measures analyzed inappropriately which fail to consider the complexities of the educational programming or the outcomes being evaluated. Handicapped learners deserve the best education we can provide, and the only way that can be established is via evaluation designed to clarify programmatic components that promote desired changes in student behaviors.

REFERENCES

Bruininks, R. H., & Rynders, J. E. Alternatives to special class placement for educable mentally retarded children. *Focus on Exceptional Children*, 1971, 3 (4), 1-12.

Burt, R. A. Judicial action to aid the retarded. In N. Hobbs (Ed.), *Issues in the classification of children (Vol. 2)*. San Francisco: Jossey-Bass, 1975, 193-218.

Cleary, T. A., Humphreys, L. G., Kendrick, S. A., & Wesman, A. Educational use of tests with disadvantaged students. *American Psychologist*, 1975, 30, 15-41.

Cohen, J. S., & DeYoung, H. The role of litigation in the improvement of programming for the handicapped. In L. Mann & D. Sabatino (Eds.), *The first review of special education (Vol. 2)*. Philadelphia: JSE Press, 1973, 261-286.

Crandall, V. C., Crandall, V. J., & Katkovsky, W. A. Children's social desirability questionnaire. *Journal of Consulting Psychology*, 1965, 29, 27-36.

Dailey, R. Dimensions and issues in "74": Tapping into the special education grapevine. *Exceptional Children*, 1974, 40, 503-507.

Dunn, L. M. Special education for the mildly handicapped—Is much of it justifiable? *Exceptional Children*, 1968, 35, 5-22.

Gardner, W. I. Social and emotional adjustment of mildly retarded children and adolescents: Critical review. *Exceptional Children*, 1966, 33, 97-105.

Gordon, R. A. Examining labelling theory: The case of mental retardation. In W. R. Gove (Ed.), *The labelling of deviance: Evaluating a perspective*. New York: Wiley, 1975.

Gottlieb, J. Public, peer, and professional attitudes toward mentally retarded persons. In M. J. Begab & S. A. Richardson (Eds.), *The mentally retarded and society*. Baltimore: University Park Press, 1975, pp. 99-125.

Gottlieb, J., & Siperstein, G. N. Attitudes toward mentally retarded persons: Effects of attitude referent specificity. *American Journal of Mental Deficiency*, 1976, 80, 376-381.

Grossman, H. J. (Ed.), *Manual of terminology and classification in mental retardation*. Washington, DC: American Association on Mental Deficiency, 1973.

Guerin, G., & Szatlocky, K. Integration programs for the mildly retarded, *Exceptional Children*, 1974, 41, 173-179.

Guskin, S. L., & Spicker, H. H. Educational research in mental retardation. In N. R. Ellis (Ed.), *International review of research in mental retardation (Vol. 3)*. New York: Academic Press, 1968, 217-278.

Jones, R. L. Accountability in special education: Some problems. *Exceptional Children*, 1973, 39, 631-642.

Jones, R. L. Problems in evaluating programs. In P. H. Mann (Ed.), *Shared responsibility for handicapped students: Advocacy and programming.* Miami: University of Miami Training and Technical Assistance Center, 1976, pp. 198-205. (a)

Jones, R. L. Evaluating mainstream programs for minority children. In R. L. Jones (Ed.), *Mainstreaming and the minority child.* Minneapolis: Leadership Training Institute/Special Education, 1976, pp. 235-257. (b)

Kaufman, M., Gottlieb, J., Agard, J. A., & Kukic, M. B. Mainstreaming: Toward an explication of the construct. In E. L. Meyen, G. A. Vergason, & R. J. Whelan (Eds.), *Alternatives for teaching exceptional children.* Denver: Love Publishing, 1975, pp. 35-54.

Koegh, B. K., & Levitt, M. L. Special education in the mainstream: A confrontation of limitations? *Focus on Exceptional Children*, 1976, 8(1), 1-11.

Kirk, S. A. Research in education. In H. A. Stevens & R. Heber (Eds.), *Mental retardation: A review of research.* Chicago: University of Chicago Press, 1964, 57-99.

Linn, R. L. & Slinde, J. A. The determination of the significance of change between pre- and posttesting periods. *Review of Educational Research*, 1977, 47(1), 121-150.

Loret, P. G., Seder, A., Bianchini, J. C., & Vale, C. A. *Anchor test study: Equivalence and norms tables for selected reading achievement tests (grades 4, 5, 6).* Washington, DC: Department of Health, Education and Welfare, 1974.

MacMillan, D. L. Special education for the mildly retarded: Servant or savant? *Focus on Exceptional Children*, 1971, 2(9), 1-11.

MacMillan, D. L. Research on mainstreaming: Promise and reality. In P. H. Mann (Ed.), *Shared responsibility for handicapped students: Advocacy and programming.* Miami: University of Miami Training and Technical Assistance Center, 1976, pp. 206-213.

MacMillan, D. L., Jones, R. L., & Meyer, C. E. Mainstreaming the mildly retarded: Some questions, cautions, and guidelines. *Mental Retardation*, 1976, 14(1), 3-10.

MacMillan, D. L., Jones, R. L., & Aloia, G. F. The mentally retarded label: A theoretical analysis and review of research. *American Journal of Mental Deficiency*, 1974, 79, 241-261.

Mercer, J. R. *Labelling the mentally retarded.* Berkeley and Los Angeles: University of California Press, 1973.

Mercer, J. R. *The who, why, and how of mainstreaming.* Paper read at the Annual Meeting of the American Association on Mental Deficiency, Toronto, June, 1974.

Meyers, C. E., MacMillan, D. L., & Yoshida, R. K. *Correlates of success in transition of MR to regular class.* Final report. Grant OEG-0-73-5263, The Psychiatric Institute, Pacific State Hospital Research Group, November, 1975.

Meyers, C. E., Sundstrom, P. E., & Yoshida, R. K. The school psychologist and assessment in special education. *School Psychology Monograph*, 1974, 2(1), 1-57.

Nihira, K., & Shellhaas, M. Study of adaptive behavior: Its rationale, method, and implication in rehabilitation programs. *Mental Retardation*, 1970, 8, 11-16.

Nystrom, K., Yoshida, R. K., Meyers, C. E., & MacMillan, D. L. *Standardized achievement measurement with the educationally handicapped—Normalization or further segregation.* Unpublished paper. Neuropsychiatric Institute & Pacific State Hospital Research Group, 1977.

Sattler, J. M. Intelligence testing of ethnic minority-group and culturally disadvantaged children. In L. Mann & D. Sabatino (Eds.), *The first review of special education (Vol. 2).* Philadelphia: JSE Press, 1973, 161-201.

Schuman, H., & Johnson, M. P. Attitudes and behavior. in A. Inkeles (Ed.), *Annual review of sociology.* Palo Alto: Annual Reviews, Inc., 1976, pp. 161-207.

Semmel, M. I., & Heinmiller, J. L. (Eds.). The education for all handicapped children act (PL 94-142): Issues and implications. *Viewpoints* (bulletin of the School of Education, Indiana University) 53(2), March 1977.

Shavelson, R. J., Hubner, J. J., & Stanton, G. C. Self-concept: Validation of construct interpretations. *Review of Educational Research*, 1976, 46(3), 407-441.

Shotel, J. R., Iano, R. P., & McGettigan, J. F. Teacher attitudes associated with the integration of handicapped children. *Exceptional Children*, 1972, 38, 677-683.

Simmons, A. & Brinegar, L. *Ethnic survey of EMR classes, 1973.* Sacramento: California State Department of Education, 1973.

Stufflebeam, D. L., Foley, W. J., Gephart, W. J., Guba, E. G., Hammond, R. L., Merriman, H. O., & Provus, M. M. *Educational evaluation and decision making.* Itasca, IL: F. E. Peacock Publishers, Inc., 1971.

Throne, J. M. Normalization through the normalization principle: Right ends, wrong means. *Mental Retardation*, 1975, *13*(5), 23-25.

Yoshida, R. K. Out-of-level testing of special education students with a standardized achievement battery. *Journal of Educational Measurement*, 1976, *13*, 215-222.

Yoshida, R. K., MacMillan, D. L., & Meyers, C. E. The decertification of minority group students in California: Student achievement and adjustment. In R. L. Jones (Ed.), *Mainstreaming and the minority child.* Minneapolis: Leadership Training Institute/Special Education, 1976, pp. 215-233.

AUTHOR INDEX

Alley, Gordon, 92

Beck, Robin, 216
Belmore, Jane, 253
Belmore, Ken, 253
Blake, Kathryn, 115
Borich, Gary D., 424
Brinkerhoff, Robert O., 351

Capps, Lelon R., 279

DuBose, Rebecca F., 73

Fanning, Peter, 325
Fine, Marvin, 5
Fitzgerald, Marigail E., 374
Foster, Carol, 92

Goff, Mary, 342
Goodstein, H. A., 34
Graubard, Paul, 236

Haring, Norris G., 216
Hatfield, Mary M., 279
Hawthorne, Linda White, 51
Hayden, Alice H., 216
Heiss, Warren, 390
Howe, Clifford E., 374

Jens, Ken G., 253
Jobes, Nancy K., 51

Kaufman, Martin J., 141
Kelly, Phyllis, 342
Keogh, Barbara K., 406

Langley, Mary Beth, 73
Levitt, Marc L., 406
Lewis, Linda, 141

MacMillan, Donald L., 446
Meyen, Edward L., 1, 139
Moran, Mary Ross, 19, 177, 294
Morrissey, Patricia A., 141
Morse, William C., 308

Rosenberg, Harry E., 236

Safer, Nancy D., 141
Semmel, Melvyn I., 446
Stagg, Vaughan, 73

Thiagarajan, Sivasailam, 198

Vergason, Glenn A., 1, 3

Walkenshaw, Margaret, 5
Whelan, Richard J., 1, 349

DEC 23 1998

DISCHARGED

DISCHARGED

DISCHARGED
OCT 1 1982

DISCHARGED
AUG 0 1983

DISCHARGED
DISCHARGED

DISCHARGED 1985

FEB 19 1986

NOV 15 1986
DISCHARGED

OCT 2 5 1988

DEC 0 7 1995
DISCHARGED

DEC 0 4 1995